ANCIENT FICTION

Society of Biblical Literature

Symposium Series

Christopher R. Matthews,
Editor

Number 32

ANCIENT FICTION
The Matrix of Early Christian and Jewish Narrative

ANCIENT FICTION
The Matrix of Early Christian and Jewish Narrative

Edited by

Jo-Ann A. Brant, Charles W. Hedrick, and Chris Shea

Society of Biblical Literature
Atlanta

ANCIENT FICTION
The Matrix of Early Christian
and Jewish Narrative

Copyright © 2005 by the Society of Biblical Literature

Cover photo of the leaf of Papyrus 46 containing 2 Cor. 11:33–12:9 courtesy of the Papyrology Collection, Graduate Library, University of Michigan.

Library of Congress Cataloging-in-Publication Data

Ancient fiction : the matrix of early Christian and Jewish narrative / edited by Jo-Ann A. Brant, Charles W. Hedrick, and Chris Shea.
    p. cm. — (Society of Biblical Literature symposium series ; no. 32)
  ISBN-13: 978-1-58983-166-7 (paper binding : alk. paper)
  ISBN-10: 1-58983-166-7 (paper binding : alk. paper)
  1. Narration in the Bible—Comparative studies. 2. Greek literature, Hellenistic—History and criticism. 3. Greek literature, Hellenistic—Jewish authors—History and criticism. 4. Bible. N.T.—Criticism, Narrative. I. Brant, Jo-Ann A., 1956– II. Hedrick, Charles W. III. Shea, Chris, 1949– IV. Series: Symposium series (Society of Biblical Literature) ; no. 32.
  BS521.7.A53 2005
  220.6'6—dc22   2005013285

13 12 11 10 09 08 07 06 05   5 4 3 2 1

Printed in the United States of America on acid-free, recycled paper conforming to ANSI/NISO Z39.48-1992 (R1997) and ISO 9706:1994 standards for paper permanence.

CONTENTS

PART 3: EARLY CHRISTIAN NARRATIVE

Acknowledgements

The editors of this volume wish to thank Gareth Schmeling and Richard I. Pervo for providing an inviting preface and introduction to this volume. In addition, while preparing the introduction, Richard read all of the essays and then offered many helpful suggestions. We also acknowledge three Goshen College students, Anita J. Hooley, Hannah M. Eash, and especially Laurel J. Yoder, for taking on the tedious tasks of preparing the lists of abbreviations and bibliographies.

We also wish to express our gratitude to Christopher R. Matthews, our editor at the Society of Biblical Studies, who encouraged us to assemble this collection and who serves as editor of the SBL Symposium Series. We also thank Bob Buller and Leigh Andersen for their assistance with the publication of this volume.

ABBREVIATIONS

SECONDARY SOURCES

AB	Anchor Bible
AEL	*Ancient Egyptian Literature*. Miriam Lichtheim. 3 vols. Berkeley and Los Angeles: University of California Press, 1971–1980.
AGJU	Arbeiten zur Geschichte des antiken Judentums und des Urchristentums
AJP	*American Journal of Philology*
ANRW	*Aufstieg und Niedergang der römischen Welt: Geschichte und Kultur Roms im Spiegel der neueren Forschung*. Edited by Hildegard Temporini and Wolfgang Haase. Berlin: de Gruyter, 1972–.
APOT	*The Apocrypha and Pseudepigrapha of the Old Testament*. Edited by Robert H. Charles. 2 vols. Oxford: Clarendon, 1913.
ASP	*American Studies in Papyrology*
AThR	*Anglican Theological Review*
BCSR	*Bulletin of the Council on the Study of Religion*
BDAG	Bauer, Walter, Frederick W. Danker, William F. Arndt, and F. Wilbur Gingrich. *Greek-English Lexicon of the New Testament and Other Early Christian Literature*. 3rd ed. Chicago: University of Chicago Press, 1999.
Bib	*Biblica*
BN	*Biblische Notizen*
BSAA	*Bulletin de la Société archéologique d'Alexandrie*
BZ	*Biblische Zeitschrift*
BZAW	Beihefte zur Zeitschrift für die alttestamentliche Wissenschaft
BZNW	Beihefte zur Zeitschrift für die neutestamentliche Wissenschaft
CBQ	*Catholic Biblical Quarterly*
CBQMS	Catholic Biblical Quarterly Monograph Series
CEA	*Cahiers d'Etudes Anciennes*

CDTS	Contributions in Drama and Theatre Studies
ChrEg	*Chronique d'Egypte*
CNI	Carsten Niebuhr Institute
CPJ	*Corpus papyrorum judaicorum*
CQ	*Classical Quaterly*
CW	*Classical World*
DSD	*Dead Sea Discoveries*
ETL	*Ephemerides theologicae lovanienses*
EPRO	Etudes préliminaries aux religions orientales dans l'empire romain
FRLANT	Forschungen zur Religion und Literatur des Alten und Neuen Testaments
HAW	Handbuch der Altertumswissenschaft
HTR	*Harvard Theological Review*
HUCA	*Hebrew Union College Annual*
JAAR	*Journal of the American Academy of Religion*
JBL	*Journal of Biblical Literature*
JHS	*Journal of Hellenic Studies*
JJP	*Journal of Juristic Papyrology*
JJS	*Journal of Jewish Studies*
JNES	*Journal of Near Eastern Studies*
JR	*Journal of Religion*
JRS	*Journal of Roman Studies*
JQR	*Jewish Quarterly Review*
JSHRZ	*Jüdische Schriften aus hellenistisch-romischer Zeit*
JSNT	*Journal for Study of the New Testament*
JSNTSup	Journal for Study of the New Testament Supplement Series
JSOTSup	Journal for the Study of the Old Testament Supplement Series
JSP	*Journal for the Study of Pseudepigrapha*
JSPSup	Journal for the Study of Pseudepigrapha Supplement Series
JTS	*Journal of Theological Studies*
LCL	Loeb Classical Library
LSJ	Liddell, Henry George, Robert Scott, and Henry Stuart Jones, *A Greek-English Lexicon.* 9th ed. with revised supplement. Oxford: Clarendon, 1996.
Neot	*Neotestamentica*
NIGTC	New International Greek Testament Commentary
NovT	*Novum Testamentum*
NovTSup	Novum Testamentum Supplements
NTS	*New Testament Studies*

ODCC	*The Oxford Dictionary of the Christian Church.* Edited by Frank L. Cross and Elizabeth A. Livingstone. 3rd ed. Oxford: Oxford University Press, 1997.
OECT	Oxford Early Christian Texts
OTP	*Old Testament Pseudepigrapha.* Edited by James H. Charlesworth. 2 vols. New York: Doubleday, 1983–85.
PG	Patrologia graeca [= Patrologiae cursus completus: Series graeca]. Edited by J.-P. Migne. 162 vols. Paris: Migne, 1857–86.
P.IFAO	Papyrus grecs l'Institut Français d'Archéologie Orientale
PW	Pauly, August F. *Paulys Realencyclopädie der classischen Altertumswissenschaft.* New edition Georg Wissowa. 49 vols. Munich: Druckenmüller, 1980.
RB	*Revue biblique*
RE	*Realencyklopädie für protestantische Theologie und Kirche*
REA	*Revue des études anciennes*
RevQ	*Revue de Qumran*
RGG	*Religion in Geschichte und Gegenwart.* Edited by Kurt Galling. 7 vols. 3rd ed. Tübingen: Mohr Siebeck, 1957–65.
RHPR	*Revue d'histoire et de philosophie religieuses*
SAC	Studies in Antiquity and Christianity
SBS	Stuttgarter Bibelstudien
SCR	*Studies in Comparative Religion*
SBEC	Studies in the Bible and Early Christianity
SBLDS	Society of Biblical Literature Dissertation Series
SBLMS	Society of Biblical Literature Monograph Series
SBLSBS	Society of Biblical Literature Sources for Biblical Studies
SBLSCS	Society of Biblical Literature Septuagint and Cognate Studies
SBLSP	Society of Biblical Literature Seminar Papers
SBLSymS	Society of Biblical Literature Symposium Series
SBLTT	Society of Biblical Literature Texts and Translations
SBLWGRW	Society of Biblical Literature Writings from the Greco-Roman World
ScrHier	Scripta hierosolymitana
SHR	Studies in the History of Religions (supplement to *Numen*)
SJT	*Scottish Journal of Theology*
SNTSU	Studien zum Neuen Testament und seiner Umwelt
TAPA	*Transactions of the American Philological Association*
TJT	*Toronto Journal of Theology*

TWAS	Twayne's World Authors Series
VTSup	Supplements to Vetus Testamentum
WMANT	Wissenschaftliche Monographien zum Alten und Neuen Testament
YCS	Yale Classical Studies
ZPE	*Zeitschrift für Papyrologie und Epigraphik*

PRIMARY SOURCES

1 En.	*1 Enoch*
1 Macc	1 Maccabees
1QDan[a,b]	*Apocryphon of Daniel*
2 En.	*2 Enoch*
2 Macc	2 Maccabees
3 Macc	3 Maccabees
4 Macc	4 Maccabees
4Q242	*Prayer of Nabonidus*
4Q243–244, 4Q245	*Pseudo-Daniel*
4Q246	*The Son of God Text* or *Aramaic Apocalypse*
4Q489	pap4Qapocalypse ar
4Q551	4QDaniel Suzanna? ar
4Q552-53	4QFour Kingdoms[a,b] ar
4QApocalypse ar	*The Son of God Text* or *Aramaic Apocalypse*
4QDan[a,b,c,d,e]	*Apocryphon of Daniel*
4QprNab ar 4Q242	*Prayer of Nabonidus*
4QpsDan[a-c] ar	*Pseudo-Daniel*
6QDan	*Apocryphon of Daniel*
Acts Thom.	*Acts of Thomas*
Aelian	
Var. hist.	*Varia historia*
Aphthonius	
Progymn.	*Prosgymnasmata*
Apuleius	
Metam.	*Metamorphoses*
Arastus	
Phaen.	*Phaenomena*
Aristotle	
Eth. nic.	*Nichomachean Ethics*
[Probl.]	*Problemata* / *Problems*
Arrian	
Anab.	*Anabasis*
Athenaeus	
Deip.	*Deipnosophistae*

Athenagoras
    Res.   *De resurrectione*
b.   Babylonian Talmud
B. Bat.   *Bava Batra*
Cicero
    Off.   *De officiis*
Clement of Alexandra
    Strom.   *Stromata / Miscellanies*
Dio Chrysostom
    Orat.   *Oration De dicendi exercitatione*
Epictetus
    Diatr.   *Diatribai (Dissertationes)*
Euripides
    Bacch.   *Bacchae*
Exod. Rab.   *Exodus Rabbah*
Hermogenes
    Progymn.   *Prosgymnasmata*
Herodotus
    Hist.   *Historiae / Histories*
Homer
    Il.   *Iliad*
    Od.   *Odyssey*
Horace
    Ars   *Ars poetica*
Irenaeus
    Haer.   *Adversus hearses / Against Heresies*
Jos. Asen.   *Joseph and Aseneth*
Josephus
    Ant.   *Jewish Antiquities*
    B.J.   *Bellum judaicum*
    C. Ap.   *Contra Apionem*
    J.W.   *Jewish War*
Justin
    1 Apol.   *Apologia i / First Apology*
Lucian
    Ind.   *Adversus indoctum / The Ignorant Book-Collector*
    Philops.   *Philopseudes / The Lover of Lies*
m.   Mishnah
Pesiq. Rab.   *Pesiqta Rabbati*
Philo
    Decalogue   *On the Decalogue*
    Flacc.   *In Flaccum*
    Moses   *On the Life of Moses*

Prob.	*Quod omnis probus liber sit*
Spec. 2	*De specialibus legibus* II
Philostratus	
Vit. soph.	*Vitae sophistarum*
Photius	
Bibl.	*Bibliotheca*
Pirqe R. El.	*Pirqe Rabbi Eliezer*
Plato	
Crit.	*Critias*
Rep.	*Republic*
Tim.	*Timaeus*
Pliny the Elder	
Nat.	*Naturalis historia / Natural History*
Plutarch	
Adul. am.	*De adulatore et amico*
Amic. mult.	*De amicorum multitudine*
Art.	*Artaxerxes*
Cleom.	*Cleomenes*
Gen. Socr.	*De genio Socratis*
Per.	*Pericles*
Prot. Jas.	*Protoevangelium of James*
Quintilian	
Inst.	*Institutio oratoria*
Seneca	
Ep.	*Epistulae morales*
Sus	Susanna
T. Levi	*Testament of Levi*
T. Ab.	*Testament of Abraham*
Tertullian	
Carn. Chr.	*De carne Christi / The Flesh of Christ*
Res.	*De resurrectione carnis*
Theon	
Progymn.	*Prosgymnasmata*
Vergil	
Aen.	*Aeneid*
Georg.	*Georgica*
Xenophon	
Anab.	*Anabasis*
Cyr.	*Cyropaedia*
Oec.	*Oeconomicus*

PREFACE

The ancient classical world of two thousand years ago looks simple when compared with our own crowded, polluted, computer-driven world, overloaded with sociologists, asphalt trucks, shopping malls, and the military-industrial complex: the classical world stretches only from Britain to eastern Turkey, south to Egypt, then west across all of north Africa, and then north to Britain. It encompasses the whole Mediterranean, taxes about 150 million people, maintains about 53,000 miles of paved roads, protects itself from migrating hordes to the north and east with about forty legions of 225,000 soldiers and a navy that guards the shipping lanes, is ruled over by one emperor, often with several announced pretenders or ambitious generals waiting in the wings, is regulated by one legal language (Latin), has been made proud by several generations of poets and historians who could rival the best of fifth-century Greece, and is unified by a tolerance for all tolerant religions.

Latin is the language in which all imperial documents become legal: 250 years after Constantine had set up a rival Greek-speaking capital of the Roman Empire on the Bosporus, Justinian (527–565) collected almost one thousand years of Roman law in Latin. For a perspective: the walls of Constantinople are not to be breached until 1453, which is 1,043 years after Rome is sacked by Alaric. Latin law, however, only apparently binds the two halves of the empire together, while the establishment of Constantinople irreparably splits the Latin West from the Greek East, a decision that will have disastrous effects in the later history of religion.

Although the greatness of Greek literature after Menander, Callimachus, and Apollonius of Rhodes gives way slowly to Latin writers, Greek is overwhelmed in the first centuries B.C.E. and C.E. by the quality of Vergil, Horace, Ovid, and Petronius. Although there are more than sixty languages (and accompanying nationalities) vying with Greek and Latin for some level of permanence, almost all disappear. But as the Roman Empire matures, the volume of Greek writing (some in the form of literature from the pens of Plutarch, Philostratus, Lucian, and the novelists) especially from Asia Minor grows and in turn overwhelms the volume of Latin. Most of this Greek, however, bears little mark of originality: it is tragic history, discussions of philosophy, rhetoric, science, scholarship, and criticism—reflections on the great work of the past. Or as L. Reynolds and N. Wilson phrase it: "second-hand learning had come to stay."[1] Far away from Rome some original material could still be produced in Latin, as we see in Apuleius and Minucius Felix. Though a pagan, Apuleius is aware of the latest religious fads; Minucius Felix, though a Christian, displays a great depth of knowledge in the classics. At this date, sometime in the second-century C.E., the pagan classical world of literature is part of the intellectual life of Christians and Jews.

The forty legions, the navy, the fairness, openness and comprehensiveness of Roman law, the paved roads, and especially the tolerance benefit all the disparate peoples of the empire. Commerce flourishes, universities thrive, ideas are rapidly exchanged, masses of books are copied and sold, and the level of literacy rises. Some of the inhabitants of Syria/Palestine can and do read and digest the best of classical literature: through their knowledge of Latin they claim their rights in court and appreciate the currents running through Roman political and social life; through their knowledge of Greek they learn to debate about the forms of the good and the beautiful, the possibility of an afterlife, the existence of a soul that lives on after the body, the notion that the body is a tomb. The eastern provinces of the empire might be a great distance in *milia passuum* from the *Urbs*, but the writings produced in the East show intellectual achievements that equal and are cognizant of everything happening to the West. People in the eastern provinces might not share equally in all facets of political power, but from their readings and discussions they know the best of what is written and thought in the whole empire.

From its beginnings with Homer through the lyricists and dramatists to its end with the novelists (Greek genius seems to have invented all four of our standard genres: epic, lyric, drama, and the novel—if science fiction is a genre separate from the novel, it begins with Lucian, the H. L. Mencken of Greek literature), ancient Greek literature has always been marked by great storytellers. And Jewish and early Christian writers seem to have stories/narratives that they desperately want to tell: many of these writers (a few of whom were to write canonical literature sanctioned later by the church) know the larger creative literature that we include in the Greek (a knowledge of which is the basis of the Greek *paideia*) and Latin classics, plus the commentaries, secondary literature, and handbooks on rhetoric, science, history, medicine, and scholarship.

---

1. L. Reynolds and N. Wilson, *Scribes and Scholars: A Guide to the Transmission of Greek and Latin Texts* (Oxford: Oxford University Press, 1974), 100.

Each of these Christian and Jewish writers has a story to tell, a narrative in prose, which according to the prejudices of others lies along a spectrum from history to fiction, from Gospels to apocrypha.

For some years now one area of Greek and Latin literature has been singled out as especially under the influence of religious thought. The canonical eight Greek and Latin novels all are credited (or discredited) with ties to ancient religions; it is clear that the stuff of which the novels are composed is often heavily religious. But these connections are not as slavishly close as R. Merkelbach would have us believe: he reads each ancient novel (except *Chariton*) as a *roman à clef* (or perhaps a *roman à these*) whose purpose can be unlocked given the right key.[2] G. W. Bowersock also points out the religious influences, borrowings, intertextuality between ancient pagan (especially the novelists) and early Christian writers.[3] By placing the narratives of the early Christian writers before those of the ancient novelists, he commits the venial sin of cart-before-the-horse.

The working relationships between religious storytelling, whether Egyptian, Jewish, or Christian, and classical narratives are not in question. But for more than a century the academic disciplines responsible for studying these narratives, classics and religion, have been divided, gone their separate ways, and failed to discuss with each other on a regular basis common material. By a happy coincidence classicists here and in Europe have begun to look anew at early Egyptian, Jewish, and Christian narratives, while at the same time scholars of religion are returning to a study of the classics. Both groups have profited by taking a holistic, rather than a disciplinary, view of the material surviving from the ancient world. Those scholars behind the creation and nurturing of the Ancient Fiction and Early Jewish and Christian Narrative Section deserve our thanks and praise for putting back together fragmented academic disciplines, which had ceased to present an understandable picture of the mosaic that is the ancient world.

Gareth Schmeling
University of Florida

---

2. Reinhold Merkelbach, *Roman und Mysterium in der Antike* (Munich: Beck, 1962).

3. Glen W. Bowersock, *Fiction as History* (Berkeley and Los Angeles: University of California Press, 1994).

INTRODUCTION

Richard I. Pervo

The Society of Biblical Literature Ancient Fiction and Early Christian and Jewish Narrative Group (now a section) began in 1992, in response to a burgeoning interest in the ancient novel among classicists and a concurrent desire of some members of the society to bring this interest to bear upon Jewish and Christian literature. From its outset the Group has sought to cross boundaries and transcend barriers that have walled off various disciplines. For this reason it has been open to new methods without attempting to establish a party line and has elected to interpret its warrant rather broadly. Testimony to this diversity can be demonstrated by listing the major authors and texts surveyed in this collection: Chariton, Shakespeare, Homer, Vergil, Plato, Matthew, Mark, Luke, Daniel, 3 Maccabees, the *Testament of Abraham*, rabbinic midrash, the Apocryphal Acts, Ezekiel the Tragedian, and the Sophist Aelian. Yet even diverse collections reveal, however unintentionally, prevalent issues and syntheses in the making. Before drawing these connecting lines it is, however, important to give every dot its day.

In "The Educational Curriculum in Chariton's *Callirhoe*," Ronald Hock applies his superb knowledge of ancient rhetorical education to an analysis of *Callirhoe*, the earliest fully preserved romantic novel. His main title evokes the famous thesis of Erwin Rohde, who viewed the Greek novels as the dubious fruit of a union between erotic poetry and the rhetorical excesses of the Second Sophistic.[1] In effect: "rhetoric makes bad romance." *Callirhoe* is what is known as a "presophistic" novel, but Hock shows that it is far from innocent of rhetoric. After a meticulous study that illustrates the congruence between the author Chariton's techniques and Greco-Roman education, Hock makes a case for viewing *paideia* as more than a status symbol—"credential" is the closest contemporary parallel. *Paideia*, a liberal arts education, produces people equipped with the skills needed to endure and eventually to master the "slings and arrows

---

1. Erwin Rohde, *Der griechische Roman und seine Vorläufer* (Leipzig: Breitkopf & Härtel, 1876; 3rd ed.; Leipzig: Breitkopf & Härtel, 1914).

of outrageous fortune," weapons that are not in short supply in the worlds of the ancient novel. In the language of traditional literary criticism, Chariton uses rhetoric to create character and not simply to facilitate the construction of episodes and the evocation of sentiment.

Hock's detailed analysis is valuable even as a restricted study of one dimension of a single book, but his essay has further applications. The more obvious of these is his implicit claim that Rohde correctly sensed the rhetorical background of the ancient novel, but improperly evaluated it. Another is an invitation to apply these tools to a wide range of narrative, including early Jewish and Christian narrative. Hock does not restrict himself to "higher education," which would leave room for the charge that authors like Mark were unlikely to have had such sophisticated, as it were, methods in their tool-chests. He indicates how each of the stages of higher education teaches the construction of narrative. If Mark had, as Dennis MacDonald aptly once said, "to leave school in the eighth grade to help his mother support the family," that does not mean that he had done no more than learn a bit of grammar. Hock's attention to different educational levels has much to offer students of ancient "popular" literature.

Chris Shea, "Imitating Imitation: Vergil, Homer, and Acts 10:1–11:18," sets her argument about the influence of Vergil upon Luke in the broader context of the influence of Vergil upon (Latin) Christianity. This is useful, not only for its information, but also because it makes an important methodological point: to understand a work—or, in this case, a hypothesis—it is desirable to look at successors as well as antecedents. Shea offers two important observations that are presuppositions to her proposal of mimesis: the first is a general comparison of the older Homeric to the later Vergilian epic. Whereas Homer celebrated individual heroes, Vergil was interested in the foundation and development of a community. His epic had political goals. If Luke and Acts are to be compared to epic, the Vergilian type provides the more suitable model, regardless of the issues of language and actual dependence. Her second observation is that Vergil and Luke had to tackle comparable problems in the transformation of their sources into the desired political/community-oriented mold. One of Luke's resources was the Greek Bible. In effect, Shea implies, Homer is to Vergil as the LXX is to Luke. These are valuable insights that will be appreciated even by those who do not agree that Luke imitated Vergil. Mimesis, which may be briefly defined as imitation of a "classic" model, is a dominant or important element in several of the essays. (See also Brant, Dupertuis, Hock, MacDonald, and Reimer.) Shea's title is a reminder that intertextuality views every text as a palimpsest. The *Aeneid* is itself an imitation of Homer (with substantial contributions from another epic, the *Argonauts* of Apollonius Rhodius). The study of mimesis must always recognize, however much it simplifies for the sake of coherence, that there are many texts in the picture, that none is likely to have a simple one-to-one relationship to another. Shea's specific example, comparison of Acts 10:1–11:18 (the conversion of Cornelius) to the narrative of *Aeneid* 8, is typically imaginative and provocative. The two stories deal with the effective resolution of problems that are not dissimilar.

With his *"Die Entführung in das Serail:* Aspasia: A Female Aesop?" Richard I. Pervo offers a companion piece to his study of the *Aesop Romance* (which also first appeared as a presentation to the SBL's Ancient Fiction Group). "Aspasia," a fictionalized story about a historical person, is the longest extant piece in Aelian's *Historical Miscellany.* Pervo examines this little-known tale in some detail, presenting it as an example of the fictionalization of history, of how to make an obscure woman the subject of an edifying little romance, with a plot worthy of an opera (whence the title). One point of comparison (and contrast) is with the *Aesop Romance,* for these two works share a number of plot features, notably an initial healing and eventual residence within a court. The narrator strongly praises Aspasia's reputation for wisdom, but has no examples that extend beyond the realm of personal relationships. Pervo finds this silence quite telling. Comparison with Esther is also revealing, since Aelian's Aspasia strongly resists the role of concubine. Aspasia gives the "women's viewpoint" on this subject, and those who read her story will never look at Esther in quite the same way again. Pervo suggests that Aelian has put the story into a "modern" perspective, in part by making his subject more like the heroines of romantic novels and, quite probably, in the light of such powerful women as the "Julias" of the Severan era (193–235). Further observations deal with the relation between novella and novel and the creation of biographical narrative, with particular reference to the Christian Gospels.

Gerhard van den Heever's dense and adventurous contribution, "Novel and Mystery: Discourse, Myth, and Society," is one of several essays that takes up the subject of "truth/history" versus "fiction/ novel" (cf. Johnson, Milikowsky, Pervo). Like Chaim Milikowsky, van den Heever regards "fiction" (or myth, fantasy, creed, etc.) as the more important of the two poles. He restates, and revises, deploying the language and tools of a number of contemporary methods, the theory which Bryan Reardon derived from Karl Kerenyi that the romantic novel is a formulation of "the Hellenistic myth."[2] In line with many others,

---

2. E.g., Bryan P. Reardon, *Courants littéraires grecs des IIe et IIIe siècles après J.-C.* (Annales littéraires de l'Université Nantes 3; Paris: Belles Lettres, 1971), 392–403; and Karl Kerenyi, *Die griechisch-orientalische Romanliteratur in religiongeschichtlicher Beleuchtung* (Tübingen: Mohr Siebeck, 1927; repr., Darmstadt: Wissenshaftliche Buchgesellschaft, 1964).

notably proponents of feminist and cultural studies, van den Heever
views romance as affirming the world as it is, most clearly in its social
structure. Yet he is also aware of the power of fantasy to promote vision
and thereby impetus for change. The ancient novel, in its broadest
sense, represents both of these poles, well illustrated in the contrast
between the romantic novels, in general, and the Christian Apocryphal
Acts, in general. Nearly all of the manifestations of the novel, however,
as his use of "Fantasy Theme Analysis" indicates, engage dreams and
thus a desire for change. This essay variously enhances every other contribution to the volume.

Judith B. Perkins's "Resurrection and Social Perspectives in the Apocryphal Acts *Acts of Peter* and *Acts of John*," turns to two of the major
Apocryphal Acts, the *Acts of John* and the *Acts of Peter*, to test a hypothesis
about the correlation between social and theological ideas. The antithesis
between (spiritual) soul and (material) body that views the former as
superior is an elitist and intellectual view that, she proposes, can be used
to support traditional social hierarchy. Early "orthodox" Christianity of
the second century rebuffed those elements of its tradition (i.e., what
would become the biblical canon) that tended to support the spiritual
view in favor of a material understanding of resurrection. Those who
supported the "spiritual" understanding were gradually marginalized as
"heretics." The Apocryphal Acts do not represent a uniform theology;
indeed, they tend to be popular and inconsistent in theological expression
(in so far as one can discern from their often revised and mainly incomplete texts). The *Acts of John* has a highly spiritualized, ultra-Johannine
view of resurrection, which takes place at conversion and of which physical resurrection is but a symbol, while the *Acts of Peter* is more concerned
with physical resurrection and its benefits to the community. Perkins
then applies her corollary. The indifference to social status of the *Acts of
John* is an elite perspective that does not challenge social hierarchy,
whereas the community envisaged in the *Acts of Peter* is more inclusive.
This is a fascinating study of what many have been inclined to regard as
one of the more boring and dubious qualities of the Apocryphal Acts:
their focus upon miraculous raisings of the dead. In both works resurrection has symbolic and social elements. The "bad guys," so to speak, are
the more dualistic, while the writing that is closer to what would become
the "orthodox" perspective is more subversive of absolute social ranking.
This is, in addition to its other merits, a useful corrective to the facile view
that "heretics" were "always" socially subversive.

Jo-Ann A. Brant, "Mimesis and Dramatic Art in Ezekiel the Tragedians' *Exagoge*," shows that changing genre also changes meaning, for
Ezekiel, one of the few Hellenistic Jewish poets whose verses survive,
albeit in fragments, had more in mind than putting the Exodus story into

dramatic verse, more also than using bits and pieces of the tragic repertory and its vocabulary. Ezekiel entered into not only what, for want of a better term, may be called "the conventions" of dramaturgy, but also, perhaps willy-nilly, into its spirit. The result, Brant argues, corrodes the univocal authority of the omniscient narrator. This mimesis of Greek drama, is, in several senses, one element of the interface between biblical narrative and ancient fiction, since drama is fiction, even when it took up historical subjects, as in Aeschylus' *The Persians* (which was one of Ezekiel's sources). Brant further demonstrates that efforts to mine these fragments for theological information while ignoring their literary qualities are fraught with danger. This observation raises questions for historical criticism to ponder and thus contributes to a dialogue between historical and literary critics.

Sara R. Johnson's study of 3 Maccabees ("*Third Maccabees:* Historical Fictions and the Shaping of Jewish Identity in the Hellenistic Period") focuses upon its use of historical data and verisimilitude as a means for investigating and giving some precision to the loosely defined category of the "historical novel" and as a tool for discerning the intention of the work. Already in antiquity there were many types of historical fiction. Johnson seeks to elucidate the how and the why of the historical material found in 3 Maccabees. She shows that historical, pseudohistorical, and "true to life" data serve the author's purpose, which is to make a case for a suitable identity for Hellenized Diaspora Jews. When all has been said and done, this self-understanding is not very different from that expressed in *Aristeas*, a work once considered to be the antithesis of 3 Maccabees. She prefers to view the book as "neither history nor novel, but something distinct from either." Johnson recognizes that this issue of identity extended beyond Jewish fictions, pointing to the old and still resonant thesis of M. Braun who posited the existence of a number of "national romances" that emerged in the wake of Hellenization and Romanization.[3] This essay thus contributes to two of the issues that reverberate through the collection: history versus fiction and the function of fiction in the creation and preservation of identity.

"3 Maccabees: An Anti-Dionysian Polemic" by Noah Hacham uses literary criticism, among other methods, to support a theological interpretation of 3 Maccabees. This unusual piece of fiction has attracted a number of conflicting interpretations, in particular attempts to delineate the political circumstances that seem to have called it forth. Hacham sagely seizes, not unlike ancient allegorical interpreters, upon an

---

3. Martin Braun, *History and Romance in Greco-Oriental Literature* (Oxford: Blackwell, 1938).

absurdity of the text, the Dionysiac brand or tattoo as a stigma, to uncover 3 Maccabees' ridicule of Dionysiac religion. He contends that the book was written for Jews, a reasonable thesis, to devalue the alleged advantages of apostasy. Whereas Johnson emphasized what 3 Maccabees was affirming, Hacham stresses what it was opposing. One may conclude that the worship of Dionysus is both historically plausible, since the Egyptian King Ptolemy IV was known to be an avid devotee, and also a synecdoche for any type of syncretism or adherence to another religion. The author supports his interpretation by a comparison with Esther. (See also Pervo's contribution in this volume.) The essays of Johnson and Hacham show that valuable insights can be made about this text when the thorny issue of date is laid aside.

"Humor and Paradox in the Characterization of Abraham in the *Testament of Abraham*" by Jared Ludlow turns to the once very popular, if, to us, somewhat tedious genre of the testament, a form found in both biblical (Gen 49; John 14–17; etc.) and classical (Plato's *Phaedo*) contexts. His purpose is to illustrate the impact of literary expectations upon expansions of the biblical narrative. Rather than portray the protagonist as a model of unassailable virtue, as in the *Testament of Joseph*, for example, one edition of the *Testament of Abraham* elects to show the patriarch as a human character, beset by conflicts and afraid of his coming death. Ludlow identifies the resultant inconsistency as "paradoxical." It is apparently humorous and certainly engaging, rather more interesting than the predictably upright final days of a paragon of righteousness. God remains steadfast, while the great saint looks rather more like one of us, a human struggling to be faithful while confronting his ultimate, and universal, fate. These findings resemble what Brant uncovered in the *Exagoge*. Both of these contributors deal with the effects of transforming "history" into fiction.

The essay of Chaim Milikowsky, "Midrash as Fiction and Midrash as History: What Did the Rabbis Mean?" directly confronts the question of what writers of fiction believed about their products. Milikowsky begins with an important observation: the tendency to generalize about rabbinic thought is unwarranted, since their literature was produced over a period of centuries. His basic question is vital for much of the literature engaged by those who study ancient narrative. Were readers supposed to believe that *Callirhoe* related actual events? Probably not, most will say, although some readers may have done so. What about the *Alexander Romance* or *Aseneth*? That is a more complicated question. A related question, in modern terms, is whether authors of works like these intended to "deceive" their readers.

Milikowsky addresses these questions with considerable erudition and careful nuance. He argues that the chronicle *Seder ʿOlam* knows (of course) the midrashic tradition, but does not utilize it to identify historical events. He thus concludes that, in at least some rabbinic circles, the distinction between "history" and "fiction" was observed. What of this? Milikowsky proposes that rabbinic Judaism participated in the heritage of Greco-Roman culture, which had long before concluded that fiction can be an important mode for communicating religious and philosophical truth. Fiction is attacked when authors consider its contents to be "bad." The irascible and irritating Jerome is a good example. Although he fulminated against the character of the lion in the *Acts of Paul* (*De viris illustribus* 7), he did not hesitate to introduce useful animals of improbable prowess and piety into his own lives of Paul, Malchus, and Hilarion. The case of Jerome intends to suggest that Milikowsky's thesis also applies, as he does not doubt, to early Christian, as well as to polytheistic, literature.

A different manner of subject receives attention from Tawny Holm's "Daniel 1–6: A Biblical Story-Collection." Holm has several objectives. One is to examine the various editions of Daniel from the perspective of story collections. Her first task is to identify the criteria for a story collection proper, to elucidate some different types, and to summarize the various literary processes that lay behind particular collections. She then turns to the Daniel-cycle, as examples of "textual fluidity" that are best examined as different "performances" or, in more conventional language, editions, rather than as descendents of a hypothetical "original." Holm is then ready to look at the literary background of the stories attached to Daniel, with particular attention to Egyptian tales about magicians, where she finds the most cogent antecedents.

Story collections, already taken into consideration by Rohde, raise important questions for the development of the ancient novel and related genres. This is most apparent in popular works like the *Alexander-Romance* and the *Aesop-Romance,* which have sometimes been viewed as more or less indefinitely expandable collections of stories. Although the "beads on a string" simile is about as valid for literature as it is for necklaces, it is undoubtedly true that there were collections of stories about Alexander, as there were about Jesus. The Gospel of Mark, for example, evidently incorporates two preexisting collections of Jesus' miracles in 4:35–8:10 (as well as controversies in 2:1–3:6, parables in 4:1–34, etc.). Even Q seems to be responding to biographical impulses, evident in the opening references to John's baptism of Jesus and the subsequent temptations (Luke 3:21–22; 4:1–13). One question, therefore, is the extent to which collections of stories may provide impetus for a "complete" narrative. This issue is related to the old question of whether a novella can be made into a novel. The scholarly tradition has tended to reject both of these proposals, but further investigation is warranted (see also Pervo).

J. R. C. Cousland has contributed a comparative study, "The Choral Crowds in the Tragedy according to St. Matthew." Although there have long been a number of general, often facile and frequently superficial, references to the "choral nature" of crowds, as well as general comparisons of Gospels/Acts to drama, meticulous examination has been rare. Cousland wishes to do more than point out interesting "parallels" between Gospel crowds and Greek choruses. One welcome feature of his contribution is an in-depth investigation of research on the chorus in Greek drama, an investigation that does not select—or stumble upon— a single theory, but a survey that reflects the conflict and diversity of interpretation.

For Cousland the study of Greek choruses provides tools for analysis rather than another list of parallels. Equipped with these, he makes a number of illuminating detailed observations and establishes a thesis that is congruent with other scholarly perspectives and also pregnant with literary insight. Although the "crowds" in Matthew do not appear to be the consistent and localized body, such as the maidservants of Creusa in Euripides' *Ion*, the identity of whom is known from the outset, it transpires that they do have an identity, "Israel," and that they play a role in the story. More than commentators and consultants, the crowd becomes a character.

Rubén Rene Dupertuis's "The Summaries of Acts 2, 4, and 5 and Utopian Literary Traditions" is a study of literary dependence. Dupertuis proposes that the descriptions of community life in Acts 2 and 4, which include the famous, or notorious, holding of property in common, are directly dependent upon the *Republic* of Plato. Scholarship has long recognized that Luke's language evokes some of the commonplaces about primitive utopias and the ideal cities proposed by various philosophers. Dupertuis's thesis has three attractive qualities. It proposes a distinct source rather than the often fuzzy "traditions," which can be a "weasel" concept. Dupertuis extends the focus from common property to other dimensions of community organization and life. Finally, this proposal tilts the argument from the widespread notion that Luke has (slightly) idealized or "Hellenized" his source toward viewing these accounts as literary fictions, since Dupertuis argues that the "whole package" came from Plato, as it were, which, if valid, would make it less likely that Luke were guilty of no more than a bit of cross-cultural sensitivity.

Dennis MacDonald's "The Breasts of Hecuba and Those of the Daughters of Jerusalem: Luke's Transvaluation of a Famous Iliadic Scene" is a contribution to a project that he has been pursuing for two decades, through three books and a number of papers and articles. MacDonald's specific argument is that some early Christians, notably the authors of Mark and Luke, imitated Greek authors, especially the Homeric epics. In the course of his labors MacDonald has gradually developed and refined an elaborate set of criteria for mimesis. "Mimesis" is not simply the sort of intertextuality that results from dependence upon a source. It is a phenomenon of an education and a culture that looks back to a "classical" past that provides models and norms for composition. MacDonald's project has two broader implications. One assaults the deep-rooted tendency to view early Christians (and Jews, not to mention devotees of Isis, etc.) as encased in blinkers that exclude all but religious texts and issues from their intellectual horizons. This assumption is fallacious, and its effect upon scholarship has been invidious. The second supports the possibility that a number of passages in the canonical Gospels are literary fictions, compositions of their authors based upon traditional models. An outstanding question is whether implied readers were expected to recognize most or all of this mimesis, as is often the case in literary texts, or, more narrowly, the "classics" were authorial resources, bridges that, once crossed, could be put to the torch. This particular essay, which includes a broad exploration of the theme of prospective suffering in ancient literature, aptly illustrates one of MacDonald's criteria, for even those who reject his thesis about mimesis will find their understanding of Luke 23:27–31 enhanced and will further appreciate the extent to which ancient audiences would find its sentiments familiar.

Andy Reimer's "A Biography of a Motif: The Empty Tomb in the Gospels, the Greek Novels, and Shakepeare's *Romeo and Juliet*" has two goals. One is to trace the *Nachleben* of the empty tomb motif in Mark, Chariton, and Shakespeare. Related to this is his support of the views of G. Bowersock and others (including G. Gamba, I. Ramelli, and T. Völker) that non-Christian novels borrowed from Christian literature (i.e., that the influence runs in the opposite direction from that generally assumed in comparative studies). All proposals that run against the grain deserve serious consideration, precisely because they challenge deeply held assumptions. Reimer's hypothesis faces at least two major challenges. One is that of chronology and accessibility. In this case the question of date is not overwhelming, for Chariton could have written later than Mark, and one could suppose that the text—or the story of the tomb—may have been known in Aphrodisias in the late first century. Another is purpose. Gamba and Ramelli, for example, argue that Petronius was attacking the Christian movement through parody. That does not seem to be the case in *Callirhoe*. Reimer must, and does, assume that Chariton knew a good story when he saw it. Many will doubt that Reimer has succeeded in making the river of research reverse its course by this one essay, but his challenge to "assured results" cannot be ignored. This is a question that is receiving vigorous attention at the present time.

* * *

Perhaps the most apparent conclusion to be drawn from a reading of these essays is the pervasive and subversive power of mimesis. Mimesis, a species of culturally honored plagiarism, links contemporary research on intertextuality with ancient literary (theory and) practice. It therefore follows the recommendation of Jesus in Matthew that scholars should utilize both "what is new and what is old" (13:52). Although mimesis may at times seem little different from traditional source criticism (e.g. Dupertuis), it is usually subversive of historicizing approaches, which presume that the text is rooted in fact and then look for greater or lesser bits of rhetorical color (e.g. Dupertuis). This is to say that, although by contemporary standards, mimesis seems uncreative, it could stimulate a high degree of creativity. A fuller understanding of this technique requires resort to later analogies, including Dante, Shakespeare, Racine et Cie., Goethe, Joyce, and, yes, even Bernstein's West Side Story and the film Clueless, to name but a few. Chris Shea peeks at this can of worms when she envisions Vergil and Luke attempting to make their respective cases through revision of the great, but irrelevant, tradition. Essays like that of Reimer are reminders that issues of source can often be argued both ways, so that ultimate decisions must rest upon which seems to be the stronger and better case in the light of the work as a whole and of its proposed purpose. Others, including Ludlow and Holm, demonstrate that the quest for the more original is often futile and not infrequently less interesting than is analysis of various editions in light of their distinctive qualities.

Brant's foray into mimesis stimulates a more direct engagement with another pervasive issue: the distinction between history and fiction. When one attempts to translate historical narrative into another form, the all but inevitable result will be a kind of fiction. This is probably no less true of authors inspired by epic, but transforming prose narrative into poetic genres makes for blatant cases. One need not doubt that Ezekiel wished to be faithful to the tradition, perhaps to compete with Greek drama, but the result is a story deprived of its formal warrant. One long-standing objection to the comparison of some Jewish and early Christian texts to ancient fiction is that readers long viewed Esther, Judith, Mark, and Acts as "straight" history. Respondents to this objection may observe that Christians long accepted the factual accuracy of at least most of the Acts of Paul and the Acts of Peter, and point as well to the large volume of mail still directed to 221 Baker Street, but it is probably better to say that this question, while important, cannot receive a full and satisfactory answer. To ask whether authors intended to deceive their readers is a difficult query to lay before those who strive for verisimilitude, who take great pains to make Callirhoe or Robert Jordan look like real people immersed in the project of living. Milikowsky shows that the rabbis did not believe all of the stories that they read (and told) and he explains why. The issue may be clouded with paternalism: people like Origen and the rabbis knew that such and such did not "actually happen" but regarded these stories as useful for the simple as simple history and for the learned as salient example. How, for instance, should cultured Egyptian Jews respond to royal pressure to show religious conformity?

Johnson reads 3 Maccabees as a story concerned with the construction and maintenance of Jewish identity in the Diaspora. Perhaps many of its original readers knew that it was not true, although this is not certain, but few of them would have failed to realize what the story was attempting to inculcate and achieve. The question of identity, implicitly or explicitly, arises in nearly every one of these essays. Hock detects the same theme in *Callirhoe*, whose author may be prepared to accept Roman rule, but not at the expense of rejecting the proud claims of ancient Hellenic culture. *Callirhoe* and 3 Maccabees have more in common than first meets the eye, even if the theme of identity is less overt, possibly less conscious, in the romantic novel. Perkins observes its working at the microlevel in her analyses of the different social and theological functions of resurrection stories. The broadest approach to the issue appears in van den Heever's exploration of the formation of new "myths" of social identity. The important half-truth that saw the origin of the novel in the "degeneration" of historiography here awakens to find itself in bed with Karl Kerenyi.[4] Kerenyi, in his *Der antike Roman*, begins to explore how novels seek to satisfy the desires and spiritual interests of the culture for which they were written. The use of history to express identity should not surprise those who have seen marginalized groups call for the study and teaching of, for example, black history and women's history. Historical fiction can be even more convenient, since it need not account for unpleasant facts or be compelled to conclude that providence, like Homer, sometimes nods. Josephus wrote for the elite (which is not to say that he did not find historical fiction useful). Shorter and more popular projects of this nature are likely to fall into or near the category of historical fiction.

---

4. Eduard Schwartz, *Fünf Vorträge über den griechischen Roman* (Berlin: de Gruyter, 1896), provides an example of the argument that the novel represents "degeneration"; see Karl Kerenyi, *Der antike Roman* (Darmstadt: Wissenshaftliche Buchgesellschaft, 1971).

Finally, it is interesting that during the Hellenistic period tales of utopia also slipped from the realm of myth into history or reality, as in the writings of Euhemerus and Iambulus. (On utopia, see the contributions of Dupertuis and van den Heever.)

This summary of some recurrent issues should not suggest that contributors were presented with a list of questions to answer or matters to address. Any coherence was unplanned, although it is far from accidental. Similarly, the résumés of individual essays lack nuance and the particularities of various methods and quests. Introductions attempt to say why the book is important and should be read. Once the book has been read, the introduction has lost its importance and may fold up its tent and vanish.

PART 1:
ANCIENT GRECO-ROMAN NARRATIVE

The Educational Curriculum in Chariton's *Callirhoe*

Ronald F. Hock

Introduction

Education in antiquity, largely known through the classic studies of H. I. Marrou and Stanley F. Bonner,[1] has recently been the object of increasing and intense investigation, through the work of Alan Booth, but especially the work of Raffaela Cribiore and Teresa Morgan. These last two have depended less on literary sources, such as Quintilian's comprehensive and idealistic treatment, the *Institutio oratoria,* and more on rigorous and comprehensive analyses of the actual classroom texts of teachers and students that have been preserved on papyri, tablets, and ostraca.[2] To be sure, literary sources are not excluded—witness Cribiore's frequent use of Herodas and Libanius;[3] nevertheless, their use can be increased and especially with respect to sources that deal with educated persons and place their educations in a broader social and intellectual

---

1. See H. I. Marrou, *A History of Education in Antiquity* (trans. G. Lamb; New York: Sheed & Ward, 1956; repr., Madison: University of Wisconsin Press, 1982), and Stanley F. Bonner, *Education in Antiquity: From the Elder Cato to the Younger Pliny* (Berkeley and Los Angeles: University of California Press, 1977).

2. See Alan Booth, "Elementary and Secondary Education in the Roman Empire," *Florilegium* 1 (1979): 1–14; Raffaella Cribiore, *Writing, Teachers, and Students in Graeco-Roman Egypt* (ASP 36; Atlanta: Scholars Press, 1996); and Teresa Morgan, *Literate Education in the Hellenistic and Roman Worlds* (New York: Cambridge University Press, 1998). Cribiore has incorporated her earlier work as well as treated education more comprehensively in her *Gymnastics of the Mind: Greek Education in Hellenistic and Roman Egypt* (Princeton: Princeton University Press, 2001). See also the collection of essays in Yun Lee Too, ed., *Education in Greek and Roman Antiquity* (Leiden: Brill, 2001).

3. Herodas's third mime, "The Schoolteacher," deserves the repeated mention she gives it (see *Gymnastics of the Mind,* 25, 68, 70, 71, 107, 108, 136, 153, 175, 179), although the truant, dyslexic boy in the mime is not Kokkalos, as Cribiore consistently calls him, but Kottalos; Kokkalos is another student in Lampriskos's class (3.60). The importance of Libanius is obvious, and it is heartening to read that Cribiore (7 n. 14) is preparing a translation of over five hundred of Libanius's letters that deal with educational matters.

world. This broader world is precisely what the Greek novels provide—
fictional, to be sure, but also lengthy, detailed, and comprehensive.
Moreover, these novels focus precisely on the sorts of aristocratic men
and women for whom ancient education was designed. As a result, these
novels are particularly valuable sources for observing educated people in
the full context of social and intellectual life in the early Roman Empire.

I restrict myself, however, to one Greek novel, namely Chariton's *Callirhoe*,[4] in part because focusing on one novel will permit fuller analysis of
it than an attempt to cover them all would and in part because Chariton—
contrary to Xenophon, Achilles Tatius, and Longus—seems more
interested in education than the others. He alone, at any rate, explicitly
identifies several of his characters—Chaereas, Callirhoe, Dionysius, and
Demetrius—as being πεπαιδευμένοι, or as being educated.[5] Chariton is
thus conscious of his characters' education, and hence his narrative should
therefore tell us something about what an educated person was expected
to be and do in the Greek East of the middle of the first century C.E.[6]

In addition, this narrative should also tell us more about Chariton's
own education, which is a matter of some debate among scholars. For
example, Antonio Scarcella attributes an excellent education to Callirhoe
and a quality education to Dionysius and by implication a like education
to Chariton himself.[7] Bryan Reardon, however, is much less effusive,
attributing to Chariton merely "a decent secondary education, perhaps
more."[8] But before delving into Chariton's depiction of his various
πεπαιδευμένοι as well as his own educational level, it is necessary to summarize briefly some of the current work being done in the study of
ancient education so as to base our analysis on the latest scholarship.

---

4. The text of Chariton used in this article is that by Warren E. Blake, *Charitonis Aphrodisiensis de Chaerea et Callirhoe Amatoriarum Narrationum Libri Octo* (New York: Oxford
University Press, 1938). Translations of Chariton's novel are available in Chariton, *Callirhoe*
(ed. and trans. G. P. Goold; LCL 481; Cambridge: Harvard University Press, 1995), and in
Bryan P. Reardon, ed., *Collected Ancient Greek Novels* (Berkeley and Los Angeles: University
of California Press, 1989), 21–124 (by Reardon himself). Nevertheless, translations of Chariton as well as of all ancient sources are my own.

5. For Chaereas, see Chariton 7.2.5; for Callirhoe, see 6.5.8; 7.6.5; for Dionysius, see
1.12.6; 2.1.5; 4.1; 3.2.6; 4.7.6; 5.5.1; 9.8; 8.5.10; and for Demetrius, see 8.3.10.

6. Dating Chariton's novel is still debated, but for a lengthy argument favoring a dating
in the middle of the first century or a little earlier, see the discussion of this issue (and much
else) by Bryan P. Reardon, "Chariton," in *The Novel in the Ancient World* (ed. Gareth Schmeling; Mnemo-syne, Bibliotheca Classica Batava, Supplementum 159; Leiden: Brill, 1996),
309–35, esp. 312–17. See also Consuelo Ruiz-Montero, "Chariton von Aphrodisias: Ein
Überblick," *ANRW* 34.2:1006–54.

7. See Antonio M. Scarcella, "The Social and Economic Structures of the Ancient
Novels," in Schmeling, *The Novel in the Ancient World*, 221–76, esp. 223 and 229.

8. See Reardon, "Chariton," 324.

GRECO-ROMAN EDUCATION IN RECENT STUDY

Recent work on ancient education has emphasized less uniformity than was presumed by Marrou and Bonner, especially at the primary and secondary levels. Booth, for example, has shown that primary education was not always taught at a school under a γραμματιστής, or primary school teacher, but sometimes at home; that even at school primary education was not always the preserve of a γραμματιστής, but sometimes of a γραμματικός, or secondary school teacher, who then was assured of students for his own more advanced curriculum; and that primary education was divided into two tiers, one for poorer students like Herodas's Kottalos and one for aristocratic children like the characters in Chariton's novel.[9]

Cribiore's studies, *Writing, Teachers, and Students in Graeco-Roman Egypt* and *Gymnastics of the Mind*, have advanced our knowledge even further. She has provided a larger and more coherently organized collection of the numerous papyri, ostraca, and tablets—now over 400—that document the actual activities of teachers and students in Greco-Roman Egypt.[10] More important, she has used this documentary material to devise a typology of school hands, which distinguishes four grades of increasing skill—zero-grade, alphabetic, evolving, and rapid. As a result, these school texts can be more precisely assigned to students at specific points in their progress through the curriculum.[11]

This typology has led Cribiore to make some significant modifications in our understanding of the primary and secondary curricula. She finds, for example, that the standard view of how students learned to read—that primary students learned to read by following a graded sequence from letters to syllables, to words of increasing numbers of syllables, to sentences, and finally to short poetic passages[12]—does not tell the whole story.[13] She shows that students learned to copy and read their

---

9. See Booth, "Elementary and Secondary Education," 1–14. His views are confirmed by Robert A. Kaster, "Notes on 'Primary' and 'Secondary' Schools in Late Antiquity," *TAPA* 113 (1983): 323–46.

10. See Cribiore, *Writing*, 173–284. Her collection supersedes the earlier collections of Roger A. Pack, *The Greek and Latin Literary Texts from Greco-Roman Egypt* (2nd ed.; Ann Arbor: University of Michigan Press, 1965), 137–40; and Janine Debut, "Les documents scholaires," *ZPE* 63 (1986): 251–78. For another collection of these documentary texts, see Morgan, *Literate Education*, 275–87. On the remarkable similarity of Egypt to other provinces of the Greek East with regard to education, see Cribiore, *Gymnastics of the Mind*, 6.

11. See Cribiore, *Writing*, 102–18.

12. For this view, based on literary evidence and illustrated by some documentary texts, see Marrou, *History of Education*, 150–59, 265–74; and Bonner, *Education*, 166–78.

13. See Cribiore, *Gymnastics of the Mind*, 161–62.

names at the same time as they began to learn the letters of the alphabet, a skill missed altogether by earlier scholars.[14] She also draws attention to the emphasis teachers placed on calligraphy, so that students with only alphabetic hands often copied short passages before they could even read what they were copying in order to improve their writing skills,[15] and, conversely, students with evolving and even rapid hands continued to practice their calligraphy on lists of words—both of which go against the strict sequencing outlined in literary sources and followed by previous scholars.[16] She also emphasizes that secondary students not only read literature and learned grammar, but also began to do some simple composing—writing summaries and paraphrases of the material they were reading as well as writing letters addressed to their parents, the latter allowing students to display their progress and permitting the γραμματικοί to justify their fees.[17]

Morgan's book, *Literate Education in the Hellentistic and Roman Worlds*, advances our understanding in yet other ways. She places the origins of the standard tripartite curriculum—primary, secondary, and tertiary—in the decades immediately following Alexander's conquests and in fact as a response to them.[18] This curriculum, set by the mid-third century B.C.E. and lasting throughout antiquity and beyond,[19] remained the preserve of urban elites, as even basic literacy, the consequence of completing the primary curriculum, never rose above fifteen percent. Consequently, completing all three stages and thereby achieving the status of a πεπαιδευμένος was rare indeed—a few percent at most.[20] Thus παιδεία, or education, along with wealth and high birth, was one of the prized social markers of Greek identity and status, which were requisites for belonging to the social and political elites of the cities of the Greek East.[21] The introduction of grammar to the secondary curriculum, she adds, occurred in the early Roman period as yet "an extra rung on the ladder of literate status,"[22] a status that those

---

14. See Cribiore, *Writing*, 40, 139–52; and *Gymnastics of the Mind*, 167–69.

15. See Cribiore, *Writing*, 43–44; and *Gymnastics of the Mind*, 169–70.

16. See Cribiore, *Writing*, 129–35.

17. See Cribiore, *Gymnastics of the Mind*, 215–19.

18. See Morgan, *Literate Education*, 21–25; cf. also Cribiore, *Gymnastics of the Mind*, 163.

19. See Morgan, *Literate Education*, 24.

20. That so few progressed through all three stages explains why so few documentary texts illustrating the secondary and tertiary stages have been discovered in the sands of Egypt (see Morgan, *Literate Education*, 57, 64, 72).

21. See Morgan, *Literate Education*, 74. See also Cribiore, *Gymnastics of the Mind*, 123: "Those who acquired a higher education became part of a network of power, in which they were enmeshed by their own educational achievements, personal wealth, and connections."

22. See Morgan, *Literate Education*, 57–63 (quotation on 63); see also Cribiore, *Gymnastics of the Mind*, 210.

who attained it could use to look down on those whose education ended at
the primary stage and up to those who had achieved even higher levels of
education.[23] Finally, Morgan proposes a core and periphery model for
ancient education, in which most students were taught only a core of skills
and authors,[24] whereas only the most advantaged of them went on to learn
more advanced skills—grammatical and rhetorical—and to read a broader
array of authors, such as those recommended by Quintilian and Dio
Chrysostom: poets of various kinds, historians, orators, and philosophers.[25]

With these corrections and modifications in our understanding of
ancient education, we can now turn to Chariton's *Callirhoe*, using the tripartite curriculum—primary, secondary, and tertiary—as an organizing
principle of analysis.

The Primary Curriculum

The primary curriculum, apart from some simple arithmetic,[26] was
concerned with basic literacy—learning to read and write the letters of the
alphabet, then lists of words, then sentences, and finally short poetic passages.[27] Chariton's romance has little to say about his characters having
learned to read and write[28] in the way that Longus explicitly tells us that
Daphnis and Chloe had at least completed the primary curriculum—were
learning their letters (γράμματα ἐπαίδευον)—when their fathers dreamed
that Eros commanded them to train their children as herders instead.[29]
Nor does Chariton refer explicitly to any of the initial exercises of the

---

23. See Morgan, *Literate Education*, 84.

24. See also Cribiore, *Gymnastics of the Mind*, 179: "Some Homer, a bit of Euripides, and
some gnomic quotations from Isocrates formed the cultural package of students at the primary level."

25. See Quintilian, *Inst.* 10.1.46–51; Dio Chrysostom, *Orat.* 18.6–17; and Morgan, *Literate
Education*, 71–72, 88.

26. See Cribiore, *Gymnastics of the Mind*, 180–83.

27. On the primary curriculum, see Marrou, *History of Education*, 142–59; Bonner, *Education in Ancient Rome*, 165–88; and especially Cribiore, *Gymnastics of the Mind*, 160–84.

28. Chariton does have something to say about preschooling. During a conversation in
which Theron attempts to sell Callirhoe to Leonas, he offers as a selling point the fact that
Callirhoe is sufficiently educated (πεπαίδευται ἱκανῶς) to be a nurse of an infant girl whose
mother has recently died (1.12.9). What Theron presumably has in mind is that Callirhoe's
education would enable her to teach the infant to speak Greek correctly as she grew up, a
recommendation of Quintilian (*Inst.* 1.1.4–5).

29. See Longus 1.8.1. Longus is aware that education of peasants was rare and explains
the anomaly by saying that they were being educated because Daphnis's and Chloe's parents
knew their children's true status was aristocratic. In any case, since Daphnis was now fifteen
and Chloe thirteen at the time of this life-changing dream, they might have progressed well
into the secondary curriculum so that γράμματα might then have meant literature.

primary curriculum in the way that, say, Herodas mentions Kottalos's difficulty in recognizing the letter alpha and his misreading the word ΜΑΡΩΝ as ΣΙΜΩΝ,[30] or in the way that Epictetus refers several times to his students having had to write the word Dio[31]—clear references to lists of words that his students had read in primary school.[32]

Chariton becomes more relevant, however, for the later exercises in the series—reading sentences and poetic passages, typically Homer. Chariton's narrative habits of citing maxims and quoting Homer may thus be attributed, in part, to these school exercises. For example, the first sentences students learned to read were usually maxims,[33] and Isocrates and Menander were core authors for collecting appropriate sentiments. Chariton's maxims likewise show a preference for Menander.[34] For example, Chariton cites a maxim to explain the ease with which one of those plotting against Chaereas could win over one of Callirhoe's slaves: "A woman is easily captivated when she thinks she's loved" (1.4.2)—a maxim that is adapted from Menander's *Naukleros*: "A man in love is by nature easily led" (*Frag.* 290 Körte), which is a play of Menander's that was praised by Quintilian (*Inst.* 10.1.70). Another of Chariton's maxims— "Eros is master of all the gods, even of Zeus himself" (6.3.2)—is similarly an adaptation of a Menandrian sentiment, this time from the *Heros:* "Nothing is stronger than Eros, not even Zeus, although he is master of all the gods in heaven; in fact, Zeus acts in all things at the behest of Eros" (frg. 2 Körte).

In addition, Chariton's one outright quotation of Menander may also derive from an educational context. Dionysius, while traveling to Babylon to prosecute Mithridates for having adulterous designs on his wife, realizes that he had too hastily taken his suspicions to the Great King and is reminded of a line from Menander (4.7.7)—"I could be (at home) and sleeping with my beloved" (*Misoumenos* 9). More papyri survive of this

---

30. See Herodas 3.22, 24–25; and J. S. Rusten, "Maron in School (P.Köln 3.125)," *ZPE* 60 (1985): 21–22.

31. See Epictetus 1.12.13; 2.2.23; 13.20; 3.24.51. For an example of the name Dio appearing in a school exercise, see Erich Ziebarth, *Aus der antiken Schule: Sammlung griechischer Texte auf Papyrus, Holztafeln, Ostraka* (2nd ed.; Bonn: Marcus & Marcus, 1913), 6.

32. For school texts with proper names in the lists of words, see Cribiore, *Writing*, 42–43, 196–203, 269–70, 274–76, 280–81, and 283. On the role of these names in inculcating cultural knowledge, see Janine Debut, "De l'usage des listes de mots comme fondement de la pédagogie dans l'antiquité," *REA* 85 (1983): 261–74, esp. 263–69.

33. For example, the primary textbook, known as P.Bour. 1, contains twenty-four maxims, one maxim for each letter of the alphabet (lines 169–239) (see Paul Collart, *Les Papyrus Bouriant* [Paris: Champion, 1926], 17–27).

34. For school texts containing Menandrian maxims, see Cribiore, *Writing*, 211, 226, 235–36, 239, 277–78.

play than any other, and one of these papyri comes from a student who had copied the first sixteen lines of the play, including this line. Chariton may have first come into contact with maxims from this play at school.[35]

One other comment regarding the primary stage of education before moving on: Chariton does not think twice about assuming literacy for aristocratic women and even for some slaves. Callirhoe, for example, is expected to be able to read a note left by Chaereas who had written that he had to go to the country (1.4.8), and Queen Statira is implicitly expected to read the letters that she and Callirhoe had resolved to exchange (8.4.8). But none of the other women in the romance—for example, the slave-confidant Plangon—is depicted as having even a basic literacy.

Literacy is assumed, however, for some highly placed slaves, specifically Leonas, Dionysius's slave manager, and Hyginus, Mithridates' slave manager, both of whom had probably been their master's σύντροφος and hence had enjoyed privileged roles since birth. Leonas is expected to read and sign papers authorizing the purchase of Callirhoe (2.1.6), and Hyginus is said to know how to speak Greek (and presumably to read it as well) (4.5.1–2). Literacy in the early Roman Empire was generally low—at most fifteen per cent—but not as restricted as it is in Chariton's novel, perhaps because so few marginal and lower level slaves play any significant roles in the story.[36]

THE SECONDARY CURRICULUM

Once students had learned the rudiments of reading, writing, and arithmetic, they moved on to the secondary curriculum offered by a γραμματικός, or teacher of grammar, literature, and simple compositions.[37] The study of literature emphasized poetry and in particular the Homeric epics,[38] and especially the *Iliad*, which students at this level read in its entirety.[39] Chariton's thorough familiarity with Homer derives in

---

35. On this papyrus, P.IFAO inv. 89, see Cribiore, *Writing*, 242–43. On Chariton's use of Menander, see also Antonios D. Papanikolaou, *Chariton-Studien: Untersuchungen zur Sprache und Chronologie der griechischen Romane* (Hypomnemata 37; Göttingen: Vandenhoeck & Ruprecht, 1973), 22–23.

36. Note, e.g., that Longus assumes that primary education was available in the chora to the young Daphnis and Chloe (1.8.1).

37. On the secondary curriculum, see Marrou, *History of Education*, 160–75; Bonner, *Education in Rome*, 189–249; and especially Cribiore, *Gymnastics of the Mind*, 185–219.

38. The core authors, besides Homer, were Hesiod, Euripides, and Menander (so Cribiore, *Gymnastics of the Mind*, 194–201).

39. Ibid., 197, 204.

large part from his secondary education. Indeed, his use of Homer pervades the novel, as he repeatedly quotes "the divine poet" as he calls him (5.5.9)—itself a view learned in school[40]—as well as adapting lines and incorporating Homeric words and phrases. Most obvious are Chariton's direct quotes of Homeric lines, twelve times from the *Iliad*[41] and nine times from the *Odyssey*.[42] By means of these quotations Chariton compares his characters and events to those of epic, comparisons that thereby redound to the credit of the former by giving them a heroic backdrop. The quotations begin early on. The first one occurs when Callirhoe learns that she is about to be married, to which young man she does not know (1.1.14), and Chariton describes her response by quoting the line—"her knees gave way and her heart as well" (*Od.* 4.703), a line used to describe Penelope's response when she learned that the suitors were intending to slay her son Telemachus (*Od.* 4.695–703); Callirhoe's response is thus intensified and clarified for the reader when it is compared to the familiar response of Penelope.

Chariton occasionally adapts a line of Homer. For example, in Chaereas's speech to the Egyptian king appealing to him not to turn in flight, he closes with a quotation from Homer, "We two, Polycharmus and I, will fight on" (7.3.5), a line in which not only is Chaereas compared to Diomedes but Polycharmus's name has been substituted for Sthenelos (cf. *Il.* 9.48).[43] Elsewhere Chariton quotes portions of lines,[44] alludes to them,[45] or uses Homeric epithets for deities[46] or Homeric phrases.[47]

This summary of Chariton's uses of Homer should be sufficient to indicate his profound familiarity with "the poet," a familiarity gained as early as the primary stage (through short passages) but more fully and rigorously at the secondary level (when the whole of the *Iliad* is read and

---

40. For the view that Homer is a god, not a man, see, e.g., Ziebarth, *Aus der antiken Schule*, 12: θεὸς οὐδ᾽ ἄνθρωπος Ὅμηρος.

41. *Iliad* 1.317 (= Chariton 6.2.4); 3.146 (= 5.5.9); 4.1 (= 5.4.6); 13.131 (= 7.4.3); 18.22–24 (= 1.4.6); 19.302 (= 2.5.12; 8.5.12); 21.114 (= 3.6.4); 22.82–83 (= 3.5.6); 22.304–5 (= 7.2.4); 22.389–90 (= 5.10.9); 23.66–67 (= 2.9.6); 23.71 (= 4.1.3); and 24.10–11 (= 6.1.8).

42. *Odyssey* 1.366 (= 5.5.9); 4.703 (= 1.1.14); 6.102–4 (= 6.4.6); 15.21 (4.4.5); 17.37 (= 4.7.5); 17.485, 487 (= 2.3.7); 18.213 (= 5.5.9); 23.296 (= 8.1.17); and 24.83 (= 4.1.5).

43. For other adaptations, see Chariton 2.5.12 (cf. *Il.* 19.302); 7.4.6 (cf. *Il.* 10.483).

44. See Chariton 2.7.4 (cf. *Il.* 5.696) and 8.5.5 (cf. *Il.* 6.474).

45. See Chariton 1.12.6 (cf. *Od.* 9.273) and 2.11.1 (cf. *Od.* 9.34).

46. See Chariton 4.1.8, where he describes Callirhoe as more beautiful than Homer's "white armed" Hera (e.g., *Il.* 1.55) and "fair ankled" Leucothea (*Od.* 5.333) or Hebe (*Od.* 11.603).

47. See, e.g., Chariton 1.7.6; 5.7.10; 8.7.9, all citing the Homeric tag ἔνθεν ἑλών (*Od.* 8.500), and Chariton 3.4.4; 7.1.11, which cite the tag οὔπω πᾶν εἴρητο ἔπος (*Od.* 16.11). On Chariton's use of Homer, see also Papanikolaou, *Chariton-Studien*, 14–16.

much of the *Odyssey*).[48] And yet, Chariton's familiarity probably goes well beyond that gained in school. Indeed, Chariton seems to exemplify Dio Chrysostom's statement that Homer is the first, middle, and last author, meaning that he is to be read as a boy, as a mature adult, and as an old man.[49] In other words, Chariton's familiarity with Homer derived from lifelong reading of "the poet."

One advance in our understanding of ancient education, already noted, is Cribiore's recognition that skills in letter writing began during the secondary stage, skills usually thought reserved for the tertiary stage.[50] To be sure, Cribiore emphasizes its peripheral role in grammatical instruction, but it is important for assessing the educations of aristocratic women.[51] Such skills learned first under a γραμματικός help to explain Chariton's easy assumption that elite women could write letters—Callirhoe writing a letter to Dionysius (8.4.5) and promising to exchange letters with Queen Statira (8.4.8). Such compositional skills are possible with a secondary education, the stage, Cribiore says, when aristocratic young women ended their education.[52]

THE TERTIARY CURRICULUM

The tertiary stage of education focused on rhetoric, by far the discipline of choice at this level, with philosophy a distant second.[53] Accordingly, skill at public speaking was the goal at this stage, but before "acquiring the wings of eloquence," to use Cribiore's apt phrase,[54] students—who

---

48. While the *Iliad* and the *Odyssey* were the principal texts of the secondary curriculum, they were used through all three stages of education (see Ronald F. Hock, "Homer in Greco-Roman Education," in *Mimesis and Intertextuality in Antiquity and Christianity* (ed. Dennis R. MacDonald; Harrisburg, Pa.: Trinity Press International, 2001), 55–71).

49. See Dio Chrysostom, *Orat.* 18.8.

50. Later references to letter writing, brief to be sure, appear in the context of one of the progymnasmata, namely, ἠθοποιία, which is an exercise of the tertiary curriculum (see Theon, *Progymn.* 10 in Christian Walz, ed., *Rhetores Graeci* [9 vols.; Tübingen: Cottae, 1832–36; repr., Osanbrück: Zeller, 1968], 1:235, 19–236, 1; and Nicolaus, *Progymn.* 10 in Joseph Felten, ed., *Nicolai Progymnasmata* [Rhetores Graeci 11; Leipzig: Teubner, 1913], 67, 2–5).

51. See Cribiore, *Gymnastics of the Mind*, 215–19.

52. See ibid., 86. Cribiore's lengthy discussion of women and education, including papyrus letters written by women, is well worth reading (*Gymnastics of the Mind*, 74–101).

53. On the clear preference for rhetoric over philosophy, see Marrou, *History of Education*, 194–96. Indeed, Cribiore says (*Gymnastics of the Mind*, 3) that she will not include philosophical education since it was not part of the ἐγκύκλιος παιδεία, or standard curriculum. Note that even students of Epictetus are assumed to have had some instruction in rhetoric before they entered his classroom (see *Diatr.* 2.2.7; 24.24–26; 3.1.1, 34).

54. Cribiore, *Gymnastics of the Mind*, 221.

were now only aristocratic young men, aged fourteen or fifteen[55]—still needed considerable preparation before they could take flight, both in reading and composition. The close reading of classic texts that they had done at the secondary stage continued, but prose writers were now added to the poets. In addition, the initial steps at composition through paraphrases, summaries, and letters under the γραμματικός were hardly sufficient to begin composing rhetorical speeches, so that students were guided through a more complex series of prerhetorical compositional exercises called *progymnasmata,* which Theon of Alexandria, a younger contemporary of Chariton, collected into the first textbook that came to be called, not surprisingly, *Progymnasmata.*[56]

But first we consider the continued close reading of classic texts at the tertiary stage. To be sure, reading poetry remained a task for students at this stage, as the *Iliad* would provide students with subjects for rhetorical treatment[57] and Homer himself was regarded as an orator and hence worth reading in that capacity as well.[58] But the focus was on prose writers, in particular historians and orators, whose works students read as sources for the vocabulary, style, and strategies of arguing that they would later use to enhance their own compositions.[59] As Theon put

---

55. Cribiore repeatedly says (ibid., 56, 86, 104) that young women, even elite young women, did not have access to rhetorical instruction, although she does not explain why. Presumably,.marriage at a younger age than their male counterparts and their inability to travel to another city to study with a Sophist kept them from going beyond the secondary stage. To be sure, Musonius Rufus argued that education should be the same for both boys and girls, but he envisions philosophy, not rhetoric, and then only moral philosophy which could be taught in a more informal manner at home (see frg. 4 [Cora Lutz, ed. and trans., "Musonius Rufus: The Roman Socrates," YCS 10 (1947): 42–49]). Such informal training seems likely in the case of Lucian's philosophically-minded Aristaenetus who named his children after famous Stoics—his son Zeno and his daughter Cleanthis; Zeno was attending a Stoic school under Diphilus while Cleanthis probably learned some philosophy from informal conversations with her father and brother, much as Hipparchia learned about Crates and Cynicism from her brother Metrocles (Diogenes Laertius 6.96).

56. Theon's *Progymnasmata* is now available in a new Budé edition: *Aelius Théon, Progymnasmata* (ed. Michel Patillon and Giancarlo Bolognesi; Paris: Belles Lettres, 1997). This edition, however, has not been available to me, so that references to Theon—by volume, page, and line(s)—will be to the older edition of Walz.

57. See Ruth Webb, "The *Progymnasmata* as Practice," in Too, *Education in Greek and Roman Antiquity,* 289–316, esp. 301–3.

58. See Quintilian, *Inst.*10.1.46–51; and Cribiore, *Gymnastics of the Mind,* 226–27.

59. Among the rhetorical handbooks that by Rufus of Perinthus is filled with gleanings from the orators, especially Demosthenes, that illustrate the language and strategies that can be used in the various parts of a speech. For the text, see *Rhetores Graeci* (ed. Leonard Spengel and Caspar Hammer; Leipzig: Teubner, 1894), 1.2:399–407. On this little-known late second-century Sophist, whose full name was T. Claudius Rufus, see Philostratus, *Vit. soph.* 597–98; and Walter Ameling, "Der Sophist Rufus," *Epigraphica Anatolica* 6 (1985): 27–33.

it, ἀνάγνωσις, or a close reading (of these texts), is the mother's milk of good style.[60]

Chariton shows that he had done such reading, for he has Dionysius refer to his having read the ποιηταί τε καὶ συγγραφεῖς, or poets and historians (2.4.8). Indeed, such reading probably accounts for Chariton's familiarity with the core group of historians and orators, and among historians Herodotus and Thucydides were the favorites.[61] Though not as pervasive in Chariton's novel as Homer, these historians do appear at several points in the narrative. Indeed, Chariton's opening words— Χαρίτων Ἀφροδισιεύς (1.1.1)—are modeled on the openings of Herodotus (1.1: Ἡροδότου Ἁλικαρνησσέος) and Thucydides (1.1.1: Θουκυδίδης Ἀθηναῖος), and his use of συνέγραψα, or "I have composed," at the end of the novel (8.8.16) may echo Thucydides' use of this same verb in his opening sentence (1.1.1: ξυνέγραψα). In between Chariton quotes these authors several times, at least for their phraseology,[62] or otherwise uses them for metaphors[63] and specific historical details.[64]

The historian, however, who provided Chariton with the most quotations and borrowings is Xenophon, another of the core authors and especially highly admired by Chariton's contemporary Dio Chrysostom.[65] In any case, Chariton clearly had read Xenophon's *Cyropaedia*. The fullest quote appears in Chariton, 2.5.7, where the words ἐλείβετο δὲ αὐτῆς τὰ δάκρυα κατὰ τῶν παρειῶν, or "but tears were flowing down her cheeks," derive from the *Cyropaedia*, 6.4.3: ἐλείβετο δὲ αὐτῇ τὰ δάκρυα κατὰ τῶν παρειῶν. Elsewhere Chariton clearly models his language on Xenophon[66]

---

60. See Theon, *Progymn.* 1 (Walz, 1:151, 9–11). Much of Theon's first two chapters (Walz, 1:145–72) consists of quotations from orators, historians, and others that might prove helpful to students in their various compositions.

61. See Quintilian, *Inst.*10.1.73; and Dio Chrysostom, *Orat.* 18.10.

62. See, for example, Chariton 1.11.1, where the words ἅπας ἄνεμος ... κατὰ πρύμναν εἰστήκει recall those of Thucydides at 2.97.1: αἰεὶ κατὰ πρύμναν ἵσταται τὸ πνεῦμα; Chariton 7.5.11, where the words ὀλίγον τε ἐπενόουν οὐδέν match those of Thucydides 2.8.1; and Chariton 1.14.6, where the words πρὶν ἐκπύστους γενέσθαι come from Thucydides, 3.30.1.

63. See, for example, Chariton 6.7.7, where the two-roads metaphor, as well as some of the language, comes from Herodotus 1.11.2.

64. See, for example, Chariton, 7.3.9, where the number 5,000,000 derives from Herodotus 7.186; and Chariton 7.5.15, where the Greek form of a Persian title, εὐεργέτης, comes from Herodotus, 8.85.

65. See Dio Chrysostom, *Orat.* 18.14–17. Cf. Quintilian, *Inst.* 10.1.82–83 (though Xenophon is regarded here as a philosopher).

66. See Chariton 4.5.3: ἔπραττε τὰ κεκελευσμένα; cf. Xenophon, *Cyr.* 4.1.3: τὸ κελευόμενον ἔπραττεν; Chariton 5.3.10: κατεφίλουν τὸν δίφρον; cf., *Cyr.* 6.4.10: κατεφίλησε τὸν δίφρον; and Chariton 6.9.5: ἐν ἐκείνῳ τῷ ἀδιηγήτῳ; cf. *Cyr.* 7.1.32: ἐν δὲ τῷ ἀδιηγήτῳ τούτῳ ταράχῳ.

or uses details to give his narrative plausibility, such as his references to the Persians' scythe-bearing chariots (6.8.7; cf. *Cyr.* 6.1.30), their taking whole households with them into battle (6.9.6; cf. *Cyr.* 4.2.2), and their word τιάρα for headgear (6.4.2; cf. *Cyr.* 8.3.13).[67]

Orators also influenced Chariton's choice of language, especially Demosthenes and Aeschines, two core authors.[68] Chariton drew, for example, on Demosthenes' *De corona*, in particular the sentence ἑσπέρα μὲν γὰρ ἦν, ἧκε δ'ἀγγέλλων τις ὡς, or "for it was evening, and someone came reporting that...." (18.169), a sentence that Chariton uses twice, more fully toward the beginning of his story: ἑσπέρα μὲν ἦν, ἧκε δὲ ἀγγέλλων τις ὅτι (1.3.1) and again near the end: ἑσπέρα μὲν ἦν (8.1.5)—a sentence, moreover, that was also culled for compositional use by Theon.[69] Also from Demosthenes and from the same speech is Chariton's language at 7.3.4, where he takes up the verb ἐγχειρεῖν, or "to undertake," as well as the phrase προβαλλομένους ἀεὶ τὴν ἀγαθὴν ἐλπίδα, or "always protecting themselves by good hope" (cf. 18.97: δεῖ δὲ τοὺς ἀγαθοὺς ἄνδρας ἐγχειρεῖν μὲν ἅπασιν ἀεὶ τοῖς καλοῖς τὴν ἀγαθὴν προβαλλομένους ἐλπίδα)—a passage that is cited in the rhetorical handbook of Rufus of Perinthus.[70] In addition, Chariton twice draws upon Demosthenes' third *Olynthiac*—ὃ γὰρ βούλεται τοῦθ' ἕκαστος καὶ οἴεται, or "what each person wishes will happen he believes will happen" (3.19), once word for word (3.9.3) and later though more loosely still quite clearly (cf. 6.5.1). Finally, the orator Aeschines is Chariton's source for the clause ὀψὲ μεταμανθάνουσα τὴν ἐλευθερίαν, or "learning late in life to forget about freedom" (3.157), a clause he likewise uses twice (2.3.6; 4.2.4) and a clause already familiar in educational settings, as shown by its appearance in one of Theon's sets of examples.[71]

Composition, however, was the principal activity at the tertiary stage, and, as already noted, it did not begin with full-length speeches but with a series of shorter but ever longer and more complex compositions called *progymnasmata*, fourteen in all: μῦθοι (fables), διηγήματα (narratives), χρεῖαι ([elaborations of] chreiai), γνῶμαι ([elaborations of] maxims), ἀνασκευαί (refutations), κατασκευαί (confirmations), κοινοὶ τόποι (general topics), ἐγκώμια (encomia), ψόγοι (condemnations), συγκρίσεις (comparisons), ἠθοποιίαι (short speeches consistent with a particular character), ἐκφράσεις (descriptions), θέσεις (theses), and νόμου

---

67. See further Papanikolaou, *Chariton-Studien*, 19–21.
68. See Quintilian, *Inst.* 10.1.76–77.
69. Theon, *Progymn.* 1 (Walz, 1.167, 2–3).
70. Rufus of Perinthus, *Rhet.* 36 (Spengel-Hammer, 1.2406, 21–23).
71. Theon, *Progymn.* 1 (Walz, 1.154, 1–2).

εἰσφοραί (proposals of a law).[72] These compositional forms—along with their definitions, classifications, differentiations from related forms, and instructions on structure and style—were collected into textbooks called *progymnasmata*. Besides Theon's, there are three other extant *progymnasmata*: by Hermogenes in the late second century, Aphthonius in the late fourth, and Nicolaus in the fifth.[73]

Chariton's training in these *progymnasmata* is apparent at various points in his narrative, but scholars have only rarely drawn attention to his use of them and even then only with brief analyses. Consuelo Ruiz-Montero has provided the fullest discussion.[74] Διήγημα is obviously the most important *progymnasma* in a novel, and her discussion of it is the longest as she notes Chariton's clear familiarity with this exercise; he frequently uses the verb διηγέομαι (1.1.1; etc.); he has knowledge of the qualities of narrative: clarity and conciseness (5.6.5); and he heeds the various instructions for writing a narrative: reporting events in sequence, avoiding lengthy digressions, and so on.[75] Ruiz-Montero also briefly discusses Chariton's use of ἐγκώμιον, σύγκρισις, ἠθοποιία, and ἔκφρασις, but then admits that this progymnasmatic material deserves a thorough investigation.[76]

Investigating all these *progymnasmata* is impossible here, too, but a more thorough analysis of one *progymnasma*, ἠθοποιία, is possible. To be sure, the appearance of ἠθοποιίαι in the Greek novel, including Chariton's, has long been known. Erwin Rohde even regarded ἠθοποιίαι as the sophistic heart of romance, but he was less interested in analyzing the use of this form than in attacking it as being lovers' pathetic emotional outbursts, which he regarded as symptomatic of the moral and spiritual

---

72. For brief discussion of these *progymnasmata*, see Bonner, *Education*, 250–76.

73. For texts of these writers, see *Hermogenis Opera* (ed. Hugo Rabe; Rhetores Graeci 6; Stuttgart: Teubner, 1913), 1–27; *Aphthonii Progymnasmata* (ed. Hugo Rabe; Rhetores Graeci 10; Leipzig: Teubner, 1926), 1–51; and *Nicolai Progymnasmata* (ed. Joseph Felten; Rhetores Graeci 11; Leipzig: Teubner, 1913), 1–79. Translations of all three as well as of Theon are now available in George Kennedy, *Progymnasmata: Greek Textbooks of Prose Composition and Rhetoric* (SBLWGRW 10; Atlanta: Society of Biblical Literature, 2003), 1–172. The best comprehensive discussion of these *progymnasmata* is that by Herbert Hunger, *Die hochsprachliche profane Literatur der Byzantiner* (2 vols.; HAW 12.5.1–2; Munich: Beck, 1978), 1:92–120. See also Webb, "Progymnasmata as Practice," 289–316.

74. See esp. Consuelo Ruiz-Montero, "Caritón de Afrodisias y los Ejercicios preparatorios de Elio Teón," in *Treballs en honor de Vergilio Bejarano* (ed. L. Ferreres, Barcelona: Publicacions de Universität de Barcelona, 1991), 709–13; much the same material is repeated in her "Chariton von Aphrodisias," 1042–44. On the *progymnasmata* in the novels, see also Ronald F. Hock, "The Rhetoric of Romance," in *Handbook of Classical Rhetoric in the Hellenistic Period 330 B.C.—A.D. 400* (ed. Stanley E. Porter; Leiden: Brill, 1997), 445–65, esp. 453–61.

75. See Ruiz-Montero, "Chariton von Aphrodisias," 1042.

76. See ibid., 1043–44.

decay that characterized imperial life.[77] Scholars have avoided Rohde's dismissive attitude, but they have also showed little interest in going on to investigate in any detail a literary form that is so central to the novel and to Chariton's in particular.[78]

Hermogenes defines ἠθοποιία as "an imitation of the character (ἦθος) of the person in question."[79] To be sure, this definition is so brief as to be obscure, but its meaning emerges from the topics that were suggested for student exercises. Theon, for example, offers these: What words a husband might say to his wife as he was about to go on a journey, or what words a general might say to his soldiers who were about to face danger.[80] In other words, an ἠθοποιία requires the student to reveal through speech a person's character as that person confronts a specific circumstance.

Aphthonius classifies ἠθοποιίαι into three types: ἠθικαί, or expressing primarily a characteristic "disposition," such as what words someone from the interior might say on seeing the ocean for the first time; παθητικαί, or expressing primarily "emotion," such as what words Hecuba might say as Troy lay in ruins; and μικταί, or a combination of disposition and emotion, such as what words Achilles might say as Patroclus lay dead and he was deliberating about returning to battle.[81] In addition, Hermogenes classifies ἠθοποιίαι as either ἁπλαῖ ("single") or διπλαῖ ("double"), terms that are obscure again, but whose meaning emerges from his following definitions in which single ἠθοποιίαι are those in which the person speaks to himself (καθ᾽ ἑαυτόν), whereas δουβλε ἠθοποιίαι are those that are addressed to another person (πρὸς ἄλλον).[82]

The structure that students were to follow when composing an ἠθοποιία is temporal, in which they express the person's response in terms of the present, then of the past, and finally of the future.[83] Thus students were to have the person respond to features of the present

---

77. See Erwin Rohde, *Der griechische Roman und seine Vorläufer* (3rd ed.; Leipzig: Breitkopf & Hartel, 1914), 353–56.

78. For what follows, see also Hock, "Rhetoric of Romance," 455–59.

79. See Hermogenes, *Progymn.* (Rabe, 9, 20, 7–8) ἠθοποιία ἐστὶ μίμησις ἤθους ὑποκειμένου προσώπου. Cf. the similar definitions in Aphthonius, *Progymn.* 11 (Rabe, 34, 2–3); and Nicolaus, *Progymn.* 10 (Felten, 64, 1–3). On ἠθοποιίαι, see Hunger, *Literatur,* 108–16.

80. See Theon, *Progymn.* 10 (Walz, 1:235, 13–15).

81. See Aphthonius, *Progymn.* 11 (Rabe, 35, 8–9).

82. See Hermogenes, *Progymn.* 9 (Rabe, 20, 24–21, 5).

83. See Hermogenes, *Progymn.* 9 (Rabe, 21, 19–20); and Aphthonius, *Progymn.* 11 (Rabe, 35, 13–14). Nicolaus's structure is modified slightly with a reference to the present again between past and future (see *Progymn.* 10 [Felten, 65, 11–66, 9]).

situation, then reflect on the person's past as a contrast to the present situation, and finally imagine the consequences of this situation for the future. Hermogenes provides some general guidelines about what a person might say in response to a calamitous situation. The student, he says, should emphasize the difficulties of the present situation, then contrast those difficulties with the happiness of the past, and finally anticipate an even worse future.[84] Theon gives instructions on how to capture the character of a person, saying that the language used should match the person's age, sex, social status, disposition, and nationality. For example, a young man's speech should combine simplicity with self-control, whereas an older man's should reflect knowledge and experience.[85] Nicolaus recommends a style that consists of short clauses rather than periodic ones, as it is distinctive of those who are rejoicing or lamenting to speak briefly, merely piling words upon words.[86] Aphthonius, finally, provides a fully worked out ἠθοποιία on the topic "What words Niobe might say when her children lay dead."[87]

With these instructions from the *Progymnasmata* in mind we can turn to Chariton's novel and begin to recognize that throughout the story his characters respond to their circumstances in what can formally be termed ἠθοποιίαι. Indeed, on reading through the novel I have identified twenty-four occasions where Chaereas, Callirhoe, and others respond to the trials and hardships of their lives by means of an ἠθοποιία. Once identified, these ἠθοποιίαι can be classified and analyzed in terms of their conformity to the prescribed temporal structure and stylistic suggestions.

Not surprisingly, παθητικαὶ ἠθοποιίαι outnumber the ἠθικαί, fifteen to nine (though some of the latter might be παθητικαί, the decision not always being obvious). Emotion is the appropriate response to many of the hardships and misfortunes the characters experience. All nine of Callirhoe's ἠθοποιίαι can be classified as παθητικαί,[88] whereas five of Chaereas'[89] and one of Dionysius'[90] can be. The eleven ἠθικαὶ ἠθοποιίαι

84. See Hermogenes, *Progymn.* 9 (Rabe, 21, 19–22, 3).

85. See Theon, *Progymn.* 8 (Walz, 1:236, 1–16).

86. See Nicolaus, *Progymn.* 10 (Felten, 66, 9–15); cf. Aphthonius, *Progymn.* 11 (Rabe, 35, 12–13).

87. See Aphthonius, *Progymn.* 11 (Rabe, 35, 15–36, 20); for English translation, see Kennedy, *Progymnasmata*, 116–17.

88. See Chariton 1.8.3–4; 11.2–3; 14.6–10; 2.9.3–5; 11.1–3; 3.10.4–8; 5.1.4–7; 5.5.2–4; and 6.6.2–5.

89. See Chariton 3.6.6–8; 4.3.9–10; 4.7–10; 6.2.8–11; and 7.1.5–6.

90. See Chariton 5.10.1–5.

are distributed among Theron,[91] Dionysius,[92] Chaereas,[93] and Mithridates.[94]

Chariton is likewise aware of the distinction between ἠθοποιίαι that are ἁπλαῖ and those that are διπλαῖ. Sixteen are ἁπλαῖ, and Chariton even echoes *progymnasmatic* language when he says in five instances that the person spoke πρὸς ἑαυτόν[95] or πρὸς ἑαυτήν.[96] Moreover, all the διπλαῖ are spoken to one other person (πρὸς ἄλλον)—for example, Dionysius to Leonas.[97]

Three examples will show that Chariton has followed the temporal structure of an ἠθοποιία as well as an appropriate style. In the first example—indeed, the first example of this form in the novel—Callirhoe had been placed in a tomb after she was thought to have died from a kick from her husband; now she revives and then responds to this frightening experience with an ἠθοποιία (1.8.3–4), which is understandably παθητική, obviously πρὸς ἑαυτήν, and structured temporally, as indicated by the temporal markers inserted at appropriate points. Callirhoe reflects on her situation as follows:

> (Present) "Oh, how terrible! I've been buried though I am alive! I'm innocent of wrongdoing. I'm dying a slow death. They are mourning me though I am perfectly healthy!
>
> (Past) "Wicked Chaereas, I do not blame you because you (thought you) killed me, but because you immediately bore me out of the house. It was not necessary for you to have buried Callirhoe so quickly, not even if she had truly died.
>
> (Future) "But perhaps you are already thinking about another marriage!"

The second example, again παθητική but now πρὸς ἄλλον, namely Dionysius, has Callirhoe responding to his news that she must appear at the trial in which he has charged Mithridates with planning an adulterous relationship with her. Her response (5.5.2–4) not only follows the temporal structure but also includes a peristasis catalogue, or list of

---

91. See Chariton 1.12.2–4.
92. See Chariton 2.4.4–5; 6.1–2; 3.2.7–9; 5.2.7–9; 6.2.5–8.
93. See Chariton 3.3.4–7.
94. See Chariton 4.4.2–5.
95. See Chariton 2.4.4; 9.3; 5.2.7; cf. 1.12.2: πρὸς αὐτόν.
96. See Chariton 2.9.3.
97. See Chariton 2.6.1; cf. 4.3.9; 4.2; 5.1.4; 5.2; 10.1; 6.2.8; and 7.1.5.

hardships, that is an especially apt way of speaking briefly and also of piling words on one another. She says:

> (Present) "This alone has been left out of my hardships—to enter into a courtroom!
>
> (Past) "I have died, I have been buried, I have had my tomb robbed, I have been sold, and I have been enslaved.[98] And now, Tyche, I am being judged! Wasn't it enough for you to slander me unjustly to Chaereas? No, you also gave Dionysius reason to suspect me of adultery. At that time you paraded my slander all the way to burial, now to a trial before the King. I have become a scandalous story in both Europe and Asia.
>
> (Future) "How will I look at the judge? What words must I listen to? Treacherous beauty, was this beauty given to me for this purpose alone—to fill the earth with slanders about me? The daughter of Hermocrates is being put on trial, and she doesn't have her father as her advocate. Others, when they enter a courtroom, pray for good will and favor, but I am afraid that I might please the judge."

The third example of an ἠθοποιία occurs earlier in the narrative than the previous one, specifically at the point where Callirhoe, having been kidnapped from Syracuse and taken to Miletus, is about to cross the Euphrates River into the interior of Asia. Before crossing, however, she pauses and with only Plangon present with her she reflects on the significance of the next step of her journey. Her ἠθοποιία (5.1.4–7) is παθητική; delivered πρὸς ἄλλον, namely to Plangon; and, though longer than the previous examples, still temporally organized. She says:

> (Present) "Baneful Tyche, you persist in doing battle against a single woman.
>
> (Past) "It was you who locked me up in a tomb while I was still alive, and it was you who got me out, although it was not out of mercy but in order to deliver me over to brigands. Then the sea and Theron effected my exile. I, the daughter of Hermocrates, was sold into slavery! And what is more burdensome to me than exile is that I became the object of a man's love, in order that, although Chaereas was alive, I might be married to another.
>
> (Future) "But now you are begrudging me even this situation, for no longer are you banishing me to Ionia, a foreign land, to be sure, but still

---

98. The piling up of words in this peristasis catalogue is more obvious in the Greek: τέθνηκα, κεκήδευμαι, τετυμβωρύχημαι, πέπραμαι, δεδούλευκα.

Greek. You gave me a land where I had a great consolation, namely, that I sat beside the sea. Now, though, you are hurling me beyond my familiar surroundings, and I am being banished from the culture of my homeland. I am being taken beyond the Euphrates, and I, an islander, am being shut up in a barbaric interior where there is no longer any sea.

"What ship sailing out of Sicily will I any longer expect to see? I will be taken from your tomb, Chaereas. Who will pour out libations for you, dearly beloved? Henceforth, Bactra and Susa will be my home and my tomb. I will cross over you, Euphrates, just once. I fear not so much the length of the journey as that I might even there appear beautiful to someone."

What makes this last ἠθοποιία especially interesting is not that it conforms to the conventions of the form, though it does so conform. No, what's interesting is that this ἠθοποιία should be seen as Chariton's μίμησις, or imitation, of an ἠθοποιία that was familiar from the schools, namely, what words a person from the interior might say on first seeing the sea.[99] Readers would, no doubt, realize that Chariton's μίμησις is an inversion of this school ἠθοποιία, though cast now as follows: What words a person from the seaside might say on first seeing the interior.

This one *progymnasma* will have to suffice to demonstrate Chariton's having gone through the progymnasmatic portion of the tertiary curriculum. Students then moved on to rhetoric proper and specifically to the rhetorical textbooks that introduced them to the three types of rhetorical speech—δικανικόν (judicial), συμβουλευτικόν (advisory), and ἐγκωμιαστικόν (celebrative)—along with their subtypes and the various parts that made up a speech—προοίμιον (introduction), διήγησις (statement of the facts of the case), ἀπόδειξις (proof), and ἐπίλογος (conclusion).[100] Familiarity with these types of speech and the parts of a speech was then

---

99. See Aphthonius, *Progymn.* 11 (Rabe, 35, 5–6). See also Hermogenes, *Progymn.* 9 (Rabe, 21, 12–13); and the Aphthonius commentator John Doxapatres (Walz, 2:500, 30–31).

100. Besides the standard rhetorical manuals—Aristotle's *Rhetoric*, the *Rhetorica ad Alexandrum*, Cicero's *De inventione*, the *Rhetorica ad Herennium*, and Quintilian's *Institutio oratoria*, all of which are readily available in the LCL, with Quintilian in a new translation by Donald A. Russell—see also the works of Hermogenes, especially those on stasis and on style (texts in Rabe, ed., *Hermogenis Opera*, 28–92 and 213–413, respectively). Translation of the former in Michael Heath, *Hermogenes, On Issues: Strategies of Argument in Later Greek Rhetoric* (Oxford: Clarendon, 1995), 28–60; translation of the latter in Cecil W. Wooten, *Hermogenes, On Types of Style* (Chapel Hill: University of North Carolina Press, 1987), 1–130. See also the minor manuals of the *Anonymous Seguerianus* and Apsines; texts and translations of them in Mervin R. Dilts and George A. Kennedy, eds., *Two Greek Rhetorical Treatises from the Roman Empire: Introduction, Text, and Translation of the Arts of Rhetoric attributed to Anonymous Seguerianus and and to Apsines of Gadara* (Leiden: Brill, 1997), 2–73 and 76–229.

mastered by having students compose practice speeches called μελέται, or declamations.[101] Upon completing the tertiary stage the students, now ῥήτορες, or orators, could speak in the assembly, in court, or at a celebratory occasion.

Knowledge of and experience with these types of rhetorical speech can be assumed for the Greek novelists. Indeed, what Graham Anderson says of Achilles Tatius—that he "has set for himself the task of making the whole rhetorical curriculum relevant to romance"[102]—is also true, not surprisingly, of Chariton, the ὑπογραφεύς, or secretary, of the ῥήτωρ Athenagoras (1.1.1). In any case, the evidence is varied and pervasive. Chariton shows knowledge of various declamatory and rhetorical conventions, such as προσαγγελία, or self-incrimination, and παραγραφή, or raising a legal objection,[103] and he shows a penchant for courtroom scenes, consistent with the dominance of the judicial speech over the others, as seen, for example, in the presentation of the handbook of Rufus of Perinthus.[104] Chariton especially delights in judicial settings and speeches, as becomes apparent with the trials of Chaereas,[105] Theron,[106] and Mithridates.

The last-mentioned trial, in which Dionysius charges the satrap Mithridates with plotting an adulterous relation with his wife (5.4.7–8.8), commands our attention, since Chariton provides details about the preparations, pretrial motions, and full prosecution and defense speeches in his narration of the trial. To set the scene: Dionysius suspected that Mithridates had designs on his wife when a letter that purported to have been written by Chaereas, Callirhoe's previous husband, who was currently with Mithridates, came into his hands. Since Dionysius presumed that Chaereas was dead, he understandably concluded that the author of the letter was really Mithridates. Dionysius communicated his suspicions to King Artaxerxes, and the latter summoned both men as well as Callirhoe to Babylon for trial (4.4.5–6.8).

Once the principals arrive in Babylon the trial takes over the city, as the city, Chariton says, becomes one big courtroom (5.4.4). On the day

---

101. See especially Donald A. Russell, *Greek Declamation* (New York: Cambridge University Press, 1983).

102. Graham Anderson, *The Novel in the Graeco-Roman World* (Totowa, N.J.: Barnes & Noble, 1984), 85.

103. See Chariton 1.5.4–5 and 5.7.3–4, respectively, on which see Russell, *Greek Declamation*, 35–37 and 38 n. 100.

104. Rufus identifies four types of speech (*Rhet.* 2 [Spengel-Hammer, 1.2.399, 4–13]) but focuses on the four parts of a judicial speech (*Rhet.* 4–41 [Spengel-Hammer, 1.2.399–407]).

105. See Chariton 1.5.2–6.1.

106. See Chariton 3.4.7–18.

of the trial Chariton's narrative pace slows down as he carefully describes the courtroom, the entrance of Dionysius and Mithridates, and the preliminary maneuvering on Mithridates' part, which results in a day's delay so that Callirhoe herself can be present at the trial (5.4.6–13).

On the next day the trial finally begins with Dionysius prosecuting Mithridates for adultery (5.6.1–10). Dionysius had awakened early that morning in order to practice his speech (5.5.6), a tactic that Quintilian considers a necessity, given the expectation of judges for carefully crafted and powerfully delivered speeches.[107] At any rate, Chariton quotes the speech in full, and it has the standard parts of a judicial speech: προοίμιον, διήγησις, πίστις, and ἐπίλογος.[108] For example, Dionysius's προοίμιον is as follows:

> I am grateful to you, O King, for the honor which you have shown me, the virtue of self-control,[109] and the marriages of all. For you have not allowed a private citizen to be plotted against by a public official. Rather, you have summoned us here in order that you might avenge the lust and insolence directed against me and so prevent such behavior toward others.[110]

This προοίμιον prompts several rhetorical observations. Dionysius's strategy is conventional, choosing to make his προοίμιον in terms of the judge.[111] Dionysius clearly fulfills the purpose of a προοίμιον by making the judge attentive (προσεχής) and securing the good will (εὔνοια) of the judge by addressing him in what has come to be called a *captatio benevolentiae*, or praise of the judge.[112] Quintilian advises, however, that this praise cannot be general but must be tied specifically to the case.[113]

---

107. See Quintilian, *Inst.* 4.1.57.

108. For analysis of this speech into its parts, see Hock, "Rhetoric of Romance," 463.

109. By my translation I reject the emendation proposed by John Jackson (see "The Greek Novelists," *CQ* 29 [1935]: 52–57, esp. 57) and accepted by the LCL editor, G. P. Goold: <τὴν τῆσδε> σωφροσύνην, or "my wife's chastity," as Goold renders this phrase (p. 257). Throughout the whole ordeal Dionysius has taken great pains to keep his wife out of the trial. It is hard to imagine that he would introduce her so explicitly here. Rather, Dionysius is praising the king for upholding the virtue of σωφροσύνη without reference to his wife.

110. Chariton 5.6.1.

111. On this strategy for composing a προοίμιον, see Rufus of Perinthus, *Rhet.* 6 (Spengel-Hammer, 1.2.400, 14–19).

112. On the purpose of a προοίμιον, see Quintilian, *Inst.* 4.1.5; Rufus of Perinthus, *Rhet.* 4 (Spengel-Hammer, 1.2.399, 17–400, 3); and *Anon. Seg.* 5 (Dilts and Kennedy, *Two Greek Rhetorical Treatises*, 2). For full discussion of the προοίμιον, see Quintilian, *Inst.* 4.1.1–79. For the *captatio benevolentiae*, see Bruce Winter, "The Importance of the *Captatio Benevolentiae* in the Speeches of Tertullus and Paul in Acts," *JTS* 42 (1991): 505–31, esp. 507–15.

Dionysius's praise conforms to this advice, since he praises Artaxerxes specifically for his commitment to σωφροσύνη and to the institution of marriage, both of which are central to the charge of adultery that Dionysius will level against Mithridates later in the speech. In addition, the words "lust and insolence" (τὴν ἀσέλγειαν καὶ ὕβριν) recall Demosthenes who had used these very words in a προοίμιον,[114] a literary echo that Chariton no doubt learned when reading the orator in school although the passage in which they occur had already been selected as an illustration for a προοίμιον based on one's opponents.[115]

Several other features of Dionysius's speech, not to mention Mithridates' defense speech with its dramatic summons of the "dead" Chaereas during the ἐπίλογος,[116] show Chariton's familiarity with the rules for composing judicial speeches and the demands of "sophistopolis," Donald A. Russell's term for the declamatory world that tertiary students, Sophists, and their audiences inhabited.[117] Chariton, though a ὑπογραφεύς, would clearly have been able to take on Athenagoras's role of ῥήτωρ. Chariton, in other words, was, like some of his characters, a πεπαιδευμένος himself.

CONCLUSION

A number of general conclusions proceed from the above analysis. First, regarding Chariton's own education, we can say the following: He "certainly," as Reardon says, "had a decent secondary education"—an obvious conclusion, to judge from his use of the Homeric epics. The habits he learned under a γραμματικός were maintained throughout his later life, allowing him to use "the poet" as adeptly and frequently as he did. But Reardon's addendum "perhaps more" sells Chariton short. His use of historians and orators for quotations, allusions, phraseology, and historical details; his sure grasp of *progymnasmata* like ἠθοποιίαι; and his relish for the courtroom and judicial speeches—all these features of the novel document a tertiary education as well. Hence Chariton deserves being called a πεπαιδευμένος.

And yet, Chariton's education must not be overestimated either. Aside from Homer's epics, which he knew intimately, Chariton's reading of other

---

113. See Quintilian, *Inst.* 4.1.16.

114. See Demosthenes, *Orat.* 21.1.

115. See Rufus of Perinthus, *Rhet.* 5 (Spengel-Hammer, 1.2.400, 9–13); and *Anon. Seg.* 7 (Dilts-Kennedy, 4, 4–5).

116. Chariton 5.7.10. On this rhetorical ploy, see Quintilian, *Inst.* 4.1.28.

117. On "sophistopolis," see Russell, *Greek Declamation*, 111, 112.

poets, historians, and orators tends to go no farther than the core authors[118] and moreover betrays a knowledge of them that derived in many instances from quotations already selected by his teachers and hence found in his school textbooks. The only exception is Xenophon's *Cyropaedia*, whose various quotes and borrowings suggest first-hand reading on Chariton's part. Consequently, Antonios Papanikolaou's conclusion, that Chariton "war ein relative belesener Mann,"[119] is overstated, although Chariton was probably far more typical of πεπαιδευμένοι in early imperial society than contemporaries like Dio Chrysostom or Plutarch. Indeed, it is Chariton's typicality that makes him historically interesting.

Secondly, from what we know about the educational curriculum it is clear that Chariton's description of his characters' education is accurate. Dionysius is most often characterized by his παιδεία, and he exhibits the full curriculum—citing maxims (4.7.7), quoting the poets and historians (2.1.5), responding to events with ἠθοποιίαι (2.4.4–5; 6.1–2; etc.), and preparing and delivering a judicial speech (5.5.6; 6.1–10). Callirhoe's παιδεία, however, is limited to what we expect of an aristocratic young woman—reading skills and training at writing letters, as already noted—but needing her father Hermocrates to be present so that he could defend her before the king (5.5.4).

Lastly, Chariton's placement of educated men and women in the full context of early imperial social and intellectual life allows us to get a sense of the functions of παιδεία. On the one hand, Chariton confirms the functions of παιδεία as suggested above by Cribiore and Morgan, namely as being a social marker, distinguishing aristocrats from all others in the society (1.12.6; 2.1.5), as well as being a cultural marker, distinguishing Greeks from others, whether Persians (7.6.5) or Egyptians (8.3.10). On the other hand, Chariton often draws attention to his characters' παιδεία functioning in a way not mentioned by scholars, namely παιδεία as the best means to assure appropriate behavior, or virtue, in all manner of situations. Specifically, παιδεία is the telling quality that Chariton attributes to Chaereas, Callirhoe, Demetrius, and especially Dionysius that allows them to act in praiseworthy ways—by responding to life's experiences with prudence (6.5.8), with inner strength (7.6.5), with dignity (5.9.8; 8.5.10), and especially with self-control, the preeminent value of the novels (2.4.1; 3.2.6; 8.3.10).

---

118. One exception would be Chariton's use (1.1.13) of Sappho by alluding to frg. 44 in *Poetarum Lesbiorum Fragmenta* (ed. Edgar Lobel and Denys Page; Oxford: Clarendon, 1968).

119. Papanikolaou, *Chariton-Studien*, 24.

Imitating Imitation: Vergil, Homer, and Acts 10:1–11:18

Chris Shea

Introduction

Recent scholars, including those of the Ancient Fiction and Early Christian and Jewish Narrative working Group, are, I believe, agreed that the ancients have in some way institutionalized imitation, that is, that their artists and authors are taught by imitation and rewarded for imitation in a significantly different way and to a significantly greater degree than in our own society. Thus, imitation in ancient works such as the ones we have studied is not simply the product of the lack of original thought or solely of a desire for profit by reproducing endlessly artistic works in the manner of Mrs. Field's cookies—each one of exactly the same composition as the last. In other words, we do not really think that the ancients set out to make *Ephesiaca, Ephesiaca 2,* and *The Absolute Last Remake of Ephesiaca.* Nor do we think that what we have in front of us is merely the product of a poorly-constructed legal-protection system, that is, that the ancients deplore plagiarism and too-close imitation but simply do not have the wherewithal to prevent abuses. Rather, we think inspired imitation is an indispensable component of their artistic aesthetic.

Therefore, it occurs to me, in a culture where mimesis is honored and ubiquitous, perhaps it would be instructive for us to privilege in our discussions the works of the great imitators as well as the Ur-works that constitute the earliest layer of a literary tradition. If the cultures of the ancient Mediterranean instill imitation as an educational value, rather than originality—the originality we might consider at the base of Art 100 or Creative Writing, for example—then perhaps the ancient educational system is also promoting a cult of the imitator, in addition to, or perhaps instead of, a cult of the innovator. In this construction, students would be taught to prize those artistic compositions that had the most commentary, that is, the deepest layering, the most furbelows. Students, then, would be taught to prize erudite, ironic versions of mythological folk epic, for example.

To explore this possibility, perhaps we might choose a passage of a clearly imitative literary text and, instead of looking for the earliest text to which the narrative seems to refer, the bottom layer of literary imitation, we might look for the most imitative imitation, as it were, the literary ancestor which has worked the most cunning changes on the original text. The Ancient Fiction Group has been accustomed to search the canonical texts of early Christianity for possible echoes of pagan, usually Greek, works. In the process scholars such as Judith Perkins, Richard Pervo, Ronald, Hock, and Dennis MacDonald have uncovered many references to the canonical texts of pagan education, particularly to Homer and the tragedians.[1] But, if we apply the principles we have just laid out above, Homer and the tragedians would appear lower on our list of possible models; those works would have been merely the starting point of a whole process of imitation that our Christian example is taking into account. In this argument, we would privilege works that had already imitated Homer, had added sophisticated layers of meaning to what, in the case of Homer, at least, is a reasonably straightforward oral folk narrative.[2]

IMITATING IMITATION

Works of the Roman Empire were precisely the works that had acquired the montage of meaning that would have appealed to the Christian writers as well as to the pagan ones. After all, they were all taught to write in an educational system that favored mimesis.[3] To test this hypothe-

---

1. I can do no better than to refer the reader to the earlier volume produced by this group, *Ancient Fiction and Early Christian Narrative* (ed. Ronald F. Hock, J. Bradley Chance, and Judith Perkins; SBLSymS 6; Atlanta: Scholars Press, 1998), and to other contributions in this volume, such as D. MacDonald's "The Breasts of Hecuba and Those of the Daughters of Jerusalem," and Richard Pervo's "Die Entführung in das Serail: Aspasia: a Female Aesop?"

2. We cannot know if the *Iliad* and *Odyssey* contain cunning references to political figures of eighth-century Athens, for example, or parodies of other oral epics, i.e., that the *Iliad* and *Odyssey* themselves are polished, sophisticated, intertextual works. But then authors of the early Roman Empire apparently did not themselves know this. Thus, I would argue, the *Iliad* and *Odyssey* are not, to the ancients, models for the art of imitation. The works of the Athenian tragedians are, of course, in a different category, since they could reasonably be considered early imitations of epic that read into folk texts coded references to political events contemporaneous with the imitation.

3. That formal education in the Roman Empire has a distinctly Greek flavor does not, I believe, require citation. As Helmut Koester sums up the evidence about Paul, for example, "The information from the letters clearly presents a man who was a Jew from the diaspora who had received a good Greek education" (*History, Culture, and Religion of the Hellenistic Age* [vol. 1 of *Introduction to the New Testament*; New York: de Gruyter, 1982], 2:99). For more on

sis, I propose to examine a passage of the canonical Acts, 10:1–11:18, where Peter and the Roman Cornelius, after concurrent dream-visions, come to an ethnic and religious accommodation.

Here, as Dennis MacDonald has pointed out in a paper to the Ancient Fiction Group, the authors of Acts seem to have chosen *Iliad* 2.3–41 as a model.[4] But the imitation is far from a reverent one: while Zeus is sending Agamemnon a dream that will lead to the destruction of Agamemnon's troops, Peter's dream will lead to the unification of warring peoples. The god of the *Iliad* sends the dream and unleashes the slaughter of the Greeks and Trojans to gratify the honor of a single favored man, Achilles. The god of Acts has sent the dream, we might argue, to put an end to bloodshed. The one favored by the god of the *Iliad* is a warrior; the one favored by the god of Acts is a heroic priest-philosopher. Thus, I argue, the imitation in Acts is in dialectic with the Iliadic model. It is critiquing the society and values of its model. It is asserting the superiority of its own society and values. Now, the question, it seems to me, might be: where did the authors of Acts learn to imitate in this fashion?

For the sake of argument, then, we are not looking at the bottom layer of tradition, the layer with the least sophisticated patina, the layer farthest in time from the heroic creators of a new testament. We are looking for a model of the act of imitation, a model of the act of remaking the heroic world. And if we are looking for a model at the top of the tradition, then I would argue for Vergil's *Aeneid* as the model—a text that, although overtly an imitation of Homer's epics, aggressively asserts the values of the early empire against the values of the Homeric heroes.[5] We

---

ancient education, see Ronald F. Hock, "Homer in Greco-Roman Education," in *Mimesis and Intertextuality in Antiquity and Christianity* (ed. Dennis R. MacDonald; Harrisburg, Pa.: Trinity Press International, 2001), 56–77; and his article in this volume ("The Educational Curriculum in Chariton's *Callirhoe*").

4. Dennis R. MacDonald, "*Iliad* 2 and Acts 10–11: Imitations of Homer in the Visions of Cornelius and Peter" (paper presented at the annual meeting of the Society of Biblical Literature, Denver, Colorado, Nov. 17, 2001). It might prove instructive to consult Vergilian criticism here, if for no other reason than that the passage I will propose to examine from the *Aeneid* and this passage in Acts seem to have some of the same Homeric exempla at heart. K. W. Gransden, *Virgil Aeneid Book VIII* (Cambridge: Cambridge University Press, 1976), ad loc.; Joseph Farrell ("The Virgilian Intertext," in *The Cambridge Companion to Virgil* [ed. Charles Martindale; Cambridge: University Press, 1997], 224–29) chronicles exhaustively the Homeric echoes in Vergil's version.

5. Although we may not yet be willing to concede that the whole of Acts is Romanized, still the example of a passage such as this one, which deals with the whole question of the Romanization of the early Christian communities, would seem to have earned a dispensation from scholarly opprobrium.

are looking at a text so layered, so rich in subtlety, so imitative that it has
been called a "vast continuous intertext."[6]

IMITATING IMITATORS

But if we are going to argue that early Christian writers sought as
models contemporary imitations providing sophisticated, philosophical
commentary on time-honored texts, that is, examples from the top layer
of the tradition, then the commentator himself takes at least some of the
prestige awarded authors in the modern cult of the artist. The
author/commentator is surely not imagined to be inspired by the same
Muses who took over the voice and body of the heroic poet—he is surely
imagined to be inspired by the art (and gods, perhaps) of philosophical
commentary. In short, he learned his craft and is thus a model for all who
would learn to do the same.

Thus, in dealing with the *Aeneid* as opposed to the Homeric epics,
there are really two narratives: the explicit narrative of the heroic culture-
founder, Aeneas, and the implicit narrative of the heroic prophetic
narrator, Vergil. Both narratives may be thought to be objects of imitation
in a work, like Acts, which is after all a heroization of the possibly historical voyages of writer-philosophers. Thus, the character Paul, for
example, is like Aeneas in his adventure-filled journey to Rome, where he
will found a new society, and, like Vergil in his creation of written works,
that will articulate the philosophical underpinnings of that new society.

The most important narratives of early Christianity are related in the
same way: the Gospels, canonical and noncanonical, relate the events of
the life of the heroic culture-founder, Jesus; the Acts narratives, canonical
or otherwise, relate the narratives of the heroic narrators. Since Paul and
Peter, in the canonical tradition, are the most important of the narrators,
the narrative of their lives is the most important.

We begin with Vergil's biography, moreover, because the figure
Vergil may have some relevance to the question of whether Acts or any
early Christian work could have a dependence on a Latin epic. First, I
might point out that there is a certain cult of the heroic writer-philoso-
pher in antiquity. Thus, for example, the letters of philosophers like Plato
and Epicurus and the Romans Cicero and Pliny and "Lives" of poets like

---

6. Farrell, "Virgilian Intertext," 236. While Farrell concedes that we may in time discover evidence which indicates all the poets of Vergil's time were as concerned with
"intertextuality," he goes on to state—perhaps to overstate—that "the Virgilian intertextuality shows every sign of being the distinct creation and in many ways the artistic signature of
classical antiquity's greatest poetic craftsman" (223).

Euripides and Vergil himself enjoyed wide currency, as much for their narratives of the authors' adventures as for their philosophical musings. And just as heroic travels or adventures are ascribed to the great authors, appealing anonymous works are attributed to heroic adventurers. The mysterious little treatise the *Peri Hypsous* (*De sublimitate*, "On the Sublime"), in our imaginations clearly bearing the stamp of an armchair professor-philosopher, was in antiquity ascribed to the gallant revolutionary Cassius Longinus. This is the age of the creation of the cult of the author, and in this age the ancients' penchant for the heroic might be thought to apply both to writing and writer.

Moreover, in these cultures writing itself conveys sacredness, an awesomeness difficult to reconcile with modern attitudes. It is not only that written prayers and requests line the walls of sanctuaries all over the Roman world, or that oracles are issued on scraps of paper;[7] in a time and place where the word of a ruler or god is imagined as having its own palpable being and sacred power (cf. the Egyptian gods' speaking the world into existence, or the opening of the Fourth Gospel), the author's pen is a magic wand.[8] Certainly Vergil and both Peter and Paul would fall into the category of magic pen-wielder.[9] Moreover, Vergil defines himself as a

---

7. The *Aeneid* itself makes reference to magical, predictive writing. Such are the predictions of the Cumaean Sibyl, which Aeneas in the beginning of book 6 begs her not to entrust to writing on leaves that will be scattered by the winds:

Great shrines await
you, priestess, too within our Latin kingdom;
for there I shall set up your oracles
and secret omens spoken to my people
and consecrate to you, generous one,
our chosen men. Only do not entrust
your verses to the leaves, lest they fly off
in disarray, the play of rapid winds:
chant them yourself, I pray. (6.71–76)

Translation by Allen Mandelbaum, *The Aeneid of Virgil* (Berkeley and Los Angeles: University of California Press, 1971). Here Vergil clearly evokes the Sibylline Books, supposedly brought to Rome by the last king, Tarquinius Superbus, and kept in the temple of Jupiter Capitolinus until a fire in 83 B.C.E. required the forging of a fresh set of oracles (cf. R. G. Austin, *P Vergili Maronis Aeneidos Liber Primus* [Oxford: Clarendon, 1971], ad loc.). The Sibylline Books also have their place in Christian lore, of course.

8. See below on the spelling of Vergil's name.

9. For 502 pages on Vergil as magician, see John Spargo, *Virgil the Necromancer: Studies in Virgilian Legends* (Harvard Studies in Comparative Literature 10; Cambridge: Harvard University Press, 1934).

priest/prognosticator/carrier of a divine message (*vates*), and certainly both Peter and Paul fall into that category, as well.[10]

VERGIL

Publius Vergilius Maro was born in 70 B.C.E., a plebeian perhaps, in the village Andes near Mantua in an area of Cisalpine Gaul that would not become officially incorporated into Italy until his adulthood.[11] From this he is often assumed to have had an outsider's or provincial's mentality; from the Gaulish connection he is sometimes (fancifully) called "the first Irish poet."[12]

His parents, although not of the higher classes, had him educated at Cremona, Milan, and Rome. He also studied with the Epicureans Siro and (perhaps) Philodemus. He wrote important poetry from an early age and attracted the patronage of Maecenas, a wealthy and influential friend of Augustus and himself an outsider in Roman society as a knight of Etruscan heritage. With the support of Augustus and Maecenas, Vergil lived quietly all the rest of his life in Campania, at Nola or at Naples. He cemented his reputation as one of Rome's greatest poets with two important works: the *Eclogues*, a collection of ten "bucolic" or "pastoral" poems, written between 42 and 37 B.C.E., and four books of *Georgics* (37–30 B.C.E.), poems in the didactic tradition, treating farming lovingly, but digressing frequently into mythology, politics, and so forth.

---

10. It has been argued many times (e.g., C. R. Beye, *Ancient Epic Poetry: Homer, Apollonius, Virgil* [Ithaca, N.Y.: Cornell University Press, 1993], 230) that, even with the first words of the epic *arma virumque cano* ("I sing of arms and the man"), the poet is coopting the sacred and prophetic powers of the Muses. (*Cano* has a magico-religious sense, as well as an artistic one.) For the poet as *vates*, see J. K. Newman, *The Concept of Vates in Augustan Poetry* (Collections Latomus 89; Brussels: Latomus, 1967), passim. For an exhaustive discussion of the first line of a poem as programmatic, see Gian Biagio Conte, *The Rhetoric of Imitation* (ed. and trans. Charles Segal; Ithaca, N.Y.: Cornell University Press, 1986), 76–87.

11. No ancient biographer tells Vergil's history in quite the way I have outlined here; to reconstruct this telling requires hobbling together pieces of the ancient lives and speculations of modern and medieval scholars. This is, however, so typical a reconstruction that R. D. Williams does not bother to footnote a single detail of his similar treatment in the introductions to his commentaries on the *Aeneid*. For the biographies of the ancients, Henry Nettleship, *Ancient Lives of Vergil* (Oxford: Clarendon, 1879), still provides the most convenient compendium. In the Christian connection, it is interesting to note that to Jerome's teacher Donatus is ascribed a life of Vergil—probably by Suetonius, in fact, but the ascription alone shows how comfortable Christians are with the idea that one of their own should research the great pagan writer.

12. I throw this in to show that even in the modern era cultural cooption colors the recording of history or biography.

Around 30 B.C.E. Vergil began a grand epic, in Homeric style and meter, and in Latin, celebrating the mighty destiny of the Caesars and Rome.[13] He worked on the *Aeneid* (its name means "tale of Aeneas" and evokes the title of the *Iliad*) steadily until 19 B.C.E. when he set out on a brief cruise to Greece for local color for his final draft.[14] He fell ill with a respiratory fever and returned to Italy. There in the port at Brundisium he died, instructing his executors to burn the unfinished epic. But Augustus, who had heard Vergil read books 2, 4, and 6, intervened and had the poem published posthumously. The text has been treated with such reverence since antiquity that we feel safe in assuming that our current text is very close to the one Vergil composed.

It is perhaps important to note that Vergil came to adulthood in a time and place that suffered from the tramp of the legions as much as any site in the Near East during the Roman occupation. From the assassination of Julius Caesar, the armies of the Second Triumvirate—the extraconstitutional alliance of Octavian, Caesar's grand-nephew who would become the Emperor Augustus, Marc Antony, Caesar's lieutenant, and M. Aemilius Lepidus, Caesar's master of the horse—raged across Italy, forcing peaceful farming communities into conflict and starvation. This is the context of Vergil's *Eclogues,* ten poems published in 37 B.C.E., which only pretend to be about the lives of simple shepherds. Indeed, it was assumed in antiquity that in this work Vergil was lamenting the loss of his own family's farm when the veterans of Antony and Octavian were resettled on his land after 42 B.C.E.

Italy in the period of the civil wars, then, endured social and political disruption on a major scale, the product of three forces which might also have had an impact on Judaea before and after the destruction of the temple: competing armies living off the land; "enemy-lists" of the victors and armies of informers that brought the knock on the door in the middle of the night; and retired legionaries paid in farmland confiscated from the conquered. The siege of the city of Perusia (in north-central Italy, modern Perugia) might be taken as emblematic: while Octavian's troops sat in siege around the town, food was allotted on a graduated scale, with slaves receiving none. They could be seen outside the walls

---

13. Other works (of the so-called *Appendix Virgiliana,* for example) apart from these three cannot with certainty be ascribed to Vergil.

14. Vergil had apparently not yet visited any of the places outside Italy, which he describes in such detail in his epic. That he intended to view them now, before the final publication of his work, leads to interesting speculation (in the absence of any hard evidence) on the question of whether he thinks his is a work of history.

foraging for grass. After the city capitulated, it was burned, perhaps on Octavian's command.[15]

Vergil's works display a deep understanding of war and longing for peace. The *Aeneid*, especially, must not be thought to be a glorification of imperial stormtroopers nor an uncritical encomium of Augustus's deeds and policies. It is a complex and ambiguous work, with plenty for the victims of empire as well as for the victors.

Currency of the Aeneid

In Vergil's own day, even before its completion, other prominent Romans were hailing the *Aeneid* as "a work greater than the *Iliad*" (Propertius, 2.34.66, post 29 B.C.E.). It was apparently used as a school text immediately on its publication (Juvenal, *Satirae* 7.226), and Quintilian in the first century C.E. advised that the entire school curriculum should be designed around Vergil's works. Quintilian also mentions that his own teacher, Domitius Afer, in the earlier generation had rated the *Aeneid* as "second [to Homer], but closer to first place than to third" (*Inst.* 10.1.86).

Moreover, accompanying the empire-wide spread of the original Latin text is a proliferation of artistic representations of the plot of the *Aeneid* and, indeed, of the figure of Vergil himself.[16] Certain episodes of the Aeneid recur in artistic representations—Dido and Aeneas taking shelter in the cave (book 4), for example—but as later Italians, intent on tracing their ancestry to characters Aeneas encounters in Italy, commissioned paintings, et cetera, with scenes from the later books, we might be forgiven for speculating that earlier generations of Italian provincial

---

15. Again, the sometimes unfortunate divisions between the disciplines has shunted the history of Vergil's *province* into a different branch of scholarship from the literary analysis of his works. But B. Miles and Archibald W. Allen, "Vergil and the Augustan Experience," in *Vergil at 2000: Commemorative Essays on the Poet and His Influence* (ed. John D. Bernard; New York: AMS Press, 1986), 13–41, have done us all a good turn in reuniting the historical background and the epic.

16. As Bristol art historian Michael Liversidge sums it up ("Virgil in Art," in *Virgil and His Influence: Bimillennial Studies* [ed. Charles Martindale; Bristol, U.K.: Bristol Classical Press, 1984], 92), "The first works of art inspired by Vergil may have appeared in his own lifetime. At any rate the popularity and wide circulation his books quickly achieved are reflected in the rapid spread of what can be regarded as a Virgilian iconography that became part of the Roman tradition generally and extended across the empire." The most important work of art of the earlier empire influenced by Vergil's epic account of the history of the Julian clan must certainly be the *Ara Pacis* (13–9 B.C.E.). But depictions of scenes of the Aeneid and of the heroized author himself can be found in a variety of media, scattered throughout even remote reaches of the empire (Lower Ham in Somerset, for example), from Vergil's death until the threshold of the Middle Ages and beyond.

nobility did so as well. In that case, book 8 with its portrayal of the Latins at the future site of Rome might be thought to have been a favorite choice of (lost) early works.[17]

Among Christians as well, Vergil is regularly admired: he is called "a second Homer" by Jerome (whose teacher was the Vergilian commentator Donatus) and mentioned with approbation by Lactantius (the first to identify Christ as the mysterious child of the Fourth Eclogue), Constantine (who mentions Christ as the child of the Fourth Eclogue in the Good Friday "Speech to the Assembly of the Saints" sometime in the 320s), Juvencus, Augustine, and Proba.[18]

Is Language a Barrier?

Are we going to be able to proffer any verbal reminiscences of the *Aeneid* to bolster our argument? Unlikely. It may be that in reviewing Jerome's Latin translation we can find some echoes of Vergilian language, but any direct quotations would long ago have been unearthed.[19] But recall that the canonical Acts and the Gospels also do not contain any direct verbal reminiscences of Homer, and the Homeric epics are in Greek. And yet—just as surely as the movie *O Brother, Where Art Thou?*— Acts is based on the plot, characterizations, concepts, and values of the *Odyssey* (and *Iliad*).[20]

In estimating the contribution to the Gospels and Acts by the works of both Vergil and Homer, it is important to remember that these works, as the essential school texts of the period, were known in their original form to all who could read and write in Greek and Latin. If we assume

---

17. For artistic representation of the *Aeneid* in general, see Liversidge "Virgil in Art" by Liversidge; and Llewellyn's "Virgil and the Visual Arts" in Martindale, *Virgil and His Influence*, 117–40.

18. For a fuller discussion of Vergil and Christianity, see, most recently, Michael Dewar, "Culture Wars: Latin Literature from the Second Century to the End of the Classical Era," in *Literature in the Greek and Roman Worlds* (ed. Oliver Taplin; Oxford: Oxford University Press, 2000), 529–32. Proba, incidentally, is credited with being the first to compose a Christian cento based entirely on lines drawn from Vergil. It is an index of the currency of Vergil's works that all of the centos composed in the West, which survive to us, are composed of lines of Vergil's poems. See Michael Roberts, *Biblical Epic and Rhetorical Paraphrase in Late Antiquity* (Liverpool: Cairns, 1985), 92–96.

19. Jerome, of course, displays a knowledge of Vergil as well; any echoes would simply be ascribed to him and not to the text he is translating; i.e., we cannot assume that he has spotted in Acts a Greek translation of Vergil's Latin text.

20. I can do no better than to refer the reader to the works of Dennis R. MacDonald, the doyen of "Homeric Christianity" (if I may call it that), listed in the bibliography.

that the Gospel-writers (and one of them is called "Mark" after all) had Latin, they had Vergil.

But, more than that, and in case the caveat be raised that we cannot prove any of the Gospel-writers had Latin, let us remember that Homer and Vergil did not only circulate widely in their original form. All three epics were imitated and parodied (the *Aeneid* from its first publication) and circulated in prose paraphrases—prose paraphrases in several languages. Thus, the *Iliad, Odyssey,* and *Aeneid* doubtless existed in "Classics Illustrated" form, and the early Christians did not require mastery of Latin or of the specialized, idiosyncratic epic language of Homer to enjoy them—any more than our own high school students do.[21]

In addition, recall that the epics also constantly resurfaced in new reworkings in each generation. Thus, Athenian tragedies of the fifth century B.C.E or the ancient romances are clearly reliant on Homer, and the epics of Lucan and tragedies of Seneca in the age of Nero are clearly reworkings of the *Aeneid.* In that sense, the values and concepts of the epics reverberate in the literature of the age, whatever the literacy rate or availability of the originals.

Archaeological finds continue to yield information on the reading habits of the common person in antiquity: mosaics with details of Vergil's *Aeneid* (however acquired) have been discovered in Taunton, England, which is just about as far as the Roman army ever traveled—although admittedly in the wrong direction.[22] It may be that archaeological digs in garrison towns in Judea will yield similar evidence of the influence of Vergil's hero. Incidentally, from what survives to us, Vergil himself has been romanticized in art almost as much as Aeneas—or as Homer. Graphic depictions of Vergil,—grave, manly, pious,—have been found in several imperial sites.[23]

---

21. It is probably worth noting here that since scholars in general find very little verbal reminiscence of even Paul's letters in Acts, most of the discussion of sources in *Acts* has been based on details which cannot be confirmed at the level of language. Thus, if we can concede, with most scholars, that the *Aeneid* circulated in a Greek prose paraphrase that preserved most of the major episodes, then we are as free to find reminiscences of the *Aeneid* in details of the "plot" of Acts as we are to find reminiscences of episodes of the Hebrew Scriptures (which, of course, were known to the authors of the Gospels in a Greek prose paraphrase, the Septuagint).

22. Let it be noted, however, that one dig in Roman Britain has yielded a letter of a Syrian stationed in England. One did move around in the Roman army.

23. The most well-known portrait of Vergil, between two Muses, is a mosaic from North Africa, currently in the Bardo Museum in Tunis.

Saint Vergil

One of the most compelling reasons to explore the works of Vergil in conjunction with the works of early Christianity is because the early Christians "canonized" him, regarding him as one of the pagan "saints" or prophets whom Jesus rescues from Satan in the "Harrowing of Hell" tale common before the Reformation. (That is one of the reasons why Vergil is Dante's guide in the *Inferno*.) It is usually argued that Vergil owes this distinction to the celebrated "Fourth Eclogue" in which he *seems* to prophesy the birth of a miraculous child who will cleanse and renew the old Roman world.[24]

Three indications (among many) of Christian veneration of Vergil as a magic-man, prophet, and miracle-worker follow.

(1) The spelling of his name: His family name was almost certainly Vergilius. In late antiquity and the early Middle Ages (the era for which we have evidence; of course, the practice may have begun earlier), Christians, apparently fascinated by its similarity to the Latin *virga* ("magic wand")—which seems to be a reference to the Golden Bough which gives Aeneas access to the land of the dead in *Aeneid* book 6—began to spell it Virgilius. This tradition continues, of course, to the modern day, with classics being the only field not willing to invest Vergil with magical powers.

(2) The *sortes Virgilianae:* Christian communities from late antiquity to the American Revolution (the era for which we have evidence; of course, the practice may have begun earlier) were accustomed to using Vergil's works alongside the Bible as magical texts, capable of answering queries or foretelling the future. The process was the same in both cases: the questioner formulated the question, let the book fall open at random, then read a verse which seemed to respond to the query.[25] In the use of both the Bible and Vergil's works, it is assumed to be the voice of God responding. Incidentally, the famous first words of the *Aeneid, arma virumque cano,* usually translated as "I sing of arms and the man," can also be translated as "I prophesy of ... the man," which doubtless led Christians to regard the whole of the work as a proto- or crypto-Christian prognostication.

---

24. Vergil is probably referring to the birth of one of Augustus's heirs. Thus, the Christians are not naïve literalists in their interpretation; they understand Vergil as referring to the birth of an actual contemporary man, and so he is. They are merely decoding his text with their own key. For the purposes of our discussion, the one question remaining is: How early did they begin to do this?

25. Thus, the Emperor Alexander Severus opened to *Aen* 6. 852 and read *tu regere imperio populos, Romane, memento;* and Charles I of England came upon *Aen.* 4. 615–620: *at bello audacis.*

(3) Constantine's dedication of the newly-founded Constantinople: On May 11, 330, a statue of the emperor, his head encircled by the rays of the sun (which were equated with the nails that had pierced Christ), was placed on a huge column in his forum. Under the column were buried what were clearly thought to be sacred objects of the Christian religion: crumbs from the bread that had fed the 5,000, saints' relics, the thieves' crosses, the alabaster ointment box, the adze Noah used to build the ark, the rock which gushed water at Moses' command, and the palladium (a cult-object) that Aeneas had brought from Troy to Italy.

Vergil's Works as Models for the Composition of Acts

It is difficult to investigate questions of authorial intent with regard to the Homeric epics, because, since the epics are the products of oral composition, composed by dozens, maybe hundreds, of "authors" over perhaps thousands of years, we can only argue for careful philosophical, social, and political consistency across the works by postulating a detailed master plan (filed on the island of Chios, perhaps) or an "inspired editor" who extensively rewrote and deleted sections to bring the epics into conformity with the views of his own precise moment in time. (Obviously, we often have the same problem in dealing with the Hebrew Scriptures.)

But the *Aeneid* is the product of a single mind, published close to the date of its composition and transmitted to us in virtually pristine form. Moreover, as a literary work commissioned by an emperor in order to articulate and make palatable his plans for a major social and political reconstruction of his state, it reeks (we might say) of its time and of point of view. In that sense, it might be expected to have more of an appeal for an author (like Luke, perhaps) who is setting out to write the story of a particular time and has the revolutionary re-creation of a whole society as his object.

Thus, if the *Aeneid* were merely what it seems to be on the surface, a spectacularly successful piece of political propaganda supporting the pretensions of a new regime, it might still have had some value as a model for the writer of Acts. But it is so much more than that. Vergil himself had the mental habits of the scholar, excellent academic training, and cosmopolitan interests. Thus, the *Aeneid* is a virtual encyclopedia of philosophical and culture lore from all reaches of the empire. Vergil displays knowledge, for example, of Egyptian cultic ritual, Ethiopian dining habits, and Phoenician goddesses. His epic contains a cosmogony, a meditation on the transmigration of souls, treatises on the obscurities of Epicurean and Neo-Platonic thought. It is, among other things, a pastiche of ideas drawn from the major Hellenistic philosophical systems—Stoicism (Aeneas is a Stoic hero, it is often argued), Epicureanism (Vergil was a great admirer of Lucretius, the major exponent of Epicureanism, and a student of the Epicureans Siro and Philodemus), Neo-Platonism (a reworking of the Myth of Er, for example), Orphic-Pythagoreanism, and others—a compendium of thought of the major competitors/contributors to Christianity.

But Vergil does not just pedantically toss his knowledge into his narrative; he blends, syncretizes, poeticizes his knowledge into a philosophical value system which was very appealing to the early Christians. Just two examples of many: (1) his cultural hero Aeneas embodies the Stoic good man, while (in opposition to Stoic values) staying engaged in the life and fortune of his city as befits a Roman patrician; and (2) his vision of the Elysian fields, obviously borrowed from Homer, alters Homer's value system: it is not only the children of gods who enjoy the rewards of paradise—anyone can earn them. Both of these ideas were common in Christian philosophy.

As you can see from these two examples, Vergil never intended his book to heroize one man, as it might be argued the *Odyssey* and *Iliad* do. Aeneas is not concerned with his own good fortune, but with the future of his people and obeying the will of the gods. Thus, he becomes a symbol of self-sacrifice, a Jesus-symbol, if you will—with the widespread appeal of the great pan-Mediterranean philosophies of the day. The *Aeneid*, then, seems to be anticipating the Christian value system.

But, even more than for the content of the work, the *Aeneid* may have been prized by the writer of Luke-Acts for the very nature of its composition. Vergil has set himself the difficult task of composing an epic that imitates the two Homeric epics (the odd-numbered books resemble the *Odyssey*; the even-numbered ones, the *Iliad*; books 1–6 are Odyssean; books 7–12 Iliadic), while in some basic way undoing and supplanting them.[26] Thus, he has borrowed the classic artifacts of an earlier culture, refitted them to his own time, and, in the process, subtly rejected them. It is completely appropriate that Aeneas, the Romans' representative, is a Trojan: Vergil criticizes the Greeks while coopting their quintessential works. Coopting the sacred tribal artifacts of a culture while advocating its demise—is not this what the Gospel-writers are doing, after all?

Thus, there are many grounds for parallels between Acts and the Roman epic: Aeneas, the self-sacrificing culture hero, bringing gods from Asia Minor to Rome, is Jesus, and Peter and Paul; Vergil himself, as the sacred prophet/poet divining the mysteries of the new age, is a model for

---

26. On the Iliadic and Odyssean books, see, for example, Gransden, introduction to *Virgil Aeneid Book VIII*, 4–11; Richard Jenkyns, *Classical Epic: Homer and Virgil* (Bristol, U.K.: Bristol Classical Press, 1992), 53; and Farrell "Virgilian Intertext," 229–30.

Peter and Paul the writers; the burning of Troy and the diaspora of the Trojans is parallel to the destruction of Jerusalem and Jewish diaspora; and the glorious new empire of Augustus, with its gifts of peace and prosperity, is the kingdom of God, on earth.

Vergil and Homer/Vergil or Homer

With all this in mind, let me turn to a concrete example, the conversion of Cornelius episode from Acts 10:1–11:18. Let me hasten to say I choose this example because of Dennis MacDonald's fine work on the Homeric parallels.[27] I am taking advantage of the arguments he has already made, so that I do not have to begin by arguing for the "epicness" of the passage.

What Homer is not—in any way the ancients could discover—is intertextual. Since it was for the ancients as for us some inconceivably ancient chronicle of old, lost wars in old, lost places, it begins at the beginning—it is the text from which other texts start.[28] Thus, for learning to "intertextuate" (if I may be so bold), it is worthless. So, if you were the product of an educational system that taught imitation—not originality, necessarily—as an aesthetic value, you might be taught to use Homer as the clay of your creation, but it would be useless as a tool of creation. For the shaping of epic stuff into something wondrous and new, Vergil's *Aeneid*—perhaps the most intertextual work ever written—would be a much better example.

Thus, I would be inclined to argue that Vergil's epic is more likely to be a model for Acts than Homer's, and I would approach both works as political documents. If we are looking deliberately for Vergil in Acts, if we are assuming Vergil is a likely model for Acts, we might start from Vergil, rather than from Acts. What, it might be argued, is the single most important political point Vergil has to make, as chief propagandist for the Emperor Augustus? He has to somehow transmogrify a rebel regime, founded by the war-lord of all war-lords, Julius Caesar, into a legitimated, community-based, history-hallowed neo-Republic. And, in the process, he has to argue that, with assumption of a new name/title ("Augustus"),[29] the old war-lord Octavian—who besieged Perusia and

---

27. See n. 4 above.

28. This argument, of course, is ignoring Gilgamesh or the Egyptian "Story of the Ship-wrecked Sailor" or other works as possible antecedents of the *Iliad* and *Odyssey*, since the ancients did not regard them as antecedents of Homer's works.

29. It can never be known what the Romans heard in this new name, which ultimately must in some way be connected with *augur* and *auguria*, which the Romans believed to be

confiscated his family's farm—has been transmuted into a community-minded, clement, responsible, and pious Princeps ("first among equals").

In the face of this formidable assignment, what need has he of heroes like Odysseus and Achilles, the ultimate war-lords? Why should Achilles be heroic when he is willing to condemn the whole of the Greek army/polity to death to satisfy a whim of personal honor—and to breach military discipline over a girl? Why should Odysseus, adrift on the ship of state, be honored for having returned home with none of the fellow citizens who set out with him—and for having slaughtered his fellow-countrymen in his own house on his return—incidentally, also because of a woman?

No, Vergil's hero may not be so much in imitation of Homer's heroes as in opposition to them. A common Irish sailor, quoted by W. B. Yeats, has perhaps said it best, "Ach, a hero? Him a hero? Bigob, I t'ought he waz a priest!"[30] With that, off to another heroic priest, Peter in Acts 10 and 11.

Acts 10:1–11:18

In this section, I will summarize the plot of Acts 10–11.18 in a way it has perhaps never been summarized before—but not unfairly or incorrectly, I think. The story starts with the captain of a troop of foreign invaders currently involved in hostilities with the locals, hostilities that the reader knows will lead to a great war.[31] This captain, a godly man, a pious man, receives a command from a supernatural visitor to send for the influential leader of a local subculture/tribe/splinter group. He sends two servants and a pious soldier for him.

Meanwhile, the local leader experiences a supernatural vision of ritually clean and unclean animals—or of in-group and out-group food animals—and a god commands him to eat them all, violating local custom. While the local leader ponders the message, a voice makes known to him that the captain's emissaries have arrived and that he is to go with them. He joins the captain in a city of the Caesars (Caesarea), which the captain's (apparent) ancestor, L. Cornelius Sulla, visited in an

---

distinctively Roman practices connected with the divining of the will of the divine. Nor can we easily determine whether the Roman world heard—in the name a title than a personal name—or when they may have changed their understanding. For uses of the name in Acts, see Colin Hemer, *The Book of Acts in the Setting of Hellenistic History* (Winona Lake, Ind.: Eisenbrauns, 1990), 107.

30. According to Ezra Pound, *ABC of Reading* (New York: New Directions, 1960), 44, Yeats was wont to say this about Aeneas and his piety.

31. We do think this was written after 70, do we not?

earlier time.[32]

The captain bows down before the local leader as a suppliant. They exchange information about the portents and vision attending their meeting. The local leader interprets the omens as signifying that his group must accept the foreign invaders—and others like them—as equals. A sign from above confirms the truth of the local leader's interpretation. The local leader tells the tale of the hero-god of his city/group/sub-culture/tribe/splinter group. In the tale the hero-god triumphs over a monster/devil and conquers death.

AENEID BOOK 8

Now I will summarize the "plot" of *Aeneid* book 8 in a way it has perhaps never been summarized before, but not unfairly or incorrectly, I think. Aeneas, captain of an invading force engaged in hostilities with the locals (which the reader knows will culminate in a great war),[33] experiences a dream-vision of a god of the place (the river Tiber).[34] The god takes him to what will be the city of the Caesars (Rome) to meet with the

---

32. The name Cornelius here is neither adventitious nor historically accurate, I suspect. The most prominent of the Cornelii in this period was Lucius Cornelius Sulla, who enters the histories of the East as a liberator from the savage aggression of Mithridates. (That he in fact financially ruined the Asian cities that had sided with Mithridates does not tarnish his reputation with those peoples who did not collaborate.) That centurions can be found bearing the *nomen* of the Cornelii is, I would argue, irrelevant here. (For the contrary view, see Joseph A. Fitzmyer, *The Acts of the Apostles* [AB 31; New York: Doubleday, 1997], ad loc.) That detail is not given to make it easier for the ancient reader to locate this event in the chronicles of history, I would contend—the ancient reader in general has little interest in and few resources for documenting the accuracy of an account. This detail contributes to the importance of this encounter and, thus, to Peter's importance, and, moreover, reenacts the first encounter between Romans and Jews in this area. Thus, Peter and his group are glazed with the patina of great antiquity—and made the brokers for relationships between Romans and Jews, an important consideration in the time in which Acts was written. For this version of a Roman name, see Hemer, *Book of Acts*, 177, 226–27.

33. A great war, both in the context of this work and in the lives of their fathers and grandfathers: the so-called Social (i.e., "allied") War between Rome and her Italian cousins. It was in this war that Marius and L. Cornelius Sulla (see n. 31 above) came to prominence. This is, of course, another example of how the *Aeneid* is "unstuck in time" (as Kurt Vonnegut would put it): most of the events of the work have echoes not only in legendary history but also in an event in Republican Roman history (past, to Vergil) and in an event in Augustan history (present, to Vergil; in this case, the civil wars) and in the Augustan plan for the Roman future (future, to Vergil).

34. The Tiber is, of course, also a god of the imperial family (Tiberius is Augustus's stepson and always a potential heir to the Principate) and a god particular to the Roman subculture/tribe/group/splinter group, (i.e., not shared with other cultures of the Mediterranean nor with the Latin tribes or Italian allied groups). Vergil may be acknowledging both

local leader of an ethnic subgroup/tribe/splinter group. To signify the vision is a true one, he prophesies that Aeneas will encounter thirty-one pigs, the ultimate Roman/gentile meat animal:

> Oh, one sprung from the race of gods, you who from the enemy bring back to us the city Troy, you who are preserving the holy heights [of Troy] for the ages, you whom the Laurentian land and the Latin fields have long awaited, here is the home secured for you, here are your household gods (*penates*) secure. [35] Do not shrink, do not be frightened by the menaces of war! All the swollen anger of the gods has subsided. [36]

> And now—lest you think sleep has fashioned empty visions—under the oaks on the shore you will find a huge sow giving birth to thirty head. White is the sow lying back on the ground, white the young at her teats. (36–45)[37]

---

of these aspects when he uses *Tiberinus*—a cult name and a form close to *Tiberius*. For Vergil's names for the river, see Richard Jenkyns, *Virgil's Experience*, 530–38.

35. Aeneas is transporting the ancestral gods of his family and of his now-destroyed city to Rome. This is the mission, surely, of the heroes of Acts—they are recovering their gods (old and new) from the ashes of Jerusalem and transporting them to Rome. The thirty piglets represent the thirty years between the founding of Aeneas's city (Lavinium) and the installation of the Trojans at Alba ("white") Longa. Alba Longa will then be the mother-city of Rome, but Aeneas will long be dead.

36. A Vergilian half-line, one of some fifty in the work and three in this book. Whether these lines represent defects in the poem that Vergil intended to edit out, whether they are intentionally incomplete, or whether they mark passages of such moment that Vergil put them aside for special attention, the text exhausts the scholarly imagination. This example does nothing to resolve the problem: *tumor omnis et irae concessere deum* ("angers that rose among the gods have passed"—Robert Fitzgerald's rather colorless translation) is a great big idea for the remnants of Troy's mighty people—and for the survivors of the sack of Jerusalem as well, I might argue.

37. All Latin citations of the *Aeneid* are from R. D. Williams, ed., *The Aeneid of Virgil: Books 7–12* (London: Macmillan, 1973). All translations of the Latin are my own, except where otherwise indicated. A caveat to the reader: Loveday Alexander has made the point in a session of the Ancient Narrative Group (November, 2002) that the *Aeneid* seems a more likely source for Acts when Latin epic poetry has been translated into (professorial) English prose. It has been argued that it is unlikely that the authors of Acts, a prose work, would have chosen an epic poem as a model. But Vergil himself makes allusion to the Greek romances, prose works, and to classical drama, poetry in different meters and intended for a different purpose. Crossing genres is apparently not forbidden by convention to pagan poets. On the Christian side, the Hebrew Scriptures and canonical Gospels are themselves pastiches of prose and poetry, and genre barriers are not respected when assembling the "story" of Jesus or the "story" of the early church. As for Jewish works, we do not hesitate to assert that Ezekiel's poetic drama about Moses, the Exagoge, must have some association with the prose Exodus although Exodus was composed in a different genre, different time,

When Aeneas and his Trojans arrive, Evander's city is celebrating a festival to the hero-god Hercules. Aeneas tells Evander that a heavenly messenger had a hand in their meeting:

> Oh, noblest of those born Greek, it is to you Fortune wished me to pray and to proffer branches bound with a sacred band (*vitta*)! I was not indeed afraid because you are a leader of the Danaans and an Arcadian, nor because you are joined by blood to the twin sons of Atreus. My courage and the holy oracles of the gods, our common ancestors, and your fame spread throughout the world have joined me to you and have driven me, a willing victim of the fates. (127–133)

Aeneas explains that he himself is there as a humble suppliant:

> Your forefather is Mercury, whom shining Maia conceived and brought forth on the cold peak of Cyllene; but that Maia—you have heard we believe something like this—Atlas fathered, the same Atlas who holds up the stars. Thus our people split in two, from the same single bloodline.
>
> Relying on these things, I sent you no envoys, made you no overtures conceived in deceit. I myself presented my own self, I offered my life to you, I came as a suppliant to your doorstep. The same people who pursue you in cruel war, the Daunians, believe that if they push us out there would be nothing to stop them from putting all Hesperia under their yoke and they would hold all the sea which washes it north and south. Take my pledge and give me one. Our hearts are brave in war. We have courage and youth experienced in action. (138–151)

Evander welcomes him warmly:

> Then he spoke to him these few words thus, "oh, bravest of the Trojans, I accept and acknowledge you gladly!" (154–155)

He then recalls an earlier encounter with Aeneas's father Anchises. Aeneas joins the feast as guest of honor.

Evander tells the tale of the hero-god of his group, Hercules—how he visited the site and defeated the monster Cacus in a fairly obvious

---

and, it is likely, a different language. It may be that the early Christian community can only assimilate the important works from both seminal cultures, Hebrew and Roman, in Greek prose paraphrases—but we are arguing the resemblances between Acts and the *Aeneid* concern plot points—which would have been preserved in a prose paraphrase—in any case.

"harrowing of hell" (8.248–290).[38] He comments that their worship of Hercules is "no empty-headed superstition, blind to the age-old gods" (248–250, trans. Fitzgerald). Aeneas spends the night as Evander's guest.

In the morning, Evander proposes that Aeneas should lead his men and an army of Etruscans against the hostile local tribes.[39] He cites a prophecy that demands the Etruscans seek a foreigner as leader:

> To these thousands, I will add you, Aeneas, as leader. For packed thick along the whole shore our ships groan. They order the signal for action, but an aged seer (*haruspex*) holds them back, chanting the fates, "Oh, young men, the best of Maeonia, the flower and the manhood of the men of old! A just sorrow drives you against the enemy and Mezentius inflames you with righteous anger, but it has been decreed that no Italian will command so great a people. Put your trust in foreign (*externos*) leaders." (496–503)

He has disqualified himself as too old, and his son Pallas is of mixed blood:

> Then the Etruscan battleline sat back down in this field, frightened by the warnings of the gods. And he sent to me spokesmen and the scepter and crown of the realm and entrusted to me the emblems of kingship did Tarchon, so I might come down to his camp and take up the rule of Tyrrhenia. But age slow as ice and worn out with its years begrudged me the *imperium*, as did a strength too old for heroics. I would have urged my son, had his mother's Sabine blood not tied him to this part of the country. You whose age and birth the fates have favored, you whom divine powers (*numina*) demand, march out, oh most mighty leader of the Trojans and Italians! I'll have join you this one, my hope and my comfort, Pallas; with you as teacher he'll learn to endure the hardship and hard work of war, he'll study your deeds, he'll look up to you from his young years. I'll give with him two hundred Arcadian horsemen, the pick of our young men, and Pallas will add just as many in his own name. (503–519)

Thus are East and West united. A sign from above confirms the truth of the local leader's interpretation:

> Scarcely had he spoken, and Aeneas, Anchises' son, and loyal Achates were still holding their eyes fixed on the ground, mulling over their

---

38. The name "Cacus" to Greek speakers of course suggests κακός, "evil" (as Gransden has observed in his introduction to *Virgil Aeneid Book VIII*, 25), rendering the Hercules-Cacus episode a "Manichean" combat between good and evil.

39. Maecenas, Augustus's best friend, mentor, master of ceremonies, etc., is an Etruscan by heritage.

many troubles with sad hearts, when Cytherea [Venus] gave a sign
(*signum*) in the cloudless sky—a lightning bolt shivered down unexpected from the ether with a clap of thunder, and suddenly wiped out
all they saw. The clangor of a Tyrrhenian [Etruscan] horn blared through
the heavens. They looked up, and again and again the huge crashes
sounded. Weapons between the clouds in a peaceful region of the sky
they saw glow red, and clang as if struck. The others stood frozen, but
the Trojan hero recognized the sound and the signs promised by his
divine parent. Then he spoke, "Truly, friend, don't fret about what
calamity these portents might bring: Olympus is calling me. My divine
mother told me she would send a sign (*signum*) when war broke out and
would bring arms of Vulcan's making through the air to help me. Ah,
what slaughter stands ready for the miserable Laurentians! What a
blood price you will pay me, Turnus! How many shields and helmets
and bodies of men will you roll under your waves, Father Tiber! Let
them seek battle and break their treaties." (520–540)

Am I going to be able to proffer any verbal reminiscences of the
Aeneid in Acts to convince you that the *Aeneid* is the source-text behind
these chapters? This is unlikely, considering the difficulties attendant in
satisfying critics that Paul's letters, a Greek text, are a source of Acts. As
was argued, now, almost a century ago, the text has been so smoothed
over (by the transmitters perhaps as well as by the author) as to have
eradicated traces of the sources that are surely there.[40]

But there is a place in book 8 that would certainly command the
attention of the early Christian communities: the celebrated tour of the
site of (the future) Rome conducted by Evander. Here, at the foot of what
will be the location of the temple of Jupiter Tonans, erected in Vergil's
present in 22 B.C.E. by Augustus, Evander speaks of an unknown god:

From this point [Evander] leads [Aeneas] to the Tarpeian Rock and the
Capitoline hill, golden now, but once all-bristly with woodland brambles.
Even as early as then a religious awe of the place set the rustics shivering
with fear, and they trembled at even the rocks and the woods. "This
grove," he said, "this hill with its leafy crown some god inhabits (what
god we're not sure). The Arcadians believe they've seen Jupiter himself,

---

40. See, for example, Ernst Haenchen's argument (*The Acts of the Apostles A Commentary*
[ed. and trans. B. Noble and G. Shinn; Philadelphia: Westminster, 1971], passim): he did not
concede that evidence of the sources of Acts would yield to the usual methods of stylistic
exegesis (p. 81), but continued to search for those sources all the same. I am merely making
an argument for searching in a different direction. Lewis R. Donelson, "Cult Histories and
the Sources of Acts," *Bib* 68 (1987): 1–21, has a lucid summary of the problem (although he
and I come to rather different conclusions).

shaking (as so often) his black aegis in his right hand and driving the clouds." (347–354)

Surely, it was just such descriptions as this that led the early Christians to the canonization of Saint Vergil. Not only has the hero been led to the site that will be occupied by the most imposing of Augustus's new temples, but it seems that temple will truly belong not to Jupiter, but to some unknown god.[41] This must seem like a reference to Jesus to the later Christians, unknown in Vergil's time, but soon to overmatch Jupiter himself. Moreover, Vergil's "prophecy" might have been taken as predicting the move of an early Christian community to Rome.

There are some other indications, perhaps, that might be mentioned based on the choice of Caesarea Maritima as a site for this encounter. In all this, let me hasten to mention that there is nothing at all in the description of Caesarea placing the story in the real Caesarea Maritima—no telling details, no brief history of the place. On some level, the Caesarea of the narrative is simply a "city of the Caesars" as the name itself suggests. Thus, Cornelius's Caesarea is no more locatable a place than any other of the stops on Peter's and Paul's journeys through Acts' symbolic/mythico-religious geography. They play the big burgs on the Christian circuit.

But if the author of the Conversion of Cornelius knows anything at all about Caesarea Maritima, he is surely likely to know that it was a Hellenistic (i.e., Greek) city refounded by Herod the Great as a spectacularly Romanophile tribute to Octavian-Augustus. Herod thoroughly Romanized the city, laying out a grand architectural plan, which some have suggested was intended to imitate directly Augustus's and Agrippa's revitalization of the Forum at Rome.[42] His most impressive addition to the city, by the way, is the splendid temple of Rome and Augustus.

Thus, in some basic way, when Aeneas is walking through the site of Evander's Rome and the Roman/Westerner follows him to see the magnificence that rose out of such humble beginnings, the Roman/Easterner could be taking a similar (imaginary) walk through Caesarea, seeing Herod's Roman city rise out of a reasonably insignificant Hellenistic foundation.[43] Moreover, because Herod specifically dedicated his architectural

---

41. For Augustus's construction of the temple of Jupiter Tonans ("Thundering"), see Gransden, *Virgil Aeneid Book VIII*, ad loc.

42. Kathryn Gleason, "Ruler and Spectacle: The Promontory Palace," in *Caesarea Maritima: A Retrospective After Two Millennia* (ed. Avner Raban and Kenneth G. Holum; DMOA 21; Leiden: Brill, 1996), 208, and passim, has suggested this.

43. At its height, Caesarea had a population of perhaps 50,000, some have argued; this would have put it among the twenty most populous cities of the Mediterranean. Its surface area also places it among the largest cities.

embellishments to his patron Octavian/Augustus, the Roman/Easterner can also imagine Augustus as accompanying them on the tour.

CONCLUSION

When we put these two passages alongside each other, I think we can see some striking similarities, points of similarity, which the Homeric models simply do not share. The most significant, in my view, include: the basic plot structure of the episode; the representative of a local culture seeking alliance with the representative of an invading culture; the emphasis on acceptance, even elevation, of a foreigner; the food animal dreams; the signs from heaven; the merger of East and West; the anticipation of conflict to come. Moreover, when I consider that (1) all these points of similarity appear in a work written by a major school author, (2) whose works would become magical objects to later Christians, (3) and at a place in that work where he just happens to prophesy the establishment of a temple to an unknown god on the top of Rome's most sacred hill, I am convinced that author of this episode of Acts had this book of the *Aeneid* in mind.

In general, I would like to argue that in analyzing a culture imbued with the values of mimesis, we might regard not only the most imitated, but the most *imitative* works as high-prestige models for the writer or artist. In this particular example, this would mean moving Vergil, as an inspired imitator, higher up on the mimetic chain. This would also be an argument for revaluing the contributions of imperial literature to the works of the earliest Christian communities.

One further point: in the modern literary-critical toolbox, the biography of the author has lost ground. Our emphasis on seeing the text as the one-and-only subject of analysis serves us well in most cases. But here, where the initial question may have been which narratives of which narrators are worthy of imitation, the prestige of the author may have been almost as crucial as the prestige of the work.

Note that this is precisely the kind of thinking that is operating in the early Christian communities: narratives produced by apostles are better than narratives produced by followers of apostles are better than narratives produced by followers of followers of apostles. Why should similar rationales not apply to the works of the great pagan authors as well? Has the narrative of Plato's life not become as important in the early empire as the narrative of Socrates'?[44]

---

44. One might mention here that, although in the modern era we tend not to regard Plato's letters with the same awe as Plato's dialogues (which we hope are Socrates' dialogues),

Thus, I would propose that in the future we put the narrative of the author's life alongside the work itself as a possible model for imitation. I make this argument apart from the question of the historicity of the narratives of authors' lives circulating in antiquity—currency of the life should take precedence over even credibility. In all this, I would remind the reader that Acts is a series of *Lives* of writers as well as of heroic missionaries.

---

in the world of early Christianity, Plato and his life in letters were clearly models for Paul. Note also that although the jury is still out on the authenticity of the letters attributed to Plato, some of them may have been written in this period.

DIE ENTFÜHRUNG IN DAS SERAIL:
ASPASIA: A FEMALE AESOP?*

Richard I. Pervo

INTRODUCTION

The subject of this exploration is not the famed Aspasia of Miletus, colleague and consort of Pericles and the Socratic circle,[1] but a somewhat younger woman from Phocaea celebrated in a passage of Aelian's *Varia Historia, Historical Miscellany,* as the editor of the recent Loeb edition renders it.[2] The miscellany, a type represented by Aulus Gellius (*Noctes Atticae*), Clement of Alexandria (*Stromata*), and (to an extent) Athenaeus (*Deipnosophistae*), sought to provide readers with an instant education, of sorts, in the hallowed format of profit with delight.[3] Aelian lived from about 170–235 C.E., apparently spending most of his life in Rome. A native Latin-speaker from Praeneste, he became a card-carrying member of the Second Sophistic, writing in atticizing Greek while firmly identifying with the empire.[4]

* I am grateful to Niklas Holzberg for his suggestions and to the Trial Balloon Society of the Twin Cities for their comments upon a draft of this essay, which was subsequently presented at Society of Biblical Literature Ancient Fiction and Early and Jewish and Christian Literature Group in Boston on November 21, 1999. This is a companion piece to "A Nihilist Fabula: Introducing the Life of Aesop," in *Ancient Fiction and Early Christian Narrative* (ed. Ronald F. Hock, J. Bradley Chance, and Judith Perkins; SBLSymS 6; Atlanta: Scholars Press, 1998), 77–120. The title plays on that of Mozart's opera "The Abduction from the Seraglio."

1. A recent study of *that* Aspasia is Madeleine Mary Henry, *Prisoner of History: Aspasia of Miletus and Her Biographical Tradition* (New York: Oxford University Press, 1995).

2. Nigel G. Wilson, *Aelian: Historical Miscellany* (LCL 486; Cambridge: Harvard University Press, 1997). See the review by Mervin R. Dilts in *AJP* 121 (2000): 328–31.

3. Gell. *Pref.* 1. *iucundiora alia reperiri queunt, ad hoc ut liberis quoque meis partae istiusmodi remissiones essent, quando animus eorum interstitione aliqua negotiorum data laxari indulgerique potuisset.* Cf. also Wilson, *Aelian,* 2: "The reader thus acquired some pleasant and instructive material."

4. In his brief life of the author (no. 31, 624–25) Philostratus cannot say enough in praise of Aelian's style.

The story of Aspasia is the longest piece in the extant collection.[5] Aelian offers two admiring portraits of women whom he evidently regards as unusual representatives of their sex: Atalanta (13:1) as your outdoorsy, athletic type and Aspasia (12.1) as one who, although by appearance and (involuntary) vocation expected to rely upon "feminine wiles," declined to do so. Women who rose to high position in oriental courts are usually viewed as having achieved their power through sexual allure, marital bonds, or close kinship. Such portraits are not always flattering; indeed, the influence of these women is most often viewed (by, needless to say, male authors) as malign and detrimental to good government.[6] Aelian presents Aspasia both as the perfect representative of what he was pleased to regard as "feminine virtue" and as a wise counselor. The latter was not his invention, for the tradition in general represents her as a sage, as bright as she was beautiful.[7] This, then, is a rather atypical story. My leading interest, however, is less what Aelian said than *how* he presented her story.

SOURCES

Xenophon (*Anabasis* 1.10.2), Plutarch (*Artaxerxes* 26.3–27.3; *Pericles* 24.7), and Athenaeus (*Deipnosophistae* 13.37, 576d) also discuss our heroine.[8] These varied authorities allow one to conclude that she was an historical character from Phocaea who was introduced into the harem of the younger Cyrus and remained as a valued and influential concubine of two or more royal personages. Other than the summary in Plutarch's *Artaxerxes*, none of these accounts is much more than a sentence in length.

---

5. 12.1 is more than twice the length of the story of Atalanta (13.1), which is similar to that of Aspasia in subject and type. The abridgment that has affected the manuscript tradition (cf. Wilson, *Aelian*, 13–14, and his references) appears to play no role in this passage.

6. Herodotus launches the Greek historical tradition with a number of stories about royal women, for example 1.8–13; 3.68–71; 3.119; and 3.133–4. After Alexander historiographical attention shifted to Greek queens, who were succeeded in the fullness of time by Roman imperial women, a number of who had the misfortune of literary attention from Tacitus. The study of Grace H. Macurdy, *Hellenistic Queens. A Study of Woman Power in Macedonia, Seleucid Syria, and Ptolemaic Egypt* (Baltimore: Johns Hopkins University Press, 1932; repr., Chicago: Ares, 1985), demonstrates not only the endurance of male bias but also the difficulty of attempting to rehabilitate such figures by traditional methods. Anthony A. Barrett has a recent and sober discussion of the problems: *Agrippina: Sex, Power, and Politics in the Early Empire* (New Haven: Yale University Press, 1996), xii–xv.

7. Xenophon, *Anab.* 1.10.2, τὴν Φωκαΐδα τὴν Κύρου παλλακίδα τὴν **σοφὴν καὶ καλὴν** λεγομένην, Athenaeus, *Deipn.* 13.37, 576d, differs only in degree: ἑταίραν οὖσαν τὴν Φωκαΐδα τὴν **σωφωτάτην** <καὶ> **καλλίστην** γενομένην.

8. The appendix cites or summarizes the sources.

Comparison of Plutarch with Aelian indicates that the two evidently shared the same source.[9] Plutarch, however, had a different interest. He states that Artaxerxes, wishing to avoid a conflict between his sons Ochus and Darius, named the latter to succeed him. Persian custom required that the crown prince receive a favor. Darius asked for Aspasia. At this point (26.3) Plutarch narrates her previous history in a brief flashback (26.3–5). Artaxerxes reluctantly agreed with the request,[10] but insisted that Aspasia was free and had to consent to this transfer. To his disappointment, she did so consent. Artaxerxes had his revenge, for he presently made her a priest of Artemis/Anaitis of Ecbatana, a position requiring chastity. Darius was not amused, and the plot quickly thickened.

Aelian, for his part, does not speak of Aspasia's connection to Darius, for he ends abruptly with a description of how she consoled Artaxerxes in his grief for the death of a friend. The Aspasia of Plutarch is a political pawn. He summarizes her story to indicate her value and attraction. For Aelian Aspasia was a pawn translated into a queen.

FORM, STRUCTURE, AND STYLE

"Aspasia" exhibits a clear and relatively simple style, with balanced periods that rarely stray from the indicative mood. The simplicity is not the result of authorial limitations; it is eminently suitable to the subject. Just as Aspasia refused to enhance her allure by cosmetic artifice and flirtatious contrivance, so Aelian affects an apparently transparent style that forsakes all the rhetorical tricks. *Ars est celare artem.* Rhetorically and formally considered, "Aspasia" is an encomiastic biographical essay that begins with the subject's birth and nurture before expounding her virtues through selected examples.[11] A well-known Lucan sentence aptly summarizes this component of the pattern: "I am a Jew, *born* in Tarsus in Cilicia, but *brought up* in this city at the feet of Gamaliel, *educated* strictly according to our ancestral law" (Acts 22:3).[12]

---

9. On these questions see Judeich, "Aspasia 2," *RE* 1:1721–22. It is less probable that Aelian worked up his account from Plutarch.

10. The theme is similar to the requests of Esther and the daughter of Herodias, Mark 6:14–29.

11. Hermogenes 7 includes a handbook outline of the encomium. See Burton L. Mack and Edward N. O'Neil in *The Chreia in Ancient Rhetoric* (ed. R. F. Hock and E. N. O'Neil; vol. 1 of *The Progymnasmata*; SBLTT 27; Atlanta: Scholars Press, 1986), 153–81, for part of the text, as well as useful notes and introduction.

12. There are a number of examples of the pattern in Willem C. van Unnik, *Tarsus or Jerusalem: The City of Paul's Youth* (trans. George Ogg; London: Epworth, 1962), 16–45, 59–72.

Table 1: The Structure of "Aspasia"

I. The Aspasiapaideia
   A. Situation:
      1. Motherless child reared in poverty but well trained. (V)
      2. Dream foreshadows good fortune.
   B. Detailed Narration: her disfigurement, which her father could not afford to have treated medically. Healing by *Aphrodite*.
   C. Summary: Description of appearance and qualities. (V)
Conclusion: the advantages of relative poverty: Aspasia is unspoiled.

II. Aspasia and Cyrus
   A. Situation: taken to Sardis to be a concubine of Cyrus.
      1. Summary: Became favorite concubine because of her qualities and intelligence (V)
      2. Illustration: Their initial encounter reveals her character. (V)
Conclusion: Cyrus loved her greatly; their relationship approached that of equals.
   B. Their Life and Love
      1. Summary: Their love is celebrated world-wide.
      2. Brief Narration: Gratitude. She builds shrine to *Aphrodite* and enriches her *father*. (V)
      3. Her own lifestyle, however, remains modest. (V)
   C. Illustration: the necklace. (V)
Conclusion: Admired even more for character than for beauty. (V)

III. Aspasia and Artaxerxes
   A. Situation: Death of Cyrus; Aspasia becomes property of Artaxerxes by design.
   B. Their Relationship.
      1. Brief Narration: Their initial encounter.
      2. Summary: She becomes "senior wife"[13] and in due course comes to love him, despite her loyalty to Cyrus and his memory. (V)
   C. Detailed illustration: the consolation of Artaxerxes. (V)

This plan shows that the work falls readily into three parts that treat her background, her life with Cyrus, and her life with Artaxerxes, respectively. Each section follows the same general pattern: a description of the general situation, summary, and detailed narration. The second section, which treats her relationship with Cyrus, is the longest and includes two

---

13. Πρώτην γε τῶν γυναικῶν. The translation is that of Wilson, *Aelian*, 355.

narrative episodes. Quantitatively, the work exhibits an A B A pattern. Section II ends with an *inclusio* to Section I, as she shows gratitude to Aphrodite and to her father. This neatly-tied bow comes undone when the story takes an unhappy turn. Be that as it may, Aspasia manages very well for herself. A story that seems to have come to a happy end comes instead to a sad end, which, time will show, is not the actual end. Rather than conclude, as in previous sections, with a generalizing statement, Aelian lets the final episode speak for itself.[14] The conclusion is a more sophisticated example of *inclusio:* the one healed in the beginning has become herself a healer. Another marker of authorial skill comes to light in the discovery that there are few detailed episodes. Only through careful analysis is the casual reader's impression of a narrative that flows rapidly and brims with incident overthrown. Aelian had only a few cards, most of them of mediocre value, but he played them so well that readers are likely to imagine that he held a full and strong hand.

The siglum (V) indicates the explicit or implicit reference to a virtue. Aspasia was not lacking in these qualities. She was, of course, modest and chaste. She also possessed generosity, courage, wisdom, piety, respect for her betters, fairness, shrewdness, loyalty, and consideration. When these attributes come in an exceptionally attractive package the result is something rather well above your run-of-the-mill denizen of a harem. None need be surprised that the subject of this exercise attracted the attention of two members of the ruling dynasty of Achaemenid Persia.

A Rose by Any Other Name Would Be a … Rose

The accounts do not agree about our heroine's given name. "Aspasia" is an adjective meaning "welcome," not the usual fate of daughters in the Greek world, many of whom were abandoned as infants. According to Aelian, our heroine was always Aspasia, although she acquired the nickname Milto in her home town because of her rosy complexion, but both Plutarch (*Per.* 24.7), and Athenaeus (13.576d, who identifies Xenophanes as his source) state that her given name was Milto and that she had been renamed by Cyrus (either after the famous *hetaira* or because she was a most welcome addition to his entourage). For Xenophon (*Anab.* 1.10.2) she is simply "the Phocean woman," a usage also found in Aelian. Of these various claims, that of Aelian is probably most suspect, for it

---

14. On the final adverb see "Conclusion," below.

would not suit his purpose to imply that every master could endow her
with a new name at his pleasure.[15]

Rosy Cheeks—and Features That Only a Mother Could Love

Beauty is no more than skin deep, to be sure. Nonetheless, it could be
said of our heroine that

> She had an abundance of charms, more than any girl of her day. She had
> blond hair with a gentle wave in it, very large eyes, a slightly aquiline
> nose, and rather small ears. Her skin was tender, and her complexion
> like roses.[16] ... [H]er lips gleamed red, and her teeth were whiter than
> snow.[17]

Those who wish to discover all that lay south of Aspasia's teeth will
be disappointed, for the narrator's eye immediately shifts to her ankles,
which were of Homeric (*Il.* 14.319) loveliness.[18] This is a rather delicate
synecdoche. Her voice, as will be suitable to one with persuasive powers,
was comparable to that of a Siren. The authors of full-length romantic
novels rarely shared detailed descriptions of their heroines, preferring to
assert that the young woman in question was as pretty as she could be,
easily mistaken for Aphrodite or Artemis.[19] Here are the readers' first
glimpses of Anthia and Leucippe:

---

15. Such a practice implies slave status. Note, however, that Jesus is said to have done
the same: Mark 3:16–17.

16. One healed by the roses of Aphrodite might well have such a complexion.

17. Translation by Wilson, *Aelian*, 343.

18. Callirhoe receives the same epithet: 4.8.1.

19. It is thus unremarkable that Judith's appearance can be described in one half of a
verse: καὶ ἦν καλὴ τῷ εἴδει καὶ ὡραία τῇ ὄψει σφόδρα. ("She was beautiful in appearance, and
was very lovely to behold"; 8:7—of eight verses devoted to her history and character). Cf.
Sus 2: καλὴ σφόδρα ("very beautiful"); Esth 2:7: καὶ ἦν τὸ κοράσιον καλὸν τῷ εἴδει ("The girl
was beautiful in appearance"). Aseneth is an unmarried woman of eighteen years
(approaching old maidhood) καὶ ἦν θυγάτηρ τῷ Πεντεφρῇ ὡς ὀκτωκαίδεκα παρθένος μεγάλη
καὶ ὡραία καὶ εὐπρεπὴς τῷ κάλλει σφόδρα ὑπὲρ πᾶσαν παρθένον ἐπὶ τὴν γῆν ("Pentephres had
a daughter of about eighteen. She was tall, lovely, and a good deal more beautiful in appearance than all the maidens in the country") Jos. Asen. 1.4. The subsequent verse reports that
she looked like the Hebrew beauties Sarah, Rebecca, and Rachel). The resources for fuller
descriptions were available. There is a lush ecphrasis of a painting of Europa in Leucippe
1.1, preceding his description of the heroine. Consider also: "and beautiful is her face! How
... fine are the hairs of her head! How lovely are her eyes! How desirable her nose and all the
radiance of her countenance.... How fair are her breasts and how beautiful all her whiteness!
How pleasing are her arms and how perfect her hands, and how [desirable] all the appearance of her hands! How fair are her palms and how long and slender are her fingers! How
comely are her feet, how perfect her thighs!" This is a description of Sarah (from an Egyptian

Anthia led the line of girls; she was the daughter of Megamedes and Euippe, both of Ephesus ... [her] beauty was an object of wonder, far surpassing the other girls'. She was fourteen; her beauty was burgeoning, still more enhanced by the adornment of her dress. Her hair was golden—a little of it plaited, but most hanging loose and blowing in the wind. Her eyes were quick; she had the bright glance of a young girl, and yet the austere look of a virgin. [20]

... [T]here appeared on her left a young maiden. Her face flashed on my eyes like lightning. Such beauty I had seen once before, and that was in a painting of Selene on a bull: delightfully animated eyes; light blond hair—blond and curly; black eyebrows—jet black; white cheeks—a white that glowed to red in the center like the crimson laid on ivory by Lydian craftswomen. [Cf. Il. 4.141–142.] Her mouth was a rose caught at the moment when it begins to part its petal lips.[21]

Curly-haired blondes had more fun—if that is a suitable term for the adventures of romantic heroines (and it is not). One should, however, probably devote some space to the guys. With Aspasia's looks one may firmly contrast the socratic Aesop:

He was truly horrible to behold: worthless, pot-bellied, slant-headed, snub-nosed, hunchbacked, leather-skinned, club-footed, knock-kneed, short-armed, sleepy-eyed, bushy-lipped—in short an absolute miscreant.[22]

This will remind many of a famous description of Paul

[Onesiphorus] ... saw Paul coming, a man small in size, bald-headed, bandy-legged, of noble mien, with eyebrows meeting, rather hook-nosed, full of grace. Sometimes he seemed like a man, and sometimes he had the face of an angel.[23]

---

perspective, evidently); The Genesis Apocryphon 20.1–6 (G. Vermes, trans., *The Complete Dead Sea Scrolls in English* [New York: Penguin, 1997], 454).

20. *An Ephesian Tale* 1.2 (trans. Graham Anderson, in *Collected Ancient Greek Novels* [ed. Bryan P. Reardon; Berkeley and Los Angeles: University of California Press, 1989], 129).

21. *Leucippe* 1.4 (trans. J. J. Winkler, in Reardon, *Collected Ancient Greek Novels*, 179).

22. *Life of Aesop* 1 (trans. L. Wills, *The Quest for the Historical Gospel* [London: Routledge, 1997], 181).

23. *Acts of Paul* 3.3 (trans. James K. Elliott, *Apocryphal New Testament* [Oxford: Clarendon, 1993], 364). This portrait has generated substantial discussion. For a recent treatment and references to earlier studies see Bruce J. Malina and Jerome H. Neyrey, *Portraits of Paul: An Archaeology of Ancient Personality* (Louisville: Westminster John Knox, 1996), 100–152. (Translation of many of the descriptive terms is debatable. The originals should be examined.)

The polymorphous apostle evokes another person—his master. The evangelists, unlike Diogenes Laertius and his authorities,[24] display no interest in the appearance or idiosyncrasies of Jesus, who is introduced with little or no information about his looks and upbringing.[25] When information begins to leak out—at about the same time as the description of Paul—it transpires that Jesus was ugly, like Socrates, or, not to make too fine a point of it, handsome, in the well-established heroic pattern. From an early date Isa 53:2–3 is cited in support of the former.[26] Those who want their Christ beautiful are urged to read Apocryphal Acts, where he can be found as a *puer speciosus* (pretty boy) and in equally attractive more mature modes.[27] Heroes, in short, may be ugly, especially if they are somehow comparable to Socrates.[28] For heroines there is less choice. Enough, the dear reader may say, of introduction. It is time for the story. So be it.

---

24. Consult, for example, D. L. 7.1.1 (Zeno).

25. This may have been just as well, considering the challenges Luke 2:52 generated for patristic authorities. The "Infancy Gospels" filled some of these gaps. On these see Oscar Cullmann in *New Testament Apocrypha* (ed. R. McL. Wilson; trans. Wilhelm Schneemelcher; 3rd ed.; Louisville: Westminster John Knox, 1991), 414–66; cf. also Elliott, *Apocryphal New Testament*, 46–122.

26. "He had no form or majesty that we should look at him, nothing in his appearance that we should desire him … and as one from whom others hide their faces he was despised." The LXX uses εἶδος repeatedly οὐκ εἶχεν εἶδος οὐδὲ κάλλος. Ps 22:7 provided other textual grounds for this view. Walter Bauer (in a contribution not in the current edition of Schneemelcher) cites Justin, Irenaeus, Clement of Alexandria, Origen, Tertullian, Cyprian, Hippolytus, all without references, as well as *APt* 24 and *Orac Sib* 8:256–257 ("Jesus' Earthly Appearance and Character," in *New Testament Apocrypha* [ed. Edgar Hennecke; trans. R. McL. Wilson; 2 vols.; Philadelphia: Westminster, 1963], 1:434).

27. *Puer speciosus: Acts of John* 73; *Acts of Paul* 7; cf. also *Acts of Thomas* 149; Clement of Alexandria, *Strom.* 2.5.21. Origen (references in Bauer, previous note) utilizes diverse traditions to argue that the earthly Jesus was polymorphic, adjusting his appearance to the capacities of those who saw him. (This is also the argument of *Acts of John* 98; 101–2.) The handsome Christ is the heavenly being, whether at the transfiguration or at some other point of polymorphic manifestation. Irenaeus states that the Carpocratians were in possession of a portrait of Christ, the exemplar of which had been painted by Pontius Pilate (*Haer.* 1.25). The Bishop of Lyons was no iconodule.

28. A second-century description of male beauty is provided by Byrrhena, Lucius's host, in her description of the protagonist: "And damn me if his appearance generally isn't just right! He is tall, but not lofty; he's slim, but there is spunk there; his colour is moderately ruddy, his hair is blonde but not foppish; his green eyes have a watchful look, quick to focus, sharp as an eagle's. His face looks healthy from every angle, and his walk is pleasing and natural." (Apuleius, *Metam.* 2.2, in Apuleius, *The Golden Ass* [trans. Patrick G. Walsh; New York: Oxford University Press, 1995], 19.)

Sagely Blonde

I stated above that "Aspasia" is formally an encomiastic biographical essay. It is not an encomium, for it is not an oration, nor is it a biography, for it omits the death of its subject, as well as much of her life. This is, moreover, as comparison with the known sources suggests, a short piece of historical fiction.[29] In modern terms "Aspasia" is a novella.[30] This novella of slightly more than 1,700 words begins by identifying Aspasia as the daughter of Hermotimus who was reared by her father in poverty, as her mother had died in giving her birth.[31] These impediments notwithstanding, she acquired modesty and self-control (ἐτράφη ... σοφρόνως ... καὶ ἐγκρατῶς).[32] Aspasia was a dreamer, experiencing one recurrent dream of future good fortune, to wit, that she would live with a καλὸς κ' ἀγαθός (handsome and noble) man. More than one attractive girl from a family of limited means, as well as others, has had such hopes, but actual dreams are distinctive. Such foreshadowing is common in the beginning of ancient fiction, which often includes a somewhat enigmatic oracle.[33] Aspasia is a Cinderella in the making. Her prospects look good.

A complication emerges, specifically an ugly growth beneath her chin. Her concerned father applied to a physician, who, it transpires, would be only too happy to remove this growth, for the apparently modest fee of three staters.[34] That sum Hermotimus does not have; the

---

29. Judeich judges Aelian's account of Aspasia to be "stark romanhaft" ("Aspasia 2," 1:1721).

30. *Novella* is used in a somewhat technical sense to characterize short, entertaining narratives located in the real world—rather than that of fairy tales, for example. Many of these stories had an oral background. A classic study is Sophie Trenkner, *The Greek Novella in the Classical Period* (Cambridge: Cambridge University Press, 1958); see also James A. K. Thomson, *The Art of the Logos* (London: Allen & Unwin, 1935).

31. Plutarch, *Pericles* 24, also supplies the paternal name. Legal parentage is proof that Aspasia was not of servile origin. Slaves were not permitted to identify themselves by parental names. This was a harsh social impediment in the Greco-Roman world.

32. ἐγκρατῶς is Hercher's emendation for the MSS καρτερῶς, which could also be rendered "discreetly." Aelian rather implies that the opposite would be expected in penury. Plutarch has the same information, with less color: ἦν δὲ φωκαῖς τὸ γένος ἀπ' Ἰωνίας, ἐλευθέρων γονεών καὶ τεθραμμένη κοσμίως ("...She was properly raised").

33. For a list of some of the "introductory oracles" in ancient novels see Richard I. Pervo, *Profit with Delight* (Philadelphia: Fortress, 1987), 164 n. 80. It is not unusual that this dream is ambiguous and slightly misleading. She would "be with" (συνέσται) a splendid gentleman. The dreamer may be forgiven for interpreting this as marriage. Aspasia will, in fact, live with more than one man.

34. Wilson, *Aelian*, 341 n., finds this a bit puzzling and wonders if gold were demanded. Aelian may simply be stressing the family's poverty.

physician lacked ample supplies of the drug and was unwilling to treat her *pro bono*.[35] Our understandably distraught heroine did something uncharacteristic: she consulted a mirror. This investigation did nothing to improve her disposition. Aspasia fell into bed without eating. Her prospects had been ruined, since her looks were all that she might offer in the way of a dowry. The wolf is not at the door, but it is contemplating a move into the neighborhood.

Sleep providentially (εὔκαιρος ὕπνος) arrived, and with it a dove.[36] This bird quickly transformed itself into a woman[37] who announced: "be of good cheer" (θάρρει). The first step toward that happiness will be to kiss doctors and their drugs goodbye. Once the medical profession has been shown to the door, Aspasia is to gather up the withered roses offered at shrines of Aphrodite, grind them (the petals?) into a powder, and apply this substance to the growth.[38] Aphrodite has taken a leaf—or a petal—from the book of Asclepius, a prescription given in a dream. Needless to say, the therapy worked like a dream.

The opening of this story may be compared to the first part of the *Aesop-Romance,* in which an individual suffering from a grievous impediment likewise receives healing by a goddess in a dream epiphany.[39] Aspasia had been restored to her place as the most beautiful girl in town.[40] This, needless, to say, is a fate shared by any number of romantic

---

35. Cf. the view of physicians in Mark 5:26–27. Such suspicions were widespread in the ancient world: Martial, 2.16; 6.31.53; 1.22; 25; 30; 40; 45; 46; 61; 78; 81; 85 (the last lumping them with other professionals); 10.77; Petronius, *Satyricon* 42 and 56; Cassius Dio 69.22; 71.33; Epictetus, *Diatr.* 3.23.27; Juvenal, *Satirae* 3.77; Lucian, *Philops.* 21; 26; *Ind.* 29. There is a lengthy description of medical ineptitude in Pliny the Elder, *Nat.* 29.8.16–18. Finally, see Tob 2:10: "I did not know that there were sparrows on the wall; their fresh droppings fell into my eyes and produced white films. I went to physicians to be healed, but the more they treated me with ointments the more my vision was obscured by the white films, until I became completely blind. For four years I remained unable to see. All my kindred were sorry for me, and Ahikar took care of me for two years before he went to Elymais."

36. A dove-like entity also appears in the opening of Mark (1:10) and parallels. New Testament scholars have all but universally determined to avoid reference to the erotic aspects of this symbol, predominant (and biblical) as these are.

37. Magicians could transform themselves into birds and back again, for example, Pamphile, Apuleius, *Metam.* 2.21.

38. Healing through the use of substances is also attested in the Jesus tradition: Mark 7:31–37; John 9:1–7; in some ways a closer parallel is Acts 19:12. The *Historia Augusta Caracalla* 5.7 states that people were condemned for wearing about their necks garlands removed from imperial busts or statues as an apotropaic against fever.

39. *Life of Aesop* 1–7, which is, of course, more detailed. The major differences are that Aesop is a speechless slave from birth and is healed in response to his kindness to a priest of Isis.

40. At this suitable point Aelian introduces his description, cited above.

heroines, and it is not necessarily something to envy. The prettiest girl is likely to be prom queen, of course but her tiara is likely to come equipped with numerous unplanned rendezvous with kidnappers, rapists, bandits, pirates, gangsters and tyrants all the way from home to Egypt or Babylonia, not to mention many points in between. Although Aelian is quite pleased to describe Aspasia's looks, he takes care to insist that Aspasia's beauty lacked the least hint of artifice. She did not, please note, possess a morsel of feminine πολυπραγμοσύνη or περιεργία.[41] One socially redeeming feature of poverty was its value for alleviating these vices. Aspasia, in short, was beautiful but not in the least little bit stuck up about it.

It came to pass that this lovely young woman "visited" (ἀφίκετο) Cyrus the son of Darius. Aspasia had not decided one fine day that she might pay a social call on the princely satrap. Neither she nor her father had the slightest desire to court royalty, as it were. There was no choice in the matter. The invitation came under a cloud of threatened violence (πρὸς βίαν). Aelian laments that such is often the case "when cities are captured or tyrants or satraps insist." Aspasia's story has a good deal in common with Esther's, and illuminates the narrative viewpoint of the biblical account.

> Then the king's servants who attended him said, "Let beautiful young virgins be sought out for the king. And let the king appoint commissioners in all the provinces of his kingdom to gather all the beautiful young virgins to the harem in the citadel of Susa under custody of Hegai, the king's eunuch, who is in charge of the women; let their cosmetic treatments be given them...." The girl was fair and beautiful, and when her father and her mother died, Mordecai adopted her as his own daughter. So when the king's order and his edict were proclaimed, and when many young women were gathered in the citadel of Susa in custody of Hegai, Esther also was taken into the king's palace. (Esth 2:2–3, 7–8, NRSV)

The narrator of Hebrew Esther does not take a moral stance about this "beauty contest." The king's subjects were effectively his slaves, and it is useless to kick against the pricks. Callirhoe, the eponymous heroine of Chariton's novel, experienced a quite similar fate, as did others; there is no dearth of material relating the adventures of beauties in the courts of oriental kings.[42] In due course Aspasia would rise to the rank of chief

---

41. Wilson, *Aelian*, 343, renders: "She was quite free of all feminine fuss and refinement." The context may justify this, but the terms characterize a *"yenta,"* a gossipy, prying, meddlesome woman.

42. Another romantic heroine so entangled is Sinonis, in Iamblichus's *A Babylonian Story*, known only in a summary by Photius. Anthia uses her ready wits to avoid purchase

concubine because of her qualities (not the least of which was that beauty unsullied by paint). She became Cyrus's counselor (σύμβολος) on weighty matters.[43] Aspasia can be compared with, among others, Mordecai, Daniel, and Aesop. One difference is that, while freely asserting Aspasia's gifts and contributions, Aelian gives no examples of particular counsel or advice. This deficit will require further attention.

Having proclaimed her ultimate triumph, Aelian returns to the scene of their first meeting. As in the book of Esther, matters began with a symposium that became a drinking bout.[44] Herodotus relates what might be expected at the Persian equivalent of such an event.[45] While being entertained at a banquet, Persian ambassadors to Macedonia took note, during the post-prandial drinking, of the absence of women. Although the presence of respectable women at symposia was contrary to local custom, the women were duly summoned. The Persians arranged for these well-bred women to be adjacent to them and proceeded to fondle their breasts and attempted to kiss them. Through a variation of the "slip into something more comfortable" theme cross-dressed boys were able to replace the women and slaughter the barbarous molesters.[46]

In such a context four Greek women were introduced to Cyrus. The narrator then flashes back to describe the beauty treatments and tuition in lovemaking that preceded these formalities.[47] Similar matters occupied Esther's narrator (2:9–15), but Aelian does not put a "positive spin" upon them. Aspasia had no fun getting ready for the ball. She did not simply refuse to get all tarted up; she could not even be induced to

---

by an Indian prince, thereby eluding the fate of the apostle Thomas (*An Ephesian Tale* 4.11). The heroes of *An Ethiopian Story* must deal with the especially wicked sister of the Great King, Arsace, who is married to the satrap.

43. Esther also served in this capacity with regard to one important issue: a proposed massacre of the Jews.

44. Other symposia in Greek fiction include *Leucippe* 1.5; cf. 1.27 *Parthenope* (in Susan A. Stephens and John J. Winkler, *Ancient Greek Novels: The Fragments* [Princeton: Princeton University Press, 1995], 84); and, in particular, *Apollonios*, which is set in the Persian court and includes a beautiful (and possibly amorous) queen, Stephens and Winkler, 391–99, 394. (Stephens and Winkler are not certain that the *Apollonios* fragment or fragments derive from a novel.) On that work see also Rolf Kussl, *Papyrusfragmente griechischer Romane: Ausgewählte Untersuchungen* (Tübingen: Narr, 1991), 141–59.

45. Q. Curtius *History of Alexander* 5.11.37–39, states that single and married women of high social standing at Babylon participated in symposia, at which their behavior was much the same as that of prostitutes in the Greek world. Specifically, if they dressed for dinner, they regularly undressed after dinner.

46. Herodotus, *Hist.* 5.18–20. The liberation of Thebes from Spartan dominion in 379 involved a similar scheme: Plutarch, *Gen. Socr.* 29–31, 596A–597A. See also his *Life of Pelopidas* 11.

47. Cf. Chariton, *Callirhoe* 5.3.4.

bathe! This was not because she was the sort who had to be spanked into taking her Saturday night bath. In her view resorting to anything with the slightest resemblance to seductive behavior would be tantamount to confession of slavery,[48] a sentiment expressed in the form of a prayer for her own death (and that of her father). Moving as her declaration may be, it is, of course, a cliché in romantic and martyr literature. Moving as her declaration doubtless was, it moved her audience not at all. Aspasia was beaten into submission. In the end and by one means or another all of the properly pampered and elegantly attired *jeunes filles* were presented to their hosts.

Whereas the other young women made advances to Cyrus, our heroine blushed, wept, and, in general, showed every sign of acute embarrassment. When kindly invited to sit beside the prince, all the women but Aspasia happily obeyed. She required the services of the satrap to be put into her place. Most have by now conceded Aspasia's virtue to the verge of diminishing returns, but, for the yet unconvinced, there will be additional evidence. The good Cyrus began to ogle and fondle his loyal subjects—except for Aspasia, who objected to the touch of his finger, and set out to leave the room when his attention turned to her bosom. Now comes the shocker: in ironically most uniranian fashion, Cyrus did not order an immediate execution or beating, but *actually praised her* nobility of character (εὐγένεια).[49] She alone, he intoned, was free and uncorrupted.[50] The others were cheap hustlers. What kind of man would prefer a depraved and submissive slave girl to the likes of Aspasia? Not Cyrus. From that moment forward, he cherished her company. Out of initial admiration there gradually developed a mutual love.

This is not the stuff of Greek romance, where love arrives in the form of a *coup de foudre*.[51] It rather suggests what we should call an adult relationship. There is more: love grew to "such a point" that they were "near to being equals and did not fall short of the harmony and morality of a Greek marriage."[52] Cyrus has become a model of bourgeois, Greek, male

---

48. Aelian states that the other three women had brought their maids with them. They, too, were free, and determined to look their best. What Aspasia viewed as slavery they regarded as opportunity.

49. εὐγένεια is a common theme in Greek fiction. See Pervo, *Profit with Delight*, 168 n. 136. A most apposite example is found in *Callirhoe* 3.1.6. The heroine has lost everything except her εὐγένεια. It will be marriage or nothing.

50. Plutarch agrees *verbatim* with this pronouncement.

51. Cf. the quotation from *Leucippe* above. This is not to say that Aelian was ignorant of the theme. Artaxerxes will fall in classic fashion: (παράχρημα ὁ Ἀρταξέρξης ἐφλέγετο καὶ κατεκτήκετο....).

52. Trans. Wilson, *Aelian*, 349.

domestic virtue. Such characterization is a large step toward the spirit of romance, reinforced in this case through a certain excess of protest by both the lady and the gentleman. Cyrus's dismissal of the actions of her colleagues is scarcely reasonable. He upbraids them for meeting the expectations of their position. Attractive, well-dressed, and elaborately made-up young women did not drop into male parties long after all the boys had become inebriated in order to discuss philosophy or to propound the blessings of chastity! The object of the incident is to show how Aspasia reformed, indeed, sobered, Cyrus and then won him by the strength of her character, more or less in spite of her looks.[53] If this is too good to be true, it must be true romance.

The fame of their storied love inundated Ionia, drenched Greece, and ultimately trickled into the ear of the Great King.[54] Aspasia had, in short, reduced Cyrus to abject monogamy. During this happy time she, like Aesop, was not unmindful of her benefactor.[55] Aspasia had a gold statue of Aphrodite erected, together with a dove, encrusted it with jewels, and made this shrine the object of daily oblation. Nor would such a paragon be liable to neglect her poor father, whom she enriched through gifts. Now none of this opulence should suggest that Aspasia had cast aside her modest life style like an old garment. "She continued to live modestly" (σωφροσύνη τε διέζη). In demonstration of this enduring virtue Aelian abandons his summary to narrate another specific incident.

Cyrus had acquired an extraordinary necklace. After showing it off to the guys, the royal personage bore this trinket to his true love, who happened to be napping just then. Waiting patiently until she awoke—as would, naturally, any male intent upon surprising his wife with a gift of jewelry—he displayed it to her with the comment that the necklace was worthy of the mother or the daughter of a king. To this assessment she assented and promptly learned that it was for her. Aspasia demurred. Cyrus really ought to give this to his *mother*; Aspasia's neck was beautiful without any decoration. (The helpful narrator intervenes to explain that this reaction was unusual, as women tend to be rather fond of jewelry.) Mama Parysatis found this action agreeable, commending Aspasia's determination not to usurp her. The grateful mother deluged Aspasia

---

53. One might compare this incident to the conversion of the drunken Polemo to the philosophic life (Diogenes Laertius, 4.16).

54. Such fame usually attends the heroine's beauty: cf. *Callirhoe* 1.1; Apuleius, *Metam.* 4.28–29 (Psyche). Reports about Callirhoe also reached the ear of the great king: 4.1.8 ἦν δὴ καὶ κλέος μέγα τῆς γυναικὸς ἐπὶ τῆς Ἀσίας πάσης καὶ ἀνέβαινεν ἤδη μέχρι τοῦ μεγάλου βασιλέως ὄνομα Καλλιρόης.

55. Aesop (123) received the honor of a statue of him with the Muses. Neglect of Apollo led to his undoing. See the essay "A Nihilist Fabula," referred to above.

with gifts, including a good deal of money.[56] Aspasia was duly grateful but, as one might expect, returned all this bounty, explaining that she had no need of such things. Her love for Cyrus was all the ornament she required.[57] These sentiments, Aelian notes, impressed the ruler to no small degree. This woman was beautiful on the outside, but even more beautiful in character.[58] All in all, it seems safe to say that Aspasia is very much a person whom other women would like to kill.

Cyrus's death on the field of Cynaxa (401 B.C.E.)[59] brought this beatitude to a rude halt. The victor, Artaxerxes (II Mnemon),[60] scooped up Aspasia with the rest of the booty and added her to his harem.[61] So one might callously describe her fate. Aelian does not align himself with the callous here. Artaxerxes had, it transpires, carefully planned for the acquisition of Aspasia as one element of his hostile takeover of the kingdom. His inspiration is the essence of romance, in which all the king's horses and all the king's men, as well as the arts of diplomacy and the machinations of treachery are enrolled for the sole purpose of securing a particular woman.[62] The nature of his intentions became apparent when he imprisoned the insensitive minions who had dragged her before him in chains. Evidently unaware of her views about such trifles, Artaxerxes replaced the chains with jewelry. After a good deal of what must by now be quite expected protestation that she was in mourning for Cyrus and simply could not don her splendid apparel, for which she did not, of course, care and of which she had, as we have learned, no need, Aspasia was finally compelled to put on the expensive dress Artaxerxes had in all innocence provided for the occasion. We have taken the point: clotheshorse Aspasia was not. The effect of this unwanted outfit was electric. Within moments another king had fallen for Aspasia. In due course she gained the unofficial status of number-one wife. So great was

---

56. When not admiring her jewelry or distributing her wealth, Parysatis served Ctesias as an eyewitness source to Persian history, according to Photius, *Bibl.* 72, 35b41–43, 42b11–13; and Diodorus Siculus, 2.32.4.

57. ἐμοὶ δὲ σὺ ἀρκεῖς φιλούμενος καὶ κόσμος μοι εἶναι.

58. This biblical (1 Pet 3:3–4) sentiment is also a Greek commonplace. See, for example, Xenophon, *Oec.* 7.42. Note also *Callirhoe* 2.5.9; 4.1.8.

59. There is an account of the battle in Xenophon, *Anab.* 1.8, shortly before his mention of Aspasia.

60. This very same king also fell in love, we are told, with Callirhoe.

61. Cf. the fate of Callirhoe, 8.1–2. The Persian practice of going on campaign with a large entourage made such captures routine. Alexander's kind treatment of Darius's harem (Arrian, *Anab.* 2.12.3–8) received high praise. It is a sign of the times that this abstinence, which formerly served as proof that Alexander was a real gentleman, is now viewed as grounds for doubting his commitment to heterosexuality.

62. *Callirhoe* is an excellent example of this focus upon an individual heroine.

her loyalty to and her love for Cyrus, however, that it took much time
and patience for Artaxerxes to win Aspasia's unqualified affections.

There perished one day, in the full blush of youth, a certain eunuch
named Tiridates. He was evidently Artaxerxes's heart-throb. In any case,
the king was heart-broken. Public mourning broke out. His grief seemed
inconsolable, and none dared seek his attention. After the good Christian
interval of three days, Aspasia did just that, putting on mourning to meet
him, keeping her tear-filled face carefully lowered. He was astonished to
see her thus, evidently, although Aelian does not say so, because she had
appeared without a royal summons. Bible readers will immediately recall
the dramatic scene of Esther's risky petition (4:9–5:4). Aspasia eventually
succeeded in her attempts at consolation, a process powerfully assisted
by the attraction she exerted when clad in the late Tiridates's cloak, which
little number she happily agreed to wear whenever she and Artaxerxes
were together. So Aspasia achieved what no one else in Asia could do:
she healed the king of his pathological grief. At this point the narrator
pulls the plug. Those who have not read (and believed) their Plutarch are
free to fancy that they lived happily ever after.

Aspasia is a species of Hellenic Esther and a kind of female Aesop, a
woman who rose to a high place in the court of two or more Persian
kings through the judicious application of her wisdom and because of the
strength of her character. Like the leading characters of many Greek
novels, she can bend without breaking, adjust without betraying her ethical principles.[63] Aesop is more like a tragic figure in that he cannot bend,
although he is a slave who must trim his principles on many occasions.
Aspasia shares with both Aesop and the heroes of some Jewish novels
and *novelle* the ability to thrive in the court of an oriental monarch
through her integrity and her sagacity.[64]

This having been said, it will scarcely escape one's attention that
Aelian provides no examples of Aspasia's advice on matters of state,
such as the resolution of international conflicts or the government of
subjects of diverse origins. Our author appears to claim that she did

---

63. Gareth Schmeling astutely contrasts the leading characters of (New Comedy and)
romance to those of the famous tragedies in terms of elasticity; tragic figures often shatter on
the rock of their inflexible commitments or principles (*Xenophon of Ephesus* [TWAS 613;
Boston: Twayne, 1980], 122, developing an observation of T. R. L. Webster). Given the limits
imposed by royal concubinage, Aspasia does a rather good job of maintaining her
"chastity," certainly in the sense of fidelity to her male master, whoever that may be at the
time.

64. On the subject note Lawrence M. Wills, *The Jew in the Court of the Foreign King:
Ancient Jewish Court Legends* (Minneapolis: Fortress, 1990), as well as his *The Jewish Novel in
the Ancient World* (Ithaca, N.Y.: Cornell University Press, 1995), esp. chs. 2 and 4.

supply such advice, but his examples relate to the governance of *self:* her refusal to stoop to seduction, her unwillingness to fly into the arms of a new master humming *la donna è mobile,* her assistance to Artaxerxes in the management of debilitating grief, her survival in conflict-ridden royal families, most notably through her adroit handling of Cyrus's mother, Parysatis, and her implicit avoidance of sexual intrigue and competition, quite clearly in her refusal to rejoice outwardly at the demise of the rival Tiridates.[65]

The contrast between Aelian's contention and his examples may be attributed to one or more of several factors, the most likely being the absence of examples to present. No doubt. The *novella* is an imperfectly successful attempt to bring an old story up to date. Aelian's values and sentiments in this text are redolent of romance and its celebration of conjugal love and personal loyalty. Those who speculate that well-educated Greek men might read romantic novels have in Aelian a promising candidate. This narrative also mirrors increased respect for the educability of women and their potential to be ethical agents who can make important contributions to domestic and civic life. Aelian wrote in the Severan era, with its crowded roster of imperial—and imperious—Julias.[66] These later values rest uneasily in the bed of a tale derived from an era when royal wives and concubines rose or fell through the ruthless application of their sexual allure in the service of intrigue. Imagine, if you would, a revision of the story of Judith in which the heroine would permit Holofernes a glimpse of her charms but rely upon moral suasion and rhetorical skill to convince the tyrant to revise his plans and leave Judea in peace.

Equally less inescapable is Aelian's desire to present a male paradigm of female virtue. His ideal would satisfy many early Christian writers.[67] Aspasia was more concerned with the inward than with the outward, cared nothing for cosmetics, clothing, or jewelry, was neither fussy nor gossipy, did not meddle and would not flirt. Nonetheless, a good deal of water has past under the dam since Xenophon wrote a

---

65. Plutarch's claim that she happily accepted translation into the arms of Darius (*Art.* 27.2) is at strong variance with Aelian's view of her character. Plutarch's *donna* is *mobile.*

66. Julia Domna is the best known of these remarkable and powerful women. One brief and generally sympathetic survey of the accomplishments of Julia Domna, Maesa, Mamea, and Soemias is John P. V. D. Balsdon's *Roman Women: Their History and Habits* (New York: Barnes & Noble, 1962), 150–64.

67. On the subject of female toilet and adornment, see 1 Pet 3:1–6 and 1 Tim 2:9–11. There is a wealth of material on this Greco-Roman (and Jewish) commonplace in Paul J. Achtemeier, *1 Peter* (ed. Eldon J. Epp; Hermeneia; Minneapolis: Fortress, 1996), 211–12. Achtemeier also notes some of the patristic references. Note also the classic anecdote about Lucretia in Livy, 1.57.8–9. (I owe this reference to N. Holzberg.)

manual on household management that expected men to train a young
wife from scratch, and, as objectionable as much of what Aelian celebrates as an ideal is, one will do well to take account of the changes also.[68]
Her exercise in "mother-in-law" management would have earned the
highest praise from Emily Post at least as late as 1960, while her ministry
to grieving Artaxerxes approaches the contemporary admiration for
women as nurturers and masters of interpersonal relations. Aelian's
examples will be more appealing to present-day readers than his philosophy. In the first of these Aspasia scorns the role of sexual object; in the
second she declines to have a "sugar daddy"; the final incident celebrates
her prowess as a healer of wounded souls. The character Aelian constructed knows how to keep her independence without making enemies
and how to win affection while avoiding abject dependence. There have
been worse models, by the lights of any era.

Aspasia and Aesop

The sub-title raises a question: is Aspasia a female Aesop? The
grounds for considering this comparison are apparent: their stories have
similar openings: a healing in the form of an epiphany that enables the
heroes to fulfill their mission. Aesop was given speech so that he might
become a teller of fables who lived by his wits. Through restoration of
her beauty Aspasia was able to become ... a woman who lived by her
wits. Aesop's wit was domestic as well as civic; he thrived in both the
household of a philosopher and in the courts of kings. Aspasia's
wisdom, insofar as instances are provided, was, following the traditional
division of labor, domestic, albeit in households where domestic affairs
had public ramifications. Both the tradition in general and Aelian in particular affirm Aspasia's sagacity, but leave a most indicative if not
atypical veil of silence over any contributions she may have made to the
public or civic spheres. The collected wisdom of Aspasia would scarcely
fill a page. Authors spanning six centuries declare that she was wise.
Here in a nutshell is the basis for deconstructive, hermeneutic-of-suspi-
cion, argument-from-silence exposition. Aelian provides both the thesis:
Aspasia was a sage; therefore female sages existed; and the silence that
has condemned all but vestiges of her wisdom to oblivion.

Differences between the two literary characters are patent. Their
formal origins vary: Aspasia was of free birth and became an unfree
person, if not technically a slave. Aesop (insofar as the tradition implies)

---

68. Xenophon, *Oec.* 7.5–14. The view is traditional: Hesiod, *Op.* 699.

was always a slave. Both, however, are truly free, even while slaves, exemplifying a fond philosophical proposition. For the fabulist speech brought a new life: his sale to the philosopher Xanthus.[69] Aspasia's beauty attracted the attention of a local satrap. Each obtained the new position by rejecting traditional approaches. Aesop was disrespectful and abusive rather than flattering and deferent. Aspasia elicited the interest of Cyrus by rejecting his attentions and protesting her virtue. Both succeeded in establishing themselves against the odds, Aesop by taking over his master's household, eventually gaining his freedom, and becoming a court adviser, Aspasia by winning the love of a prince for whom she was to be a simple sexual object, eventually becoming a court adviser herself. In other respects their careers reflect quite different personalities. Aesop romped from scrape to scrape, never very far from the lash or the noose, and he fell more than once. His fateful dealings with the citizens of Delphi were utterly devoid of diplomacy. That was a subject in which Aspasia could have given Aesop valuable lessons. She tiptoed through the shifting minefields of harem and court with flawless ease, while Aesop would walk two hundred meters out of his way to detonate a mine.

That the two met quite different ends is consonant with the foregoing. Aesop unwisely decided to challenge Apollo, whom he had offended, on his home court, as it were, and visit Delphi. Jesus did much the same. Both met with an apparent lack of success.[70] Aspasia had to learn to accept the love of another king into whose harem she had come by way of capture. According to the brief summary of Plutarch, Aspasia was sent to a convent, as it were, to prevent her transfer to Darius. Crueler fates than that can be identified. Plutarch's account demonstrates her lack of freedom—she was not offered the priesthood as a reward, after all. The disparity between these very different conclusions highlights Aesop's tragic end; the Aspasia of Aelian is rather more like a heroine of romance. The point at which Aelian determined to conclude his story (whatever his sources or powers of invention) establishes her character. It is also equivalent to ending the story of Jesus with Peter's statement that he is the Messiah or the story of Julius Caesar with "*Alea iacta est.*"[71]

Aspasia is also unlike most heroines of romance. Identification of these differences is one way of listing the elements that make this novella somewhat "realistic." Callirhoe, whose *curriculum vitae* had a lot in

---

69. *Life of Aesop* 22–28.

70. In "A Nihilist Fabula" (see above) I compare the fates of Aesop and Jesus. See also Lawrence M. Wills, *The Quest for the Historical Gospel* (London: Routledge, 1997), 23–50.

71. Mark 8:29, which is almost exactly halfway through the book.

common with Aspasia's, supplies an obvious basis for comparison. A free woman of Syracuse, Callirhoe was captured and sold in Ionia, where she attracted the attention of more than one satrap and eventually bewitched the Great King, himself. Like Aspasia, Callirhoe would later find herself part of the booty following a battle. Callirhoe, distinct in this decision from all other heroines of romance, compromised her chastity by marrying one Dionysius, a satrap, and leading him to believe that the child she carried was his.[72] Both of these heroines had to come to terms with the death of their true love and did so with the flexibility noted.[73] Everyone fell in love with Callirhoe, very much against her will. She, to unleash an ineptly phallic metaphor, was, like her sisters in other romantic novels, the very incarnation of Cupid's arrow. Aspasia was no doubt pleased that she could attract powerful Persian men, as long as it was on her own terms, terms that prove—quite happily for those intent upon illustrating a moral—more rewarding than wantonly seductive behavior. Her triumph was to achieve the position of honorary wife, in truth a status nearly approaching equality (ἰσοτιμία) in a relation marked by fidelity and mutuality (ὁμονοία καὶ σωφροσύνη), which are, Aelian assures his readers, qualities more typical of Greek marriages than of Persian unions.[74] Be that as it may, Aspasia knows how to win the hearts of prominent men. Aelian relates that she did this in just the manner her mother, had she had one, or her nurse, had her father been able to afford one, would have recommended: by "playing hard to get" and insisting upon her virtue. No one will write off Aspasia as a mere passive object. Finally, romantic heroines typically begin at the pinnacle of social and personal standing and happiness, plunge precipitously to the bottom, and, in the last volume, regain all that they had lost and quite possibly more. Aspasia had little to begin with, lost that, and in the end did very well for herself in rather inauspicious circumstances. Aphrodite was her

---

72. Although the narrator does not make this explicit, Callirhoe must have had marital relations with Dionysius. Chariton has prepared his soil well. Callirhoe elects marriage to preserve the life and freedom of her and Chaireas's unborn child, not to make her life less repugnant. Moreover, readers are likely to hold a bit of a grudge against the hero, who attacked his wife in a fit of temper (brought on as the result of a plot, to be sure, but still indefensible).

73. Callirhoe's husband Chaireas was not actually dead, but she could only assume that he had perished.

74. Twentieth-century analyses of ancient Greek marriages are a bit less sanguine than is Aelian, and with good reason. It should nonetheless be recognized that Aelian's ideal is that of the romantic, "companionate" marriage, scarcely an invention of the Renaissance, as Margaret Doody notes (The True Story of the Novel [New Brunswick, N.J.: Rutgers University Press, 1996], 5).

benefactor and received appropriate devotion. Athena remains unnamed, but she did her part.

Novella into Novel?

So long as ancient novels were an oddity requiring explanation the quest for their origins was the dominant subject of research. One venerable answer to that question looks to more or less realistic *novelle*.[75] The story of Aspasia is an example of what happens when this metamorphosis is attempted. The technique does not easily work, for few stories deconstruct so readily as that of Aspasia. Length is not an issue; plot is. To make a proper romantic novel about Aspasia one would need to endow her with wealth, prominence, and a handsome true love of equal position, ascertain that none of those ardent Persians ever quite got her into a lawful marriage or any other bed, and return her after suitable vicissitudes to Phocaea and conjugal bliss. Very little of the "original story," other than some names[76] and places, would remain.

The Descent of the Dove

The foregoing has pointed out that the story of Aspasia and the *Life of Aesop* have similar openings: misfortune relieved through an epiphany. The most famous New Testament parallel is the epiphany inaugurating the conversion of "Saul" from maniacal persecutor to fervent supporter, an event symbolized by his blinding and the healing of that illness (Acts 9:1–19a). Epiphanies also mark the call of Moses and various prophets, who often report some impediment or disability (e.g.,: Exod 4:10–11; Isa 6:5–7; Jer 1:6). Beginnings that portray mastery over an initial moral or physical impediment before ascending the path to greatness are ever so typical. This observation underscores the extent to which Christian tradition, which has found such "conversion" highly desirable for Paul, Matthew, Thomas, and Augustine, and saints of every era and clime, staunchly evades it in relating the story of Jesus. Matthew alone takes a slight step in that direction by detailing the existence of a

---

75. Erwin Rohde proposed that one of the two sources of the romantic novel was the love stories recounted by Hellenistic poets (*Der griechische Roman und seine Vorläufer* [Leipzig: Breitkopf & Hartel, 1876; 3rd ed.; ed. Wilhelm Schmidt; Leipzig: Breitkopf & Hartel, 1914], 12–123). Bruno Lavagnini developed a more sophisticated approach by focusing upon local legends (*Le Origini del romanzo Greco* [Pisa: Mariotti, 1921]). For a brief discussion, see Pervo, *Profit with Delight*, 92–93.

76. This is a somewhat ironic fate for a heroine of uncertain name.

plot intended to prevent Jesus from growing up to be the Messiah (2:13–18). The possibility of sin hovers over the story of Jesus' baptism, of course, but without suggestion of any noteworthy fault. Mark alone is insensitive to that issue, while Matthew faces it most squarely.[77] Christology appears to have eliminated the option of beginning with a hero in need of help.

There are many changes rung upon this simple melody. Historical novels in the stricter sense often introduce a national calamity. When his prophetic powers indicate the conquest of Egypt by Persia, the last Pharaoh moves *incognito* to Macedon, where he will sire/arrange for the conception of a king destined to overthrow Persia. Thus begins the *Alexander Romance*.[78] The biblical books of Esther and Judith revolve about the threatened destruction of the Jewish people or nation. Romantic novels prefer, as one might suspect, individual ailments. That ailment is always the same: love-sickness, the cure for which may involve some type of revelation.[79] Developments of this cliché are not lacking in creativity. Variations include the humorous, the salacious, and the macabre.[80] For historians of religion the most interesting example may well be the Habrocomes-like blend of love-sickness and repentance that launches Aseneth onto a new spiritual trajectory. "Aseneth saw Joseph on his chariot and was strongly cut (to the heart), and her soul was crushed, and her knees were paralyzed, and her entire body trembled, and she was filled with great fear."[81] The *Metamorphoses* of Apuleius endow this theme with its most elaborate—and entertaining—manifestation. The hero, Lucius, suffers from unholy and unhealthy curiosity (among other things), is punished by reduction to a bestial state, and will

---

77. Mark 1: 4–9; Matt 3:14–15.

78. *Alexander Romance* 1.1–14.

79. The slam-bang approach of Xenophon of Ephesus (*An Ephesian Tale*) provides, as so often, broad illumination within a narrow compass. Anthia and Habrocomes fall in love at first sight (in church, as it were). He is punished by Eros for his pride, in a passage (1.4) reminiscent of the punishment of θεόμαχοι (as was Paul, despite the views of his alleged teacher: Acts 5:35–39). For her part Anthia can only lament feelings unsuitable for a young girl (she is fourteen; ibid.). The two continue to decline, in separate symmetry, until their parents seek the aid of Apollo, who issues a revelation (1.6).

80. Longus's *Daphnis and Chloe* features young lovers who cannot resolve the pains of love because they are unfamiliar with "the facts of life"; illness takes the form of impotence in the *Satyrica* of Petronius. Consummated passion for a daughter launches the plot of *Apollonius of Tyre*.

81. *Joseph and Aseneth* 6:1 (trans. C. Burchard; *OTP* 2:177–247); chapters 8–17 recount her repentance and "cure."

not be rescued until, as the novel approaches its climax, he repents and receives (like Aesop) an epiphany of Isis.[82]

If the descent of the dove does not make the otherwise unremarkable Jesus of Nazareth the Son of God, and so forth, a similar event (the gift of the Spirit) serves to transform rather cowardly and impercipient apostles into effective agents of their Lord in Luke's second volume (Acts 2). Reflection about the kind of a beginning found in the stories of Aesop and Aspasia (among others) will not lead to Luke or to Mark, but it can throw some light upon Pentecost. The various Acts may begin with some personal obstacle or defect; Gospels do not.[83] This difference has now been duly noted and widely, albeit not deeply, explored. There are also a few similarities worthy of a glance.

By the third line of her story Aspasia is receiving premonitions of future success. Her dreams, together with the subsequent epiphany of an "angel," as it were, of Aphrodite, evoke a narrative world like that of the openings of Matthew, Luke, and the *Protevangelium of James*, for example. As a dreamer she may be compared to Joseph. Both are relatively humble but upright people.[84] Her (recurrent) dream brings hope of a bright future; Joseph's offers hope to a benighted people. To him comes the promise that his fiancée's child "will save his people from their sins" (Matt 1:21).[85] Aspasia did not dream of a χρῖστος (messiah) but of the χρηστόν (good). She would live with a "handsome and noble" man.[86] These similarities place the differences in relief: Jesus' story is oriented toward and identified with that of a people; the tale of Aspasia is about an individual. She exemplifies how a person may triumph over adversity through virtue. The Gospels also provide guidance for individuals, but their messages and their ethics are first and foremost constitutive of communities. Aspasia's story is a testament to a perennial anti-Iranian prejudice that would eventually cost the civilization of Greece (and that

---

82. Christoph Burchard has a synoptic chart comparing *Aseneth*, Apuleius, and Acts 9: *Der dreizehnte Zeuge* (FRLANT 103; Göttingen: Vandenhoeck & Ruprecht, 1970), 59–86.

83. Cf. the opening of the *Acts of Thomas*, in which the hero accepts his mission in the spirit of Jonah. Since the *Acts of Thomas* alone retain their original beginning, analogies from Apocryphal Acts are hard to find. The *Acts of John* quite possibly opened with an epiphany that prevented the future apostle from committing matrimony.

84. She is described as chaste and self-controlled; Joseph is characterized as "righteous" (δίκαιος).

85. In addition to this illustration from Matthew, note also Luke 1:13–17, 76–79 (John the Baptizer); 1:31–33 (Jesus); *Prot. Jas.* 4.1 (Mary the mother of Jesus).

86. See n. 31 above. The adjectives καλός and ἀγαθός together constituted a revelatory Greek cliché, for the (male) Greek ideal sought to identify physical and moral excellence.

of Persia) a great deal. The piece reflects common Hellenic standards but only indirectly nourishes a kind of "Hellenism."

CONCLUSION

This essay has multiple objectives. There is a probe toward women's history and the no less patent fact of the construction of female characters to meet male ideals. The latter is a kind of fiction, and the history uncovered can be summarized in a sentence, if not a word. Another project is explorations of the border and shadowland between "history" and "romance," including the rewriting of history to meet the demands of fiction and the process by which flesh is given to the most exiguous of narrative bones. "Aspasia" is a minor witness to the upward social climb of the novel. Her re-creator endowed her story with qualities that suggest, although they cannot prove, that the romantic heroine was gaining status.[87] Aelian wished to produce a flattering portrait of Aspasia. That in itself is interesting. In order to do so he was obliged to resort to fiction. That in itself is not surprising. Interest, if not surprise, arises in the way his fictional portrait testifies to changing views of women in high places and in the influence of the ideal Greek romantic heroine. As a fictional biography "Aspasia" is also comparable to the *Life of Aesop (Aesop-Romance)* up to a point in structure and in theme. These comparisons are meritorious in that they reveal that Aelian had to repress the end of the story, which presented neither endless beatitude nor glorious martyrdom, and that he could draw upon very few examples of Aspasia's celebrated wisdom, none of which illustrated her alleged acumen on matters of state.

Comparison with early Christian literature produced a number of dissimilarities and similarities. Luke and Aelian follow somewhat similar paths, in neither case solely motivated by love of invention. The villain and savior of those with scanty sources in the Greco-Roman world was rhetorical education, which taught students how to fashion a mountain from a mole hill (through elaboration of a *chreia*[88]) and how to stir up a tempest in a tea-pot, if circumstances required a tempest. The more pressing question is not *whether* ancient writers concocted material to fill in gaps but *how* they did so.

---

87. A more certain example can be seen in the portrait of Apollonius of Tyana produced by Aelian's colleague Philostratus, which is a biographical novel influenced by a range of fictional types.

88. Cf. the reference to Hock and O'Neil, *Chreia in Ancient Rhetoric*, n. 11 above.

This study has noted two ways of writing a fictionalized biography. One, found in the *Alexander Romance*, as well as in many stories of rulers, endows the subject with divine origins. Matthew and Luke (and, in some ways, John) follow, for whatever reasons, this model. Another, more characteristic of prophets and sages, begins with a conversion or healing.[89] Luke's story of Paul—and of all the apostles—appropriately takes the second model. So, apparently, does Mark. These choices of beginning—and ending—cannot serve as primary grounds for distinguishing among biography, Gospel, Acts, and novel.

Aelian wisely ends with an adverb: συνετῶς. One crafter of early Christian narrative who would probably have approved of this tactic is the author of Luke and Acts.[90] There is a weightier resemblance. Each author elected to end at an artistic, "high" note rather than proceed to a less congenial dénouement. Luke chose not to narrate the death of Paul, of which he was quite aware (Acts 20). If one can assume that Aelian knew what Plutarch knew (if not the text of Plutarch), the explanation for his deliberate omission is not far to seek. There is general agreement that Acts ends where it does because the author so elects (rather than, for example, that it was composed ca. 60 C.E.).[91] The argument will henceforth revolve about the reasons for making this choice. To what extent was this decision dramatic or artistic in inspiration? If the motive is primarily ideological, what tenet is in the driver's seat?

Both Luke and Aelian are sovereign over their material, ending where it suits them, not least when the continuation might be detrimental to their case. This is a valid observation whether one sees Acts as something like the story of Paul with a long preface or as the march of the Christian message to Rome. The latter is, for a variety of reasons, the more appealing option at present and evokes sympathy from readers of various stripes. The implications of the view that Luke brought Acts to its rousing end by choice rather than because of the lack of further

---

89. If the story is more picaresque and/or "realistic," the "healing" may come at the end, quite dramatically in the story of Lucius.

90. Act 28:31: κηρύσσων τὴν βασιλείαν τοῦ θεοῦ καὶ διδάσκων τὰ περὶ τοῦ κυρίου Ἰησοῦ Χριστοῦ μετὰ πάσης παρρησίας ἀκωλύτως.

91. Of the making of arguments on the end of Acts there is no end. Two relatively recent examples, representing somewhat different points of view, are Daniel Marguerat, *La première histoire du christianisme: Les Actes des apôtres* (Paris: Cerf, 1999), 301–34; and William F. Brosend II, "The Means of Absent Ends," in *History, Literature and Society in the Book of Acts* (ed. Ben Witherington III; Cambridge: Cambridge University Press, 1996), 348–62. Colin Hemer summarizes the various options with a review of research in his *The Book of Acts in the Setting of Hellenistic History* (Winona Lake, Ind.,: Eisenbrauns, 1990), 383–87. Hemer would prefer to assign a very early date to Acts, but he does not depend upon the ending for his argument.

knowledge cannot be evaded. "Aspasia" is, to at least a degree, a tale of the triumph of Greek breeding and virtue in foreign parts exemplified in the story of one woman. Acts tells the story of the triumph of the Christian Gospel in the Roman Empire by focusing upon the chief instrument (9:15) of that triumph. Such selections may be either factual or fictitious. In either case, they are artistic—i.e., literary in function. There is no need to choose between the ideological and the artistic; the latter can be in the service of the former. The presence of literary art, including the selection of beginnings and endings, certainly does not identify a work as fiction, but to conclude a book with a substantial *suppressio veri* that conveniently allows an author to establish a thesis inconveniently unsupported by facts is either falsehood or fiction. Aelian's Aspasia is to a large degree his own creation, although most of the story has roots in data taken from history and biography. It is none the worse for that. One challenge this study raises for those who study Christian origins is to be quite candid about what it means to speak of "Luke's literary artistry" or "Lucan narrative skill." A word like "artistry" is abused when it is merely a cloak to cover the presence of fiction.

APPENDIX: SOURCES ABOUT ASPASIA IN TRANSLATION

1. Xenophon, *Anabasis* 1.10.2. The King and his men seized, among much other booty, Cyrus's mistress, the Phocaean girl, who was said to be both beautiful and intelligent.[92]

2. Plutarch, *Artaxerxes* 26.3–27.3 [After describing the custom that the heir should receive a favor]. Accordingly, Dareius asked for Aspasia, who had been the special favourite of Cyrus, and was then a concubine of the king. She was a native of Phocaea, in Ionia, born of free parents and fittingly educated. Once when Cyrus was at supper she was led in to him along with other women. The rest of the women took the seats given them, and when Cyrus proceeded to sport and dally and jest with them, showed no displeasure at his friendly advances. But Aspasia stood by her couch in silence and would not obey when Cyrus called her; and when his chamberlains would have led her to him, she said: "Verily, whosoever lays his hands upon me shall rue the day." The guests therefore thought her a graceless and rude creature. But Cyrus was delighted, and laughed, and said to the man who had brought the women: "Dost thou not see at once that this is the only free and unperverted woman thou has brought me?" From this time on he was devoted to her, and loved her above all women, and called her The Wise. She was taken prisoner when Cyrus fell in the battle at Cunaxa and his camp was plundered. 27. This was the woman for whom Dareius asked, and he gave offence thereby to his father … [but] he said that she was a free woman, and bade his son take her if she was willing, but not to constrain her against her wishes. So Aspasia was summoned, and contrary to the hopes of the king, chose Dareius. And the king gave her to Dareius under constraint of the custom that prevailed, but a little while after he had given her, he took her away again. That is, he appointed her a priestess of the Artemis of Ecbatana, who bears the name of Anaitis, in order that she might remain chaste for the rest of her life.…[93]

3. Plutarch, *Pericles* 24.11 [The famous mistress of Pericles]. Aspasia, they say, became so celebrated, that even Cyrus, the prince who fought his brother, the king, for the sovereignty of the Persian Empire, gave the name of Aspasia to his favourite concubine, who had previously been called Milto. She was a Phocaean by birth, the daughter of a man named

---

92. *Xenophon: The Persian Expedition* (trans. Rex Warner; Harmondsworth, U.K.: Penguin, 1949), 57.

93. *Plutarch's Lives XI* (trans. Bernadotte Perrin; LCL 101; Cambridge: Harvard University Press, 1926), 191–93.

Hermotimus, and when Cyrus was killed in battle, she was captured and brought to the king and later gained great influence with him at court.[94]

4. Athenaeus, *Deipnosophistae* 13.37, 576D. And as for Cyrus, who made the expedition against his brother, did he not have with him on the expedition the woman of Phocaea, who was a prostitute, though she was called the most wise and most beautiful? Of her Zenophanes says that she had formerly been called Milto, but her name was changed to Aspasia.[95]

******

Comparison of these sources in Greek with the account of Aelian will dispel any doubt that, at the very least, they share common traditions.[96] Verbal similarities, in particular those between Aelian and Plutarch's *Artaxerxes*, establish a high probability that the relationship is intertextual. For the purposes of this essay it is not necessary to attempt to determine whether these two authors shared a common source or Aelian used Plutarch.[97] These excerpts probably contain all the data that was available to Aelian, in whatever form.

---

94. *The Rise and Fall of Athens: Nine Greek Lives by Plutarch* (trans. Ian Scott-Kilvert; Harmondsworth, U.K.: Penguin, 1960), 191.

95. *Athenaeus The Deipnosophists VI* (trans. G. B. Gulick; LCL 235; Cambridge: Harvard University Press, 1937), 113. Athenaeus adds a detail about another concubine that is also found in Xenophon.

96. Consult the notes for some examples of verbal identity among the sources.

97. Judeich, "Aspasia 2," 1:1721, believes that the two shared a common source.

NOVEL AND MYSTERY:
DISCOURSE, MYTH, AND SOCIETY

Gerhard van den Heever

INTRODUCTION

The discussion of the relationship between ancient fiction and religion has been frustrated by an inadequate circumscription of the genre of the novel as well as an inadequate theorizing of religion. When fictional discourse is understood as one performative discourse among many, meaningful discussion of the relation of ancient fiction to late Antique mystery religions can resume. This paper will demonstrate that the Roman Empire created the conditions in which the novel could flourish. When one considers the nature of religion and the mysteries in the late antique world, one begins to see that, rather than frivolous, far-fetched, romantic, adventure stories, the Greek novels are encoded narratives of survival in a politically and socially fragile world.

ANCIENT FICTION AND RELIGION

In his *Die griechisch-orientalische Romanliteratur in religions-geschichtlicher Beleuchtung,* Karoly Kerenyi argued for an origin for the ancient novel in religion based on his reading of the *Romanfiguren* (the characters populating the novels). He held that the novels represent the accounts of the suffering of the gods.[1] Reinhold Merkelbach took up the project of a religio-historical interpretation of the ancient novel and in the process went one step further to include not only the Isiac mystery cult, but also all the major mystery cults of the early empire. Not only do the novels present the reader in narrative format with Egyptian myths, but also with Mithraic, Dionysiac, Pythagorean, and Helios myths, the narrative texts themselves *are* mystery texts, or are themselves mythologies. Since the origins of epic, lyric and drama should be sought in

---

1. Karoly Kerenyi, *Die griechisch-orientalische Romanliteratur in religionsgeschichtlcher Beleuchtung* (Tübingen: Mohr Siebeck, 1927).

religion, it follows that the same should hold for the novel.[2] According to Merkelbach, "The ancient romances are intimately connected to the mysteries of antiquity in decline, namely the cults of Isis, Mithras, Dionysus, and the sun god. The novels constitute the principal sources for these religions, about which we would otherwise have very little evidence."[3] In effect the novel romances are the scripts for the performances of mystery rituals, our only source for the "beliefs" held by these mystery cults, which were traditionally, of course, secret societies.

Merkelbach's controversial thesis placed the issue of religion *and* fiction as well as religion *in* fiction firmly on the agenda of studies of the ancient novel, even though his thesis was not generally accepted.[4] Even Kerenyi distanced himself from Merkelbach's "much too simplistic statement of the case."[5]

Nevertheless, one can point to numerous instances of contact between the ancient novel and its religious world or the religious values reflected or assumed in the novel. And here, for instance, one can use as an illuminating test case the parallel between the myth of Isis and Osiris and its "use" as plot framework in *Leucippe and Clitophon*. There is an uncanny, but very real similarity between the plot of Achilles Tatius's *Leucippe and Clitophon* and the portrayal of the myth of Isis and Osiris in Plutarch's *De Iside et Osiride*. As an example, one can start by considering, among other possibilities, the sacrifice scene of Leukippe in *Leucippe and Clitophon* 3.15–25.[6] Kleitophon watches from a distance from the Roman (Egyptian cavalry)

2. Reinhold Merkelbach, *Roman und Mysterium in der Antike* (Munich: Beck, 1962), preface.

3. "Die antiken Liebesromane hängen eng mit den Mysterien des sinkenden Altertums zusammen, mit den Kulten der Isis, des Mithras, des Dionysos und des Sonnengottes: Die Romane werden zu Hauptquellen für diese Religionen, über die wir sonst nur wenige Zeugnisse haben" (ibid., preface).

4. See Niklas Holzberg, *The Ancient Novel: An Introduction* (London: Routledge, 1995), 30: "There is no need for us to examine this theory in any depth, since its underlying assumptions have already been disproved several times, and it is now almost unanimously rejected by scholars."

5. Isolde Stark, "Religiöse Elemente im antiken Roman," in *Der antike Roman: Untersuchungen zur literarischen Kommunikation und Gattungsgeschichte* (ed. Heinrich Kuch; Berlin: Akademie Verlag, 1989), 147 n. 69, referring to Kerenyi's *Der antike Roman: Einführung und Textauswahl* (Darmstadt: Wissenschaftliche Buchgesellschaft, 1971), in which Kerenyi softened his original argument somewhat by viewing the Greek romance novels as a "parallel phenomenon to the spread of initiations into foreign mysteries in the Roman empire," as a kind of secularization. Stark lists other authors who also repudiated Merkelbach's thesis.

6. I have retained the dual spelling of Leukippe and Kleitophon in the narrative, and *Leucippe and Clitophon* in the title of the work, in accordance with the translation of John Winkler in *Collected Ancient Greek Novels* (ed. B. P. Reardon; Berkeley and Los Angeles: University of California Press, 1989), 170–284.

camp how the bandits are sacrificing Leukippe. He sees how she is led to an earthen altar with a coffin near it. A libation is poured over her, and she is led around the altar to the accompaniment of a flute while a priest intones what sounds like an Egyptian hymn. Then she is tied to stakes in the ground, and the sacrificer plunges a sword in her and cuts her open from the heart to the abdomen while Kleitophon, horrified, watches her entrails "leaping out." Her entrails are pulled out and carried to the altar and the bandits share a meal of it.

Some time later Kleitophon learns that his beloved Leukippe escaped her would-be gruesome fate. His slave-companion Satyros and their travel-companion, Menelaos, an Egyptian native to that region, had been captured by the *Boukoloi* (the brigands or "Desperadoes") and initiated into the banditry, a process that required them to perform the human sacrifice. So they obtained by happy coincidence the stage props of a Homer actor-reciter (a sword with retracting blade) and they set out to prepare the elaborate scam. An animal bladder was stuffed with the entrails, sewed shut and hid beneath Leukippe's robes. After the mock-sacrifice, "Leukippe's" liver was roasted and shared among the bandits and what was deemed left of her, interred in the coffin.

Then the cavalry arrives and destroys the band of bandits and Kleitophon is united with Satyros and Menelaos, and eventually also with Leukippe. Menelaos performed some hocus-pocus, recited magic words, and removes the contraption from Leukippe's stomach. The book ends with a parable of the phoenix as (unintended?) commentary on what has occurred.

I would like to contend that this is a "refictionalized" version of the myth of Isis and Osiris. According to the myth, Osiris reigned over Egypt and "delivered them from their destitute and brutish manner of living." He later traveled through the world spreading civilization. Then Typhon killed him "by a treacherous plot." Osiris was tricked and locked into a chest specially made to measure. The chest was dropped in the river and so sent off to sea. The chest washed up, shipwrecked at Byblos, where Isis eventually found it and brought it back to Pelusium in the Delta area of Egypt. Here Typhon stumbled across the chest, recognized who was inside, and dismembered Osiris's body and scattered the parts in different places. Isis dutifully searched the swampy delta area, found the parts (save for the phallus) and buried them. Isis's son, Horus, eventually avenged Osiris's death and dismemberment by defeating Typhon in battle.

---

7. *De Iside et Osiride* 27.

Plutarch sees within Isis's representation of her experiences "a lesson in godliness and an encouragement for men and women who find themselves in the clutch of like calamities."[7] Later in the same commentary Plutarch, after exploring the etymology of "Osiris" as joy and fructifying and regenerating moisture, claims that this whole narrative "is an image of the perceptible world."[8]

The myth of Isis and Osiris and the romance of *Leucippe and Clitophon* create the same narrative world. And this can be seen in a number of illuminating points of contact between the two narratives. Both stories include shipwrecks, hints of adultery, dismemberment, uncivilized foes, and geographical locales between Phoenicia and Egypt. But there are also several inversions. Unlike in the myth, in the novel it is the female heroine who faces dismemberment. The direction of travel is inverted; in the myth it is from Egypt to Phoenicia and back, whereas in the romance it from Phoenicia to Egypt and back via Asia Minor.

Nonetheless, the romance of *Leucippe and Clitophon* can be understood as a refictionalized version of the myth, perhaps not directly as a mystery text, but definitely as a reappropriating and reconfiguring of the folklore motifs and narratives underlying the myth itself. And one should remember, myth only ever existed as narrative and in different versions: in the world of oral transmissions of folklore we do not have a fixed and stable "original." Even in antiquity, people like Plutarch were aware of the intersections between myth and fiction. After recounting the myth to his interlocutor, Clea, Plutarch turned his nose up (ever the snob) at the popular fictions feeding off the myth or repackaging the myth in novelistic fashion:

> That these accounts [that is, the recounted myth] do not, in the least, resemble the sort of loose fictions (μυθεύμασιν ἀραροῖς) and frivolous fabrications (διακένοις πλάσμασιν) which poets and writers of prose (λογογράφοι) evolve from themselves, after the manner of spiders, interweaving and extending their unestablished first thoughts, but that these contain narrations of certain puzzling events and experiences, you will of yourself understand.[9]

By arguing for a qualitative difference between his recounted version of the myth and the other, fictional, versions of it (calling them by the derogatory term "empty/idle concoctions"), Plutarch actually witnesses to the existence of story plots that encapsulate or imitate the

---

8. *De Iside et Osiride* 54.
9. *De Iside et Osiride* 20; 358f.

mythic narrative. If the πλάσματα of the Plutarch citation indeed refers to what we now call novelistic fiction (as I think it does), then these words attest to the existence side by side of Greek novel and the myth/mythic narrative of mystery cults. When he later interprets the plastic representation of Osiris as an erect male member to be the signification of his creative power and the representation of Isis by means of lunar symbols (the moon governing love affairs) as signifying her presiding role in love affairs, Plutarch himself establishes the link between the myth of Isis and Osiris and adventure love romances.[10] In light of the characteristics of oral folklore it is in any case difficult to distinguish between the pure myth of the mystery and the fictional versions of it. Therefore, the main question raised by these convergences, and the one that concerns me here, is how one should theorize the similarities and "points of contact" between ancient fiction and religious myth.

So, however one wishes to approach the question, the issue of the relation of ancient fiction and religion will not go away. In addition, in order to account for the genesis of the novel as literary genre, recourse is still often taken to the religious mentality of late antiquity, a putative degenerated "age of anxiety." But this is too vague (even misleading) and does not help to describe in greater detail and is perhaps theoretically more appropriately the phenomenon of ancient fiction vis-à-vis the Greco-Roman world of the late first century onwards, but also the religious mentalities of that world. The topic of the ancient novel in its relation to late antique religion can be reconceptualized and redescribed, but for that one needs to approach the question from a different theoretical framework, and this essay is an experiment in that direction.

RELIGION, FICTION, AND GENRE

Characteristic of the novel, modern and ancient, is the way it represents a deliberate confluence of reality and fantasy, fact and fiction. If it is the vividness of the narration that compelled belief in the veracity of the historical account,[11] then equally it is the conventions of realism

---

10. *De Iside et Osiride* 51.

11. See Timothy P. Wiseman, "Lying Historians: Seven Types of Mendacity," in *Lies and Fiction in the Ancient World* (ed. Christopher Gill and Timothy P. Wiseman; Exeter: University of Exeter Press, 1993), 140–45.

12. John R. Morgan, "Make-Believe and Make Believe: The Fictionality of the Greek Novels," in Gill and Wiseman, *Lies and Fiction in the Ancient World*, 195–96.

employed in the novel that create the "illusion of belief" in fiction as if it were fact.[12] The cluster of rhetorical devices that combine to create the verisimilitude and believed-veracity of fiction, called realism, include historiographic form,[13] real geography,[14] authentic detail, pretense to historical authenticity,[15] closeness to social reality, and manner of narration.[16] What we have in the ancient novel is fiction in the form of history.[17]

As theorists such as Michel de Certeau have demonstrated, the distinction between history as what is true, reliable and credible, and fiction as frivolous lies cannot hold.[18] Both history and fiction are discursive practices that create a past that can be studied or understood from the present. History, like myth, is a vehicle for the construction of social identities, for fashioning and authorizing ordinary human lived in and "believed in" worlds, and for the transformation of collective agreements of a people into truths held to be self-evident. Following Paul Veyne's study on the myths of the Greeks, one can say that truth is not a transhistorical invariant but a work of the constitutive imagination.[19]

The upshot of this, of course, is that generic classifications that pit fiction against other genres as something in a class of its own (and then divorced from historical reality) are not very helpful in answering questions as to the connections between ancient fiction and religion. Rather, what is needed is to understand fictional discourse as one performative discourse among many others. Only then will it be possible to come to any kind of meaningful conclusion as to the relation of ancient fiction to

---

13. The titles of novels such as *Aethiopica, Ephesiaca, Babyloniaca* occurred as titles of historical works too. Other novels' titles pretend to relate real events, as in Chariton's novel "Events concerning Chaereas and Callirhoe." So too the beginnings of the novels situate the following tales in the midst of purported real events: "The Syracusan general, Hermocrates, the man who defeated the Athenians, had a daughter, Callirhoe" (Chariton); "There's a city in Lesbos called Mytilene" (Longus), to name only two examples. See J. R. Morgan, "Make-Believe and Make Believe," 197–98.

14. "The entire geography of the novel's world—distances, directions, sailing times—approximates reality so closely that there seems nothing odd when the recent Budé edition of Chariton includes a map tracing the fictitious movements of its fictitious characters" (Morgan, "Make-Believe and Make Believe," 198).

15. According to Morgan (ibid.), the novelists deliberately emulate the style of historians like Herodotus.

16. Morgan (ibid., 205) claims they not only emulate the diction of Herodotus or Thucydides, but also use archaicizing and Atticizing diction and declamatory descriptions (ἔκφρασις).

17. Ibid.

18. See in particular, Michel de Certeau, "History: Science and Fiction," in *The Certeau Reader* (ed. Graham Ward; Oxford: Blackwell, 2000), 37–52.

19. Paul Veyne, *Did the Greeks Believe in Their Myths? An Essay on the Constitutive Imagination* (trans. Paula Wissing; Chicago: University of Chicago Press, 1988), 117–18.

late antique mystery religions—the Merkelbachian question this essay started off with.

We must also refrain from reading the ancient novels through modern eyes, eyes accustomed to viewing fiction as "that which one reads for relaxation," that is, nonserious reading, or readings without social and political consequences.[20] When fiction or the novel is contrasted to history, science, philosophy, and religion as something by nature intentionally designed not to relate to reality outside it, scholars such as David Konstan, treat it as having "referential autonomy" that deliberately suspends referentiality.[21] When the genre of the novel is thus circumscribed, it becomes impossible to contemplate with any seriousness the theories of Merkelbach and Kerenyi, for by definition fiction cannot refer to religious reality. When novels do reflect their religious context, religion provides part of the scenic context.

In order to proceed in the discussion of fiction and religion, we need to rethink fiction, this time as performative discourse and as discursive artifact. In fact, ancient fiction projects a world by referring to cultural and social codes, by adopting conventional ways of speaking and conventional ways of presenting social and cultural phenomena. Ironically, the putative "escapism" and fantasy world of ancient fiction can also be read differently and lead to an almost exact opposite conclusion. The very same "escapism" and fantasy world that divorced the ancient novel from its context can also be understood to ground it in that very historical context. Thus Heinrich Kuch has argued that the happy endings following on the characters' travails and travels with their triumph over misery so characteristic of ancient fiction (and not only of the "true novels" or romances) represent for its readers an imaginary triumph over the harshness, miseries, and dangers that constitute the threatening environment of their (real) daily lives. The utopian nature of the ancient novel resides in its erection of a counter state to the contemporary state of affairs.[22] The essence of this argument is that the reference of a work of fiction can be

---

20. See, for examples of authors who equate fiction with escape into a make-believe world, Berber Wesseling, "The Audience of the Ancient Novels," in *Groningen Colloquia on the Novel* (ed. Heinz Hofmann; Groningen: Forsten, 1988), 77; Holzberg, *Ancient Novel;* and Albrecht Dihle, *Greek and Latin Literature of the Roman Empire: From Augustus to Justinian* (London: Routledge, 1994), 236.

21. David Konstan, "The Invention of Fiction," in *Ancient Fiction and Early Christian Narrative* (ed. Ronald F. Hock, J. Bradley Chance, and Judith Perkins; SBLSymS 6; Atlanta: Scholars Press, 1998), 6, 14.

22. Heinrich Kuch, "Funktionswandlungen des antiken Romans," in *Der antike Roman,* 75–76.

veiled in that it is ostensibly about the story facts, that is, the contents of the work, while on another level it speaks to and into its social context of origin. This essay is concerned with this complex interplay of dual reference in literature.

Through fiction we can read history in a different fashion than is normally taken to be the case: through fiction we can read a society's sense of self, its own existence as discursive formation displayed in the multitude of narratives it generates. Therefore, ironically, the "lies" of fiction tell us the factual truth about how a society imagines itself.[23] Fiction (and by extension, the novel) is not just fiction. It is a social discourse and it makes a world of difference to read the ancient novels or love romances in this way.

FICTION AND CONTEXT, RHETORIC AND SOCIAL DISCOURSE

John R. Morgan suggests that both fiction and religion "were operating in the same general market" and "cater to the same need to reassure the individual of his personal worth and discover meaning in the tangled web of his daily experience."[24] While he raises an important question—What does it mean to "operate in the same market?"—he betrays a common tendency to treat fiction as an object of individual consumption and religion as an individual interior state. The task, then, is to identify the social and political context that produces a demand that is satisfied by the particular kind of fiction represented by the ancient novel and religious cults such as the mystery religions.

Text production and text reception are two sides of the same communication coin united by cultural scripts or cognitional frames; that is, social and cultural codes that include authoritative traditions and canons, mores and values, conventional styles of communication, and typical scenes and topics for specific purposes. Interpretation, then, requires that we be on the look out for the schemata or frames that conditioned the author's reception of prior tradition and production of a new text. While we can, of course, have no empirical data on the representation of the text by the original readers, we can at least imagine, given the frames or schemata, how the author envisages them and their context.

One of the schemata of imperial literature is the depiction of the colonized world as both a romantic entity and simultaneously as a

---

23. See Keith Hopkins, "Novel Evidence for Roman Slavery," *Past & Present* 138 (1993): 12.

24. John R. Morgan, "Introduction," in *Greek Fiction: The Greek Novel in Context* (ed. John R. Morgan and Richard Stoneman; London: Routledge, 1994), 8.

region of high adventure and threatening danger to be overcome, where heroism is a highly valued trait, and where through these heroic deeds civilization is restored (or extended to new territory). In fact it is part of the imperial mentality or world outlook that popular cultural production and cultural artifacts should be designed to circulate stock images of heroic taming of the wild "other," as well as the rescuing of the distressed and extending (or restoring) civilization to the world of the afflicted.

The political integration of the Mediterranean world in the Roman Empire went hand in hand with the preservation of the cultural integrity of the Greek provinces of the empire and the simultaneous eulogizing of Rome (the histories charting the rise and progress of the Roman Empire were written by Greeks—"from Appian, to Cassius Dio and Herodian, for the best part of a century Roman history was written by Greeks for Greek speakers, in Greek.").[25] The historical works set the stage or a panorama against which another set of narratives, novelistic fiction, could be projected. It is not by coincidence that the Greek novels are, apart from being love stories or romances, also adventure narratives of swashbuckling heroes and dramatically rescued heroines, the ancient equivalent of *The Princess Bride* (1987), or the graphically gruesome, more recent *Pirates of the Caribbean: The Curse of the Black Pearl* (2003), to name only two examples of a well-established genre. As a typical feature of adventure tales, the hero setting off on a journey beset by dangers, life-threatening circumstances, and eventual overcoming of these in joyous reuniting with a loved one and the home city evince the positive character of imperial fiction. The world had been turned into a fantasy playground where the (geographically distant) other represented the romantic (and romanticized) exotic that not only fires and draws the imagination, but also in comparable circumstances (such as the British empire of the high Victorian age) caused many young men to seek honor and fortune in far lands, through minor imperial offices or military careers. The romantic imperial fantasy generates the category of adventure narratives, which not only reflects the imperial fantasy but also contributes to the maintenance of imperial values, ethos, and practices.[26]

Historians of literature note that the novel arose in imperial contexts, first in the first through third centuries of the Christian era, and then again from the seventeenth century onwards.[27] The reason for this,

---

25. Peter Garnsey and Richard Saller, *The Roman Empire: Economy, Society and Culture* (Berkeley and Los Angeles: University of California Press, 1987), 183.

26. John A. McClure, "Late Imperial Romance," *Raritan* 10 (1991): 111–30.

27. Edward Saïd, *Culture and Imperialism* (New York: Vintage, 1993), 69–70.

according to John A. McClure, is that the romance/love adventure
needs "regions rich in the 'raw materials' of adventure, magic, mystery,
Otherness."[28] For the greater part of the last four centuries of European
history, the relation between romance and imperialism was symbiotic
and mutually generative. McClure makes the following observation:

> Imperial expansion created new heroic professions (explorer, colonial
> soldier, and administrator) but also provided new sites for the playing
> out of old stories: quests for wisdom and treasure, struggles with
> demons and magicians, tests of strength against monstrous enemies. It
> provided an endless stream of material for writers of popular historical
> and literary romances. And popular romance in turn provided a valoriz-
> ing vision of expansion.[29]

Hence, imperialism generated the literature that inspired the need for
young men to sustain and expand the empire.

The birth of the modern novel, furthermore, coincided with an explosion in travel narratives.[30] Spanish, Portuguese, English, and French
travel narratives were widely distributed, read, and translated into other
European languages. By the end of the sixteenth century, when the rush
to colonize and build empires was on its way, European travelers had
already been on every continent, except Australia, and the various
descriptions of campaigns, conquests, strange and far away lands, peoples and their customs had begun to feed an almost insatiable demand
for knowledge, but more pointedly for the thrills, of the exotic and the
marvelous.[31] Of even greater relevance is the fact that the accounts of the
gold-hunting, colonizing, missionary, and discovery voyages and campaigns of the Spanish, the French, and the English were often very
thrilling (recall the ἐνέργεια of ancient historiography) and close to fic-

---

28. McClure, "Late Imperial Romance," 112.

29. Ibid., 113.

30. The travel narrative, of course, had an ancient pedigree from Xenophon, to Pausanias, to the many early Christian and later medieval pilgrims' guides (including Egeria and
the Bordeaux Pilgrim), to late antique lists of antiquities, city plans, road and route maps,
local guidebooks (like Polemo of Ilium), to Bede, to Petrach, the *Crusades's Manual*, and the
very many travel accounts following on the "discovery" of the New World and the onset of
the great scramble for colonies; see Percy G. Adams, *Travel Literature and the Evolution of the
Novel* (Lexington: University Press of Kentucky, 1983), 39–80.

31. Adams, *Travel Literature*, 38–80. See also Matthew Sweet, "A Defence of the Freak
Show," in his *Inventing the Victorians* (London: Faber & Faber, 2001), 136–54. Sweet demonstrates how the opening of strange new far away places created a market for the freakish,
often putatively found in some exotic far-off location.

32. Adams, *Travel Literature*, 52.

tion.[32] In fact, these travel accounts often provided the settings and contents of the early (modern) novels.

Glen Bowersock has suggested that we consider prose fiction in the broader context of the Greco-Roman Empire.[33] I contend that just as empire is the context that gives rise to the modern novel, the Roman Empire is the generative matrix for the Greek novel. The political consolidation of the Greco-Roman world under the control of the Roman Empire provided a context for Greeks to assert themselves culturally with great self-confidence once more. This went hand in hand with a renewed sense of the cultural and ethnic diversity of the make-up of the empire (a revival in the early empire of a Herodotean interest in other peoples and other places), which in itself may arguably have been one of the main motivations for empire building, namely to include the new and the exotic in the boundaries of the empire even as the horizons opened up.[34] Fiction was a well-suited vehicle to satisfy the flowering interest in other peoples and places, for ancient fiction (like its modern counterpart) entextualized a betraveled cosmos, either into other far away and exotic places, or into the weirdly exotic imaginary space of fantasy. Imperial fiction is concerned with the inhabitants and events on the margins, with going away (by choice or through force), and with confrontation with the unknown.[35]

If the Greeks and Romans had long had a notorious taste for the freakish, it was certainly the case that freaks announced themselves significantly only in Hellenistic and especially in Roman imperial art and society.[36] Human curiosities were as sought after as exotic animals like ostriches and giraffes,[37] and according to Plutarch there existed a "monster market" (τέρατον ἀγορά) alongside the normal slave market.[38] Human oddities populated the world of the Roman emperors as intimate companions, informers, erotic love-slaves (used as *deliciae* by aristocratic women), alongside anomalous animals.[39] Not only were freak shows held, but museums were set up to house life-size models of human curiosities, much like the "Hottentot Venus," Saartje Baartman, in a Paris

---

33. See Glen W. Bowersock, *Fiction as History: Nero to Julian* (Berkeley and Los Angeles: University of California Press, 1994), 15.

34. Ibid., 31–33.

35. Ibid., 33.

36. See especially Robert Garland, *The Eye of the Beholder: Deformity and Disability in the Graeco-Roman World* (London: Duckworth, 1995).

37. Bowersock, *Fiction as History*, 33.

38. *Marcellus* 22 and *Moralia* 520c. See Garland, *Eye of the Beholder*, 47.

39. Garland, *Eye of the Beholder*, 48–54.

40. Pompey was the first to set up such a museum. See ibid., 54–55.

museum at the beginning of the nineteenth century.[40] A more elevated level of interest in the customs and cultural oddities of foreign peoples (as well as a quite modern tolerance for them)—Chinese, Indian Brahmins, Persians, Medes, Bactrians, Edessenes, Arabs, and Germans—is represented by the wide ranging curiosity of the Syrian Christian sage of the late second, early third century, Bardaisan.[41] Add his knowledge of Egypt to the mix, and you describe the physical world that appears in various configurations in the novels and other works of fiction like the Apocryphal Acts of the Apostles and the *Life of Apollonius of Tyana*. Moreover, the opinions expressed by Bardaisan and his students were in accord with the tales about the foreign "other" told in contemporary Greco-Roman fiction.[42]

The bizarre characters that populate imperial fiction from Petronius's *Satyricon* to Antonius Diogenes' *The Wonders Beyond Thule* and Lucian's *True History*, testify, alongside the combination of travel to far-away and fantasy destinations with romantic plots, to a growing fascination with the fictional and the marvelous from the first century onwards.[43]

The literature of the early imperial period presents the first imperial century as a carnivalesque, exuberant, excessive celebration of imperial good times (for the classes who produced this literature represented themselves as the upper fraction of society for whom the times could be said to be good). It was the return of the mythical golden age, the *Saturnia regna*, the *Saturnia saecula*, or the *saeculum aureum*, the long gone age of Kronos or Saturn restored in the reign of the historical Augustus.[44] In the utopian, panegyric choruses of Vergil, Ovid, and Horace (sung *in unisono*), the earth will give her bounty, animals will live in harmony with one another and man will not feel the strain of hard work (Vergil), peace and refuge replace the ravages of the civil war, nature is beautiful, the earth fecund, weather ideal, and harmony reigns among all living creatures

---

41. Bowersock, *Fiction as History*, 46–48.

42. Ibid., 48.

43. Ibid., 37.

44. The principal mythographer of this returned golden age is Vergil in the *Fourth Eclogue* and the *Aeneid*, but there is also Ovid's *Metamorphoses* and the *Carmen Saecularum* of Horace. Augustus himself had a hand in this by commissioning and eventually finishing the *Aeneid*, as well as instituting the *Ludi Saeculares* in 17 B.C.E.—well outside of official calculations—to mark and celebrate the beginning of a new era. See on this topic the excellent discussion of Henk S. Versnel, "Two Carnivalesque Princes: Augustus and Claudius and the Ambiguity of Saturnalian Imagery," in *Karnivaleske Phänomene in antiken und nach-antiken Kulturen und Literaturen* (ed. Siegmar Döpp; Stätten und Formen der Kommunikation im Altertum 1; Trier: Wissenschaftlicher Verlag, 1993), 99–122; and *Inconsistencies in Greek and Roman Religion II: Transition and Reversal in Myth and Ritual* (Studies in Greek and Roman Religion 2; Leiden: Brill, 1993), 89–227.

(Horace). Social harmony, natural fecundity, political peace, economic security, personal happiness, a time noble and simple, rustic and blissful prevail (Ovid).[45] Realistic dreams of justice restored under an ideal ruler were quickly swept away in a surge of enthusiasm for the fantastic, topsy-turvy, hyperbolic fairy tale vistas of a genuine utopia. Witness the flowering of panegyric language in dedicatory inscriptions and edicts pertaining to the position of the emperor. Whatever Augustus may have thought about the adulation at the start of his reign, in the way he was constructed by sycophant-elites (especially in the Greek eastern provinces), early in the principate he cast aside the bonds of mortal humanity and earth to take up his abode among the gods. The super-abundant blessings and benefactions bestowed by the emperor placed him among the gods.[46] With the blurring of the dividing lines between divine and human, the whole world within the reach of the empire, adding to that the real, Saturnalian behavior of emperors,[47] the emperor himself became a freakish character in the official freak show that was the empire. The persona of the princeps and imperator, had now itself become a marvel and a παράδοξον. This opened the sluice-gates for an avalanche of the fantastical.

While the art of spectacle and the triumphal procession were not Roman inventions, they gained a particular significance in the context of the empire.[48] Spectacle and triumph, far from sedate and sober occasions, constituted extreme and overwhelming experiences.[49] Greeted by vociferous

---

45. See A. Bartlett Giamatti, *The Earthly Paradise and the Renaissance Epic* (New York: Norton, 1966), 24–30, for an overview.

46. For a description of the escalation of divine honors for the emperors in Ephesus, and by implication the geographical area mentioned in the novels and in which they originated, see ch. 2 of Sjef Van Tilborg, *Reading John in Ephesus* (NovTSup 83; Leiden: Brill, 1996), 25–57.

47. There are possible indications in the narrative that knowledge of contemporary events in Rome and of the emperor's behavior was presupposed among the readership of the novel, for instance the references to theatrical spectacles and gladiatorial contests; see Niall W. Slater, "From *Harena* to *Cena*: Trimalchio's *Capis* (*Sat.* 52.1–3)," *CQ* 44 (1994): 549–51.

48. See Jonathan C. Edmondson, "The Cultural Politics of Public Spectacle in Rome and the Greek East, 167–166 B.C.E.," in *The Art of Ancient Spectacle* (ed. Bettina Bergmann and Christine Kondoleon; Studies in the History of Art 56; New Haven: Yale University Press, 1999), 77–95, for a description of the interplay between Roman and Greek forms of spectacle at the crucial period of Roman ascendancy in the Greek world, after the defeat of Macedon and the battle of Pydna. The point being that the over-the-top nature of the spectacle was a vehicle for announcing, advertising, and promoting Roman hegemony in the Greek East.

49. If the earliest Roman triumphs were more sober, by the time of the late Republic and the advent of the Principate they had become noisy and boisterous extravaganzas, costly, carefully scripted theatrical events ("ostentatious display," "visual splendor"); see Richard Brilliant, "'Let the Trumpets Roar!' The Roman Triumph," in Bergmann and Kondoleon, *The Art of Ancient Spectacle*, 224–25.

response and shouting from both audience and soldiers, the triumphant victor, made up in the image of Jupiter Capitolinus, paraded by leading defeated generals and royalty, as well as captured images of their gods and looted trophies carried on portable platforms—treasures on display. In his wake followed placard bearers, troupes of musicians and large brass bands of trumpets and horns, herds of exotic animals like tigers, lions, and especially elephants, paintings depicting battle scenes, models of destroyed cities, moving mechanical set-pieces portraying important campaign events or mythic episodes and animated statues,[50] and tableaux-vivant in which mythical and historical scenes were enacted in a kind of allegorical commentary on the present celebrated event.[51] These assaults on the senses not only grew more elaborate (each new staged procession aiming to surpass the previous), but also preserved, and consciously evoked, the *pompa triumphalis* of Dionysus (the god's "raucous epiphany," so Brilliant) as described by Callixenos and preserved in Athenaeus's *Deip.* 5.25).[52] Add to these the enacted military campaigns, naval battles (with ships in flooded amphitheatres), performed violence (gladiatorial fights, killings of various kinds of undesirables), wild beast fights, displays in theatres and amphitheatres, and one finds oneself within the broad sweep of narrative scenery encountered in the novels, but which existed everywhere for public consumption.[53] In a very real sense the enacted and performed spectacle, as

---

50. Ann Kuttner, "Hellenistic Images of Spectacle, from Alexander to Augustus," in Bergmann and Kondoleon, *The Art of Ancient Spectacle*, 99: "similar fabulous machinery marked Hellenistic stage effects and was taken to a high pitch in Rome."

51. Compare also Claudius's spectacle as part of a triumph in the Circus Maximus in Rome, in which he presided, dressed in military cloak, over the enacted storming and sacking of a town and the subsequent surrender of the British kings: a reconquest of Britain to justify his claim to the title Claudius Imperator Brittanicus (Suetonius, *Divis Claudius* 21.6), Brilliant, "Roman Triumph," 228.

52. Brilliant, "Roman Triumph," 223. Dionysus's triumphal procession from India to Greece through Asia Minor is not a reflection of the "original" myth of Dionysus, but a Hellenistic invention, one that became very important in the maintenance of imperial ideology, in which the figure of Dionysus is crafted as an imperator himself. See Brian Bosworth, "Augustus, the *Res Gestae* and Hellenistic Theories of Apotheosis," *JRS* 89 (1999): 2–3.

53. See David L. Balch, "The Suffering of Isis/Io and Paul's Portrait of Christ Crucified (Gal. 3:1): Frescoes in Pompeian and Roman Houses and in the Temple of Isis in Pompeii," *JR* 83 (2003): 24–55; and Kuttner, "Hellenistic Images of Spectacle," 100–101, for descriptions of an exotic Nilotic scene preserved in mosaic (ca. 125 B.C.E.) with a Romanized cuirassed imperator enjoying a spectacle victory banquet (with an automaton—a moving statue of Victory—pouring the wine) and the famous Dionysiac marriage scenes from the Villa of the Mysteries in Pompeii, which prefigured by about half a century the enactment of the marriage (and banquet revel) of Aphrodite/Cleopatra and Dionysus/Antony, when Cleopatra came to meet Antony on barge, imitating Aprodite "in the manner of a painting," surrounded by a costumed crew of "Nymphs," "Graces," and "Erotes."

well as the textualized and the graphic and plastic portrayals of spectacle, forms the diorama of the discursive world in which the ancient novels had their home.

If one must take the *Satyricon* of Petronius as the first novel of imperial times, then the celebration of παραδόξα and the weirdly marvelous occur at a time when news of other marvels also started to circulate in the Roman Empire: tales of an imposter king crucified yet risen from the dead ... and deified. It is not by coincidence that depictions of revivifications also turn up in the Greek novels. The difference in terminologies (ἀνάστασις [Christian literature] versus αναβίωσις [Greek writers]) should not blind us to the range of possibilities in which the boundaries between divine and human, between heaven and earth can be breached. From *Scheintode* and other "resurrections" and reappearances in the novels,[54] to real revivifications,[55] to tours of heaven and hell reported in such widely divergent types of texts as Jewish and Christian apocalypses and paradoxographies like Antonius Diogenes' *The Wonders Beyond Thule*, to the apotheoses of dead and/or living emperors, we are looking at a massive entextualized freak show. It is literally a world turned upside down.

In this, a world redolent with the marvelous fictional, "truth" becomes stranger than fiction. In a topsy-turvy world the truth is everything but plain, "there is something sinister going on behind the scenes ... which is actually the truth"—tabloid truth![56] The literary production of the empire resembles the modern day tabloid press, when viewed through these lenses. Is the world, then, not good enough? Invent one!

It is in this context that the large-scale refictionalizing and remythologizing characteristic of the period should be understood. If in earlier times Thucydides, and during the transition to the Roman period, Polybius, wrote histories stripped of fable, myth, and fantasy to provide examples and paradigms for the exercise of civic and political responsibility in the context of the πόλις (i.e., "political history"), in the late Hellenistic period and in the empire, history once again embraced divine

---

54. Each of the novels contains a description of a coming to life of some sort: Achilles Tatius's *Leucippe and Clitophon* (three times), Antonius Diogenes' *The Wonders beyond Thule* (more than one), Heliodorus's *Aethiopica*, Chariton's *Chaereas and Callirhoe*, and Apuleius's *Metamorphoses*. On the whole phenomenon, see Bowersock, "Resurrection," in *Fiction as History*, 99–119.

55. See, for instance, the reported miraculous resurrections in Christian literature as well as in Philostratus's *Life of Apollonius* and the *Heroicus*.

56. See Fiona Black, "Lost Prophecies! Scholars Amazed! *Weekly World News* and the Bible," in *Culture, Entertainment and the Bible* (ed. George Aichele; JSNTSup 309; Sheffield: Sheffield Academic Press, 2000), 20–43, for the similarities between biblical tradition and tabloid truth.

and heroic genealogies, mythic and legendary accounts of prehistory, and generally all kinds of exotic and fantastic tales.[57] Following the expansion of geographic and cultural horizons as a result of Alexander's conquests and the interest in the strange, miraculous, and exotic generated by the accounts of the new generation of geographers and historians, history thus became a handmaiden to myth and tall tales. When credibility of recounted phenomena or facts is disregarded, the boundaries separating history and fiction get blurred to such an extent that history itself becomes fiction, just as fiction, in this case the novels, started off life as history-like writings.

The result of this was a genre of literature in which myth, heroic legend, historical and geographical data, and scientific information were scrambled with the exotic, portentous, and the abnormal.[58] The first-century C.E. mythographer and paradoxographer, Ptolemy Chennos, could label his history *New History*. Lucian could spoof the genre with some tall tales himself—*True History* (a utopian fantasy involving a travel to the moon). He then went on to produce a "serious theory of historiography" and to ridicule the fashion in history writing in *How to Write History*, covering such topics as mythology, genealogical and heroic legends. Diodorus Siculus included in his five volumed history of the Mediterranean world, the *Historical Library*, the utopian tales of Dionysius Skytobrachion, Euhemerus and Iambulus, and these were taken seriously as history. Albrecht Dihle observes, "Such so-called paradoxographical writing was a fairly important branch of philosophical-scientific as well as of entertainment literature."[59]

The implicit social discourse inherent in this historico-paradoxographical literature is demonstrated by the island settings chosen for late Hellenistic and early Roman description of utopias. These include Euhemerus's story of the inhabitants of Panchaea, an island in the Indian Ocean, Iambulus's account of his stay on the Island of the Sun, a pseudo-scientific description of utopian life on an island in a state of nature where inhabitants are welcome so long as they reach their own level of perfection, and Dionysius Skytobrachion's account of two islands: Hesperia, inhabited and ruled by the Amazons, and Nysa, where Dionysus

---

57. Emilio Gabba, "True History and False History in Classical Antiquity," *JRS* 71 (1981): 52–53: "In the Hellenistic period, changing cultural interests and the responses thereto of historians meant that historical research lost much of its political element and returned to traditional narrative forms" (52).

58. Ibid., 53.

59. Dihle, *Greek and Latin Literature*, 238.

60. Gabba, "True History and False History," 58.

was supposedly raised.[60] These utopias are located outside the normal order of things, where nature and social order are inversed. They constitute imaginary, topsy-turvy worlds where nature gives up its bountiful fruits automatically without the need for human toil and agriculture, where humans live in egalitarian harmony without a particular social organization, in blissful isolation uncorrupted by contact between communities. In spite of being the kind of accounts satirized by Lucian as extravagant fantasies, these narratives present the reader with a social critique of contemporary imperial society (the late Hellenistic empires with the Roman Empire in the ascendancy).[61] Importantly, they were not confined to a Greek readership. These and similar utopian fantasies circulated in Latin as well.[62] These utopian fantasies had their longest and most far-reaching influence in the world of Latin literature. If the Roman general Sertorius (a younger contemporary to the senator-paradoxographer, Manilius) desired to escape from the horrors of the civil war to the Islands of the Blessed beyond the Columns of Hercules, he did so on the strength of sailors' tales about their gentle climate and luxuriant growth of edible fruits.[63] He was acting out the utopian and social fantasies that were beginning to circulate in Saturnalian visions of the golden age espoused by writers like Horace (the *Sixteenth Epode,* written in the spring of 38 B.C.E. during the civil war), and his contemporary, Vergil (whose *Fourth Eclogue* dates from 40 B.C.E.).

As the extremities of the known world, these islands represent the transgressed boundaries into the world of the fantastical, as seen in Antonius Diogenes' *The Wonders beyond Thule.* But they also play a role in the emerging imperial myths that justified the apotheosis of the emperor (especially when one compares the self-promotion of Augustus's *Res Gestae* with the Hellenistic doctrine of apotheosis).[64] The myth of the eastern triumphs of Dionysus was a creation of Alexander, triumphs which he surpassed in the conquest of India, and which caused

---

61. And apart from the fantastical utopian islands, Diodorus also described historical islands in utopian terms: Corsica, Sardinia, the Balearic islands: see Gabba, "True History and False History," 59.

62. See, for example, Euhemerus and the *Admiranda,* a work of antiquarian curiosity written by G. Licinius Mucianus, consul and king-maker of Vespasian.

63. Recounted by Plutarch *Sertorius* 8.2–5, 9.1. See Gabba, "True History and False History," 59.

64. Bosworth, "Augustus." The mythology by which the apotheosis of the Roman emperor was argued was, of course, not a Roman invention. In this they continued a mythological and ideological program set in motion by Alexander the Great. The Roman "invention" lay in promoting the idea that the Roman emperor, Octavian/Augustus, went *far beyond* the achievements of his predecessors.

him to be hailed as even more successful than Herakles and Dionysus, and which justified his recognition as divine. The theme was developed by Hellenistic writers such as Megasthenes (who presents Dionysus as the *fons et origo* of Indian civilization and kingship) and Hecataeus of Abdera (who elevated Osiris as the Egyptian counterpart of Dionysus into a world conqueror of Arabia, India, and Greece). The theme was demonstrated in the famous pageant of Ptolemy Philadelphus—testimony to the attraction of the newly created legend for rulers and subjects. Callixenos provides a description of the pageant with its visual construction of the return of Dionysus, complete with an eighteen-foot statue of the god, testifying to the appeal of newly created legend to both rulers and subjects.[65] Vergil, in his description of Augustus's triumphal march across the East, has him surpass the achievements of both Alexander and the god by letting him reach the natural limits of the world, and transcend them (the conquests include Mount Atlas, the *Axis Mundi*, the southern fringes of the Sahara desert, the northern ocean beyond the Caspian and Azov Seas and the Rhine, colonies on the Atlantic coast of Africa and beyond, even beyond the stars and the sun).[66] Greater than Alexander, greater than the conqueror-deities Herakles, Dionysus, and Osiris, and surpassing their labors for the benefit of humankind, in true paradoxographical fashion Augustus became a god himself.

The ideology operative in this remythologizing portrays Augustus as the climax of Roman history, but also the existence of Rome and the imperium as the acme of Greek history. The invention of history characteristic of this mythological reconceptualizing of history is amply demonstrated by Vergil's magnum opus, the *Aeneid*, but also in such openly mythologizing fictions as the two rewritings of the Trojan conflict, the *Ephemeris belli Troiani* of Dictys of Crete, and the *Acta diurna belli Troiani* by Dares the Phrygian.[67] The latter two works are especially relevant in this connection because they demonstrate the dual aspect of Greek thinking about the Roman Empire.[68] In the Dictys text the Greeks are portrayed as culturally, morally, and militarily superior to the Trojans, who are depicted in negative terms as morally inferior. The epic makes the following two statements about the war: the Trojan War is a campaign by a civilized and peaceful nation that had suffered injustice at the hands of

---

65. Ibid., 3.

66. *Aen.* 6.756–853. Cf. Bosworth, "Hellenistic Theories of Apotheosis," 4–6.

67. Stefan Merkle, "Telling the True Story of the Trojan War: The Eyewitness Account of Dictys of Crete," in *The Search for the Ancient Novel* (ed. James Tatum; Baltimore: Johns Hopkins University Press, 1994), 183–96.

68. For a description of these works, see Dihle, *Greek and Latin Literature*, 368.

unscrupulous barbarians and, in the process, the Greeks underwent a moral decline themselves.[69] If Dictys wished to describe Troy (the mythological forebears of the Romans) as barbarian (and anti-Roman sentiment was probably the point of the Dictys epic), later Greek writers would tend in the other direction in their versions of the Trojan conflict.

Most Greek writers at the time reacted to the imperial hegemony of Rome by concentrating on a glorious Greek past, ignoring the Romans completely.[70] But for others, such as Dio Chrysostom and Philostratus, it was a different matter, and here a comparison with the Dictys epic is enlightening. According to Dio in his *Troikos Logos* (*Orationes* 11). Troy had never been sacked by the Greeks, in fact, it was the Greeks who lost the war because of their unprovoked attack on Troy, and in this Dio expressed his sympathy for the heirs of Troy, the Romans.[71] Philostratus's *Heroicus* is probably to be considered, in part, a direct polemic against the Dictys epic in which a positive picture of the Trojans is drawn.[72] If it was a reinvention of myth that created the ideological basis for the creation of the empire, then it is significant that the whole era is characterized by the wholesale reinvention of history.

Why all this production of histories? And why the increase in production of foundation histories of Greek cities in the Roman world? What we are looking at is essentially a search for roots, socio-cultural, ideological, and political—a discourse to define the place of Greek elites in a Roman world. It is now customary to observe that the novel as well as the flowering of historiographical and other literature is to be situated in the wider cultural context of revival of Greek culture from the late first/early second century C.E. onwards through the period known as the Second Sophistic. Far from being merely a leisure time activity, the literary production of the period signifies the way in which the Greek elites of the empire juxtaposed the Roman present on their Greek past, thereby

---

69. Merkle, "Telling the True Story," 191. The love affair of Achilles and Polyxena serves as the central focus of the work through which to describe the changing character of the Greeks (from controlled and civilized to equally cruel and destructive).

70. And this is certainly true of the novels, which contain no references to the imperial context in which they were conceived and received. Cf. Merkle, "Telling the True Story," 193.

71. Ibid.

72. Ibid., 193–94. As instances of polemic: according to the *Heroicus*, Protesilaus declares that Idomeneo did not take part in the Trojan War (*Heroicus* 30), and then in *Heroicus* 26.10 it is stated that writing did not exist at the time of the Trojan War, so destroying the frame narrative of the Dictys epic.

73. Jaap-Jan Flinterman, "De Tweede Sofistiek: Een Portie Gebakken Lucht?" *Lampas* 29 (1996): 135–54.

appropriating the values of the empire as well as participating in it.[73] The Second Sophistic as re-creation of the present in the light of the distinguished Greek past, as a revival movement of the recovery of Greek heritage, was also for that very reason a redesigning of the past in the image of the present. Historical themes had always played an important role in rhetorical declamation and formed the basis of local ruling elites' self-conception of their position in society.[74] In a context that Simon Swain describes as the "most successful period of urbanization known anywhere in the ancient world" (the mid-first to mid-third century C.E.)[75] the successes of local Greek elites in climbing the Roman imperial career ladder (both in the provinces and in the capital, Rome, itself) found extensive expression in Greek cultural hegemony, renewed consciousness of their cultural superiority, and their political involvement and patronage in the local setting.[76] This was the world of the past, the Hellenistic world after Alexander.[77] The past provided the justification of the power and position of the Greek elites in the cities of the eastern provinces of the empire.

On the one hand, the Greeks played along with the creation of an empire, as ideology and as practice, as a world and opportunity for the advancement of class interests, but on the other hand they occulted the very vehicle of those opportunities, Rome, from their literature, that is, apart from the "panegyrists" who lauded the fact of the empire. Evidence of this duality can be discerned in the so-called epistolary novels in which Greeks engaged the empire as their social and political context.[78] Especially relevant are the *Letters of Socrates and the Socratics*, written at the end of the second or beginning of the third century C.E., in which the Greek author addresses other Greeks from the imperial age. The topic that dominates is the relationship between intellectual and political potentate. Despite the near unanimity of late Hellenistic and early imperial philoso-

---

74. Simon Swain, *Hellenism and Empire: Language, Classicism, and Power in the Greek World AD 50–250* (Oxford: Clarendon, 1996), 112.

75. Ibid., 108. In light of literary sources as well as archaeological evidence, it was far from a period of decline; see also H. S. Versnel, "Religieuze Stromingen in het Hellenisme," *Lampas* 21 (1988): 111–36.

76. See Swain, *Hellenism and Empire*, 109. In addition, the new focus on marital fidelity exhibited in the novels arose out of an increasing value put on control of the self and the body (important topics in imperial political philosophy), as well as the fact that the local elites supported their position and ensured their survival as class through marital alliances: Swain, *Hellenism and Empire*, 118–30.

77. For historical references in the Greek novels, such as Ninus, Parthenope, Sesonchosis, Callirhoe's father (the Syracusan general Hermocrates), the allusions to the Hecatomnid dynasty ruling Caria in Chariton's novel, see ibid., 110–12.

78. Niklas Holzberg, "De griekse Briefroman," *Hermeneus* 67 (1995): 71–77.

phies on the issue of the art of living (to abandon the fruitless search for the unattainable: power and wealth), philosophers regularly clashed with Roman imperial authority, or at least existed in a tense relationship with it (Nero and Domitian both banished philosophers from Rome). This confrontation between Greek culture and Roman power politics, however, found expression in literature, where, not to sharpen the conflict, the antagonism was projected into the past.[79] Coming at a time when narrative prose fiction also flowers (the early empire), with Greeks living under absolute monarchy despite local constitutional pretensions to the contrary, Greek authors experience nostalgia for the lost glory of the Greek past. The double and contradictory aspect of Greek comportment with respect to the empire—acceptance and critique—can be seen in the absence of Rome from the novels, as well as in the images of survival and triumph over adversity in myth, fiction, and graphic arts. And this is my theory: the Roman Empire created the conditions in which the fictional, the fantastical, the marvelous, the paradoxographical, and the novel could flourish. The novel flourished especially in the Greek-speaking provinces of the eastern Roman Empire due to the "imperial reach" of the imaginary narrated worlds, where the provincial Greek-speaking elite both bought into the imperial ideal and sublimated their disempowered position. In other words, to take up the theoretical perspective above, far from "just" romantic adventure stories, the Greek novels are encoded narratives of survival in a politically and socially fragile world, an aspect that becomes visible when one considers the nature of religion and mysteries in the late antique world.

And So We Come to Religion

One of the problems that bedeviled past thinking on the relationship of fiction and religion stemmed from the way religion was conceptualized. Underlying past debates on Merkelbach was an unspoken assumption about religion as an interior state of belief as assent to truths, parallel to the way literature was relegated to the private enjoyment of the individual.[80]

---

79. Ibid., 76.

80. In recent years this has been exposed as the (Christian) theological legacy of, mainly, William James and Mircea Eliade (and before them, Rudolf Otto), which was immensely influential in over half a century of theorizing about religion. See for a short overview of the issues involved Burton L. Mack, "A Radically Social Theory of Religion," in *Secular Theories on Religion: Current Perspectives* (ed. Tim Jensen and Mikael Rothstein; Copenhagen: Museum Tusculanum Press, 2000), 123–36; and Russell T. McCutcheon, "Redescribing 'Religion' as Social Formation: Toward a Social Theory of Religion," in *What Is Religion? Origins, Definitions, and Explanations* (ed. Thomas A. Idinopulos and Bryan C.

By treating them both as species of social discourse one can entertain a new perspective on the topic. As Burton Mack put it, "Religion thought of as traffic-with-the-divine implicitly works with an anthropology of the autonomous individual, not with a social anthropology."[81] Seeing ancient religion as a social formation brings us closer to understanding religion in the ancient world. Reading the ancient religious context as an age in decline, an age of anxiety for the lost individual in search of contact with the divine, makes it impossible to see the complex relationship between fiction and religion in the Greco-Roman world. So we need to reconceptualize religion for our purposes. Following Burton Mack, one can profitably study religion as a set of social actions in the intersection between social formation and mythmaking.[82]

To study religion as social formation is to pay attention to the social forces that generate the specific religion(s) as active and ongoing social processes.[83] In this sense, social formation refers to a "specific and coordinated system of beliefs, acts, and institutions that construct the necessary conditions for shared identities."[84] Mythmaking refers to the way in which images, stories, and exempla from the past (ancestors, events, concatenated strings of events as history) are configured and used to construct and shape a collective imagination about the present and to make a world in which to live. World in this sense is understood as a *habitus*, an imagined order of things as social context for the present, so that the symbols of the mythic world not only act as vehicles for political and cultural representations but also for the social interests generating the whole process.[85]

Wilson; Leiden: Brill, 1998), 51–72. Consider also Philip A. Harland, *Associations, Synagogues, and Congregations: Claiming a Place in Ancient Mediterranean Society* (Minneapolis: Fortress, 2003), 120: "The traditional view reflects modern distinctions between politics and religion, that, as Simon Price also stresses, do not fit the ancient context, where the social, religious, economic, and political were intricately interconnected and often inseparable. Second, the view involves the imposition of modern notions concerning 'individualism,' 'private' vs. 'public,' and related definitions of religion (such as those offered by William James and Rudolf Otto) stress emotions or feelings of the individual as the heart of religion, emphasizing an equation between 'personal' or 'private' and genuine religiosity, and there is a tendency among some scholars to apply this to antiquity ... However, such individualistic and (sometimes) antiritualistic definitions of religion are problematic when applied to non-Western (or even non-Protestant) religious phenomena, modern or ancient."

81. Mack, "Radically Social Theory," 129.
82. Ibid., 131.
83. McCutcheon, "Redescribing 'Religion,'" 58—a reference to the work of Jonathan Z. Smith.
84. Ibid., 59.
85. Mack, "Radically Social Theory," 133.

Late antique religion, including the mysteries of the Hellenistic and imperial age, did not lead to a growing individualization but rather to the reverse, to a "heightened, if redefined, social reality."[86] Hellenistic cultural fragmentation led not to individualism but to a plurality of subcultures. Participation in religious activities was a kind of socialization, the opposite of which was to be a wanderer.[87] So, to cease to be a wanderer is to be socialized into a religious association. Salvation had to do with status conferred through group membership.

In the formation and maintenance of such religious groups secrecy played an important constitutive part. However, far from having as its purpose to hide the myth of the religious or mystery cult group, the keeping of secret had a social function, namely to strengthen social cohesion and to serve as a facilitator in the imagination of a second world alongside the manifest world.[88] So the mysteries to which the novels are related as myth are social formations organized in the same manner as other religious groups in antiquity, functioning in the same manner, that is, they were focused more on ritual enactments than on secret teachings. Piety and religion in antiquity were more attuned to the performance of rituals within group or communal settings as ways of establishing and maintaining the correct relationships with the gods than with individual, solitary experiences.

When viewed like this, the whole question of the relationship of the Greek novels with mystery religious cults can be redefined: the novels are not coded remains of mystery cult secrets we would not otherwise have known, but part of the same social construction of reality in which all the other instances of imperial era literary production, iconographic portrayals, and religious cult groups, including the mysteries, were embedded. What we should consider are the intersections between various ensembles of images, imagined histories, imagined social space, and social actions. On this score, it is not so important to attempt to relate the various novels to specific mysteries or mystery cults as Merkelbach did in his *Roman und Mysterium*, for what is important is the social discursivity of

---

86. Luther H. Martin, "The Anti-individualistic Ideology of Hellenistic Culture," *Numen* 41 (1994): 125.

87. See ibid., 127, for a discussion of the wanderer terminology in mystery religions (examples: Apuleius's *Golden Ass* 11.20 and the *Homeric Hymn* to Demeter 133; a Mithraic inscription promises "life to wandering humans").

88. Luther H. Martin, "Secrecy in Hellenistic Religious Communities," in *Secrecy and Concealment: Studies in the History of Mediterranean and Near Eastern Religions* (ed. Hans G. Kippenberg and Guy G. Stroumsa; SHR 65; Leiden: Brill, 1995), 108: "The 'doing' of secrecy, in other words, is not primarily a concealing of some knowledge, but rather embodies the ritual procedures necessary for the formation and maintenance of social boundaries" (110).

the cult and its "cultic technologies," and at this level there is a large
overlap and similarity between the various mysteries.

It is not by coincidence that the mysteries experienced a flowering
exactly in the imperial era, and furthermore, it is not by coincidence that it
is exactly those mysteries that flower that have imperial overtones—Dionysus, Isis, Helios/Mithras, and the imperial mysteries themselves. In fact
there is evidence of considerable overlap between them; imperial mysteries
were often inserted into other mysteries, and the emperors integrated into
the other cults, so that being a Demetriast, or Dionysus *mystikos* often
meant simultaneously being an imperial *mystikos*. (Although there is no
direct evidence of the incorporation of imperial mysteries into cult associations of Isis or Sarapis in Asia, we do have an inscription from Rome about
a group of παιάνισται [paean singers], probably originally from the Greek
East, who chose both the Sebastoi gods and Sarapis as their divine patrons.
This might suggest that rituals for the imperial gods were a normal part of
the activities of this group.)[89] A well-known inscription of the Demetriasts
at Ephesus demonstrates how the imperial gods could be important for the
self-identity and practices of the group concerned:

> To Lucius Mestrius Florus, proconsul, from Lucius Pompeius Apollo-
> nios of Ephesus. Mysteries and sacrifices are performed each year at
> Ephesus, lord, to Demeter Karpophoros and Thesmophoros and to the
> revered gods (*theois Sebastois*) by initiates with great purity and lawful
> customs, together with the priestesses. In most years these practices
> were protected by kings and revered ones, as well as the proconsul of
> the period, as contained in their enclosed letters. Accordingly, as the
> mysteries are pressing upon us during your time of office, through my
> agency the ones obligated to accomplish the mysteries necessarily peti-
> tion you, lord, in order that, acknowledging their rights....[90]

The imperial gods are incorporated within the ritual life or mysteries
of this group, and if we can state with Philip Harland that "the mysteries
were among the most respected and revered acts of piety in the Greco-
Roman world, and that few actions so effectively maintained fitting
relations between the realm of humans and that of the gods," then we
must conclude that the empire formed the core of all symbolic constructions of reality.[91] If ritual is "action wrapped in a web of symbolism" and
if through ritual a conceptualization of the world is constituted, then the

---

89. *IEph* 213; cited by Harland, *Associations*, 131.

90. Ibid., 117–18.

91. Imperial mysteries themselves could be consciously modeled on other mysteries
such as those of Dionysus, Demeter, Kore and so on; see ibid., 129.

mythical discourse that accompanies ritual enwraps the action with numerous instances of story/narrative and graphic portrayals.[92] That is not all: the invention of new myth, new prose narratives, exuberant utopian fantasies can all be linked to the unleashed creativity that was the early empire. The symbolism is the same everywhere: to survive and overcome in an adventurously dangerous world.

It is in this sense that one should understand the statement by Averil Cameron that novelistic literature provided the emerging Christian world with a kind of mythic structure and so served to create a new worldview.[93]

A final consideration must be given to the prosopography of both the novels and the mysteries. There is no direct evidence that ties any of the novels with any mystery cult group, but there is some indirect evidence regarding the personages involved in both. For example, Chariton, the author of *Chaereas and Callirhoe*, not only reflects the realities of cultic politics of his home city, Aphrodisias in Caria, but also the city promotes itself as imperial cult center making an intimate connection between Aphrodite of Aphrodisias, the Julio-Claudian house (Venus Genetrix being an ancestor), and Rome. Chariton himself is a member of the city elite, and secretary to the lawyer Athenagoras. Similarly the novelist, Antonius Diogenes (*The Wonders Beyond Thule*) comes from Aphrodisias.[94] The mysteries of Mithras may have been invented by military and civilian dependants of the dynasty of Commagene as it made the transition from client rulers to Roman aristocrats in the mid to late first century C.E. Moreover, with regard to the cult of Isis, inscriptional evidence would suggest that it was the elites (scholars, statesmen, generals, courtiers, priests, ambassadors) that formed the majority of adherents of the cult (not least because of the high costs involved in becoming an initiate), with a minority from the lower classes.[95] Similarly, the archaeological evidence with regard to the mysteries of Dionysus suggests that these mysteries involved the well-to-do rather than any

---

92. See, for instance, the interplay between myth and ritual in a Mithras cult artifact in Roger Beck, "Ritual, Myth, Doctrine, and Initiation in the Mysteries of Mithras: New Evidence from a Cult Vessel," *JRS* 90 (2000): 145–80. If the imperial mysteries can be taken as normal case for what went on in other mysteries, then the audience/participants would have seen drama/tableaux-vivant, dances, mythical portrayals, processions with showings of sacred objects and images, hymn singing and choruses, and spectacular light effects; cf. H. W. Pleket, "An Aspect of the Imperial Cult: Imperial Mysteries," *HTR* 58 (1965): 337–44.

93. Averil Cameron, *Christianity and the Rhetoric of Empire: The Development of Christian Discourse* (Berkeley and Los Angeles: University of California Press, 1994), 89–119.

94. Bowersock, *Fiction as History*, 38–39.

95. Cf. Sarolta A. Takacs, *Isis and Sarapis in the Roman World* (Leiden: Brill, 1995).

kind of underclass.[96] If we add what we know of the imperial mysteries, where priesthoods and other offices were occupied by the local elites, then we can safely say that the two groups—those who played a leading role in the mysteries and those who produced literature—came from the same social niche.[97]

All the same, despite benefiting from an imperial peace in a period of cultural efflorescence, the way to live meaningfully in a Roman world was to face backward into a glorious Greek past. It is therefore not unwarranted to state, somewhat akin to Matthew Arnold's "English" as literature of the new ideology and mythology of the English middle classes,[98] that the social and cultural matrix that generated both the mysteries and the novels is the same. The social discourse that generated the novels is the same discourse that generated the mysteries of the imperial era. And it is the latter, the imperial context, that provides the link between the two. In a very roundabout way it can indeed be maintained that the Greek novels are mystery texts, provided one reinterprets both literature/fiction and religion. And then Merkelbach was right after all, but in ways he did not imagine.

96. Martin P. Nilsson, *The Dionysiac Mysteries of the Hellenistic and Roman Age* (Lund: Gleerup, 1957), 146.

97. See Christine M. Thomas, "At Home in the City of Artemis. Religion in Ephesos in the Literary Imagination of the Roman Period," in *Ephesos Metropolis of Asia: An Interdisciplinary Approach to Its Archaeology, Religion, and Culture* (ed. Helmut Koester; Harvard Theological Studies 41; Valley Forge, Pa.: Trinity Press International, 1995), 115.

98. Terry Eagleton, *Literary Theory: An Introduction* (Oxford: Blackwell, 1983), 24.

PART 2:
JEWISH NARRATIVE

MIDRASH AS FICTION AND MIDRASH AS HISTORY: WHAT DID THE RABBIS MEAN?

Chaim Milikowsky

INTRODUCTION

To determine what people believe is never an easy task.[1] To determine what a large cultural-social entity believes seems to me to be impossible—unless that entity is both extremely homogeneous and also very successful in closing itself off from ideas and beliefs existing outside of it. Even on the level of formal, socially-constructed acts, we know well that very often the same act in one cultural context can have many different meanings to the various actors who perform that act. To state the obvious then, there is rarely one answer as to "what the rabbis thought" or "what the rabbis meant" on just about any subject. While concerning a few basic points of dogma, there was complete agreement, even with regard to the rabbis of one generation it would be foolhardy to conclude "what they believed." Most assuredly, this is true for all the rabbis of some five or so centuries. The range in time between the beginning and end of rabbinic culture is equivalent to our distance from Columbus, or to take a closer parallel, from the time of Jerome and Augustine, at the turn of the 5th century, until the 9th century. Thus when I say I want to determine "what the rabbis mean," I refer only to what some rabbis mean. I admit—indeed, I assert—that I am presenting only one side of a multi-faceted picture—an image purposely skewed to emphasize a side of rabbinic discourse, which seems to me to have been neglected.

To phrase my question in the most vulgar way possible: Did the rabbis believe in the historicity and facticity of the stories found in

---

1. This paper was presented on November 24, 1997, at the Annual Meeting of the Society of Biblical Literature in San Francisco. It has been only mildly revised, and very minimal annotation has been added. Were I to write the paper anew today (September 6, 2004), I would change some of the emphases. I deal at length with some of these questions in my forthcoming critical edition of, commentary on, and introduction to *Seder 'Olam* (Israel Academy of Sciences and Humanities, in press).

midrashic literature? Phrasing the question this way presumes that the notions of "historicity" and "facticity," notions which I assume are understood by my contemporaries, were also understood by the rabbis, and that this question would have meaning for them. This implicit presupposition of my question, now just made explicit, will be an important factor in our deliberations and will come to the fore shortly. My answer is no; the rabbis about whom I am talking did not believe that the stories we find in midrashic literature actually depict the events of the past.

To our modern temper, this answer seems obvious and is the answer we desire; this of course is the nub of the problem. Perhaps we tend to give this answer because we desire it. After all, we can pick up pointers from midrash itself, as well as from the larger cultural context surrounding rabbinic midrash—specifically, from patristic references to rabbinic historical exegesis—which seem to imply that rabbinic midrash was meant to be taken as historical fact. Hence, it may appear that we ignore the evidence and find what we desire.

I will engage my above conclusion in dialogic—or if you prefer, rabbinic—style, by detailing some possible objections to my conclusion that the rabbis did not believe midrashic literature depicted events of the past, and my responses to these objections. These responses will lead me to the analysis of one of the several passages found in midrashic literature, which prompted the conclusion stated so boldly above.

Exegesis versus Historiography

Most immediately, a strong objection to my position is the fact that most premodern societies accept the veracity and facticity of their traditions. Countless passages could be cited to illustrate this central difference between the premodern, on the one side, and the modern and post-modern on the other.[2] There is, of course, some validity to this argument. I do not want to argue that all the events detailed in rabbinic literature lacking biblical warrant were not accepted as historically true. I have little doubt that stories of venerable antiquity were accepted and no one would think to doubt them. The crucial point here, however, is that

---

2. Excellent in this regard are Paul Veyne, *Did the Greeks Believe in Their Myths? An Essay on the Constitutive Imagination* (trans. Paula Wissing; Chicago: University of Chicago Press, 1988); Geoffrey E. R. Lloyd, *Demystifying Mentalities* (Cambridge: Cambridge University Press, 1990); Ruth Morse, *Truth and Convention in the Middle Ages* (Cambridge: Cambridge University Press, 1991); and Christopher Gill and Timothy P. Wiseman, eds., *Lies and Fiction in the Ancient World* (Austin: University of Texas Press, 1993).

this is true only for "stories of venerable antiquity," an ambiguous phrase. Anyone who has read extensively in rabbinic literature knows that the overwhelming majority of midrashic additions to the Bible story-line are not presented as independent narrative, but are rather presented in an exegetical mode.[3]

For example, the midrash says that Abel had defeated Cain in their struggle and was about to kill him when Cain begged for mercy; Abel released him, and Cain then "got up" and killed Abel. How do we know this? Because the Bible says וַיָּקָם קַיִן אֶל־הֶבֶל אָחִיו וַיַּהַרְגֵהוּ, "And Cain got up onto his brother Abel and killed him" (Gen 4:8). If it says that Cain "got up onto his brother," that means that previously he was under his brother; after all, if all the Bible had wanted to say was that Cain killed Abel, it could have simply said, וַיַּהֲרֹג קַיִן אֶת הֶבֶל אָחִיו, "And Cain killed his brother Abel" (Genesis Rabbah 22:8).[4]

Another example: Moses killed the Egyptian by means of pronouncing the Holy Ineffable Name. In many midrashic texts, this tradition is connected to the statement of the Hebrew addressed to Moses in Exod 2:14: הַלְהָרְגֵנִי אַתָּה אֹמֵר כַּאֲשֶׁר הָרַגְתָּ אֶת־הַמִּצְרִי, "Will you kill me, you say, as you killed the Egyptian?" The words אַתָּה אֹמֵר, "you say," are a bit perplexing: Why should they refer to "saying" or "speaking"? The midrashic explanation is that Moses killed the Egyptian by speaking, that is, by means of the Divine Name; thus his blow against the Egyptian was spiritual in nature, not physical (Exodus Rabbah 1:30).[5]

The emphasis on the exegetical basis for much of midrashic narrative is not new: it has been known for thousands of years. More recently, much of James Kugel's book, In Potiphar's House, deals with just such matters: showing how so many narratives found in midrashic literature are generated out of exegetical tensions in the text.[6] These midrashic stories then are not presented as traditions that have been received from one's predecessors but rather as being the result of creative activity by those who craft new cultural matter.

It is difficult to generalize on these matters. On the one hand, there is little doubt that many exegetical traditions represented by the midrashic text were not generated for the first time at that moment; on the other hand, other exegetical traditions are clearly new creations, ex nihilo. This,

---

3. Let me note that I am dealing with early rabbinic midrash here, not late works like Tanhuma or Pirqe Rabbi Eliezer, where storyline is more often a dominant element of the text.

4. Bereshit Rabbah [Hebrew] (ed. Theodor-Albeck; Jerusalem: Wahrman, 1965), 214.

5. Midrash Shemot Rabbah [Hebrew] (ed. A. Shinan; Jerusalem: Dvir, 1984), 91.

6. James Kugel, In Potiphar's House: The Interpretive Life of Biblical Texts (San Francisco: HarperSanFrancisco, 1990), passim.

however, brings me to the second point I wish to refute. In that sprawling essay of Paul Veyne, *Did the Greeks Believe in Their Myths,* there is a wonderful passage about Hesiod: "Because of the dissymmetry that characterizes knowledge based upon faith in another, Hesiod knows we will take him at his word, and he treats himself as he will be treated: he is the first to believe everything that enters his head."[7] This is a perspective that cuts to the heart of one of the great chasms between our mode of understanding the past and the essential premodern understanding of the past. A medieval historian who invented events or documents was neither necessarily intent on deceiving his audience, nor had he failed to understand the difference between history and nonhistory. Rather, his basic presuppositions concerning God's working in history caused him to be the first to believe the "history" he is presenting. Similarly, Hesiod's presuppositions about his relationship with the Muses make him believe the "history" he is presenting.

So, perhaps the rabbis in the same way also believed the "history" they are presenting. Though much of it was original, and not traditional material to be accepted unquestioningly, we can nonetheless sustain the position that, in various contexts, new traditions were accepted as historical facts, even by those who created them. Indeed, in a sense, this point borders on the obvious: all human cultural traditions are at one time new creations. Thus from a theoretical perspective, a good case can be made in favor of the claim that midrashic narrative was accepted as historically true by the rabbis.

Before we respond to this basic point and before we turn to those elements of rabbinic literature that lead to the conclusion that midrashic narrative was at its base fiction; that is, it was not meant to represent the historical past, we must return to that presupposition mentioned above— that it is valid to distinguish in the rabbinic cultural world between (a) a mode of retelling the past where everything being retold is, from the perspective of the teller, truthful and factual, and (b) a nonfactual representational mode of retelling the past.

In general, there is at present a strong tendency in the study of ancient historiography to collapse together history and fiction. To quote a recent one-line summary of Detlev Fehling's book, *Herodotus and his "Sources,"* by Kraus and Woodman: "'scholarly' [i.e., ancient scholarly] conventions of historiographic narrative are purely mendacious."[8] A few

---

7. Veyne, *Did the Greeks Believe in Their Myths,* 29.

8. Christina S. Kraus and Anthony J. Woodman, *Latin Historians* (Greece: New Surveys in the Classics 27; Oxford: Oxford University Press, 1997), 4; cf. Detlev Fehling, *Herodotus and His "Sources": Citation, Invention and Narrative Art* (trans. J. G. Howie; Leeds: Cairns, 1989).

pages later, when discussing Woodman's own book, *Rhetoric in Classical Historiography,* the claim is presented that when Roman historians profess to be telling the "truth," they are not denying that they are doing what in our terms would be called "fabrication."[9]

Many reviews of these two works fall into the "yes but" category. Yes, there is a lot of mendacity and fabrication in classical historiography—more than the modern (I use modern here as an ideological term, not as a temporal term) desire to see ancient historiography as the close forerunner of our historiographic method would allow—but this does not justify the complete rupture of any barrier separating history and fiction in the ancient mind.

This tendency of some modern historians to redefine ancient historiography as more connected with the literary than with what we call the historical has refocused critical discussion in many important ways. First, to quote from Stephen Greenblatt's comments regarding a medieval travel narrative called "Mandeville's Travels:"

> There is something at once misleading and sentimental about this saving invocation of art. Misleading because it detaches the work from its truth claims and from the history of its reception, a history based not upon a willing suspension of belief but upon trust; sentimental because it reinforces familiar modern conceptions of intentionality and originality exactly where they are most powerfully challenged.[10]

Second and much more important for our purposes, I do not think this entire discussion is relevant to our question. The difference between the perception of the facticity of the events of the past in the Greco-Roman world and the perception of the facticity of the events of the past in the Jewish world was immense: as is obvious to any reader of rabbinic literature, or for that matter, of Josephus. No one in this cultural world questioned the facticity of the events described in the Bible, not necessarily for reasons of religious piety, but primarily because they were a given.[11] Contrast this to the extreme discomfort caused by the Homeric corpus. As is well known, though no one in the ancient world questioned the fact that there had been a Trojan War, many did question the

---

9. Kraus and Woodman, *Latin Historians,* 6; cf. Anthony J. Woodman, *Rhetoric in Classical Historiography: Four Studies* (London: Routledge, 1988).

10. Stephen Greenblatt, *Marvelous Possessions: The Wonder of the New World* (Chicago: University of Chicago Press, 1991), 33.

11. Note that rabbinic literature does recognize the validity of the claim that the events told in the book of Job never took place and that the entire book is only a parable.

facticity of both the divine and human tales contained in the *Iliad* and the *Odyssey*.

Thus, in the Greco-Roman world, the very foundation of its retelling of the past (i.e., the stories of Homer), combined already at an early time, for many of its readers, elements of fact and fiction. In the Jewish world, on the other hand, the foundation of its retelling of the past (i.e., the Bible) contained only fact. I would therefore be much more hesitant in claiming that Jewish culture collapsed together history and fiction, as did a prominent strand—if not the predominant strand—in Greco-Roman historiography.

Furthermore, the idea that historical retelling permits the conjunction of past event with fiction presupposes an interest and need in reconstructing the past—for whatever purpose. This purpose in the classical world is often related to their present, but nonetheless it is past event that is being retold. If the actual facts that the reconstructor "knows" are not sufficient for the necessary reconstruction or can lead to the incorrect reconstruction—that is, the incorrect reconstruction from the perspective of the reconstructor—then it is necessary to devise what we would call fiction.

Returning now to midrash, it is quite possible that this interest in reconstructing the past simply does not exist. Without denying that there is a strand in midrashic literature that does want to depict the past, it seems immediately obvious that, from a formal perspective, midrashic narrative is not to be identified as historiographical narrative. As we can see in the two examples I discussed briefly, not only is the story generated by the exegesis, but it is formally blocked off from the biblical verse which is being utilized as its source. We make, in our minds, a narrative out of the text in front of us; on its own, it is not narrative but exegesis.

The question facing us has to move therefore from a historiographic context to a more hermeneutic context. The historiographic question centers on the relationship of this additional story drawn from the biblical text to the story that was drawn from the biblical text before this new story was added, and the hermeneutic question centers on the relationship of midrashic exegesis to nonmidrashic exegesis.

Midrashic Distinctions between Historical and Nonhistorical Events

There is a well-known tendency among certain schools of thought to flatten out the differences among various modes of interpretation. To quote one of many possible representations of this view: "Literal meaning is the product of the application of a norm, social in nature, hence arbitrary, rather than a result of the operation of a law."[12] This mode of conceptualization about text and meaning, although sometimes useful, is definitely of questionable utility when dealing with rabbinic exegesis. It is the very nonliteralness of God's message, the opacity and mystery of it, which makes the rabbis' role in proclaiming God's word to the people so central.

Thus the very fact that the history-type narrative found in midrash is connected formally to a midrashic exegetical operation and is presented in contrast to the biblical flow of events should convince us that the narrative does not make claims of facticity and historical veracity. I think it worthwhile to contrast the mode of representation found in midrash with the mode of representation found in *Jubilees*, or Artapanus, for that matter. These latter books treat the events depicted in the Bible together with the events not depicted in the Bible indistinguishably; indeed from reading their works one would not know which event had a biblical pedigree and which not.

Quite plausibly, however, many will not be convinced that this formal argument is sufficient to indicate that the rabbis themselves were distinguishing between the historical events of the Bible and the nonhistorical events of the midrash. I will try now to buttress my position.

First of all, there is the very fact of the existence of one work in the rabbinic corpus that is historiographic in nature—though a very specific type of historiography. This work is called *Seder ʿOlam*.[13] It is a chronography of the world detailing the dates of biblical events from the creation until the end of the biblical period, when Alexander conquered the Persian Empire. What is especially important is the fact that this work contains almost no storyline additions to the biblical narrative. Just about every sentence not directly derived from the Bible is concerned with details of the biblical story: How old was Isaac at the time of the binding? How long did the Israelites remain in Egypt? How many years did Joshua lead the nation?

It cannot simply be a coincidence that not one of the midrashic plot lines so well known from midrashic literature is found in *Seder ʿOlam*: not Noah and his neighbors, not Abraham and the idols, not Moses as a child

---

12. Hayden White, *The Content of the Form: Narrative Discourse and Historical Representation* (Baltimore: Johns Hopkins University Press, 1990), 115; White was paraphrasing Foucault.

13. See note 1. This work is often wrongly called *Seder ʿOlam Rabbah*. *Seder ʿOlam* is the title of this work in the Babylonian Talmud and in the vast majority of medieval citations. The name *Seder ʿOlam* Rabbah (the greater *Seder ʿOlam*) was generated many centuries later to distinguish this early rabbinic composition from a late Geonic composition entitled *Seder ʿOlam Zuta* (the lesser *Seder ʿOlam*) and unfortunately entered common usage because the printer of the *editio princeps* used it.

in Pharaoh's house. Quite clearly, *Seder 'Olam* does not consider these midrashic additions to the biblical narrative as historical events needing dating as do the binding, the exodus, and the leadership of Joshua. Note well: *Seder 'Olam* has no hesitation in adding his own exegetetically-derived data to the biblical data. His claim that the binding of Isaac took place when Isaac was twenty-six years old would not be considered in his own eyes as being on the same level of historical veracity as the very fact of the binding or the biblical statement that Abraham was one hundred years old when Isaac was born, yet he has no problem in presenting his reconstruction as historical fact.[14] Nonetheless, of typical midrashic additions to the biblical story line, there are none. Note also the exegetical additions to the Bible are presented not as exegetical discourse but as narrative; the statement that details the age of Isaac at the time of the binding is not marked off formally from the statement that Isaac was bound.

The very fact that this book is part of the rabbinic corpus indicates that at least for some elements in the rabbinic cultural world, there was a clear demarcation between what is considered a historical reconstruction of the past and the midrashic use of the biblical text to create a new story having no aspirations to talk about the past.

Let us now turn to a famous story found in the Babylonian Talmud, *b. Ta'anit* 5b. While sitting together at a meal Rav Nahman asked Rabbi Yitzhaq to expound on some subject. After some preliminary diversions, Rabbi Yitzhaq said in the name of Rabbi Yohanan, "Our father Jacob never died." Rav Nahman was taken aback by this claim and said, "But he was embalmed and buried." How is possible to do such things to someone who has not died? Rabbi Yitzhaq responds and says, מקרא אני דורש, "I am engaged in Bible elucidation," and he then cites Jer 30:10, "Therefore fear not, my servant Jacob, says the LORD; be not dismayed, Israel, for I will save you from afar and your seed from the land of their captivity." He continues, "Israel is compared to his seed; just as his seed is alive so too is he alive."

At first sight, it appears that the midrashic statement denying Jacob's death is being derived from Jer 30:10. However, if we look closer at the passage, we will find a fascinating distinction between the biblical deathbed scenes of Abraham (Gen 25:8) and Isaac (35:29), on the one hand, and that of Jacob (49:33), on the other. In the former scenes, two verbs, גוע, "expired," and מות, "died," and one phrase, וַיֵּאָסֶף אֶל־עַמָּיו, "was gathered to his people," are used to describe their deaths. Regarding

---

14. *Seder 'Olam* 1. None of the presently available editions of *Seder 'Olam* have twenty-six as Isaac's age at the time of the binding.

Jacob, however, only two verbs appear: expiring and being gathered to his people. For the midrashist, the absence of any verb from the root מות, "to die", in the description of Jacob's death cannot be by chance, but must be understood as communicating to us the Bible's message that Jacob did not die.

According to the story, Rabbi Yitzhak's statement to Rav Nahman was made in a completely neutral context—that is, outside of any context whatsoever. Consequently, Rav Nahman understood this claim as being functionally parallel to a claim such as "Elijah did not die." The characteristic position of rabbinic Judaism is, of course, that Elijah never died but is still alive; indeed, according to the rabbis, he is the heavenly recorder of human deeds.[15] Rav Nahman therefore asked Rabbi Yitzhak: But Jacob was embalmed and buried, so how can you claim he did not die. Rabbi Yitzhak's response, מקרא אני דורש; "I am engaged in Bible elucidation," and the citation of Jer 30:10, is not given to tell us the source of his previous statement, for as we have just seen, its source is the absence of any mention of death in Jacob's deathbed scene. What he is doing is saying the following: "You have misunderstood me; my statement that Jacob did not die is not to be understood as a literal-historical depiction of historical facts, but as midrash." Midrash comes to tell us a story placed in the biblical text by God, having no necessary relationship to the actual historical events, but whose purpose is to give us a message from God. That message is being explained to Rav Nahman by Rabbi Yitzhaq's citation of Jeremiah. God's exclusion of any mention of Jacob's death is a promise found midrashically in Genesis and explicitly in Jeremiah: for Rabbi Yitzhaq, Jacob's nondeath is a promise that his seed shall exist forever.

This midrash and its surrounding narrative are important because they give what we desperately need in reading midrash: a cultural and theoretical context. The original misunderstanding by Rav Nahman and the final exposition by Rabbi Yitzhak show, as clearly as possible, that midrashic narrative is explicitly demarcated from the historical-literal reconstruction of past events. Midrash is the rabbis' reconstruction of God's word to the Jewish people and not the rabbis' reconstruction of what happened in the biblical past.

---

15. See *b. B. Bat.* 121b and *Leviticus Rabbah* 34:8 (ed. Mordecai Margulies; Jerusalem: Wahrmann, 1972), 790–91.

WHY THE RABBIS USED FICTION

The issue, then, is as follows. As noted above, never in rabbinic literature is the facticity of the events described in the Bible questioned. The rabbis, like most other social groupings in Judaism of the ancient world, postulated a direct one-to-one correspondence between the biblical narrative and the events of the past. Yet we have just shown that rabbinic literature itself contains narratives that are clearly understood to be nonfactual in terms of the "story" they tell. Why should the rabbis develop a mode of discourse that tells the truth by means of fictional events, when the only literature they have in front of them is the Bible, which tells the truth by means of true historical events?

What is fascinating is to compare this rabbinic objective to something Plato says quite openly in the *Republic*. At the end of the second book, after his vigorous attack on Homer and Hesiod, Socrates says, "therefore it is most important that the tales which the young first hear should be models of virtuous thoughts," but immediately adds in reply to Adeimantus' question, "You and I, Adeimantus, at this moment are not poets, but founders of a State: now the founders of a State ought to know the general forms in which poets should cast their tales, and the limits which must be observed by them, but to make the tales is not their business."[16] Already we see that composition of stories about the gods is too important to be left to the impious or to the vagaries of chance.

A few paragraphs later, the point is made—still hidden—but explicit. When talking of the possibility of God lying, Socrates says, "Also in the tales of mythology, of which we were just now speaking—because we do not know the truth about ancient times, we make falsehood as much like truth as we can, and so turn it to account. But can any of these reasons apply to God? Can we suppose that he is ignorant of antiquity, and therefore has recourse to invention?"[17]

As strange as this idea of "creating new myths" seems to us from our modern anthropological perspective, it seems that the rabbis did something very similar to what Plato proposed—and it worked! I am not suggesting that reading Plato was part and parcel of rabbinic culture; the idea is preposterous. Nonetheless, I do want to propose that there is some sort of a relationship between the subject of Plato's discussion and the beginnings of rabbinic narrative midrash. Plato had a problem: he recognized that a culture needed stories that portray ultimate meaning in

---

16. Plato, *Resp.* 378e–379a (Benjamin Jowett, trans., *The Republic of Plato: An Ideal Commonwealth* [New York: Willey, 1901], 59).

17. Plato, *Resp.* 382 c-d (Jowett, *Republic of Plato*, 64).

various ways. Much of his cultural matter—the myths of Homer and Hesiod—he rejects out of hand, not because they are fictions, but because they are immoral fictions. As is well known, the rejection of traditional myth as a valid mode of depicting the gods spread through larger and larger segments of the population during the late Hellenistic and early Roman period. These tales, having been generally seen throughout Greek history as having ultimate moment for mankind, were now seen by many as fictions, either harmful fictions, as we saw above with Plato, or innocuous fictions, like the romances, which began to develop just about this time, or ultimate fictions, which is of course dependent upon transferring the truth value of the myth from the historical tale to some underlying sublime claim.

These various ways of judging and valuing the traditional stories of myth were widespread and popular and very plausibly penetrated rabbinic culture in Palestine. I would like to suggest, therefore, that the rabbinic presentation of their responses to ultimate issues by means of fictional tales—that is, their creation of midrashic narratives—developed in consequence of the broad identification of large segments of Greek traditional tales as fiction. From the Greek world, the rabbis took the basic idea that fiction is a valid way of projecting and proclaiming one's beliefs and practices.

CONCLUSION

Midrashic literature contains countless storyline additions to the biblical narrative, and the rabbis could and did demarcate between midrashic plot-additions whose function was to present God's word and historical-literal reconstruction of past events. In our modern terms, then, these midrashic plot-additions are indeed fiction, though perhaps a better term, based upon Plato's usage, would be "creative mythology."

Mimesis and Dramatic Art in Ezekiel the Tragedian's *Exagoge*

Jo-Ann A. Brant

Introduction

Adaptations of texts for a different medium are never simply retellings of stories. When Ezekiel the Tragedian adapts the story of Moses found in the biblical narrative for the stage, like other ancient dramatists, he kills the narrator and brings characters closer to his audience by putting them dramatically before our eyes. The characters speak for themselves and reveal the workings of their minds.[1] The plot becomes less about what characters do than "what they are told, and how they feel at the telling."[2] Narrative becomes embodied memory and, therefore, personal experience of suffering, and the action becomes the language of the characters, their debate and expression of internal dispositions, their conflicting viewpoints and shifting perceptions.[3] These features of Ezekiel's dramatic art have implication for how we treat the significance or purpose of any creative activity or deviation from the biblical account in which Ezekiel engages.

Preliminary Matters

Before getting to my argument, I will quickly lay out the nature of our extant version of the *Exagoge* and presuppositions about Ezekiel's use of particular Greek tragedies as hypotexts and the rationale for those assumptions.

---

1. Stephen Halliwell, "Traditional Greek Conceptions of Character," in *Characterization and Individuality in Greek Literature* (ed. Christopher Pelling; Oxford: Clarendon, 1990), 58.

2. Richard Lattimore, *The Poetry of Greek Tragedy* (Baltimore: Johns Hopkins University Press, 1958), 331.

3. P. E. Easterling, "Constructing Character in Greek Tragedy," in Pelling, *Characterization and Individuality in Greek Literature*, 91.

Preservation of the Exagoge

Little is known about the author of the *Exagoge* or its provenance, and
little remains of the play. The work was written in Greek sometime
between the appearance of the Septuagint and an extant citation of the
play in the first century B.C.E. Howard Jacobson, in his important monograph, *The Exagoge of Ezekiel*, reviews various arguments and concludes
that the play was written in Alexandria during the latter half of the
second century B.C.E.[4] The fourth-century church historian Eusebius preserved the following fragments:

— Moses, in a monologue, reports the events of Exod 1:1–2:15
  (1–59)
— Sepphora greets Moses (60–65)
— Sepphora's dialogue with a man named Chum about her mar-
  riage to Moses (66–67)
— Moses relates his vision of a heavenly throne and his own
  coronation to Raguel (Jethro) (68–82)
— Raguel interprets the dream as a good sign from God (83–89)
— Moses and God's dialogue at the burning bush (90–119)
— Moses and God's dialogue about the miraculous rod and lep-
  rous hand (120–131)
— God reports the action of Exod 4–8 (132–174)
— Moses instructs the Hebrews on how to perform the Passover
  (175–192)
— An Egyptian messenger reports the events at the Red Sea
  (193–242)
— A Hebrew scout reports about the oasis at Elim and the sight-
  ing of a strange bird. (243–269)

Eusebius gave no idea and was, perhaps, unaware of how the play ended.

In general, the extant fragments of Hellenistic Jewish writers were
preserved by authors who had no interest in their literary merit. While
Eusebius preserved 269 lines of metered verse, his interest lay not in
Ezekiel but in Alexander Polyhistor (ca. 105–35 B.C.E.), a Greek historian,
whom he quoted.[5] Eusebius intended to demonstrate that famous Greeks
were familiar with Jewish history and interested in Jewish authors,
rather than to affirm this volume's hypothesis that Jewish authors were

---

4. Howard Jacobson, *The Exagoge of Ezekiel* (Cambridge: Cambridge University Press,
1983), 5–17.

5. Eusebius, *Preparation for the Gospel* 9.1.203b–c.

interested in Greek literature. Polyhistor used Ezekiel as a source for Jewish history and probably obscured the plot of the play in the way he excerpted material. The two remaining ancient sources provide nothing beyond what is found in Polyhistor. Clement of Alexandria (ca. 150–215 C.E.) cited material from the prologue to substantiate his claim that Moses had an extensive Hellenistic education.[6] Eustathius, bishop of Antioch (ca. 324–330 C.E.), preserved the last extant fragment because he considered it a reference to the Phoenix.[7] Modern scholars tend similarly to be disinterested in Ezekiel's dramatic art and treat the *Exagoge* as a source for earlier Jewish mythology or hagiography concerning the person of Moses.[8] Other than interest in Ezekiel's anachronistic use of iambic meter, little attention has been given to the genre of his work except insofar as its form as a tragedy makes the identification of mimesis possible.

Established Proof of Ezekiel's Mimesis of Greek Tragedy

Whereas many biblical scholars are reticent to recognize the influence of Greek literature upon canonical texts, scholars who have treated the *Exagoge* have no qualms about detecting imitation of the classics in the fragments, which for the most part follow the events of the biblical exodus. Scholars of the *Exagoge* conclude that Ezekiel had before him Aeschylus's *Persians* and *Suppliant Women* and appropriated Euripides' usage and dramatic techniques. Howard Jacobson, building upon the foundational work of Joseph Wieneke and others, provides extensive evidence of verbal echoes and direct borrowing of content from the *Persians*.[9] John Strugnell supplements this work by demonstrating that Ezekiel's metrics are closer to those of Euripides than to his contemporary tragedians.[10] Their findings satisfy the six criteria for determining mimesis set out by Dennis R. MacDonald.[11] Satisfying the criterion of accessibility,

---

6. Clement of Alexandria, *Strom.* 1.23.

7. PG 18:729.

8. Rare exceptions to this statement include B. Snell, "Die Jamben in Ezechiels Moses-Drama," *Glotta* 44 (1966): 25–32; and John Strugnell, "Notes on the Text and Metre of Ezekiel The Tragedian's *Exagôgê*," *HTR* 60 (1967): 449–57.

9. Howard Jacobson, *Exagoge of Ezekiel*, passim; Joseph Wieneke, "Ezechielis Iudaei poetae Alexandrini: Fabulae Quae Inscribitur" (Ph.D diss., University of Münster, 1931); Snell, "Die Jamben in Ezechiels Moses-Drama," 25–32; Peter M. Fraser, *Ptolemaic Alexandria* (3 vols.; Oxford: Oxford University Press, 1972).

10. Strugnell, "Notes on the Text," 453.

11. Dennis R. MacDonald, *The Homeric Epics and the Gospel of Mark* (New Haven: Yale University Press, 2000), 8–9.

Ezekiel, as a playwright and Jew with a Hellenistic education, would have had access to the classic Greek tragedies. Jacobson meets the criterion of analogy by listing numerous cases of Hellenisitic and Roman use of Aeschylus as a hypotext.[12] Proof for fulfillment of the third criterion, density, obtains in the number of verbal echoes (no less than fourteen within forty-nine verses) from the *Persians* found by Jacobson within the messenger speech.[13] Jacobson demonstrates that the fourth criterion, order, is satisfied when he outlines the striking similarities between the messenger speeches in the *Persians* and the *Exagoge*.[14] Both contain inquiries and explicit expressions of confidence about the numbers of the army, both attribute the victory to divine intervention and attach importance to the cycle of day and night, and both describe their enemy crying out to their god. Evidence for the fifth criterion, distinctiveness, may lie in Ezekiel's use of compounds such as εὐάνδρου (203) and Aeschylus's use of πολυάνδρων (533, 899) found in other parts of the *Persians*.[15]

MacDonald's final criterion is interpretability or intelligibility; that is, some purpose for using the hypotext must be evident in the hypertext.[16] Jacobson argues that Ezekiel hoped to win favor for the Jews from a Greek audience by showing "that Greek-Persian history could be seen as an analogue to Jewish-Egyptian."[17]

Evidence against a Greek Pagan Audience

A number of observations about the habits of Hellenistic theatre-goers and about the *Exagoge* as a theatre piece puts into question the hypothesis that Ezekiel wrote for a Greek audience. First, the wholesomeness of the *Exagoge* contrasts with the fragments we have of other Hellenistic plays. Extant fragments of Hellenistic plays suggest that the Hellenistic audience preferred comedies and mimes containing ribald plots about the lives of the lower classes.[18] A fragment of a work by

---

12. Jacobson, *Exagoge of Ezekiel*, 27.
13. Ibid., 136–40.
14. Ibid.
15. Ibid., 137.
16. MacDonald, *Homeric Epics and the Gospel of Mark*, 9.
17. Jacobson, *Exagoge of Ezekiel*, 138.
18. John R. Green, *Theatre in Ancient Greek Society* (London: Routledge: 1994), traces the development of Greek theater by examining archaeological evidence. Mosaics such as the ones found at Pompeii depicting scenes from Menander (111–12), monuments indicating that substantial sums of money were invested in the staging of New Comedy (113), and kraters depicting comic actors as slaves (118–19), as well as the absence of fragments of tragedies other than that belonging to Ezekiel, point to the popularity of comedy.

Herondas from third century B.C.E. Egypt contains a discussion between two middle-class women about the virtues of a particular dildo. Another fragment from Herondas dramatizes a mother and schoolmaster flogging a truant son. While Hellenistic audiences may have mustered the energy to attend a revival of a classical tragedy, it is difficult to imagine that they would have been attracted to this new play written in anachronistic language.

Secondly, the prologue presupposes an audience familiar with the biblical narrative. The ancient audience had no playbill and no elaborate sets. The prologue of a play oriented the audience to the setting and identified the characters upon the stage. The first line of the play, "[w]hen Jacob left Canaan," provides the first point of orientation, the end of the patriarchal narrative.[19] If the audience members were Greek, one would expect more detail about Jacob, for example that he was the father of the twelve tribes of Israel, the ancestor of the Jews, or some such epithet. In the *Exagoge,* Moses delivers the prologue by summarizing Exod 1:1–2:15, but first offers his name thirty lines into the speech. The design of the prologue resembles those delivered by familiar characters from mythology or Homeric epics. For example, in the prologue to *Alcestis,* Apollo begins by greeting the, "House of Admetus," and then refers to his past encounter with that house; he refers to his son Asclepius, and a number of other markers of his identity are given. Although we do not hear his name until he is addressed by Death thirty lines into the play, an audience even minimally familiar with Greek mythology already has put a name to the character.[20] This gradual unfolding of information in the *Exagoge* is designed to give the audience the pleasure of recognizing Moses before he introduces himself. Much of the entertainment and suspense of classical drama depends upon precognition of the audience.

Finally, the *Exagoge* stands in continuity with classical tragedy in that it does not mediate tradition. As the following analysis will demonstrate, the *Exagoge* plays with tradition.

---

19. All quotations from the *Exagoge* are taken from Jacobson, *Exagoge of Ezekiel.*
20. In addition, Apollo carries a bow and arrows—added clues to his identity.

Ezekiel's Mimesis of the Form and Function of Tragedy

The Prologue and Discrepant Awareness[21]

An examination of Moses' lines illustrates how Ezekiel has shifted the action from the plot of the exodus; that is, he shifts focus from a description of God's deliverance of his people to Moses' experience of that event. The action of the play begins in *media res:* Moses is a wandering fugitive in foreign territory that Sepphora identifies as Libya, a land occupied by black Ethiopians (Ezekiel seems to have constructed his geography from assorted literary sources rather than a map or personal experience). Moses delivers a prologue that draws the audience into the eternal present of the stage by giving it a role: the audience becomes the people to whom Moses justifies his presence in Libya. As we come to understand his predicament, the story of the Israelite experience in Egypt becomes the unfolding action upon the stage with Moses as its focal point. The striking feature of his representation of the past is his insistence upon his identity as a Hebrew over against a possible Egyptian identity:

> Till this day we have been ill-treated....
> Pharaoh ... saw our people increasing in numbers,
> devised many plans against us. (5–8)

In Moses' retelling of his own story, he emphasizes that his Hebrew education happens before his Egyptian education:

> When my infancy had passed,
> my mother brought me to the princess' palace,
> after telling me all about
> my lineage and God's gifts. (32–35)

The first-person pronoun emphasizes Moses' Hebrew identity for the audience.

Keir Elam argues, "the drama consists first and foremost precisely in this, and I addressing a *you here* and *now*" and assigns these little words the status of the "most significant linguistic feature—both statistically

---

21. According to Froma I. Zeitlin, discrepant awareness is a form of irony in which "one character knows and the other doesn't or ... none of the characters know but that the audience does" ("Playing the Other: Theater, Theatricality, and the Feminine in Greek Drama," in *Nothing to Do with Dionysos? Athenian Drama in Its Social Context* (ed. John J. Winkler and Froma I. Zeitlin; Princeton: Princeton University Press, 1990), 74. Discrepant awareness provides pleasure and suspense for an audience that knows things about the protagonist that he himself does not know.

and functionally—in the drama."[22] Use of personal pronouns can also signify conflict by creating opposition. This is seen most clearly in dialogue when the "I" is opposed to a "you," but it is also apparent in the contrast that Moses constructs between his royal upbringing and acts of his own volition:

> [T]he princess gave me a royal upbringing and education,
> as if I were her own son.
> But when I grew into an adult,
> I went forth from the royal place
> at my spirit's urging (θυμός μ᾽ ἄνωγε), to see the deeds and devices
>   wrought by the king. (36–41)

Moses repudiates the identity imposed upon him as the object of his royal Egyptian upbringing by becoming the subject of his syntax and making the designs of Egyptian royalty his subject.

With one exception, little in Moses' narration of his childhood contradicts the biblical account. In Moses' version he is left dressed but exposed by the bank of the river, and he makes a telling comment about the source of his knowledge: "mother hid me for three months (so she has told me) (ὡς ἔφασκεν)" (14–15). The audience knows a slightly different and perhaps more dangerous story in which Moses is placed in a basket. In the *Exagoge*, Jochebed, unlike the biblical narrator, is not completely trustworthy. Jacobson treats this discrepancy between the exodus and the *Exagoge* as evidence of Ezekiel muting unsavory elements of the biblical story for an unassuming Greek audience, but if one takes this approach to Ezekiel's departures from the Bible, one misses his use of the dramatic technique of discrepant awareness.

Discrepant awareness comes into play again when Moses relates why he has fled Egypt. He describes a conflict between an Egyptian and a Hebrew but says nothing about an imbalance of power between the two men:

> First, I saw two men fighting,
> one a Hebrew, the other an Egyptian.
> I saw that we were alone, no one else was present.
> So I rescued my kinsman and slew the other. (42–45)

He eliminates the moral grounds for killing the Egyptian and makes his motivation his own ethnic identification with the Hebrew. In contrast, the author of Acts emphasizes the moral grounds for striking the Egyptian in Stephen's recount of the story (Acts 7:23). Philo provides foreground to the

---

22. Keir Elam, *The Semiotics of Theatre and Drama* (London: Routledge, 1980), 22.

murder by describing Moses' exhortations to the Egyptian to stop beating the Hebrew and his belief that the destruction of the Egyptian was a pious act (*Moses* 1.44). In the *Exagoge*, Moses glosses over the ethnic identity of the second of the two men (i.e. the "other") obscuring the fact that in the biblical account he flees Egypt because he fears exposure by the Hebrews.

Recognition of Moses' Role as a Feature of Plot

The puzzle that Ezekiel's changes present must be solved by the action into which the prologue takes us. Unfortunately we have only two lines of dialogue with which to reconstruct what that initial action is. Chum, a character whom Ezekiel seems to have invented, states "Sepphora, you must reveal this" (ὅμως κατειπεῖν χρή σε, Σεπφώρα, τάδε) (66), to which Sepphora responds. "My father has given me as spouse to this stranger" (ξένῳ πατήρ με τῷδ᾽ ἔδωκεν εὐνέτιν) (67). Polyhistor implies that these lines belong to a longer dialogue lacking in the present text. The telltale marks of dramatic conflict are found in our two short lines in the use of personal pronouns. Chum makes an offensive move with his demanding use of the pronoun σε and Sepphora a defensive one with her use of the first-person με. Jacobson suggests that Chum is the thwarted suitor of Sepphora and argues that the *Exagoge* follows the action of Aeschylus's *Suppliant Women* in which the daughters of Danaus flee Egypt in order to escape marriage from the sons of Aegyptus. Ezekiel inverts Aeschylus's plot by having the suitor flee Egypt and denying his Egyptian identity in order to be recognized as a suitable groom.[23] Jacobson grounds his speculation in the dramatic similarity between the initial encounters in both plays. I find support for his hypothesis, however, in the next fragment of the *Exagoge* in which Moses relates a dream to Raguel, his father-in-law. Raguel's reception of the dream provides further evidence that the action of the play centers upon Moses' suitability as a spouse for a daughter of Libya (Midian). We, the audience, cast in the role of residents of Libya, are meant to weigh the reception of Moses based upon what he has told us from our vantage point above the action in which we know Moses will play a part unanticipated by the denizens of the play.

The Dramatic Function of Moses' Dream and Its Interpretation

Moses' dream coupled with his father-in-law's interpretation and the encounter with the portent of the burning bush are stock conventions in

---

23. Jacobson, *Exagoge of Ezekiel*, 24–25.

Greek tragedy.[24] While scholars such as Carl Holladay recognize them as such, treatments of these elements typically ignore their dramatic function. Carl Holladay argues: "Since it was a stock stylistic device to incorporate a dream into the narrative of Greek tragedies, it is clear that Ezekiel includes the dream-scene to impress his readers with a knowledge of Greek literary conventions as well as his finesse in handling them."[25] Wayne Meeks finds in the *Exagoge* "a witness to traditions of the second century B.C.E. that God gave to Moses unique powers as king and prophet," but he concedes that no other piece of literature, which he considers, combines "the offices of kingship and prophecy so directly."[26] Historical critics such as Meeks and Holladay attempt *to reconcile the tension* between the dream and the interpretation to determine what portrait of Moses Ezekiel intends "to emerge." The dramatic role of the dream and interpretation *is to produce tension* by allowing characters to construct different dramatic worlds. The tension in the drama or the interest of the audience is sustained along the projected and conflicting possibilities of these two worlds. Which one will prove reliable, whose expectations will

---

24. Aeschylus makes the most frequent use of this convention. See for example, *Persians,* 176–214 (Atossa's dream is accompanied by the portent of an eagle flying for refuge to Apollo's temple); *Prometheus Bound* 645–667 (Io's dream is followed by an clear oracle from Loxias commanding her father Inachus to expel her from his home); and *Libation-Bearers* 32–80, 170–210 (the chorus' dream of the earth calling out for vengeance is followed first by the request for an avenger as a sign that the earth's demands should be satisfied and then the discovery of signs of Orestes' return, first a lock of hair and then his footprints in the sand).

25. Carl R. Holladay, "The Portrait of Moses in Ezekiel the Tragedian," *Society of Biblical Literature 1976 Seminar Papers* (SBLSP 15; Chico, Calif.: Scholars Press, 1976), 447–52.

26. Wayne Meeks, *The Prophet-King: Moses Traditions and the Johannine Christology* (NovTSup 14; Leiden: Brill, 1967), 149–50. According to Meeks, "The meaning of this divine investiture is probably no different from the more common apocalyptic imagery in which the ascended hero is seated at God's left or right or shares God's throne, that is Moses becomes God's vicegerent." The concept of a vicegerent with whom God shares the signs of his majesty does not appear in any conclusive form until *Midrash Rabbah.* Pieter W. van der Horst, "Moses' Throne Vision in Ezekiel the Dramatist," *JJS* 34 (1983): 25–27, while recognizing the conflict between dream and interpretation, contends that the scene implies a "deification of Moses." John J. Collins, *The Scepter and the Star: The Messiahs of the Dead Sea Scrolls and Other Ancient Literature* (Garden City, N.Y.: Doubleday, 1995), 145, argues that the vision is "the virtual apotheosis of Moses" and uses this as a datum to support Wayne Meeks's contention that the tradition of Moses as god and king is older than Philo's *Moses:* "For he was named god and king of the whole nation. And he was said to have entered into the darkness where God was, that is, into the formless and invisible and incorporeal archetypal essence of exiting things, perceiving things invisible to mortal nature." Collins makes an important point, "While the enthronement of Moses can be grounded exegetically, it is not demanded by exegesis, and would hardly have occurred to an exegete who was not already familiar with some traditions of heavenly exaltation, though not necessarily the particular ones that are attested in the Christian era."

be proven wrong or what new reality will emerge?[27] Ezekiel's plotted world is no longer that "truthful" representation of reality offered by the biblical narrator, but rather the worlds offered by the various characters. Both Moses' representation of his vision and his father-in-law's interpretation make his dream the story of Moses' fate or glorification. The audience "on high" balances this with the story told in the Bible and perhaps with a growing Intertestamental tradition of visions of a heavenly throne.[28]

Moses' Self Revelation in His Dream

Moses' dream differs from Daniel and 1 and 2 *Enoch*, which focus upon descriptions of a heavenly throne and end with a revelation about eschatological judgment.[29] It is like the vision found in the *Testament of Levi*, where the narrator describes what happens to himself before the throne. Levi describes putting on the vestments of the priesthood and the crown of righteousness, the oracle of understanding, the robe of truth, the breastplate of faith, the miter for his head, and the apron for prophetic power (*T. Levi* 8). Unlike Levi, however, who recognizes the presence on the throne to be that of God, Moses sees only a noble man (γενναῖόν) with a crown and a large scepter in his left hand (70). Neither Moses nor Raguel identify the noble man with God. Ezekiel exploits the dramatic irony of Moses' inability to understand his own dream and to explain his ambivalent reaction to it.

Moses begins by describing his own enthronement and coronation. An audience familiar with the biblical story should easily recognize that the dream lines up with Moses' experience on Mount Sinai, which he does ascend, where he has a vision of God and from whence he returns transformed. In Moses' retelling of the dream, the object in the noble man's hand becomes a scepter, the instrument of royal power. Set within the plot of the exodus, and perhaps the *Exagoge* as well, Moses receives the instrument of divine rule, the Torah, or a rod, an instrument of divine power. Ezekiel may be employing a hermeneutical technique similar to that found in the midrashic literature whereby he takes what is in the Bible and something analogous to human experience and then con-

---

27. Elam, *Semiotics of Theatre and Drama*, 114–5.

28. Ithamar Gruenwald (*Apocalyptic and Merkavah Mysticism* [Leiden: Brill, 1980], 128–30) and van der Horst ("Moses' Throne Vision," 21–29) both locate the dream within the Merkavah tradition, but Howard Jacobson rejects this interpretation in his article, "Mysticism and Apocalyptic in Ezekiel's Exagoge," *Illinois Classical Studies* 6 (1981): 272–93.

29. Dan 7:1; *1 En.* 37–71; and *2 En.* 24–36.

fuses the two. For example, midrashic literature takes Moses' radiance to mean he is wearing a crown.[30] Ezekiel seems to have used the same technique when Moses identifies the object in the noble man's hand as a crown that is then handed to him. The same strategy may be at work when Moses describes the multitude of stars that fall before his knees and his attempt to count them. A knowledgeable Jewish audience ought to contextualize Moses' dream within the narratives of Abraham and Joseph where stars represent people. David Winston disagrees and situates this reference in the developing Merkavah tradition arguing that Ezekiel depicts Moses as a cosmic figure of semidivine stature.[31] In the later midrashic tradition, the smoke enveloping Sinai through which Moses must pass in order to descend to the people becomes an angelic army with which Moses does battle.[32] Given the association of stars with angels, it is possible that Moses is expected to see angels but what he reports is stars; nevertheless nothing in the fragments of the play sustains this interpretation. Ezekiel's interest, true to the tragic form, seems to lie in the tragic characterization of Moses. When Moses says, "They [the stars] paraded past me like a battalion of men," he does not see them as the people whom he will deliver from bondage, but rather as a military force and as a result he reports that he awoke in fear (82). As in other dramatic retellings of dreams, his speech serves to dramatize emotion and characterize him as a timid leader.[33]

The Questionable Interpretation of Moses' Father-in-Law

In the tragic convention of allegorical dreams, interpretations are misleading and favor the dreamer. For example, in the *Persians*, Atossa rightly responds to her dream in which she sees, with a sense of foreboding, her son yoke a Persian and a Greek woman: "These signs have struck my eyes with dread, your ears no less" (210–211). The chorus of *The Persians* puts a positive spin on Atossa's dreams saying, "we predict that, be

---

30. Rimon Kasher, "The Mythological Figure of Moses in Light of Some Unpublished Midrashic Fragments," *JQR* 88 (1997): 30.

31. David Winston, "New Light on an Old Drama," *Jud* 35 (1986): 113.

32. *Pesiq. Rab.* 20; *Sipre* 306; *Pirqe R. El.* 46; and *Exod. Rab.* 28; 42:4. This tradition is treated at length in Kasher, "Mythological Figure of Moses," 19–42.

33. In *Iphigenia at Tauris*, Euripides uses the tension between Iphigenia's dream, which she relates in her prologue and interprets to mean that Orestes is dead (42–60), and the audience's knowledge that Orestes is alive to create dramatic tension. The dream also points to her cold resignation to her role as a priestess who performs sacrifices and her lack of hope. In his *Rhesus*, the driver of Rhesus's chariot, who is given to paranoia that they will be harmed by allies, dreams of being attacked by wolves, and then interprets the dream as a sign that some injury has been done to them by friends (756–803).

these omens good or bad, all will be well" (225–226).[34] The juxtaposition of Atossa's fear with the chorus' optimism provides dramatic tension. Raguel's pronouncement, "My friend, this is a good sign from God" (83) and his wish, "May I live to see the days when these things are fulfilled" (84), serve a similar purpose by setting in tension the emotions of the two figures on stage. The dream that terrifies Moses pleases Raguel. This sort of tension is the stuff of drama. A sister grieves on stage over a dead brother who stands before her in disguise secretly celebrating reunion.[35] A daughter rejoices in her self-sacrifice to her country, while her mother laments her child's fate.[36] One sister sees honor in violating a law to bury a brother; the other, only more grief in flouting the will of the people.[37] And in the *Exagoge*, Moses wakes in terror from a dream over which Raguel rejoices.

Rather than contextualizing the dream within the Jewish tradition, Raguel seems to set it within the Greek traditions of Zeus' throne and of Apollo and the powers of his prophet. When Ezekiel writes that Moses' vision of the world below and the heavens above signify that he "will see what is, what has been and what shall be," (ὄψει τά τ' ὄντα τά τε πρὸ τοῦ τά θ' ὕστερον (89), he may have as his hypotext *Iphigenia at Tauris* or the *Iliad*. In Euripides' play the chorus sings a stasimon to Apollo in which they describe his ascent to his father's throne and how Apollo sits upon that shrine and through dreams reveals "to the mass of mortals both things that once were and things destined to later fulfillment" (1265–1267).[38] When Homer describes the gifts of Kalchas in the *Iliad*, he uses remarkably similar language, "Kalchas ... who knew all things that were, the things to come and the things past" (*Il.* 1.70).[39] Raguel's insistence that Moses will establish a great throne and become a judge and leader of men express his confidence in a world in which there is a direct correspondence between what one dreams and what happens. But neither the Greek literary tradition nor the biblical tradition supports this confidence.[40] The fact that Raguel does not attribute his interpretation to

---

34. Translation by Philip Vellacott, *Prometheus Bound, The Suppliants, Seven Against Thebes, The Persians* (Harmondsworth, U.K.: Penguin, 1961), 128.

35. Sophocles, *Electra* 1126–1170.

36. Euripides, *Iphigenia at Aulis* 1433–1444.

37. Sophocles, *Antigone* 67–79.

38. *Euripides IV* (ed. and trans. David Kovacs; LCL 10; Cambridge: Harvard University Press, 1999), 291.

39. *The Iliad of Homer* (trans. Richard Lattimore; Chicago: University of Chicago Press, 1950), 61.

40. In Homer's *Odyssey*, Penelope describes the two gates of dreams: "My friends, dreams are things hard to interpret, hopeless to puzzle out, and people find that not all of

God ought to lead a Jewish audience to question his view of the world. Past interpreters of the *Exagoge*, the most influential of whom is Wayne Meeks, have led us in the wrong direction by ignoring the genre of the *Exagoge* and hence the purpose of its conventions. In the dream and its interpretation, Ezekiel is not drawing from tradition but is engaging in the sort of activity that generates haggadic midrash. He is exploiting the ambiguities and the language of the text to explore various worlds that might open out from it, in particular, the way the characters depicted in the text view the world.

The Play of Perspective in the Remaining Fragments

The Burning Bush

The next series of fragments present the scene at the burning bush into which Ezekiel has collapsed a great deal of the action of Exod 4:18–13:16. In this scene, Ezekiel emphasizes the distinction between the divine perspective and that of Moses. Picking up on the characterization of Moses as the reticent leader found in the biblical narrative, Ezekiel dramatizes this through the sounds and words that come from Moses' lips. He greets the sight of the burning bush with a gasp by vocalizing the sound ἔα. When the rod becomes a snake, Moses pleads with God:

Oh Master, be merciful.
How dreadful, how monstrous. Have pity on me.
I shudder at the sight, my limbs tremble. (124–126)

The longest preserved speech in the *Exagoge* belongs to God who narrates the story of the plagues and the observance of the Passover as a prediction of events to come. The lack of dramatization of the plagues does several things. First God's narration becomes a boast about what he will accomplish, and Moses' role in the conflict disappears from view:

I shall bring a multitude of frogs and lice upon the land.
Thereafter, I will sprinkle on them ashes from a furnace....
I will bring darkness for three whole days

---

them end in anything. There are two gates through which the insubstantial dreams issue. One pair of gates is made of horn, and one of ivory. Those of the dreams which issue through the gate of sawn ivory, these are deceptive dreams, their message is never accomplished. But those that come into the open through the gates of the polished horn accomplish the truth for any mortal who sees them. I do not think that this strange dream that I had came to me through this gate" (19.560–569; *The Odyssey of Homer* [translation by Richmond Lattimore; New York: Harper & Row, 1967], 296–97).

and will send locusts which will destroy...
Thus, I shall bring to an end the arrogance of this evil people. (135–148)

This litany of plagues serves a second purpose. By describing the plagues in quick succession and ignoring the dialogues between Moses and Pharaoh, Ezekiel moves the play away from the central conflict of the biblical narrative—that is, the contest between the divine will represented by Moses and that of Pharaoh. Enough of the play remains to show that the action of the play is not what happens off-stage but rather the pathos and reversals of those who experience the action off-stage.

The Crossing of the Red Sea

The crossing of the Red Sea is told in retrospect through the convention of a messenger speech, a survivor of the Egyptian army. This speech with its antithetical structure and its dramatic turns in emotion provides us with evidence of Ezekiel's competence as a dramatist. Like the speeches of the great tragedians, the messenger has subjective participation in the story by focalizing the army through the use of certain epithets and head counts. While the action is in the past, the messenger moves through the account as though the action were unfolding in order to emphasize the dramatic turns, the reversal of emotion.

The messenger begins with a detailed description of the Egyptian force including military formations (193–201) and troop strengths:

I inquired as to the total number of the army:
it came to one million men. (202–203)

As in classical messenger speeches, the report is more than an account of the action. Simple devices, such as the inclusion of the adjective "awesome" (φρικτὸς, 197) and the provision of an unnamed authority for the size of the army to provide credibility to his account, point to the messenger's lack of objectivity. He represents the action not from a position of hindsight, but rather with the emotions and from the perspective of someone who witnessed the scene. Similar strategies can be found in the messenger speech in Euripides' *Suppliant Women*, which narrates the battle that ensues when Theseus attempts to recover the dead bodies of Polynices and six Argive champions who have been defeated by Creon, the king of Thebes (650–730). In this text, the messenger corroborates his report by explaining where he stood to see what he claims to have seen, by appealing to information given to him by others, and by providing first person quotations. He betrays his subjective reporting through his own reaction to events and by frequently praising Theseus and imputing cowardly motives to Creon. Ezekiel's messenger embodies the arrogance of the Egyptian army in his description of it and his claim "my army overtook the Hebrews" (204). His confidence in an Egyptian victory is dramatized in the contrasting picture he paints of the disarray and turmoil of the Hebrew camp. The Egyptian army moves in ordered formations, whereas the Hebrews "were lying in groups by the shore of the Red Sea.... Flocks and household utensils were all around" (205–209). He contrasts the Israelite fear and panic with the Egyptian desire for battle and patience:

> We in contrast were delighted ....
> Since the sun was on the verge of setting,
> we waited, desiring a morning battle:
> we were confident in our numbers and our fearsome weapons. (215–219)

The mood of the speech changes suddenly with the account of the pillar of cloud. The Israelites become the ones described with positive epithets and the Egyptians, the ones overcome by panic. The messenger brings the past to the present and confirms his own interpretation of the event, "It seemed that God was helping them," (235–236) by relating the words of one Egyptian soldier in the first person:

> Let us run back home and flee the power of the Supreme One.
> For He is helping them, but is wreaking
> our destruction. (239–241)

In this statement, Ezekiel replaces the words of the Egyptians found in Exodus prior to the surge of water (φύγωμεν ἀπὸ προσώπου Ισραηλ· ὁ γὰρ κύριος πολεμεῖ περὶ αὐτῶν τοὺς Αἰγυπτίους LXX 14:25) with the cry of a single drowning soldier. Of course, the words reflect Ezekiel's convictions; they could hardly have been those of an Egyptian soldier.

In the biblical account, no Egyptian survives to comprehend fully what has happened. The significance of the Egyptian messenger's recognition of God's role in the salvation of the Israelites and the destruction of his army to the action of the play becomes clear when, in the last remaining fragment, the Israelites seem unable to recognize the divine hand that is guiding them. Once again, the audience enjoys the irony that, even though an Egyptian could recognize God's agency, the Israelites do not. Moreover, given that the Egyptian has recognized God agency, it seems likely that Ezekiel would include in the conclusion of his action some form of recognition of God by the Israelites.

The Scout's Report

Into the last scene that Polyhistor preserves for us (the return of scouts to the Israelite camp), Ezekiel seems to have conflated a number of biblical events. It appears to be a conflation of Exod 15:27, in which the

Israelites camp briefly at Elim before setting out on their desert wanderings, and Num 13 where scouts are sent out to explore Canaan. While the extant ending does not provide evidence for how the play comes to an end and leaves us wondering whether the receipt of the law at Sinai played any role in it, the fragment with its contraction of the longer storyline of the exodus does give hints about the central action of the play.

In the last scene, once again, Ezekiel employs the conventions of the messenger speech to relate events not easily staged. But again, the purpose of the messenger speech is not simply a way around a technical difficulty for the dramatist. The messenger through his speech clarifies the discrepancy between how characters upon the stage perceive the action and what the audience understands. Jacobson, I think rightly, argues that Ezekiel turns the scene into a "Hellenistic Utopia." The scout describes something more enticing than the small oasis capable of sustaining only twelve trees described in Exod 15:27. He describes a spot by a verdant valley with seventy fruit bearing palms fed by twelve springs flowing from a single rock (244–252). He begins, "Great Moses, take note of the place we have discovered" (243–244). While the scout does note that they saw "some sort of sign, a pillar of light" (247), he repeats once more "we discovered a shady meadow and springs of water" (248). God's agency is all but ignored. For the scout, the number of springs and palms signify the fertility of the space beyond the stage. When he observes, "There is grassland with water around about, forage for our animals" (252–253), he sees a physical rather than a spiritual reality. The numbers twelve (the tribes of Israel) and 70 (the elders of Israel) cannot be insignificant for a Jewish audience and suggest a symbolic interpretation of the space. Where the scout sees only pasture for beasts, his words point to a place in which the Israelites, God's people, can dwell. The audience sees the promised land itself.

The remainder of the fragment seems to be a continuation of the scouts' report and describes a fantastic bird as an object of curiosity. In an extensive study of the ancient tradition of the phoenix, R. Van den Broek observes that when ancient authors wished to proclaim an event significant they tied it to the appearance of a phoenix.[41] If Ezekiel's bird is meant to be a phoenix, as Eustathius and many modern readers take it, then the scout fails to recognize that what he has seen is a portent of a significant event. The action of the scene, the dramatization of ignorance, suggests that what follows ought to be a scene in which the Israelites

---

41. R. van den Broek, *The Myth of the Phoenix according to Classical and Early Christian Traditions* (trans. I. Seeger; Leiden: Brill, 1971), 113.

recognize their mistake. The action of the earlier fragments, Moses' anxious reception of his dream and divine portents, Raguel's divergent interpretation of that dream as Moses' rise to power, the pathos at the Red Sea when the false hubris of the Egyptian army leads to their destruction, and the misinterpretation of the scouts anticipates some sort of disappointment and reversal. The action is conflated so that the crossing of the Red Sea anticipates the crossing of the Jordan. It is logical to surmise that the *Exagoge* ends as the Pentateuch ends: Moses does not enter into Canaan to ascend a throne and rule over the Israelites. Instead, he ascends Mount Nebo and dies in sight of the promised land.

EZEKIEL IN THE CONTEXT OF EARLY JEWISH FICTION

Through his imitation and exploitation of the conventions of tragic drama, Ezekiel opens the door for the sort of first person interpretation that becomes characteristic of midrashic literature. This development is seen in the *Testament of the Twelve Patriarchs* and the *Genesis Apocryphon* in which the omniscient narrator is replaced, altogether or in part, by the monologue of a character from the biblical narrative. For example, in the *Genesis Apocryphon* the fictitious voice of Abram allows for the sort of apologetic about his behavior in Egypt that would be required by readers sympathetic to Abram. Abram recounts how the men who return to Pharaoh describe Sarah:

> and beautiful is her face! How ... fine are the hairs of her head! How lovely are her eyes!! How desirable her nose and all the radiance of her countenance.... How fair are her breasts and how beautiful all her whiteness! How pleasing are her arms and how perfect her hands .... When the king heard the words ... he sent out at once to take her ... and took her to be his wife, but me he sought to kill. Sarai said to the king, "He is my brother," that I might benefit from her, and I, Abram, was spared because of her and I was not slain. And I, Abram, wept aloud that night, I and my nephew Lot, because Sarai had been taken from me by force. (20)[42]

Abram then prays to the Lord for justice:

---

42. Translation by Geza Vermes in *The Dead Sea Scrolls in English* (4th ed; London: Penguin, 1995), 218.
    43. Ibid., 219.

Judge him for me that I may see Thy mighty hand raised against him
and against all his household, and that he may not be able to defile my
wife this night. (20)[43]

The third-person narrative, which embellishes the biblical account, shifts
dramatically to the first person. This allows Abram to gloss over his own
role in handing Sarah over to Pharaoh by having him verbalize his private emotions, prayers and desires.

In its final manifestation, rabbinic midrash veers away from the unity
of the tragic form. It continues to represent the voice of characters including the divine voice but diminishes the authority or power of fiction to
represent reality in competition with the authority of scripture by frag-
menting the unity of the dramatic representation. The treatment of Exod
3:3 in *Exodus Rabbah* provides a typical example of rabbinic midrash. To
Moses' line "I must turn aside and see why the bush is not burned up,"
R. Simeon b. Lakish provides God's first person fictitious response, "This
man is worthy to tend Israel." The authority of God's voice is immediately undercut by an alternative version of God's speech provided by R.
Issac, "this man is downcast and troubled at seeing Israel's affliction in
Egypt, he is, accordingly, worthy of being their shepherd." Several explanations of the doubling of Moses' name then follow. One of these
includes a short *mashal*.[44] As Chaim Milikowsky explains, the rabbis created fictions to elucidate the Bible rather than to talk about the past.
Layers of alternative versions and divergent retellings and interpretations, lists of scriptural citations, and digressions to illustrative *mashalim*
allow a polyphony of interpretation, but the rabbinic narrators must
point back to the text rather than a hypothetical reality of their own creation in order for the midrash to have coherency.[45] The biblical narrator
retains control of the unity of the narrative.

Aristeas closes with a question put by king Ptolemy Philadelphus to
Demetrius, the president of the king's library, and his answer, both of
which may shed light on why Judaism did not embrace the dramatic
form of tragedy. The king asks:

How is it that after such great works were (originally) completed, none
of the historians or poets took it upon himself to refer to them? (312)

Demetrius responds:

---

44. *Exod. Rab.* 2.6 (trans. H. Freedman and Maurice Simon; London: Soncino, 1939),
54–55.

45. Chaim Milikowsky, "Midrash as Fiction and Midrash as History: What Did the
Rabbis Mean?" pages 113–23 of this volume.

Because the legislation was holy and had come from God, and indeed, some of those who made the attempt were smitten by God, and refrained from their design. (313)

He then provides two illustrations, the last of which brings Ezekiel to mind:

I have also received from Theodectus the tragic poet (the report) that when he was about to include in a play a passage from what is written in the Bible, he was afflicted with cataract of the eyes. He suspected that this was why the affliction had befallen him, so he besought God for many days and recovered. (316)[46]

In response to these stories, the king "bowed and gave orders for great care to be taken of the books and for their hallowed preservation" (317). This story seems to be an apologetic suggesting why pagan poets do not refer to Moses and so does not deal with whether a Jewish author should write a play about Moses. While one did, neither posterity nor archaeology provides us with other contemporary Jewish plays. The tragic form in its representation of divine reality competed too directly with the authority of scripture to be tolerated.

Conclusion

The *Exagoge* is an example of a "faithful" retelling of a biblical story that makes use of Greek hypotexts, as subtly as the Gospel writers may have made use of Homer, but here it is made obvious because the genre of his work can clearly be identified as tragedy. Ezekiel's purpose in this mimesis of Greek tragedy is to accomplish what the biblical narrative does not do, that is to bring to exterior expression the pathos that lies in the background of the Hebrew narrative. Ezekiel exploits the elements and the ambiguity of that narrative to generate a world of divergent perspectives represented by the characters within it rather than by a detached narrator who controls the story.[47] The excitement of expectations to which diverse perspectives give rise and their subsequent realization or disappointment become the action of the play, rather than the deliverance of the Israelites from bondage.

---

46. Translation by R. J. H. Shutt, *OTP* 2:33–34.

47. I borrow the language for this description of the biblical narrator from Meir Sternberg, *The Poetics of Biblical Narrative* (Bloomington: Indiana University Press, 1987), 84–85.

DANIEL 1–6: A BIBLICAL STORY-COLLECTION

Tawny L. Holm

INTRODUCTION

An aspect of the book of Daniel that has received only minor atten-tion is its uniquely episodic nature, in that it seems to be a collection of discrete and separable stories and visions. One of the few who has remarked on this, Alexander Di Lella, writes:

> The Book of Daniel is logically divided into ten sections.[1]... This book is unique among all the books of the Bible, Old and New Testament, in that each of these sections forms a distinct unit separable from the rest. Any one of the ten sections could have existed independently of any of the others and would have been virtually as intelligible, or unintelligi-ble, as it now stands in the Book of Daniel. Or put differently, any one or more of the sections could have been lost, and the remaining sections would not have suffered in any significant way at all. Superficially, the book seems to be a collection of once isolated mini-works brought together by some unknown editor or redactor who despite his work as compiler could hardly claim the title of author of the whole book.... Yet there are certain features in the book that seem to point to one author or at most two for the whole work.[2]

Other scholars have not paid much attention to this particular aspect of the book of Daniel. Some simply state that the Daniel stories and visions are a "collection," or that the stories are even an *Erzählsammlung* or story-collection, but these seem to be mere terms of convenience with-out reference to any concrete genre or typology.[3] This is in spite of the

---

1. This includes the six stories that roughly correspond to each of chs. 1–6, and the four visions found in ch. 7, ch. 8, ch. 9, and chs. 10–12. Note that the division by language is as follows: Dan 1–2:4a and Dan 8–12 are in Hebrew, while Dan 2:4b–Dan 7 are in Aramaic.

2. Di Lella's introduction to Louis F. Hartman and Alexander A. Di Lella, *The Book of Daniel* (AB 23; Garden City, N.Y.: Doubleday, 1978), 9.

3. See for example: Reinhard G. Kratz, *Translatio imperii: Untersuchungen zu den aramäischen Danielerzählungen und ihrem theologiegeschichtlichen Umfeld* (WMANT 63; Neukirchen-Vluyn: Neukirchener, 1991), 5; and Rainer G. Albertz, "Bekehrung von oben

influence of Hermann Gunkel, Walter Baumgartner, and other scholars in the early twentieth century, who called Aḥiqar and the biblical narratives of Esther, Joseph, 1 Esdr 3, and Daniel "court tales" and compared them to similar tales in, for example, Herodotus and the *Arabian Nights* (*Alf laylah wa-laylah*, or the *Thousand and One Nights*).[4] Many subsequent biblicists have since understood the Daniel stories as Near Eastern "court tales," but few have dwelt long on the fact that the genre regularly appears in collected form, as in the *Arabian Nights*.[5]

Daniel (especially MT chs. 1–6) should be set against the background of the story-collection genre. The genre occurs in the well-known compositions of fourteenth-century European literature, such as Chaucer's *Canterbury Tales*, Boccaccio's *Decameron*, and Gower's *Confessio Amantis*, but its precursors are found in the literatures of the ancient Near East and India, as well as classical Greece and Rome. Among these antecedents one notes, for instance: the "Tales of Wonder" in the Egyptian *Papyrus Westcar* (containing perhaps the oldest frame narrative ever, dating to the first half of the second millennium B.C.E.), the *Aetia* of Callimachus (third century B.C.E.), Ovid's *Metamorphoses* (1–8 C.E.), and other famous but less datable compositions, such as Aesop's *Fables*,[6] the Indian *Pañcatantra*,[7]

als 'messianisches Programm': Die Sonderüberlieferung der Septuaginta in Dan 4–6," in *Theologische Probleme der Septuaginta und der hellenistischen Hermeneutik* (ed. H. Graf Reventlow; Veröffentlichungen der Wissenschaftlichen Gesellschaft für Theologie 11; Munich: Kaiser & Gütersloher, 1997), 48. Note also Jan Wim Wesselius's term "composed dossier," which reflects the segmented nature of Daniel but neglects the narrative aspect; see Wesselius, "The Writing of Daniel," in *The Book of Daniel: Composition and Reception* (ed. John J. Collins and Peter W. Flint; 2 vols.; VTSup 83; Leiden: Brill, 2001), 2:291–310.

4. See, for instance, Hermann Gunkel, "Esther" in *RGG*[2] 2:378–79; Walter Baumgartner, *Das Buch Daniel* (Giessen: Töpelmann, 1926), 9; and Curt Kuhl, *Die drei Männer im Feuer* (BZAW 55; Giessen: Töpelmann, 1930), 58.

5. For the most recent and thorough treatment of Daniel as part of a Near Eastern "court tale" genre, see Lawrence M. Wills, *The Jew in the Court of the Foreign King: Ancient Jewish Court Legends* (HDR 26; Minneapolis: Fortress, 1990). See also Susan Niditch and Robert Doran, "The Success Story of the Wise Courtier: A Formal Approach," *JBL* 96 (1977): 179–93; and W. Lee Humphreys, "A Life-Style for Diaspora: A Study of the Tales of Esther and Daniel," *JBL* 92 (1973): 220.

6. Aesop himself was said to have lived in the sixth century B.C.E., and already in the fifth century he was attributed with certain fables. The earliest extant collection of Aesopic *Fables* (the Rylands Papyrus 493) is dated by F. Rodríguez Adrados to the first century C.E., although it is probably ultimately based on a (lost) 300 B.C.E. collection by Demetrius Phalereus. See Adrados, *History of the Graeco-Latin Fable* (trans. Leslie A. Ray; 3 vols.; Mnemosyne, Bibliotheca Classica Batava, Supplementum 201; Leiden: Brill, 1999), 1:48–66, 410–21.

7. The Pañcatantra was perhaps written in Sanskrit in ca. 300 C.E., but its fables are commonly accepted to go back to 200 B.C.E. There was a Pahlavi translation in ca. 550 C.E. (now lost), from which the extant Syriac translation derived in ca. 570 C.E. The Arabic translation *Kalilah wa-Dimnah* is from ca. 750 C.E. (see Adrados, *History of the Graeco-Latin Fable*, 1:308–9).

and the *Book of Sindibad*.[8] Since some of the earliest antecedents are to be found in the same literary *milieu* from which Daniel arose, and because of Daniel's unique characteristics, a restudy of the book with the story-collection genre in mind seems fruitful.

When the book of Daniel is set against an explicit definition of the story-collection, it affects our conception of diverse aspects of textual criticism, the history of composition, and the overall nature of the book. The divergent texts (especially the Masoretic Text, the Theodotion version, and the Old Greek/Septuagint) of the narrative parts of Daniel are to be described as variant editions, or tellings, of common core material, rather than as translations of older written texts with clearly demonstrable genealogies or relationships. The ancient audience of Daniel probably expected creativity and not consistency between versions of a story.

In contrast to other approaches that look to Hellenistic Greek literature to illuminate Jewish and Christian texts, one may propose a closer look at the ancient Near East, particularly to Hellenistic Egypt, for literature in Aramaic and Egyptian with morphology and motifs similar to Daniel. The courtier stories from Egypt about "magicians," which often appear in story-collections and story-cycles, share significant correspondences with Daniel. The relationships between Daniel and its analogues do not necessarily fit into the narrow boundaries of intertextuality, but rather suggest the existence of common structural models of narrative and motifs, which shaped independent processes of textualization in these different literary traditions.

1. THE STORY-COLLECTION GENRE

It is within studies of medieval European story-collections, especially of the *Canterbury Tales*, that one finds a sound methodical approach to the story-collection genre.[9] Helen Cooper provides the following definition:

See also Hertel, *Das Pañcatantra: Seine Geschichte und seine Verbreitung* (Leipzig: Teubner, 1914), 9–11, 20–25.

8. The stories in the *Book of Sindibad* may go back to the fifth century B.C.E., but the earliest text is in Syriac dating to the tenth century C.E. (see Morris Epstein, *Tales of Sendebar* [Philadelphia: Jewish Publication Society of America, 1967]). Yet it is mentioned already by Arab writers in the eighth and ninth centuries C.E. who say that the origin of the Arabic version was Persia. The later western versions (e.g., the Greek *Syntipas*), which lack the sage Sindibad, are collectively known under the name *The Seven Sages of Rome*. The bridge between the earlier eastern versions and the western versions was probably the Hebrew *Mishle Sendebar*.

9. Especially Helen Cooper, *The Structure of the Canterbury Tales* (Athens: University of Georgia Press, 1983); idem, *The Canterbury Tales* (Oxford: Clarendon, 1989); and Piero Boitani,

A story-collection is a collection of separable tales compiled and written,
or more probably re-written, essentially by a single author; and it circu-
lates in a recognisably coherent form. It is different, therefore, from an
anthology or a manuscript miscellany, or from a collection of separate
works by a single man, where the different items do not necessarily
belong together; and it is different from works such as interlaced
romances, where there may be a number of stories but they are not at all
easily extractable. The stories must be essential to the work, not incidental, and so a sermon with a generous use of story *exempla* is not in itself a
story-collection.[10]

Cooper's definition emphasizes both the individuality of the stories as
well as their coherence within the literary form as a whole. Each story is
complete unto itself and can be easily isolated from the collection, yet it
gains new meaning and sense when it is taken together with the other
stories in the collection. Cooper also posits that there is usually a single
hand behind each story-collection, belonging to someone who in some
sense is an author as well as a compiler. That is, the author did not merely
gather random material together; the "story-collection" is really a composition reflecting an individual's intentions, and often the individual has
reworked the stories with the whole collection in view. Cooper also
explains that, although individual story-collections might share features
and material with others, coherence is imposed upon each story-collection
through some kind of structure or ordering scheme. This scheme may be
as basic as a common theme or genre shared by the stories or a chronological or other progressive arrangement of the stories, and as elaborate
as framing material, such as a prologue, epilogue, or a fully developed
frame narrative with links and connectives between stories.[11] Finally,
while some great compositions of the fourteenth century such as the

---

English Medieval Narrative in the Thirteenth and Fourteenth Centuries (Cambridge: Cambridge
University Press, 1982).

10. Cooper, *Structure of the Canterbury Tales*, 24.

11. Many fourteenth-century story-collections, such as the *Canterbury Tales*, the
Decameron, and Don Juan Manuel's *El conde Lucanor*, have a frame narrative, but other story-
collections such as the *Gesta Romanorum*, which contained 180 stories with a moralization
attached, or the *Alphabetum narrationum* (*Alphabet of Tales*), arranged in alphabetical order by
catchwords, had no linking or framing material at all. Story-collections with prologues and
epilogues but no real frame include *The South English Legendary*, Petrarch's *De viris illustribus
vitae*, Boccaccio's *De casibus virorum illustrium* and *De claris mulieribus*, and Chaucer's *Legend
of Good Women*, among many others. The most elaborate frame narrative is the "Chinese
box" or "Russian doll" structure displayed in story-collections such as the Indian *Pañcatantra*
or its Arabic version *Kalilah wa-Dimnah* in which there are several levels of narration. The
framing story itself contains another story or stories that in turn frame other stories.

Canterbury Tales may well be judged sophisticated or artistically self-conscious in comparison to earlier story-collections, according to Cooper, the story-collection genre actually exhibits "no clear lines of chronological development."[12] The frame narrative, which one might mistakenly suppose to be a late feature, is present alongside other collections that have no framing material at all.

Other features common to story-collections are: the dual function of both "instruction" (or "wisdom") and entertainment at the same time; a close interaction between oral performance and written composition since the stories themselves are often of a "popular" nature; and a specific set of literary processes behind their compositional and textual history. These processes include certain principles of selection behind the assembling of the stories (such as choosing stories from a common theme or genre), the borrowing of stories from other sources (especially other story-collections),[13] an open-endedness in the number and final arrangement of the stories,[14] and the nonfixity or fluidity of the texts of an individual story-collection.[15]

---

12. Cooper, *Structure of the Canterbury Tales*, 24.

13. Among those story-collections from which Chaucer pulled several of his own stories in the *Canterbury Tales* were Gower's *Confessio Amantis* and Ovid's *Metamorphosis*. As for Boccaccio, Chaucer never cites him by name, but at least six of Chaucer's twenty-four stories (the Reeve's, Clerk's, Merchant's, Franklin's, Shipman's, and Man of Law's Tales) have parallels in Boccaccio's *Decameron*, and he probably got his basic idea for the mini story-collection in the "Monk's Tale," as well as the subtitle *De casibus virorum illustrium*, from Boccaccio's work of the same title. See Leonard M. Koff, *Chaucer and the Art of Storytelling* (Berkeley and Los Angeles: University of California Press, 1988), 37; and Leonard M. Koff and Brenda Deen Schildgen, eds., *The Decameron and the Canterbury Tales: New Essays on an Old Question* (Madison, N.J.: Fairleigh Dickinson University Press, 2000), 11.

14. It often seems that more stories could be fit into the collection; the medieval histories could contain more of the same, and the legendaries of the saints have not run out of saints to include. In the *Canterbury Tales*, for example, the host announces that each pilgrim will tell two stories coming and going from Canterbury, however, the pilgrims never reach Canterbury and only twenty-two of them tell stories before the Parson says only one tale is left. The precise number of pilgrims is unknown; twenty-nine people are said to be at the Inn (I.24), but later three priests are mentioned (I.164) and the Canon and his Yeoman join the party after the journey has begun. These oft-debated phenomena have been variously explained, but one possibility is that Chaucer intentionally left his work incomplete or open-ended, a maneuver not necessarily unanticipated by his audience. (Chaucer's *Legend of Good Women* is also incomplete or unfinished.) The last story is followed by Chaucer's retraction—a traditional medieval conclusion to a work—recanting his writing of the tales and even apologizing for all his other works. "The Retraction leaves us in no doubt that, unfinished, unpolished, and incomplete as *The Canterbury Tales* may be, Chaucer is finished with it" (Larry D. Benson, *The Riverside Chaucer* [3rd ed.; Boston: Houghton Mifflin, 1987], 22). See also Edward I. Condren, *Chaucer and the Energy of Creation: The Design and the Organization of the Canterbury Tales* (Gainesville: University Press of Florida, 1999). It has also

2. Application to the Book of Daniel

Daniel 1–6 possesses certain overt features in common with the story-collection genre. Six discrete episodic tales belong together by reason of their connection to the figure Daniel and their common setting and themes. Moreover, these tales were probably compiled and circulated together as an independent collection in the late Persian or early Hellenistic period before being connected to the visions of Dan 7–12 in around 164 B.C.E. Furthermore, these tales exhibit various elements of structure and arrangement, such as a prologue and narrative links, and an open-endedness in the number and arrangement of the stories. When the equally discrete four apocalyptic visions were added to the stories, the collection underwent a transformation of genre that meant a lessening of the entertainment factor and a heightening of the didactic to indicate God's sovereignty over human affairs even in the difficult times of Antiochus IV's persecutions of the Jews. The individual court tales in chapters 1–6 emphasize God's support of righteous Jews, and the aggregation of stories, in which the wise and righteous courtier defeats his rivals at their own skills and contests in the foreign court, provides further support for the (mostly *ex eventu*) visions said to be from Daniel, the wise courtier, himself.

Structure of the Daniel Narratives

The collection of stories in Dan 1–6 compares to the more simply structured kinds of story-collections, rather than those with a full framework introducing and surrounding the stories. One notes that there is a kind of prologue (ch. 1 in Hebrew, which can be seen to anticipate both the Aramaic stories alone and the book as a whole since it gives the length of Daniel's career in v. 21), some limited connections between the

---

been suggested that Chaucer emulated Arabic or Near Eastern precedents in this open-endedness; however, this is a feature also found in the classical collections, such as the *Metamorphoses* of Ovid; see Katharine S. Gittes, *Framing the Canterbury Tales: Chaucer and the Medieval Frame Narrative Tradition* (Contributions to the Study of World Literature 41; New York: Greenwood, 1991), 50–51, 109–11.

15. The situation with the *Canterbury Tales* is well known to medievalists; the thirty-one surviving manuscript witnesses have different orderings of stories in the ten groups or fragments, as well as different orderings of the fragments themselves. Certain variants can perhaps be traced back to changes made by Chaucer himself, but there are few explicit external links between the fragments; see Benson, *Riverside Chaucer*, 5. The Decameron also "encouraged alterations and omissions and insertions of new tales, as well as coupling with other narrations"; see Vittore Branca, *Boccaccio: The Man and His Works* (trans. Richard Monges; New York: New York University Press, 1976), 202.

stories, and several layers of narration. In Daniel, however, the prologue
is not the kind in which an author states his or her intentions, nor does it
introduce an explicit storyteller or storytellers, i.e., characters in the first
layer of narration who tell the individual stories that follow. The organization and coherence of the stories are provided by similar motifs and/or
genre, the centralization on a main character Daniel, and an imposed
chronological progression.[16] The few cross-references between stories also
aid coherence; yet one notes that the links are rather sporadic. For
instance, in Dan 5 King Belshazzar is told of Daniel by his mother, who
recounts events from the story in Dan 4, but in Dan 2 King Nebuchadnezzar meets Daniel for the first time as if the events of Dan 1 never took
place. This stresses the discrete and self-contained nature of the stories as
opposed to a novelistic or linear development of plot running through
Dan 1–6.

On the other hand, when one considers the addition of the visions
(Dan 7–12) to the stories, the situation becomes nuanced. In 7:2, the third-
person stories about Daniel switch to the first-person visions of Daniel:
the Daniel of the stories speaks. Then, in Dan 11 and 12, especially in the
angel Michael's command to Daniel to keep the words and the book
hidden or sealed, an implied audience is indirectly addressed in the
secretive language of apocalyptic. One may assume the audience is the
מַשְׂכִּילִים ("wise") who "will give understanding to many," although
they may "fall, so that they may be refined, purified, and cleansed, until
the time of the end" (11:33, 35). These מַשְׂכִּילִים "will shine like the stars"
(12:3) and "shall understand" Daniel's words when the wicked do not
(12:10). But here, the Greek versions of Daniel subvert the visions because
of their ordering—in both Theodotion and the Old Greek (OG), the book
of Daniel does not end with the visions of Dan 7–12, but with an additional story or stories that are again told in the third person. In the case of
Theodotion Daniel, the book is ordered almost as a *vita*, since it book-ends
its version of the entire Masoretic Text (MT) of Daniel (chs. 1–12, stories
and visions) between the story of Susanna, in which Daniel is portrayed as
a young man, and Bel and the Dragon, in which Daniel is an old man.[17]

---

16. As Lawrence Wills has noted, the kings were imposed on the stories (which originally
lacked them), in order to follow the cycle of kingdoms in the oracle of ch. 2. See Lawrence M.
Wills, *The Jewish Novel in the Ancient World* (Ithaca, N.Y.: Cornell University Press, 1995), 50.

17. Pap. 967, one of the three extant OG manuscripts, may also be attempting the form
of a *vita* by arranging the twelve chapters in chronological order, in that it places chs. 7 and
8 between chs. 4 and 5. (This is in contrast to the MT, Theodotion, and the two other OG
manuscripts, which order the stories separately from the visions, resulting in the fact that
the story of ch. 6 is set in the time of Darius the Mede and anachronistically intrudes
between the Belshazzar story of ch. 5 and the visions during Belshazzar's time in chs. 7 and

Text-Critical Problems of Daniel

The text-critical problems of Daniel arise from the existence of two major text types, a situation made still more complex in that within one of these types, one specific family stands apart from its type and in certain sections follows more closely the opposite type.[18] The Hebrew-Aramaic MT and its eight witnesses from Qumran (1QDan[a,b], 4QDan[a,b,c,d,e], and 6QDan), belong to the one text type containing the short edition of Daniel, with six stories and four visions. The Greek versions (Old Greek and Theodotion) belong to the other text type containing the long edition of the book of Daniel—the additions in Dan 3, plus the appended Daniel stories, Susanna and Bel and the Dragon. However, in Dan 4–6 (and to a smaller extent, in Dan 3), the Greek text of Theodotion Daniel follows the MT against the Old Greek. Scholars have traditionally confronted this problem of the divergent texts of Daniel with attempts to ascertain the authority or priority of a particular text or its (presumably Semitic) *Vorlage.*

This strategy of searching for the *Urtext,* the authoritative and original text, has until recent years been considered by scholars to be the central task in any attempt at critically establishing biblical texts. The assumption was that the history of a text can be diagrammed as a sort of genealogical tree possessing a trunk from which all textual groups branch. Recently, however, scholars such as Eugene Ulrich, Emanuel Tov, and Bertil Albrektson, to name only a few, have demonstrated the simplicity of this view and have begun outlining the multidimensional aspects of textual composition and development.[19] The evidence of

---

8.) However, the concern for chronology in Pap. 967 ends at ch. 12; Bel and the Dragon and Susanna are merely appended afterward.

18. This terminology is taken from the suggestions made by Eugene Ulrich, "Pluriformity in the Biblical Text, Text Groups, and Questions of Canon," in *The Madrid Qumran Congress: Proceedings of the International Congress on the Dead Sea Scrolls, Madrid 18–21 March, 1991* (ed. Julio Trebolle Barrera and Luis Vegas Montaner; 2 vols.; Leiden: Brill, 1992), 1:38.

19. See, e.g., Eugene Ulrich, "Double Literary Editions of Biblical Narratives and Reflections on Determining the Form To Be Translated," in *Perspectives on the Hebrew Bible: Essays in Honor of Walter J. Harrelson* (ed. James L. Crenshaw; Macon, Ga.: Mercer University Press, 1980), 101–16; idem, "Horizons of Old Testament Textual Research at the Thirtieth Anniversary of Qumran Cave 4," *CBQ* 46 (1984): 613–36; idem, "From Literature to Scripture: Reflections on the Growth of a Text's Authoritativeness" *DSD* 10 (2003): 3–25; Emanuel Tov, "Criteria for Evaluating Textual Readings: The Limitations of Textual Rules," *HTR* 75 (1982): 429–48; idem, "A Modern Textual Outlook Based on the Qumran Scrolls," *HUCA* 53 (1982): 11–27; idem, *The Text-Critical Use of the Septuagint in Biblical Research* (Jerusalem Biblical Studies 3; Jerusalem: Simor, 1981); and Bertil Albrektson, "Reflections on the Emergence of a Standard Text of the Hebrew Bible," in *Congress Volume: Göttingen, 1977* (ed. John A Emerton; VTSup 29; Leiden: Brill, 1978), 49–65.

diversity in texts from Qumran and elsewhere shows that "no standardization of the text had taken place" in the Second Temple period; translations of the OG move "toward greater stereotyping and closer proximity to the parent text of the MT tradition in late antiquity."[20] Ulrich has argued for a pluriformity, or multiple literary editions, of certain biblical texts that cannot be traced back to an original or archetype as such. These editions likely existed alongside each other from earliest times and did not develop from each other.

Dean Wenthe has utilized these considerations in his careful assessment of the character of the OG in Dan 1–6. In his overview of the OG's word selection and word order, Wenthe takes up the challenge of deciding whether the OG can rightly be described as a paraphrastic free translation of a Semitic text, as it so often has been described. One of his conclusions is that the OG is consistent throughout the book of Daniel, even in most portions of Dan 4–6.[21] This is to say that, while the OG has a "larger vocabulary and translates with flexible literality, it is not accurate to describe it as paraphrastic."[22] In addition, "there is no evidence of *Tendenz* or Midrashic activity on the part of the translator. The MT displays similar pluses to those in the OG."[23]

Wenthe argues that each of the Daniel stories of Dan 4–6 in its separate edition took on a different form with its own length and pluses. Therefore, one cannot regard either of the textual traditions of these chapters as superior to the other. Rather, Wenthe concludes that two editions and two collections of Dan 4–6 (MT/Th versus the OG) circulated independently of each other at an early period.

Wenthe also goes on to describe these two editions of the three stories as "different tellings of the legend[s] in varied contexts," and adds that each edition of a story points to an earlier common core legend.[24] His description of the editions in these terms is suggestive for the present approach and is supported by our knowledge of story-collections. Story-collections do indeed often contain stories that possess multiple editions

---

20. Dean O. Wenthe, "The Old Greek Translation of Daniel 1–6" (Ph.D. diss., University of Notre Dame, 1991), 5, 30.

21. These conclusions are similar to those of Sharon Pace Jeansonne for Dan 7–12. Jeansonne concluded that the OG of those chapters was most likely not operating on its own *Tendenz*, but rather the translator "attempted to translate accurately the *Vorlage* available of the day" (*The Old Greek Translation of Daniel 7–12* [CBQMS 19; Washington, D.C.: Catholic Biblical Association of America, 1988], 132).

22. Wenthe, "Old Greek Translation of Daniel 1–6," 247.

23. Ibid., 87.

24. Ibid., 97.

elsewhere, each maintaining the central core common to all but without a fixed text.

There is no need to posit one Semitic original or *Urtext* from which all versions of the Daniel stories descended. One may better speak, as does Wenthe, of core material behind each "telling" of the story. However, in contrast to Wenthe, who states "the evidence points to the variant of Semitic *Vorlagen* rather than *de novo* Greek compositions," we cannot say that the OG is necessarily a *translation* of a Semitic text.[25] The observed Semitic or Semitizing features (use of parataxis, etc.) occur alongside features that seem Greek rather than Semitic and would in fact be difficult to render back into Hebrew or Aramaic. As Bludau noted long ago, it is difficult to tell the difference between Semitizing Greek and a translation of a Semitic *Vorlage*.[26] Intentional contraction or expansion of what occurs in a different text are processes that can be entirely different than interpretation or *Tendenz*.[27] To limit ourselves to only one example, we can look at the description of the world tree in Nebuchadnezzar's dream in Dan 4 of both the MT and the OG.

MT 4:7b–9/OG 4:10b–12

The MT reads:

> Behold, (there was) a tree (אִילָן) in the midst of the earth, and its height was great. The tree grew great and strong; its height reached to heaven, and the sight of it (חֲזוֹתֵהּ) to the end of all the earth. Its foliage was beautiful, its fruit abundant, and food for all was in it. Beneath it the beasts of the field found shade; the birds of the sky lived in its branches. From it all flesh was fed.[28]

The OG reads:[29]

> Behold, a tall tree (was) growing on the earth. Its appearance (ὅρασις) was great and there was not another like it. Its branches were about thirty stadia long; all the wild beasts of the earth found shade under it,

---

25. Ibid., 96.

26. August Bludau, *Die alexandrinische Übersetzung des Buches Daniel und ihr Verhältnis zum massoretischen Texten* (Freiburg: Herder, 1897), 210. See also John J. Collins, *Daniel: A Commentary on the Book of Daniel* (Hermenia; Minneapolis: Fortress, 1993), 6.

27. Wenthe, "Old Greek Translation of Daniel 1–6," 35.

28. Translations of MT 4:7b–9 and OG 4:10b–12 are my own.

29. Following Ziegler's order of verses: Joseph Ziegler, ed., *Susanna, Daniel, Bel et Draco* (Septuaginta: Vetus Testamentum Graecum 16; Göttingen: Vandenhoeck & Ruprecht, 1999), 292.

and the birds of the heaven made their nests in it. Its food was plentiful and good and it supported all living things. Its appearance was great. Its crown came close to heaven and its trunk to the clouds, filling the region under heaven. The sun and the moon dwelt in it and it illumined the whole earth.

The details added by the OG are employed to amplify our wonder at this marvelous tree, and to reinforce the cosmic imagery behind the story. This tree is so great that no other tree has ever been like it, its branches are approximately thirty stadia long (about five miles), and it takes up so much space in both heaven and earth that the sun and the moon are said to live in its branches. It is not easy to say whether the OG text here is simply "expansionistic" or "paraphrastic" in comparison to the MT. And the fact that no scholar can produce a *Vorlage* or *Urtext* for this passage may be due, not to the fact that it was lost sometime in the past, but to the fact that there never was one. In regard to the book of Daniel, textual (lower) criticism and historical (higher) criticism go hand in hand, especially when one remembers that the Hebrew-Aramaic Daniel of 164 B.C.E. is only a few decades older than the first Greek edition (the OG), which may be as old as the end of the second century B.C.E.[30]

Compositional History

With regard to the compositional history of Daniel, it is clear that there was a cycle of stories and visions centered around a Jewish courtier in the Hellenistic period that became attached to the figure Daniel. To illustrate this, not only do we have the additional stories of Susanna and Bel and the Dragon (as well as the *Prayer* and *Song* inserted into Dan 3) found in the Greek additions, but also other Daniel stories and visions in parabiblical manuscripts from Qumran in Aramaic (perhaps up to seven compositions in nine manuscripts),[31] as well

---

30. Bludau, *Die alexandrinische Übersetzung des Buches Daniel*, 8; Hartman and Di Lella, *Book of Daniel*, 78; and Jeansonne, *Old Greek Translation of Daniel 7–12*, 16–17.

31. According to Peter Flint: "this new material, none of which was known previously known [sic] to scholars, bears powerful testimony to several traditions related to 'Daniel' among at least some Jews in the last century B.C.E. and the first century C.E."; see Peter Flint, "The Daniel Tradition at Qumran," in Collins and Flint, *Book of Daniel*, 2:329. These include at least the *Prayer of Nabonidus* (4Q242 or 4QPrNab ar); *Pseudo-Daniel* (4QpsDan^{a-c} ar or 4Q243–244, 4Q245; three manuscripts but probably two compositions); *The Son of God Text* or *Aramaic Apocalypse* (4Q246 or 4QApocalypse ar); 4Q489 (pap4Qapocalypse ar); possibly

as one or more other traditions about Daniel found in Josephus's *Ant.* 10.263–281.[32]

All the parabiblical Daniel manuscripts are in a very fragmentary state, and so only a little may be said about their relationship to the biblical Daniel. *The Prayer of Nabonidus* (4Q242) does not mention Daniel by name, but refers to a Jewish diviner (גזר) who has a hand in healing the Babylonian king *Nabonidus* (*Nbny* or Nabunay) of a disease after seven years of affliction. This text, plus other information from Babylonian sources about Nabonidus' unpopular devotion to the moon-god Sîn and strange self-imposed exile to *Taymāʾ* in north Arabia, make it possible that 4Q242 is the source for the story of Nebuchadnezzar's madness in Dan 4. The two *Pseudo-Daniel* compositions (4Q243–244 and 4Q245) both mention a certain Daniel and seem to review history in some way, although they probably were influenced by the biblical Daniel rather than the other way round. The first *Pseudo-Daniel* even refers to a Babylonian court-setting, King Belshazzar, eschatological prophecy, and a prophetic review of Hellenistic history, while the second *Pseudo-Daniel* mentions "a book that was given." Other compositions have a slightly looser connection to biblical Daniel, in that the name Daniel is not preserved, and the motifs are less specifically similar. For example, the *Four Kingdoms* composition contains an unnamed seer who tells of his vision of an angel and four speaking trees that symbolize four kingdoms, and 4Q551 mentions a judge in a court setting.[33] The so-called *Son of God Text* (4Q246), describes someone who is "son of God" and "son of the Most High," who is obeyed by all nations (cf. Dan 7). While the identity of the figure is unclear in this fragmentary text, it seems that someone utters the information about him in the presence of a Gentile king.

4Q551 (4QDaniel Suzanna? ar); and 4Q552–553 (4QFour Kingdoms[a,b] ar). See also John J. Collins, "New Light on the Book of Daniel from the Dead Sea Scrolls" in *Perspectives in the Study of the Old Testament and Early Judaism: A Symposium in Honour of Adam S. van der Woude on the Occasion of His 70th Birthday* (ed. Florentino García Martínez and Ed Noort; VTSup 73; Leiden: Brill, 1998), 180–96.

32. Josephus relates that Daniel was responsible for the building of a burial tower in Ecbatana in Media. He adds that in his day the kings of Media, Persia, and Parthia were still being buried in the tower, and that a Jewish priest was entrusted with the care of it.

33. Milik supposed it was part of the Susanna story; see Józef T. Milik, "Daniel et Susanne à Qumrân," in *De la Tôrah au Messie: Etudes d'exegèse et d'herméneutique bibliques offertes à Henri Cazelles* (ed. Maurice Carrez et al.; Paris: Desclée, 1981), 337–59. But now George W. E. Nickelsburg, "4Q551: A Vorlage to the Story of Susanna or a Text Related to Judges 19," *JJS* 48 (1997): 349–51.

3. The Daniel Collection and Its Ancient Near Eastern Analogues

The "Daniel" character was probably an ancient Syro-Palestinian hero of legend, known to the author of the Daniel stories from Ezek 14:14 and 28:3, and given the identity of a Jew exiled to Babylon.[34] However, some of the closest analogues to the morphology and motifs of Dan 1–6 are within the Hellenistic-period continuum between Egyptian literature and Aramaic literature, especially from Egypt. In his investigation of the ancient Near Eastern court tale genre used in the book of Daniel, Lawrence Wills looks to court tales set in Persia and Mesopotamia, such as those in Herodotus, the biblical stories of Esther and Daniel, and to the story of Aḥiqar, a sage in the Assyrian court (written in Aramaic in the fifth century B.C.E. in Egypt, but also found in later Demotic fragments, not to mention later recensions in several languages).[35] Wills pays little attention to the biblical court tales set in Egypt, such as the Joseph narratives in Genesis and the story of Moses and Aaron competing with Egyptian magicians in Exodus, and he only briefly mentions the Egyptian Demotic story of the sage ʿOnchsheshonqy.[36] However, there are also other court tales, story-collections, and story-cycles in Egyptian literature, either not so well-known to biblical scholars or only just recently published, that center around famous sages and magicians at court and that begin to appear as far back as the mid-second millennium B.C.E. These figures are usually termed in Egyptian ḥry-ḥb (ḥry-tp) "(chief) lector priest" or "magician."[37] Remarkably, some of these stories occur in both Egyptian and Aramaic. This material in both languages, as well as the existence of the *Papyrus Amherst* 63, a twenty-two-column Aramaic text in Demotic

---

34. Most scholars agree that the righteous judge *Dnʾil* in the Ugaritic story of *Aqhat* from the mid-second millennium B.C.E. has to be an early form of a long Syro-Palestinian tradition surrounding the figure Daniel (see, e.g., Collins, *Daniel*, 1–2). Neither the Ezekiel author nor the Daniel author probably knew directly of the Ugaritic story. However, note that the inclusion of Daniel beside Noah and Job as righteous worthies in Ezek 14:14 hints that Daniel was thought to be an ancient non-Jewish character of legendary fame, like the other two.

35. Wills, *Jew in the Court of the Foreign King*, 39–74. For the three Demotic fragments, see Karl-Theodor Zauzich, "Demotische Fragmente zum Ahikar-Roman," in *Folia Rara* (ed. Herbert Franke et al.; Wiesbaden: Steiner, 1976), 180–85; and Max Küchler, *Frühjüdische Weisheitstraditionen* (OBO 26; Fribourg: Universitätsverlag, 1979), 333–37. For the Aramaic text, see Bezalel Porten and Ada Yardeni, *Textbook of Aramaic Documents from Ancient Egypt* (3 vols.; Jerusalem: Hebrew University of Jerusalem, 1993), 3:22–53.

36. Wills suggests that this story of an Egyptian courtier only occurred in Egypt because of Persian influence (*Jew in the Court of the Foreign King*, 43).

37. The lector-priest, known for reading incantations, was understood to be a magician; see, for instance, Robert K. Ritner, *The Mechanics of Ancient Egyptian Magical Practice* (SAOC 54; Chicago: Oriental Institute of the University of Chicago, 1993), 220–33.

script, are witnesses to literary and linguistic interaction in Hellenistic Egypt between Aramaic speakers and Egyptians.[38]

Probably the earliest use of the story-collection as a device anywhere in the world is actually found in Egyptian literature with the *Papyrus Westcar*, which perhaps dates to the Twelfth Dynasty.[39] The setting of the composition is the royal court of the long-past Fourth Dynasty (ca. 2600–2450) when the sons of King Khufu are entertaining their father with stories of magicians. Another example of the story-collection genre is the recently published *Story of Petese Son of Petetum and Seventy Other Good and Bad Stories* from Papyrus Petese in Demotic, dating from the fourth century B.C.E. to the end of the first century C.E. Although the text is only partially preserved, its editor, Kim Ryholt, believes it to be similar in many respects to the *Arabian Nights*.[40] The text is fragmentary but contains large sections of a long frame story in which the protagonist, Petese, who is designated a prophet of Atum at Heliopolis, performs certain magical acts and proposes the telling of seventy stories (three of which are also partially preserved, but are appended to, rather than enclosed by, the frame narrative). One also notes stories and story-cycles surrounding various other Egyptian courtiers from the first centuries B.C.E. and C.E., such as: the magician Horus-son-of-Paneshy or Hor-son-of-Pawenesh (who appears, like *Aḥiqar*, in both Aramaic and Demotic texts),[41] the

---

38. The papyrus contains several compositions from various genres. See Sven P. Vleeming and Jan W. Wesselius, *Studies in Papyrus Amherst 63: Essays on the Aramaic texts in Aramaic/Demotic Papyrus Amherst 63* (2 vols.; Amsterdam: Juda Palache Instituut, 1985–90); and for a more recent translation, see Richard C. Steiner, "An Aramaic Text in Demotic Script," COS 1:309–27.

39. *LÄ* 4:744. Another example of a frame-narrative, this time a mythological text with inset fables, is the *Myth of the Sun's Eye*; see Wilhelm Spiegelberg, *Der ägyptische Mythus vom Sonnenauge (Der Papyrus der Tierfabeln, "Kufi") nach dem leidener demotischen Papyrus I 384* (Strassburg: Strassburger Druckerei und Verlagsanstalt, 1917), and Françoise de Cenival, *Le Myth de l'oeil du soleil* (Demotische Studien 9; Sommerhausen: Zauzich, 1988). The main texts are in Demotic and Greek from the second and third century C.E.; however, there seems to also be a fragment from the late second millennium B.C.E.

40. Kim Ryholt, *Carlsberg Papyri 4: The Story of Petese Son of Petetum and Seventy Other Good and Bad Stories (P. Petese)* (CNI Publications 23; Copenhagen: Museum Tusculanum Press, 1999); idem, "An Elusive Narrative Belonging to the Cycle of Stories about the Priesthood at Heliopolis," in *Acts of the Seventh International Conference of Demotic Studies, Copenhagen, 23–27 August 1999* (ed. Kim Ryholt; CNI Publications 27; Copenhagen: Museum Tusculanum Press, 2002), 361–66.

41. *Ḥr-p3-nšy* or *Ḥr-p3-wnš* in Demotic, and *Ḥr br pwnš* in Aramaic. The Aramaic text was first published by Arthur E. Cowley in *Aramaic Papyri of the Fifth Century B.C.* (Osnabrück: Zeller, 1967), 179–82; Papyri Blacassiani = *AP* 71 or Cowley 71. The papyri were rearranged and retranslated by Porten and Yardeni, *Textbook of Aramaic Documents*, 3:54–57. The Demotic character *Ḥr-p3-wnš* is found in *Setne II* and in an unpublished text under

magician Ḥi-Ḥor (in Demotic),[42] Setna Khamwas, a priestly prince, and Si-Osire, a magician (both in *Setna I and II* and in other Demotic texts),[43] and the magician Merire in the hieratic *Papyrus Vandier* (and perhaps also in a Demotic fragment),[44] among others.

This new material shares similar motifs and morphology with the Jewish Hebrew and Aramaic Daniel stories: (1) Concerning genre, the Egyptian magician stories are often court tales wherein a wise courtier succeeds over his rivals at court or triumphs over an ordeal. The categories "tales of court contest" and "tales of court conflict" that have been applied to the Daniel stories can be applied also to the Egyptian and Egyptian Aramaic courtier stories.[45] In addition, there exist Egyptian story-collections (the *Papyrus Westcar, Petese,* and perhaps *Setna II*) from different periods that seem to compile stories about magicians for entertainment. Finally, some of the same characters show up across many different texts, forming interwoven story-cycles gravitating around those figures. Daniel 1–6, the collection of stories about the Jewish Daniel and his friends, exhibits these generic features, as does the book of Daniel as a whole to some extent. In addition, the fact that there is a large pool of extrabiblical material about Daniel, hints at the popularity of this figure to Hellenistic Jews.

(2) In the book of Daniel, Daniel is designated as one of the sages at court who are given several professional titles, and is himself called a חַרְטֹם *ḥarṭōm* "magician" or "dream interpreter" (Dan 2:10, 27; 4:4), and even רַב חַרְטֻמִּין *rab ḥarṭummîn* "chief of the magicians/interpreters" (Dan 5:11) in the Hebrew and Aramaic of the Daniel stories. The term חַרְטֹם *ḥarṭōm,* used here as well as in the Joseph narratives in Genesis (41:8, 24), and in the narratives about Moses and Aaron's competition with the Egyptian magicians (Exod 7:11, 22; 8:3, 4, 15; 9:11), has long been recognized as a Demotic loanword, as has the Akkadian *ḥarṭibi,* which is used in two Neo-Assyrian texts to designate professional dream interpreters

---

preparation by Karl-Theodor Zauzich; see Ritner, *Mechanics of Ancient Egyptian Magical Practice,* 70–71.

42. Wilhelm Spiegelberg, *Demotische Texte auf Krügen* (Demotische Studien 5; Leipzig: Hinrichs, 1912), jar-text A, 1–9.

43. For Setna I and II, see *AEL* 3:125–51. First published by Francis Llewellyn Griffith, *Stories of the High Priests of Memphis: The Sethon of Herodotus and the Demotic Tales of Khamuas* (Oxford: Clarendon , 1900). Si-Osire may also shows up on a jar-text; see Spiegelberg, *Demotische Texte auf Krügen,* jar-text B, 1–9.

44. Georges Posener, *Le Papyrus Vandier* (Cairo: Institut Français d'Archéologie Orientale, 1986).

45. Humphreys, "Life-Style for Diaspora," 211–23.

brought from Egypt.[46] The use of this loanword from Demotic does not argue on its own for Egyptian influence on the Daniel tales, since it may have been picked up from the Joseph or Moses narratives. However, it does indicate Daniel the sage or "magician" performs and competes at court as a recognized professional among others, in a way paralleling the Egyptian magician stories. Egyptian magicians vie with each other in their attempts to out-perform each other and thereby win the favor of the king, but it is the exceptionally skilled and wise magician who is marked to succeed over the others.

(3) In addition to having success over rivals or a conflict, the Egyptian court tales also possess the recurrent motifs of the wise magicians solving problems or puzzles for the king, or performing marvelous deeds. They are able to read sealed documents (e.g., *Papyrus Westcar* and *Setna II*), animate clay figures (e.g., *Papyrus Vandier*, *Papyrus Westcar*, *Hi-Hor*), find lost items by upheaving a lake (*Papyrus Westcar*), reattach the head of an ox onto its body (*Papyrus Westcar*), and they have knowledge of cures for mysterious illnesses (*Papyrus Vandier*), etc. In the Daniel stories, the wonders performed by Daniel and his friends are all done with the aid of their God and are not really "magical" in terms of manipulative strategies (even if Daniel is called the chief of the magicians). However, Daniel interprets dreams in Dan 2 and 4; the three friends are able to survive a fiery furnace in Dan 3; Daniel is able to read and interpret the mysterious writing on the wall in Dan 5; and Daniel is able to survive a period of time in the lions' den in Dan 6 and in Bel and the Dragon. In Dan 4, Daniel is on hand when Nebuchadnezzar regains his senses, while in 4Q242 (*Prayer of Nabonidus*), the possible source for the Dan 4 story, the Jewish diviner apparently intercedes with God to cure the king of his disease.

(4) Egyptian magicians sometimes predict future events, as in Dan 2, 4, and 5 (and the visions). For instance, it is notable that the *Papyrus Westcar* uses the story-collection device to launch some *ex eventu* predictions about the coming of the Fifth Dynasty. Certainly *Papyrus Westcar* is much older than Daniel, but it should be noted that its themes of magicians and others who predict the future survive, or rather flourish, in the later literature that is closer to or contemporary with the Daniel stories. The

---

46. *CAD* Ḫ:116; *AHw* 1:328. On the term *ḥrṭm* in Hebrew and Aramaic as a loanword from Egyptian *ḥr(y)-tp* (Demotic *ḥr-tb*), see Yoshiyuki Muchiki, *Egyptian Proper Names and Loanwords in North-West Semitic* (SBLDS 173; Atlanta: Society of Biblical Literature, 1999), 245. Against the translation "dream interpreter," see, e.g., J. Lanckan, "*Ḥarṭummîn*—die Traumspezialisten?" *BN* 119/120 (2003): 101–17.

fragmentary Aramaic papyrus, Cowley 71, links Ḥor-son-of-Pawenesh to certain apocalyptic predictions before a king.[47]

Space does not permit here further elaboration of other shared motifs between the Daniel stories and the Egyptian court tales, such as the punishment of death by fire in a furnace or brazier for courtiers who displease a king (cf. Dan 3, ʿOnchsheshonqy, Papyrus Vandier). Suffice to say that it now seems possible to posit a greater connection between the book of Daniel and Egyptian literature than usually thought.[48] It has typically been supposed that the Daniel stories were connected to the eastern diaspora in provenance and themes, since they are conspicuously given a Babylonian or Persian setting by the author.[49] We are continually gaining more and more evidence that in fact writers in Egypt, whether they were native Egyptians or Aramaic-speakers displaced from Syria-Palestine or Mesopotamia,[50] did sometimes choose to place their compositions in Mesopotamia or the East, and they knew enough about eastern traditions to aspire to verisimilitude in their fiction.[51] Without disputing all the

---

47. In the Aramaic fragments it appears that Ḥor-son-of-Pawenesh announces some coming disasters against a king. On the obverse of the text, which is not at all easy to read because of its fragmentary state, someone has had someone else's sons executed by hanging, a deed for which they should be punished (perhaps it is the king who has wronged Ḥor-son-of-Pawenesh in this manner). A list of disasters to come includes the king's succession by another. Ḥor-son-of-Pawenesh seems to be casting a spell against the king, yet it is not clear whether the king in question is the pharaoh of Egypt or a foreign monarch. On the reverse of the papyrus, further disasters are enumerated. However, there is no mention of Ḥor-son-of-Pawenesh or the king on the reverse, and thus the reverse may not belong to the same composition as the obverse. As fragmentary as the obverse is, it seems to represent "apocalyptic" themes. See Porten and Yardeni, Textbook of Aramaic Documents, 3:54–57.

48. A few scholars, such as Lebram, Müller, and Wilson have argued for some parallels between the Daniel stories and Egypt. However, the connections made are with Egyptian prophetic texts in which a sage predicts the future before a king, but not with Egyptian court tales other than the Papyrus Westcar. See Jürgen-Christian Lebram, Das Daniel Buch (Zürich: Theologischer Verlag, 1984), 20; Hans-Peter Müller, "Mantische Weisheit und Apokalyptik," in Congress Volume: Uppsala, 1971 (VTSup 22; Leiden: Brill, 1972), 291; and Robert R. Wilson, "From Prophecy to Apocalyptic," Semeia 21 (1982): 91.

49. John Collins has stated that "none of the analogies, however, is so close as to require Egyptian provenance, and there is no apparent reason why tales composed in Egypt should be set in Babylon" (Collins, Daniel, 50 n. 417).

50. See Bezalel Porten, "Settlement of Jews at Elephantine and Arameans at Syene," in Judah and the Judeans in the Neo-Babylonian Period (ed. Oded Lipschits and Joseph Blenkinsopp; Winona Lake, Ind.: Eisenbrauns, 2003), 451–70.

51. Among other works in Egyptian, we have the story on the Bentresh stela that is set in Bakhtan (possibly Bactria), and the "Doomed Prince," set in Nahrin (Mitanni). In Aramaic we have the examples of the story of Aḥiqar, which is set in Assyria, and the "Revolt of Babylon" on Papyrus Amherst 63 (cols. 18–23), a historical poem written with the Demotic script, set in Babylon and based on historical events during the days of Shamash-shum-ukin and

parallels that have been made between Daniel and Mesopotamia, one can suggest that the historical inaccuracies and confusions in the Babylonian and Persian setting of the Daniel stories (such as the confusion of Nebuchadnezzar with Nabonidus in Dan 4, the title of "king" granted to Belshazzar, the statement that Darius was a Mede, etc.), may well argue for greater distance between the author and the East.

There seems, thus, to be an even larger Near Eastern tradition of court tales than previously thought, especially in Aramaic and Egyptian literature from Egypt. To view Daniel in the light of the story-collection genre, sheds new light on our understanding: it brings new literary parallels to our attention, and new evidence (some previously little-known Egyptian courtier stories), to bear on questions of textual criticism, composition, and literary traditions and processes. There are not only analogues to Daniel's structure, but to the morphology and motifs of its court narratives.

Assurbanipal. See the edition of Richard C. Steiner and Charles F. Nims, "Ashurbanipal and Shamash-shum-ukin: A Tale of Two Brothers from the Aramaic Text in Demotic Script, Part 1," *RB* 92 (1985): 60–81; and Vleeming and Wesselius, *Studies in Papyrus Amherst 63*, 1:31–37.

3 MACCABEES: AN ANTI-DIONYSIAN POLEMIC

Noah Hacham

INTRODUCTION

The document known as 3 Maccabees, an apocryphal book, that is, a book included in the Septuagint and not in the Hebrew Bible, was apparently written by an Alexandrian Jew, probably in the first half of the first century B.C.E.[1] Until recently, the obviously fictional content of the book has led to its neglect by scholars seeking to reconstruct a picture of the history of the Jewish Diaspora in Hellenistic-Roman Egypt. This study reexamines the value of 3 Maccabees to historical research by adopting the tools of literary critical studies in order to reveal the role that the depiction of the Dionysian cult plays in the development of the community's identity.

The book describes two confrontations between Ptolemy IV Philopator (221–204 B.C.E.) and the Jewish people. The first occurs after Philopator's victory in the battle in Raphia when he visits Jerusalem on a triumphal tour through the reoccupied territory of Coele Syria and Phoenicia (217 B.C.E). Astonished at the marvelous temple and its orderly arrangements, he desires to enter the holy of holies, but the Jews refuse to let him enter, claiming that only one person—the high priest once a year on the Day of Atonement—is allowed to do so. The king insists, in spite of protests from the citizenry of the city and his own companions, and continues to march towards the sanctuary. After Simon the high priest prays at length (2:2–20), God scourges the king by inflicting him with a

---

1. On the different views on the date of the composition of 3 Maccabees see Erich S. Gruen, *Heritage and Hellenism: The Reinvention of Jewish Tradition* (Berkeley and Los Angeles: University of California Press, 1998), 225–26; Noah Hacham, "The Third Book of Maccabees: Literature, History and Ideology" [Hebrew] (Ph.D. diss., The Hebrew University of Jerusalem , 2002), 221, nn. 89–92. The best Greek edition of 3 Maccabees is Robert Hanhart, *Maccabaeorum liber III* (2nd ed.; Septuaginta, Vetus Testamentum graecum 9/3; Göttingen: Vandenhoeck & Ruprecht, 1980). The common English translations (with introductions and commentary) are Cyril W. Emmet, "The Third Book of Maccabees," *APOT* 1:155–73; Moses Hadas, *The Third and Fourth Books of Maccabees* (JAL 3; New York: Harper, 1953), from whom translations are taken for this essay; Hugh Anderson, "3 Maccabees," *OTP* 2:509–29.

violent seizure that leaves him near death and lying on the ground. The king's bodyguards speedily draw him out of the sanctuary; some time later, he recovers and returns in anger to Egypt. The temple is, thus, saved from desecration.

The king's failure in Jerusalem leads to a second confrontation with the Jews in Egypt. Philopator orders that all Jews be required to enroll in the census and be reduced to the condition of slaves. Those who did enroll would be branded by fire on their body with an ivy leaf, the emblem of Dionysus. However, if any of the Jews voluntarily chose to be initiated into the mysteries, they would be on the same footing as the citizens of Alexandria. Most of the Jews, however, excuse themselves from the census and remain faithful to their religion.

The king, when told about this, is enraged and orders that all the Jews of Egypt be assembled to the hippodrome near Alexandria where they were to be trampled to death under the feet of five hundred drunken elephants. The Jews are indeed assembled in the hippodrome, but a chain of providential events hamper fulfillment of the king's intent. His clerks cannot register the Jews because of a lack of papyri and pens. Twice the already drunken elephants cannot be led to the hippodrome, on the first day because the king cannot be awakened to give the final command, and on the second day because the king is afflicted with amnesia and cannot recall his own command. On the third day, when the king enters the hippodrome and the beasts are brought in, God reveals his face opening the gates of heaven, and sending two angels to confront the Jews' adversaries. The elephants turn back and trample and destroy the forces that had followed them, and the king repents and orders all the Jews be freed and sent home safe and sound. The king and the Jews then celebrate their liberation, and three hundred Jews who transgressed against God and his law by accepting Philopator's order are put to death by the faithful Jews, with the king's permission. In the happy ending, the Jews return to their homes all across Egypt, under God's protection, safer than anytime before. The book concludes with the blessing: "Blessed be the deliverer of Israel forever and ever! Amen" (7:23).

This story can hardly be viewed as an historical account of Philopator's, or any other Ptolemaic king's, reign because of its fantastic and imaginary character. No serious history can include a story about five hundred drunken elephants designated to kill *all* the Jews of Egypt in the Alexandrian hippodrome. No doubt, this character is one of the factors leading to the neglect of 3 Maccabees in modern research.[2] But it is pre-

---

2. Third Maccabees is one of the most neglected texts of Second Temple Judaism. Only in the last decade has research begun to devote more attention to 3 Maccabees. See, e.g., the

cisely these stories, with their allusions to the cult of Dionysus that a literary approach renders promising subjects of analysis. Indeed, literary approaches have proven fruitful in a number of recent studies on the book.[3]

It is well known that the cult of Dionysus is a central theme in 3 Maccabees.[4] Nevertheless, only a few scholars have focused on Dionysus's cult as a central clue to solve the question of the purpose of the book.[5] In an article published forty-five years ago, Yehoshua Gutman, although stating that 3 Maccabees should not be viewed as historiography, looks for the historical kernel of the story, which he connects to the centrality of Dionysus's cult in the days of Philopator.[6] In a more recent article, J. R. C. Cousland also notes the central role of Dionysus's cult in 3 Maccabees. He, in contrast, focuses on literary aspects, isolating echoes of the *Bacchae* in 3 Maccabees and concluding that part of the purpose of 3 Maccabees is the aretalogical claim that the God of Israel is the real and the only ruler of the world.[7]

---

bibliographies of Andreas Lehnardt (*Bibliographie zu den Jüdischen Schriften aus hellenistisch-römischer Zeit* [JSHRZ 6/2; Gütersloh: Gütersloher Verlagshaus, 1999], 153–57) and Lorenzo DiTommaso (*A Bibliography of Pseudepigrapha Research* [JSPSup 39; Sheffield: Sheffield Academic Press, 2001], 673–91).

3. See, e.g., Sara R. Johnson, "Mirror, Mirror: Third Maccabees, Historical Fictions and Jewish Self-Fashioning in the Hellenistic Period" (Ph.D. diss., University of California at Berkeley, 1996); D. S. Williams, "3 Maccabees: A Defense of Diaspora Judaism?" *JSP* 13 (1995): 17–29; and J. R. C. Cousland, "Dionysus *Theomachos?* Echoes of the *Bacchae* in 3 Maccabees," *Bib* 82 (2001): 539–48.

4. On the Dionysian religion in general, see Walter F. Otto, *Dionysus: Myth and Cult* (Bloomington: Indiana University Press, 1965).

5. These were postulated in different directions. Some scholars have focused mostly upon the book's reflection of the Jews' situation in Roman Egypt—whether at the outset of Roman rule (so Tcherikover) or in the days of Gaius Caligula (so Grimm and Collins). More recently, scholars have focused upon the book's role as a statement concerning the self-identification of Diaspora Jews. Thus, D. S. Williams has emphasized the book's defense of the Jews in the Diaspora vis-a-vis the Jews of the Land of Israel, while Sara Johnson has focused more on the Alexandrian context, suggesting that the purpose of the book is "to assist pious Jews to steer a middle ground between the evils of separatism and the perils of assimilation" (Johnson, "Mirror, Mirror," 63).

6. Yehoshua Gutman, "The Historical Value of 3 Maccabees" [Hebrew], *SXOLIA* [Eshkolot] 3 (1959): 49–72. His views were not widely discussed, probably since they were written in Hebrew. Aryeh Kasher followed in his footsteps; see his *The Jews in Hellenistic and Roman Egypt: The Struggle for Equal Rights* (Tübingen: Mohr Siebeck, 1985), 211–32.

7. Cousland, "Dionysus *Theomachos*," 539–48. Thus, he concludes (547), "the author of 3 Maccabees ... draws on the literary heritage of the Greeks to skewer the Ptolemaic ruler cult and particularly Philopator's Dionysian pretensions." However, just the last few lines of his article hint at a possible conclusion that can be drawn on the religious life of the Jews of Ptolemaic or Roman Egypt. This hint demands a lengthy discussion as will be done here.

The Dionysian cult in 3 Maccabees has not received the discussion it merits. In this paper, I examine how the Dionysian cult is presented in 3 Maccabees and make the case that the literary and historical purpose of that representation is to ridicule the cult. In my opinion, the fiction called 3 Maccabees reveals the author's polemic against contemporary Jews who were inclined towards the cult of Dionysus. Thus, by literary analysis of 3 Maccabees, new historical conclusions on the religious life and self-identity of the Jewish Diaspora in Egypt in the Hellenistic period can be drawn.

PHILOPATOR AND THE JEWS:
THE CULT OF DIONYSUS AND THE GOD OF ISRAEL

The first story of 3 Maccabees seems to contrast liberal access to Dionysus in comparison to limited access to the Jewish God, but this liberality becomes a subtle point of ridicule.

In Philopator's first epistle (3 Macc 3:12–29), the king presents his own characterization of the differences between his and the Jews' behavior. He states that for reasons of hypocrisy and hostility, the Jews did not allow him to enter the temple (3:17–19). The king, however, forgives the Jews in magnanimous philanthropy, granting them civil rights and allowing them to be appointed to the group of the priests (3:20–21).[8] These differences have religious significance: the king, in stark contrast to the Jews, enables everyone who so desires to participate in worship (3:21).[9] The king and the Jews are differentiated in two important details: (a) While the Jews claim that their cult is restricted, the king's cult is not restricted at all. (b) While even the high priest is allowed to enter the holy of holies only once a year, the king emphasizes the eternal (ἀεί) or constant nature of his service.

Philopator's invitation ("if any of them should prefer to join those who are initiated in the mysteries according to the initiation, they would have equal rights with the citizens of Alexandria" [2:30][10]) makes clear

---

8. The contrast between the king and those Jews who obeyed him on the one hand and those who did not accept his demands on the other is also evident in the language of these verses. See in detail Hacham, "3 Maccabees," 18.

9. ἐβουλήθημεν καὶ πολιτείας αὐτοὺς Ἀλεξανρέων καταξιῶσαι καὶ μετόχους τῶν ἀεὶ ἱερέων καταστῆσαι. The word μέτοχος has also the technical meaning of "member of the group that wields power" (see Friedrich Preisigke and Emil Kiessling, *Wörterbuch der griechischen Papyrusurkunden* [Berlin: Erben, 1925–31], 2:94, s.v. μέτοχος.] With Hanhart, I prefer the version ἱερέων.

10. ἐὰν δέ τινες ἐξ αὐτῶν προαιρῶνται ἐν τοῖς κατὰ τὰς τελετὰς μεμυημένοις ἀναστρέφεσθαι, τούτους ἰσοπολίτας Ἀλεξανδρεῦσιν εἶναι. The English translation is based on

that membership in the mysteries is a consequence of joining the priests (see 3:21).[11] That these are Dionysus's mysteries is stated explicitly when the ivy leaf with which the Jews are branded is identified as the emblem of Dionysus (2:29).

The nature of the king's invitation to the Jews to join the mysteries of the Dionysian cult has bothered many historians.[12] It is well known that joining the mysteries of the Dionysian cult was restricted and that not anybody who so desired could do so.[13] Since the mysteries of this cult were restricted, how could it be possible that any Jew who so desired could join them? Various attempts have been made to reconcile the story with known facts,[14] but the simple solution is that the described offer is, indeed, not a historical fact. The question then becomes to what end did the author of 3 Maccabees ignore the fact that the Dionysian cult was restricted. What message does the author want to convey by contrasting the Jews' prohibition of the foreign king to enter the temple with the foreign king's offer to anyone who so desires to join the mysteries of Dionysus?

The key to the significance of the contrast lies in Philopator's royal decree: "that those who were registered should be branded by fire on their persons with an ivy leaf, the emblem of Dionysus, and that they should be recorded in their former limited status" (2:29).[15] Dionysius's emblem symbolizes the return of the Jews to their former limited and

---

Hadas's translation with an additional phrase ("according to the initiation") translating the words κατὰ τὰς τελετὰς.

11. Carl L. W. Grimm, *Die zweite, dritte und vierte Buch der Maccabaer* (vol. 4 of *Kurzgefasstes exegetisches Handbuch zu den Apokryphen des Alten Testaments*; Leipzig: Hirzel, 1857), 247, has already noted that the ritualistic significance of the verses of the letter in ch. 3 is connected to the royal edict in ch. 2. Cf. Jakob Cohen, *Judaica et Aegyptiaca, de Maccabaeorum libro III Quaestiones historicae* (Groningen: M. De Waal, 1941), 8.

12. See, e.g., Cohen, *Judaica et Aegyptiaca*, 8–12, 18, 22–23; J. Tondriau, "Les thiases dionysiaques royaux de la cour ptolémaïque," *ChrEg* 21 (1946): 155; Hadas, *Third Maccabees*, 17–18, 44–46; Yehoshua Gutman, *The Beginnings of Jewish-Hellenistic Literature* [Hebrew] (Jerusalem: Bialik Institute, 1958), 143–47; Victor A. Tcherikover, "The Third Book of Maccabees as a Historical Source of Augustus' Time," *ScrHier* 7 (1961): 1–26, esp. 2–5, 17; Kasher, *Jews in Hellenistic and Roman Egypt*, 211–32; and A. Paul, "Le Troisème livre des Macchabées," *ANRW* 2.20.1: 315.

13. See J. Tondriau, "Un Thiase Dionysiaque à Péluse sous Ptolémée IV Philopator," *BSAA* 37 (1948): 4, and the sources mentioned there.

14. Some suggest limiting the range of membership (not in the mysteries but in the public cult [so Tondriau and Kasher]) or the quantity of joiners (i.e., not everybody, but only soldiers or a selected group [so Cohen and Hadas]). Yet others view this as the author's misunderstanding and as a result of source-mixing and rewriting (so Tcherikover).

15. τούς τε ἀπογραφομένους χαράσσεσθαι καὶ διὰ πυρὸς εἰς τὸ σῶμα παρασήμῳ Διονύσου κισσοφύλλῳ, οὓς καὶ καταχωρίσαι εἰς τὴν προσυνεσταλμένην αὐθεντίαν.

servile status. However, *Etymologicum Magnum* provides us with the name of another person who bore the sign of Dionysus, none other than Ptolemy IV Philopator himself.[16] Moreover, many literary and archeological sources document Philopator's special attachment to Dionysus's cult.[17] Thus, by his own decree, Philopator proclaims the symbol he bears is the mark of servitude and, thereby, makes himself a slave! Erich Gruen identifies this joke against Philopator as characteristic of the author's highly developed sense of humor.[18] However, not just the king but all worshipers of Dionysus become the brunt of the joke since all who bear this prominent marker of the cult are now marked as inferior. The absurdity of the king's orders becomes an implicit argument against joining the cult. It is not worth belonging to this cult because, with membership, comes a decrease in one's status.

The contrast between the gates of the Dionysian cult being open to all and the gates of the holy of holies in the temple in Jerusalem being closed to all save one proves the superiority of the worship of the Jewish God over the Dionysian cult. Whoever opens the gates to everyone and does not restrict entrance to the cult does not really care about his dignity and honor. The restricted worship of the Jewish God is, therefore, more honorable than the Dionysian cult since it is not open to everyone. The point becomes clear. If a Jew succeeds in joining the Dionysian cult, he will not benefit but allies himself to a practice that is worthless and contemptible.

Dionysian Motifs in 3 Maccabees

Through allusions to various components of the mystery cults, the author of 3 Maccabees, on the one hand, creates a picture of Dionysus's cult that threatens Judaism and, on the other hand, fights against it. His goal is to lead his reader to recognize the superiority of Judaism over the cult of Dionysus.

It is well known that wine drinking and parties were common features of Dionysus's cult.[19] Such parties and wine drinking are mentioned

---

16. *Etymologicum Magnum*, s.v. Γάλλος: Ὁ φιλοπάτωρ Πτολεμαῖος· διὰ τὸ φύλλοις κισσοῦ κατεστίχθαι ὡς οἱ γάλλοι.

17. For summary of sources and bibliography, see Peter M. Fraser, *Ptolemaic Alexandria* (3 vols.; Oxford: Oxford University Press, 1972), 1:203–4, 344–48; Martin P. Nilsson, *Geschichte der Griechischen Religion* (2 vols.; Munich: Beck, 1967–74), 2:161; and Hacham, "3 Maccabees," 22–25.

18. Gruen, *Heritage and Hellenism*, 234–36.

19. Note, for example, the wine drinking in the *Anthesteria*. Specifically about the nature of the Dionysian cult in Alexandria, see Fraser, *Ptolemaic Alexandria*, 1:202, 205.

a number of times in conjunction with the preparations to kill the Jews and are central in this narrative.

Simultaneously with the census of the Jews, the king organized drinking parties in the temples of all his idols (4:16).[20] In these parties, he praised "creatures dumb and impotent to answer or help, and uttered things unseemly against the Greatest God."[21] This mockery that anticipates the act of killing the Jews is intended to prove that the king's gods are superior to the Jewish god. Thus, the entire event is portrayed as a religious struggle and the drinking parties are the king's way of worshiping his idols.

In chapter 5, descriptions of drinking parties held by the king and his friends are repeated three more times before the narration of the attempted executions of the Jews.[22] The description of the third and final party (5:36) [23] is comparable to that of the party in 4:16, discussed above. Both verses contain a combination of the predicate συνίστημι, the object συμπόσιον, and the subject βασιλεύς. Furthermore, both drinking parties are connected to joy (εἰς εὐφροσύνην or χαρᾷ), and both occur in conjunction with execution of the Jews. In light of the similarities between the two verses, apparently the author implies that the purpose of the party that took place on the third day is similar to that of the parties that are mentioned in 4:16, namely, the king's worship of his idols, especially Dionysus.[24] Set within the frame of two Dionysian parties, the middle two parties (5:3; 16–17), also connected to the attempt to kill the Jews, also seem to connote Dionysian rites.

An echo of the king's praise of the idols and mockery of God at the drinking party in chapter 4 can be found in Eleazar's prayer (6:11): "Let

---

20. ἐπὶ πάντων τῶν εἰδώλων. Literally: "before all his idols." This means, as most translators and interpreters agree, that the drinking parties took place in the temples themselves (see, e.g., Emmet, "Third Book of Maccabees," 168 and Anderson, "3 Maccabees," 523). Probably this is another hint of the possibility that all Dionysus's worshipers appear freely "before" their gods in contrast to the prohibition to enter the Jewish temple.

21. Τὰ μὲν κωφὰ καὶ μὴ δυνάμενα αὐτοῖς λαλεῖν ἢ ἀρήγειν ἐπαινῶν, εἰς δὲ τὸν μέγιστον θεὸν τὰ μὴ καθήκοντα λαλῶν.

22. 5:3, 16–17, 36.

23. κατὰ δὲ τοὺς αὐτοὺς νόμους ὁ βασιλεὺς συστησάμενος πᾶν τὸ συμπόσιον εἰς εὐφροσύνην τραπῆναι παρεκάλει.

24. Probably, the unclear term in this verse κατὰ δὲ τοὺς αὐτοὺς νόμους (= according to the same rules) can be explained better according to this outlook. The problem is to which "same rules" does this phrase relate. The previous verses contain no rule connected to organizing drinking parties. In light of the linguistic parallelism between 5:36 and the parties in 4:16, it seems that the hint of "the same rules" in this case alludes to the religious customs and laws prevalent in such drinking parties like this of 4:16. See Hacham, "3 Maccabees," 27–29.

not those whose thoughts are vanity bless their vanities for the destruction of those beloved of Thee saying: Neither did their God deliver them."[25] It seems that Eleazar refers to the "vanities" of Dionysian ritual during which the Jews' enemies indeed despised the God of Israel (4:16). As I have shown elsewhere, all the historical precedents in Eleazar's prayer (6:4–8) allude to the story of the persecution of the Jews in 3 Maccabees.[26] Verse 6:6 mentions the three companions that "freely give their life to the flames that they should not serve vain things."[27] This seems to be an allusion to the Egyptian Jews who did not worship the "vanities" and were ready to surrender their lives. Given that the only idol mentioned in 3 Maccabees is Dionysus, the service of vain things to which Eleazar refers must be that of Dionysus.

The king's desire to kill the Jews using elephants also reflects a Dionysian mythos. Various ancient sources report that when Dionysus returned from his triumphant conquests in India, he brought elephants with him and, according to one source, he even rode one.[28] For this reason, elephants were symbolically connected to Dionysus and were displayed together with him in various contexts.[29] One of the most famous descriptions is that of the procession ('*Pompe*') staged by Ptolemy Philadelphus, in which Dionysus's return from India was represented.[30] Hence, it seems that the elephants in 3 Maccabees symbolize Dionysus and his threat to Judaism.[31]

According to 3 Maccabees, the elephants are given wine and frankincense (5:2, 10, 45) in order to incite them to kill the Jews. The elephants are given wine three times (5:2, 10, 20, 45) in parallel to the king's three drinking parties. The effect of the wine upon the elephants, namely, loss of control (5:2, 45), is parallel to the ecstasy and loss of control characteristic of the Dionysian cult. The association of the elephants' drunken rampage

---

25. μὴ τοῖς ματαίοις οἱ ματαιόφρονες εὐλογησάτωσαν ἐπὶ τῇ τῶν ἠγαπημένων σου ἀπωλείᾳ λέγοντες Οὐδὲ ὁ θεὸς αὐτῶν ἐρρύσατο αὐτούς.

26. See Hacham, "3 Maccabees," 124–29.

27. πυρὶ τὴν ψυχὴν αὐθαιρέτως δεδωκότας εἰς τὸ μὴ λατρεῦσαι τοῖς κενοῖς.

28. See, e.g., Diodorus Siculus, *Bibliotheca historica* 3.65.7; Pliny, *Naturalis historiae* 8.4; and Nonnus, *Dionysiaca* 26.295ff.; 329; 36.315.

29. See Jocelyn M. C. Toynbee, *Animals in Roman Life and Art* (Baltimore: Johns Hopkins University Press, 1973), 39, and Howard H. Scullard, *The Elephant in the Greek and Roman World* (London: Thames & Hudson, 1974), 124–25, 255–57. See also summary in Hacham, "3 Maccabees," 31–32.

30. Athenaeus, 5:197–208. On the elephants, see ibid., 200d–f.

31. On this Dionysian meaning of the elephants, see also J. Moreau, "Le troisième livre des Maccabées," *ChrEg* 16 (1941): 111–22; Cousland, "Dionysus *Theomachos*," 545–46.

with Dionysian rituals serves the goals of the author to ridicule and denigrate the cult.[32]

I can find no reference to the addition of frankincense to wine (5:2, 10, 45) in any other source. Frankincense is a ritualistic element, usually used in sacrifices.[33] The amount of frankincense described by the word "handful" (δράκος; 5:2) is reminiscent of two verses in *Leviticus* (2:2; 6:15[8]) that use these two words (λίβανος, δράξ) to describe the way meal offerings were burnt on the altar.[34] Therefore, it seems likely that the use of frankincense in the wine mixture is meant to suggest that the whole picture is portrayed as ritualistic in nature, namely, that the elephants are representing the cult of Dionysus.

The time when the elephants were supposed to trample the Jews, early in the morning,[35] may also be connected to the Dionysian cult. Early morning is when the Bacchae (female Dionysus worshipers) chase their victims[36] and the time of beginning the Dionysian celebrations of welcoming Dionysus.[37] Given that night is also important in the Dionysian cult,[38] it is hard to claim with certainty that the early morning hour mentioned in 3 Maccabees alludes to the Dionysian cult. Nevertheless, the frequent repetition in the story of the hour decreed for the elephants' sortie (5:10, 20, 23, 24. 26, 46) and the killing of the Jews, and the fact that after the king's slumber and forgetfulness, the execution had to be postponed until the next day, points to the importance of this hour, probably because of the religious significance attributed to it.

---

32. In contrast to Fausto Parente ("The Third Book of Maccabees as Ideological and Historical Source," *Henoch* 10 [1988]: 166), I think that giving wine to elephants is unusual and therefore this is proof for the Dionysian nature of the event.

33. See LSJ s.v. λιβανωτός.

34. The word δράκος is considered the nominative form of the dative form δράκεσι, which appears in 3 Macc 5:2. This form is unique in the *Septuagint*. It could be an alternative form of the word δράξ (which appears in the two verses in Leviticus), whose genitive form is δρακός. According to Grimm, *Kurzgefasstes exegetisches*, 258, the word appearing here is δράξ, and he seems to assume that the dative form δράκεσι is a slight variation of the usual dative form δράξι (= δράκσι, thus in our verse the only addition is ε). Our claim regarding the connection between this verse and the verses in Leviticus is, therefore, based on these analyses.

35. The exact time is defined in different formulations: ὄρθριος (at daybreak) 5:10, 23; τὴν ἐπιτέλλουσαν ἡμέραν (the day approaching) 5:20; πρωία (early morning) 5:24; οὔπω δὲ ἡλίου βολαὶ κατεσπείροντο (the rays of the sun were not yet scattered abroad) 5:26 and περὶ τὴν ἕω (about dawn) 5:46.

36. Euripides, *Bacchae* 678–679.

37. Aeschines, *In Ctesiphon* 76; Demosthenes, *In Meidias* 74. Cf. Gutman, "Historical Value of 3 Maccabees," 70.

38. See, for example, Pausanias 2:37.6. See also Tondriau, "Un Thiase Dionysiaque," 8 and n. 2.

While presenting the "Gentiles arguments" about the unsocial Jewish behavior, 3 Maccabees says, "such people were not bound in loyalty to the king or his army" (3:7).[39] As Barclay notes the word ὁμοσπόνδους (bound in loyalty) "perhaps echoes the use of libations (σπονδαί) at meals as well as in oaths of loyalty."[40] If the meaning of ὁμοσπόνδους is connected to the libation of wine, it is hard to ignore the connection between this word and the central place allocated to wine and drinking feasts in 3 Maccabees. It was customary to make libations of wine before drinking parties.[41] It is, therefore, plausible that the reference to not being "bound in loyalty" refers to the Jews' refusal to drink libations to Dionysus.

Taken alone, the mention of elephants, wine, frankincense, sunrise, drinking parties or libations may seem insignificant, but the density of these elements associated with the cult of Dionysus cannot be coincidental. They point to the religious basis for the annihilation of the Jews; the worship of God is threatened to be replaced by a particular pagan cult, that of Dionysus.

Ridiculing Dionysus

As mentioned above, the author narrates at length the failed attempts to kill the Jews and their successful redemption by God making evident the Jewish God's power and Dionysus's disgrace. Each of the ludicrous reasons for the plot's failure happen through God's agency (5:11–12, 28) and mock features of Dionysian ritual. Euripides (*Bacchae*, 282–283, 385) praises the wine drinking in the Dionysian cult, which begets sleep and forgetfulness of the day's evils. Sleep and forgetfulness are, therefore, good things emanating from Dionysus. But in this story, the king loses his self-control: he oversleeps (5:11–12) and he forgets what happened (5:18–20) and what he has ordered (5:26–32). The narrator describes sleep as a benign gift from God to his chosen ones (5:11), but since Philopator cannot be numbered among the chosen, the sleep that Philopator would normally deem a gift from Dionysus becomes a covert weapon in God's defeat of Dionysus. Finally, on the day following the third drinking party, the angels appeared, and the Jews were saved (6:18–19, 27). If every one of the king's drinking parties is part of Dionysus's cult, then the king's failure after every party indicates the worthlessness of this cult and the inability of Dionysus to help his believers. Instead of supporting the king

---

39. μήτε τῷ βασιλεῖ μήτε ταῖς δυνάμεσιν ὁμοσπόνδους... γίνεσθαι.

40. John M. G. Barclay, *Jews in the Mediterranean Diaspora: From Alexander to Trajan (323 B.C.E.–117 C.E.)* (Edinburgh: T&T Clark, 1996), 199.

41. LSJ s.v. σπονδή.

in carrying out his scheme, the ritual wine drinking of Dionysus produces side effects associated with the cult that prevent the king from implementing his order.[42]

Frequent reference to the binding of the Jews in chains may be another allusion to Dionysus's symbols used to express the inferiority of the Dionysian cult in comparison to the worship of God.[43] For example, the king orders that the Jews with their women and children be fettered in iron chains (δεσμοῖς σιδηροῖς) (3:25). The motif of imprisoning and chaining is also found in literary references to Dionysian rites.[44] In the Bacchae, Euripides recounts that when Pentheus chased the worshipers of Dionysus, he imprisoned and chained both Dionysus and a flock of Bacchae.[45] For example, he recounts that the women were chained (226: δεσμίους χέρας) and Pentheus threatened to catch other women in iron traps (231: σιδηραῖς ... ἐν ἄρκυσιν).[46] Another work dealing with the persecution of Dionysus, a Homeric hymn to Dionysus, also describes a failed attempt to chain Dionysus.[47] In this poem, pirates attempt to chain Dionysus on their ship similarly to the chaining of the Jews on ships described in 3 Macc 4:9.

The document known as 3 Maccabees subverts this Dionysian theme by making the detractors of Dionysus's cult, rather than the participants, the victims of bondage and the God of the Jews the liberator rather than Dionysus. According to the Dionysian narrative, Dionysus releases (Bacchae 613: ἐλευθερόω) himself and the bacchae from their chains, thereby

---

42. Cousland, "Dionysus *Theomachos*," 543, notes this affinity between 3 Maccabees and the Bacchae and calls it "an obvious parody." However, he views the sleep and forgetfulness of 3 Maccabees as the beginning of the punishment imposed on the evil king Philopator, while in my opinion they should be viewed as mockery of the Dionysian cult, whose benefits for his devotees are really negative and ridiculous.

43. See 3 Macc 3:25; 4:7, 8, 9; 5:5, 6; 7:5. Hadas, *Third Maccabees*, 60 (commentary on 5:5), notes the problem arising from the numerous repetitions of the Jews' chaining. Our account explains the repetition easily.

44. The motif of chains and the release from them is not unique to Dionysian works. Chaining criminals is a frequent motif in various sources from the Hellenistic and Roman periods; see, for example, Philo, *Flacc.* 74; Josephus, *Ant.* 18.195. Thus, the motif of chains in itself suggests nothing. The main argument derives from the numerous repetitions that accentuate this motif in 3 Maccabees in parallel to its centrality in the Dionysian works, and from the release from chains, which is common to both sources.

45. Cousland, "Dionysus *Theomachos*," 542 and n. 19, explains this point as a part of the evidence for his opinion that Philopator's figure is depicted similarly to that of Pentheus. I think that the focus of the issue is characterizing Dionysus's cult as the cause of the persecutions and danger facing the Jews of Egypt.

46. Euripides, *Bacchae* 355, 443–448, 518, 615–616, 643, 648, 792.

47. Thomas W. Allen, ed., *Homeri Opera* (5 vols.; Oxford: Oxford University Press: 1946), 5:76, lines 12–13.

overcoming his persecutors. In 3 Maccabees, the Jews of Egypt are also freed from their chains by Ptolemy Philopator's new edict (6:27), which acknowledges the Jews are the descendents of the living God who protects the state and the king. Ptolemy Philopator, who is dedicated to the Dionysian cult, by ordering the release of the Jews from their bonds, implicitly acknowledges the Jewish God's supremacy over Dionysus. By denying Dionysus's power to liberate, once again, the author of 3 Maccabees negates the benefits of joining his cult.

One more possible association with Dionysus adds to the parody. The description of the incarceration of the Jews on the ships portrays some Jews chained with unbreakable shackles (πέδη) on their legs (4:9). In contrast, the angels who appeared bind the king's army in immovable chains (πέδη) (6:19), after which the elephants trample the soldiers. Thus, the persecutors of the Jews themselves are injured in a way identical to the manner they had wanted to injure the Jews. Whereas God delivers believers and releases them, Dionysus the deliverer or liberator does not succeed in saving the soldiers, dispatched in his name, from the elephants, which were guided by God's angels. Or, from another point of view, the elephants which symbolize Dionysus, were not guided by him, but rather were controlled by the Most High God, the God of Israel.

The defeat of Dionysus can be shown in an additional way. At the end of 3 Maccabees, we are told that those Jews who surrendered to the king's edict and joined Dionysus's cult were killed (7:10–12, 14–15). Thus, there is no reason or benefit whatsoever in joining Dionysus's cult. In fact, it might even be dangerous.

Erich Gruen has recently drawn our attention to the highly developed sense of humor of 3 Maccabees—as well as of other Jewish-Hellenistic literature.[48] J. R. C. Cousland has also called one of the points mentioned above an "obvious parody," and defined the book as "profoundly ironic" and "comic."[49] In contrast to Gruen, our study reveals that the humor serves more than as "comic relief" that "subverted the aura of foreboding and fear."[50] The humor functions as a weapon in a religious and cultural struggle. The author ridicules the Dionysian cult in order to convince the reader of its worthlessness. Cousland's view that we have here ironic *theomachy* seems more appropriate.[51] Clearly 3 Maccabees is a polemic

---

48. Gruen, *Heritage and Hellenism,* 234–36 (on 3 Maccabees), 327 (index s.v. "Humor and irony").

49. Cousland, "Dionysus *Theomachos,*" 543, 547, and n. 46.

50. See Gruen, *Heritage and Hellenism,* 236.

51. Cousland, "Dionysus *Theomachos,*" 547.

against the Dionysian cult, but this leads to the question: To whom is the polemic directed?

POLEMICS AGAINST JEWISH WORSHIPERS OF DIONYSUS

In order to solve this puzzle, let us turn briefly to the well-known comparison between 3 Maccabees and the book of Esther. It is well known that Esther, like 3 Maccabees, abounds with drinking parties and that the Jews' feasts celebrate the turn of events and the salvation of the Jews.[52] However, whereas in Esther these drinking parties express the Gentiles' stupidity and materialism, in 3 Maccabees the Gentiles' parties express their idol worship. In contrast to 3 Maccabees, Esther's Jewish feasts are not described as an expression of thanksgiving to God or as an expression of prayer. The decree against the Jews in Esther names men, women, and children (3:13) and, therefore, calls for genocide. In 3 Maccabees, the original decree prescribes the death punishment only for those who speak against the king's decree (2:28). Only later, when the Jews refuse to accept the king's offer to join Dionysus's mysteries and to receive civil rights, are all in danger of being killed (2:32–3:1). In other words, in Esther the danger of annihilation is physical and unconditional, whereas in 3 Maccabees the physical danger emanates from a religious decree imposing idol worship. Thus, in Esther the decree is against Jews and in 3 Maccabees it is against Judaism.

In both books, the Jews injure members of other groups, but the groups are substantially different. In Esther, the Jews kill all those who sought to kill them (9:2, 5, 6). In 3 Maccabees, the Jews kill the three hundred Jews who agreed to the king's decree and joined the mysteries (7:14–15). In contrast to Esther, the Jews did not harm or kill even one evil Gentile.[53] Thus, the main danger facing the Jews in 3 Maccabees does not emanate from foreigners but from those Jews who abandon their faith and turn to Dionysus.

This short comparison between Esther and 3 Maccabees accentuates the significance of the subtle allusions to Dionysus's cult in 3 Maccabees. Although 3 Maccabees describes the Jews' persecution by the king, the central problem that seems to bother the writer is the danger facing Judaism

---

52. 3 Macc 6:30–32, 35, 36, 40; 7:15, 18, 19–20; Esth 8:17; 9:17–18, 19, 22.

53. Cf. Hadas, *Third Maccabees*, 7; Tcherikover, "Third Book of Maccabees," 23; and John J. Collins, *Between Athens and Jerusalem: Jewish Identity in the Hellenistic Diaspora* (2nd ed.; Grand Rapids: Eerdmans, 2000), 128. Gentiles were indeed killed according to 3 Maccabees, but this was God's act through the drunken elephants who trampled the soldiers following them (3 Macc 6:18–21). No Jew even imagined harming any Gentile.

from within its ranks. The author struggles against those Jews who are not loyal to their ancestral tradition and who are tempted to abandon it in order to join the mysteries, especially that of Dionysus. His conclusion is that it is inconceivable to abandon Judaism in favor of the Dionysian cult, since Dionysus failed when he faced the God of Israel, and those tempted to convert their religion were killed. Even the king, who is dedicated to the Dionysian cult, acknowledges God's powers (7:2) and has a feast in his honor (6:33). Judaism is represented as a religion recognized by the authorities that one would be unwise to reject for worship of another god. In short, 3 Maccabees seems to be an anti-Dionysian fiction that serves to polemicize any Jew's inclination toward Dionysus's cult.

DIONYSUS THE JEW

Although 3 Maccabees struggles against the Jews' inclination toward Dionysus's cult, the work appropriates elements of Dionysian worship in its description of the actions of faithful Jews. Juxtaposed with the four drinking parties organized by the king, stand the parties Jews hold after their redemption.[54] Emphasizing the reversal of fortune, the author sets the festival of deliverance in "that place where they had expected destruction to overtake them" (6:30). In contrast to the pagan parties of the king, the Jews held parties "not for the sake of drinking and gluttony, but for the deliverance that had come to them through God" (6:36).[55] Thus, the feasts are not part of the brutish cult of Dionysus, but a thanksgiving to God for their redemption. Moreover, in contrast to those Jews who submitted to the decree and abandoned God's path "for their belly's sake" (7:11), the faithful Jews erect a house of prayer where the feasts had been held (7:20). In other words, the faithful Jews also drink, but their drinking is better than that of the brutish Dionysians, since its main purpose is to direct one to prayer and thanksgiving.

Dancing, an activity common in Dionysian ritual,[56] is also mentioned in conjunction with the Jews' parties (6:32, 35). Once again they stand in contrast to the Dionysian practice of losing self-control, for these dances

---

54. It seems that it is not coincidental that the verb συνίστημι, which is used twice to describe the organization of the king's drinking parties (4:16; 5:36), is also used in ch. 6 to describe the Jews' feasts and dances (6:31, 32, 35).

55. οὐ πότου χάριν καὶ λιχνείας, σωτηρίας δὲ τῆς διὰ θεὸν γενομένης αὐτοῖς. For Jewish Hellenistic parallels to this idea, see Josephus, C. Ap. 2.195–196; Philo, Spec. 2.148.

56. Dances were part of ritual in general, but they are a prominent motif in Dionysian ritual. See, for example, Euripides, Bacchae 21, 63, 114, 220, etc.

signify joy and peace (6:32) and are accompanied by thanksgiving and psalms (6:35).

Other details in the description of the Jews' redemption and celebration hint at Dionysus's cult as well. When returning home the Jews are described as "crowned (κατεστεμμένοι) with all manner of the most fragrant flowers (ἄνθεσι)" (7:16).[57] In the Homeric hymn to Dionysus, the god causes flowers to bloom as one of the miracles he performs while imprisoned on the ship.[58] The word ἄνθεσι is probably reminiscent of a Dionysian festival, the Anthesteria (Ἀνθεστήρια).[59] The participle κατεστεμμένοι is suggestive of crowning (στεφανόω) with ivy leaves in Dionysian ritual.[60] While the author seems to imply that the people of Israel are also crowned when worshiping their God, he marks a significant difference. Philopator's decree stipulates that the ivy leaf must be branded onto the Jews' flesh (2:29), but the redeemed Jews only crown themselves with garlands and do not harm their bodies. Moreover, the flowers crowning the Jews are described as "most fragrant" (εὐωδέστατος). The same word used to describe the beverages that brought the elephants to a state of seeming craziness (5:45). That means that the perfuming in the Dionysian cult is reckless intoxication, and the Jews' perfume is a delicate smell that crowns them. Thus, in the description of these details as well, the writer of 3 Maccabees claims that the Jews have what the Dionysian cult has, but in a pure, gentle, Jewish way and not in a vulgar, disgusting way.

Another clue can be interpreted in a similar way. At the end of the book it is said that the Jews returned home ἐλεύθεροι (free, 7:20). As Gustav A. Deissmann noted, this is in contrast to their situation and feelings during the persecutions against them.[61] It should be emphasized that a similar word is used to describe the reward for those who persecute the Jews in 3:28, suggesting that the persecutors would be crowned in the

---

57. παντοίοις εὐωδεστάτοις ἄνθεσι κατεστεμμένοι.

58. Allen, *Homeri Opera*, 77, l. 41: ... ἄνθεσι τηλεθάων....

59. The name of this holiday, Anthesteria, is documented from the second century B.C.E.; see Richard Hamilton, *Choes and Anthesteria: Athenian Iconography and Ritual* (Ann Arbor: University of Michigan Press, 1992), 5–6. If we accept Hamilton's opinion (ibid., 57) that a custom of crowning children with flowers is connected to the Anthesteria, it may be possible that the hint in 3 Maccabees is not only of the association arising from the sound of the word but also to customs of this holiday. However, I did not find sources that report that this holiday was celebrated in Alexandria.

60. See, for example, Euripides, *Bacchae* 81.

61. Gustav A. Deissmann, *Bible Studies* (Edinburgh: T&T Clark, 1901), 345.

62. The exact text of this verse is uncertain; see Hanhart's appartus (52). However, many scholars prefer the text and interpretation connecting it with Dionysus's cult. See Grimm, *Kurzgefasstes exegetisches*, 249; P. Perdrizet, "Le Fragment de Satyros sur les dèmes

Dionysian festival Eleutheria.[62] Thus, the use of the word ἐλεύθεροι for describing the Jews' situation after their deliverance not only accentuates the reversal in the Jews' situation, it also means that the author of 3 Maccabees contrasts the crown of the Dionysian festival with the real freedom felt by the Jews when they were delivered. Thus, the Jews do not require Dionysus to feel ἐλεύθεροι, because they have their God's deliverance to bring them freedom.

Besides ridiculing the Dionysian cult, the author of 3 Maccabees claims that Judaism offers preferable rewards by appropriating features of Dionysian worship in the representation of Jewish celebrations. The conclusion is, therefore, that if a Jew is attracted by the Dionysian cult, he or she should not abandon his faith and transfer to Dionysus's cult since Judaism has benefits superior to those of Dionysus.

Conclusions

If I am correct, the story of the three hundred apostates and the ridicule and imitation of the Dionysian cult in 3 Maccabees indicates that some Egyptian Jews were inclined towards Dionysus. Other sources substantiate this claim. Martin Hengel points to several sources that report the interest of Diaspora Jews in the mysteries and the Dionysian cult.[63] Thus, 3 Maccabees should be added to those sources reporting pagan influence upon Judaism and Jewish syncretism.

The fact that the data point to an appeal to the Jews by the mystery cults, especially that of Dionysus, raises the question precisely what appealed to them. I will limit myself to two suggestions. To begin with, the cult of Dionysus was the state religion, and it was a prevalent and important cult in Ptolemaic Egypt.[64] Therefore, avoidance of the Dionysian cult may have been interpreted as an act of disloyalty to the state and the dynasty. Third Maccabees suggests that the Jews who participated in the cult did it for reasons other than piety: those who "transgressed the divine commandments for their belly's sake would never be well disposed to the king's estate either" (7:11). The line implies that they acted out of political self-interest, that is their motivation was rooted in their participation in the state. On the other hand, for some

---

d'alexandrie," *REA* 12 (1910): 235; Emmet, "Third Book of Maccabees," 167; Hadas, *Third Maccabees*, 52; Anderson, "3 Maccabees," 522; and Hacham, "3 Maccabees," 50–52.

63. Martin Hengel, *Judaism and Hellenism: Studies in Their Encounter in Palestine during the Early Hellenistic Period* (2 vols.; Philadelphia: Fortress, 1974), 1:202, 2:135 n. 611; see also Hacham, "3 Maccabees," 58–63.

64. Fraser, *Ptolemaic Alexandria*, 206.

Jews, participation in the cult may have offered an opportunity to express genuine religious feelings. Without direct access to the rituals of the temple and the opportunity to make frequent offerings, some Egyptian Jews may have sought a tangible context in which to express themselves. This motive would provide an explanation for a particularly difficult verse in the king's edict: "none of those who did not sacrifice should be allowed to enter their temples" (2:28), namely, those who did not sacrifice are not true worshipers of God. It must have been difficult for the Jews to persuade their neighbors that they were devotees of a God to whom they were never seen making offerings or providing service.

Treating 3 Maccabees as a fiction enables its analysis as such. This analysis exposes one of the problems that has troubled this author, namely, the Jews' inclination toward Dionysus's cult, and one of the purposes of the book: an anti-Dionysian polemic.

THIRD MACCABEES: HISTORICAL FICTIONS
AND THE SHAPING OF JEWISH IDENTITY
IN THE HELLENISTIC PERIOD

Sara Johnson

INTRODUCTION

When Philopator learned from those who returned that the regions he
had controlled had been seized by Antiochus, he gave orders to all his
forces, both infantry and cavalry, took his sister Arsinoe, and marched
out to the region near Raphia, where the army of Antiochus was
encamped. (3 Macc 1:1 NRSV)[1]

The battle of Raphia (217 B.C.E.) is well known to Hellenistic historians as the Egyptian victory that marked the end of the Fourth Syrian War
between Ptolemy IV Philopator and Antiochus III. The above-cited sentence is not from a historian such as Polybius, however, but is rather the
opening verse of 3 Maccabees, a wholly fictional story of persecution happily averted. The incongruity of the tale's opening and its subject matter
is only one symptom of a deeper problem that has long puzzled readers
of 3 Maccabees and other quasi-fictional Jewish texts: What sort of narrative did the author of 3 Maccabees set out to write?

The author of 3 Maccabees does not merely mention the battle of
Raphia as his starting-point, a chronological anchor for the story; he gives
a detailed account of the battle, which agrees for the most part with that
given by Polybius.[2] Indeed, the level of detail provided seems strangely

---

1. ὁ δὲ Φιλοπάτωρ παρὰ τῶν ἀνακομισθέντων μαθὼν τὴν γινομένην τῶν ὑπ' αὐτοῦ κρα-
τουμένων τόπων ἀφαίρεσιν ὑπὸ Ἀντιόχου παραγγείλας ταῖς πάσαις δυνάμεσι πεζικαῖς τε καὶ
ἱππικαῖς καὶ τὴν ἀδελφὴν Ἀρσινόην συμπαραλαβὼν ἐξώρμησε μέχρι τῶν κατὰ Ῥαφίαν τόπων,
ὅπου παρεμβεβλήκεισαν οἱ περὶ Ἀντίοχον. All Greek citations from 3 Macc are taken from
Robert Hanhart, *Maccabaeorum liber III* (2nd ed.; Septuaginta, Vetus Testamentum graecum
9/3; Göttingen: Vandenhoeck & Ruprecht, 1980).
2. 3 Macc 1:1–7, cf. Polybius 5.79–86. It does not in fact agree with Polybius's account in
every respect, leading to speculation that the author of 3 Macc used another source (see n. 3).

irrelevant to the main narrative of the book. Some scholars see here evidence of the author's clumsy use of some lost Hellenistic historian, perhaps the sensationalist Ptolemy of Megalopolis.[3] This prepares the reader for a tale firmly rooted in the known facts of the past. Philopator's tour of the surrounding cities of Syria to offer sacrifices in their temples also finds its place in the historical account of Polybius (5.86). When Philopator arrives in Jerusalem, however, we soon find ourselves jerked from the dry facts of history into the fantastic world of Jewish legend. Philopator, in a scene suspiciously reminiscent of Heliodorus's experience in 2 Maccabees,[4] attempts like many an arrogant conqueror to force his way into the temple and is struck down by God's wrath. Legend follows upon legend. Carried from the scene, indignant and breathing threats against the Jews, Philopator prepares a horrible death for the Jews at the feet of a pack of drunken elephants, only to be foiled at the last moment by the appearance of angels. The unforgettable role played by the elephants is likewise suspiciously familiar to the modern reader: Josephus knew at least two forms of the legend.[5] The substance of 3 Maccabees is unquestionably fiction, not history.

For a more detailed comparison of 3 Macc 1:1–7 with the account of Polybius, see Sara R. Johnson, *Historical Fictions and Hellenistic Jewish Identity* (Berkeley and Los Angeles: University of California Press, 2004), 192–202.

3. Cyril W. Emmet, "The Third Book of Maccabees," *APOT* 1:159; Elias J. Bickermann, "Makkabaerbucher (III)," PW 27:799; Victor A. Tcherikover, "The Third Book of Maccabees as a Historical Source of Augustus' Time," *ScrHier* 7 (1961): 2–11; Hugh Anderson, "3 Maccabees," *OTP* 2:513; and Joseph M. Modrzejewski, *The Jews of Egypt* (trans. Robert Cornman; Philadelphia: Jewish Publication Society, 1995), 147. However, it is not really necessary to posit a lost source; the author of 3 Macc may in fact have used the same sources as Polybius, if not indeed Polybius himself, but altered the details to suit his narrative (Johnson, *Historical Fictions*, 200–201).

4. 3 Macc 1:8–2:24, cf. 2 Macc 3:9–40.

5. Josephus, C. *Ap.* 2.53–55, locating the persecution under Physcon in 145 B.C.E. In this passage, Josephus gives details from at least two different versions of the legend (Tcherikover, "Third Book," 8; John J. Collins, *Between Athens and Jerusalem: Jewish Identity in the Hellenistic Diaspora* [2nd ed.; Grand Rapids: Eerdmans, 2000], 123; Johnson, *Historical Fictions*, 184–85). Although Josephus's version has often been thought by modern scholars to be more historically reliable than that found in 3 Maccabees, both versions are equally tendentious, and it is more likely that both Josephus and the author of 3 Maccabees are attempting in different ways to locate in historical context a legend whose historical origins, if there were any, had already been lost. For the argument in favor of the historicity of the incident as recorded by Josephus, see Carl L. W. Grimm, *Das zweite, dritte und vierte Buch der Maccabaer* (vol. 4 of *Kurzgefaßtes exegetisches Handbuch zu den Apokryphen des alten Testaments;* Leipzig: Hirzl, 1857), 216, 218; Moses Hadas, *The Third and Fourth Books of Maccabees* (JAL 3; New York: Harper, 1953), 10–11; Tcherikover, "Third Book," 8–9; Geroge W. E. Nickelsburg, *Jewish Literature between the Bible and the Mishnah* (Philadelphia: Fortress, 1981), 170; Emil Schürer, *The History of the Jewish People in the Age of Jesus Christ* (rev. ed. and trans. by Geza

Readers from Josephus to modern times have been consistently bewildered by the deliberate combination of two elements that appear (at least to us) to be incompatible with each other, historical precision and blatant fiction. The narrative is replete with carefully drawn historical detail. The portrait of the tyrannical and headstrong Philopator is compatible with the villainous portrait of his character found in all the historical sources for the period. The same historical sources confirm, in lurid detail, the life of idleness and debauchery led by the king back in Alexandria and the evil character of his accustomed drinking-companions.[6] The insistence that the Jews of Alexandria consent to be branded with the ivy leaf of Dionysus recalls Philopator's known penchant for the cult of Dionysus, which he reformed and promoted.[7] Lest the reader be left in any doubt as to the reliability of the tale, the author includes verbatim decrees that precisely imitate the tortured style of the Ptolemaic chancery—although, to be sure, the style they imitate is that of the author's own day, not Philopator's.[8] The author is knowledgeable about the facts of Philopator's reign and the details of Ptolemaic court procedure.[9] Yet this same author, at other times, seems to have no concern for

---

Vermes, F. Millar, and Martin Goodman; 3 vols.; Edinburgh: T&T Clark, 1986), 3.1:539; Modrzejewski, *Jews of Egypt*, 147; John M. G. Barclay, *Jews in the Mediterranean Diaspora* (Edinburgh: T&T Clark, 1996), 38, 194; and Collins, *Between Athens and Jerusalem*, 124. For doubts about the historicity of either version, see Bickermann, "Makkabaerbucher," 799–800; Anderson, "3 Maccabees," 510–11; Erich S. Gruen, *Heritage and Hellenism* (Berkeley and Los Angeles: University of California Press, 1998), 228–29; and Johnson, *Historical Fictions*, 184–87.

6. Our principal sources for Philopator's character are Polybius 5.34; Plutarch, *Cleom.* 33; and Justin, *Historiae Philipicae* 30.1–2. See also incidental references in Aelian, *Var. hist.* 13.22, 14.31; Pliny, *Nat.* 7.56; and *Etymologicum Magnum*, s.v. Γάλλος.

7. In addition to the primary sources cited above, the extent of Philopator's devotion to the cult of Dionysus is revealed by Satyrus frg. 51 and Berlin Papyrus 6.1211. See P. Perdrizet, "Le fragment de Satyros," *REA* 12 (1910): 217–47; J. Moreau, "Le troisième livre des Maccabées," *ChrEg* 16 (1941): 111–22; Furio Jesi, "Notes sur l'édit dionysiaque de Ptolémée IV Philopator," *JNES* 15 (1956): 236–40; Tcherikover, "Third Book," 4–5; Modrzejewski, *Jews of Egypt*, 149–52; and Johnson, *Historical Fictions*, 205–9.

8. The allegedly verbatim decrees are 3 Macc 3:12–29 and 7:1–9. For the dating of the formulae used in the letters to the late Hellenistic period, see Bickermann, "Makkabaerbucher," 798; Emmet, "Third Book," 157–58; Tcherikover, "Third Book," 11; D. S. Williams, "3 Maccabees: A Defense of Diaspora Judaism?" *JSP* 13 (1995): 20; and Collins, *Between Athens and Jerusalem*, 124 (though Tcherikover and Collins would date 3 Maccabees itself even later, in the early Roman period). For the implications of the formulae for the dating of 3 Maccabees, see further Johnson, *Historical Fictions*, 139–40; for the implications of the letters for the author's historical-fictional methodology, see Johnson, *Historical Fictions*, 209–16.

9. See notes above; it has also been argued that the figure of Dositheus, allegedly an apostate Jew who saved Philopator from an assassination plot at 3 Macc 1:2–3, may be based on a historical figure by the same name who actually served at the court of Philopator. On

the exigencies of historical fact, or even historical plausibility. He has no qualm about asking us to believe that the crowd of Jews whom Philopator marked for death was so numerous that the king's scribes had to give up registering them when they had entirely exhausted the kingdom's supply of papyrus and ink and, at the same time, to believe that this innumerable horde could nevertheless be fitted into one (admittedly large) hippodrome.[10] In short, the author adopts all of the outward mannerisms of a serious historian and, yet, seems unconcerned by the fact that the fictional character of his work would be apparent to any reader who was historically sophisticated enough to appreciate his use of the conventions of Hellenistic historiography. How can we make sense of this paradox?

A Jewish Novel?

One suggestion that has gained in popularity of late is to label 3 Maccabees a member of a genre like "romance" or "ancient novel."[11] It is not uncommon to find in the Greek sentimental novel apparently precise, but inaccurate, historical details sprinkled throughout the narrative with promiscuous abandon. Chariton sets his novel ostensibly in Syracuse in the time of the general Hermocrates (contemporary with the Peloponnesian War) but makes no effort to present a consistent historical setting, instead mixing and matching real and invented historical events and personages of the fifth and fourth centuries at will and, apparently, at random.[12] The reader of Hellenistic Jewish texts can likewise supply a number of parallels from among the so-called "Jewish novels." One thinks, for instance, of the seemingly accurate portrayal in the book of

Dositheus, see CPJ 127d–e, 230–36; Hugo Willrich, "Dositheos Drimylos' Sohn," *Klio* 7 (1907): 293; Hadas, *Third and Fourth Books*, 32–33; Alexander Fuks, "Dositheos Son of Drimylos: A Prosopographical Note," *JJP* 7–8 (1954): 205–9; Joseph M. Modrzejewski, "How to Be a Jew in Hellenistic Egypt?" in *Diasporas in Antiquity* (ed. Shaye J. D. Cohen and Ernest S. Frerichs; Atlanta: Scholars Press, 1993), 83–85; idem, *Jews of Egypt*, 56–61; and Barclay, *Diaspora*, 32, 104. Polybius 5.81 reports the assassination plot but makes no mention of a Dositheus, apostate Jew or not. Although it is often assumed that the historical Dositheus was a Jew, the sources do not actually say that he was; the only evidence of his ethnicity is his theophoric name and the possible connection with the account in 3 Maccabees. See further Johnson, *Historical Fictions*, 195–96.

10. 3 Macc 4:17–21.

11. The most systematic treatment of Jewish texts as "novels" is found in Lawrence M. Wills, *The Jewish Novel in the Ancient World* (Ithaca. N.Y.: Cornell University Press, 1995).

12. See, e.g., Bryan P. Reardon, *Collected Ancient Greek Novels* (Berkeley and Los Angeles: University of California Press, 1989), 18; and George P. Goold, trans., *Chariton: Callirhoe* (LCL 481; Cambridge: Harvard University Press, 1995), 10–12.

Esther of the blustering tyrant Ahasuerus (Xerxes), which is undermined
by a host of anachronisms, not least his willingness to take as his queen a
woman of humble and unknown origin.[13] Even more strikingly, one
might cite, from the book of Judith, the wholly fictional attack on the fictional town of Bethulia by Holofernes, the general of the strangely-named
Nebuchadnezzar the Assyrian. Nebuchanezzar is campaigning to enslave
the western nations, not in 587 B.C.E., but in the days when the Jews had
recently returned from exile and rebuilt their temple.[14] It is becoming
increasingly common today to label such Jewish texts "Jewish novels," in
no small part because in such Jewish texts, as in the Greek novels, imaginary historical details are used playfully to indicate that the story is
meant to be read as fiction.[15] Consequently, scholars have sought primarily literary motives, such as dramatic considerations or irony, for the
inclusion of fiction in purportedly historical accounts.[16]

The similarities between 3 Maccabees and other so-called Jewish
novels, such as Esther and Judith, are undeniable and highly significant.
Scholars have drawn our attention to the literary art with which these stories are constructed. These efforts to define the aesthetic principles of
ancient fictions lay the groundwork for other considerations. Numerous
recent works examine how narratives with strong touches of fiction help
to shape the identity of communities represented by their protagonists.[17]
The ancient novels should not be dismissed as mere entertainments, nor
should the use of fictional historical details be characterized as a playful
"marker" of such texts as fiction and nothing more. In 3 Maccabees, and
to a varying degree in many other Jewish fictions, the invention of history
is designed to support and further the author's own ideological agenda,
the creation of a particular view of Jewish identity.

---

13. For the identification of Ahasuerus as Xerxes, see Carey A. Moore, *Esther* (AB 7B;
Garden City. N.Y.: Doubleday, 1971), 3–4; for accurate details, ibid., xli; for anachronisms,
ibid., xlv–xlvi. See also (on all three issues) Jon D. Levenson, *Esther: A Commentary*
(Louisville: Westminster John Knox, 1997), 23–27.

14. For the problem of historical and geographical errors in Judith, see Carey A. Moore,
Judith (AB 40; Garden City, N.Y.: Doubleday, 1985), 37–38, 46, 52–56, 123–24.

15. So, in the case of Judith, Moore, *Judith*, 79, 85, 124, 129; Toni Craven, *Artistry and
Faith in the Book of Judith* (SBLDS 70; Chico, Calif.: Scholars Press, 1983), 65–74.

16. For example see, Wills, *Jewish Novel*, 134–39.

17. For example, see Judith Perkins, *The Suffering Self: Pain and Narrative Representation
in the Early Christian Era* (London: Routledge, 1995), in which the representation of suffering
in early Christian narratives serves to form a new human self-understanding, and Simon
Swain, "The Greek Novel and Greek Identity," in idem, *Hellenism and Empire: Language, Classicism and Power in the Greek World A.D. 50—250* (Oxford: Clarendon, 1996), 101–31, which
analyzes the role of the sentimental novel in the development of Greek identity during the
Second Sophistic.

Genre and Identity

Re-creating a sense of national identity often involves reinventing that nation's past. The invention of self-consciously historical fictions about the past is a widespread phenomenon in the works of many Jewish authors. While Jewish fictions about the past are certainly highly entertaining, they were not written merely to entertain.[18] They serve more importantly as a means through which to articulate a particular view of the past and therefore of Jewish identity in the contemporary Hellenistic world.

The Jewish texts in which scholars have identified elements of fiction vary in content, language, and genre. They include not only 3 Maccabees but also the *Letter of Aristeas*, Esther, Daniel, Judith, Tobit, 2 Maccabees, the tales of the Tobiads and of Alexander's visit to Jerusalem, Artapanus's history of the patriarchs, the *Testament of Joseph* and *Joseph and Aseneth*. Some seem to be based on legends that first originated in the Hellenistic period, while others contain elements of legends that go well back into the Persian period. They take for their subject a wide variety of historical topics, some drawn from life under Greek rule, some from life under Persian rule, some going back to the traditions surrounding Joseph and Moses. Some were composed in Greek, while others were composed originally in Hebrew or Aramaic and only later translated into Greek. Esther and 3 Maccabees are essentially etymological legends that trace the origin of particular religious festivals. The *Letter of Aristeas* is written in the form of an eyewitness narrative account of the translation of the Septuagint, addressed to the author's brother. Daniel consists of a series of apocalyptic prophecies, somewhat awkwardly joined with several chapters of historical narrative. Second Maccabees is an epitome of a work of Hellenistic historiography that contains within the narrative several episodes that have been labeled as "romance." The tales of the Tobiads and the stories of Alexander the Great's visit to Jerusalem are preserved only in the lengthy historical narrative of Josephus's *Antiquities*, and it is

---

18. While I think most readers of Jewish texts would agree that even the most light-hearted Jewish tales have a serious didactic purpose, it is often alleged that the specific use of historical anachronisms in texts like Esther, Daniel and Judith was intended only to entertain the audience and signal the fictional nature of the text. With particular regard to Judith, where the anachronisms are so outrageous that virtually every reader would have noticed them, it has been argued that the historical absurdities were, first and foremost, a deliberate signal to the audience to read the narrative as fiction; in Moore's phrase, the author launches the narrative with a "sly wink." See Moore, *Judith*, 85, 124, 129; Craven, *Artistry and Faith*, 72; and Wills, *Ancient Novel*, 134. My argument is that the use of history itself in all the Jewish fictions, no matter how "realistic" or "absurd" the details, should be regarded not primarily as entertaining narrative coloration, but as an essential part of the author's didactic purpose.

hard to say what their original form was. The sensational account of Joseph's encounter with Potiphar's wife turns up unexpectedly in the otherwise sternly moralizing context of the *Testaments of the Twelve Patriarchs*. Artapanus's history of the patriarchs, which survives only in fragments, appears to build Moses up as a highly eccentric national hero, in a manner very reminiscent of the Alexander Romance. *Joseph and Aseneth* most strongly resembles the genre of the Greek sentimental novel, with its focus upon the star-crossed romance of its hero and heroine, although unlike the typical sentimental novel, it is really much more interested in the conversion of the Egyptian heroine Aseneth to Judaism than in the love affair or developing an understanding of marriage.

It should be clear, even from this short survey, that the attempt to collapse all of these diverse texts into a single genre could result in a meaningless abstraction. Yet, as varied as these texts are, they do have one thing in common: they all, regardless of the language or the genre in which the authors happen to be writing, employ fictions about the past in order to make a particular didactic point about identity. The point being made is not always the same. Jewish identity in the late Hellenistic period was far from monolithic. There were Jews who spoke Greek and Jews who spoke Aramaic, Jews living in Palestine and Jews living in the Diaspora, those who lived under or looked to Hasmonean rule and those who thrived under foreign rule, those who sought to carve out a niche in the wider Hellenistic world and those who looked to the coming of God's kingdom to sweep that world away and replace it with a better one. Thus it should not surprise us that the so-called Jewish romances reflect an infinite variety of ideas about the nature of Hellenistic Jewish identity. What is interesting is that all employ self-conscious historical fictions to get their point across. It would appear that the technique was infinitely adaptable.

MODELING THE BOUNDARIES OF ASSIMILATION

How then does the author of 3 Maccabees manipulate history, not merely to entertain or to signal the fictional nature of the story, but in order to support his particular didactic purpose?

It is generally agreed that the author of 3 Maccabees was a Greek-speaking Egyptian Jew who was writing primarily for an audience of Greek-speaking Alexandrian Jews.[19] It is usually further agreed that an

---

19. The literary style of the text makes it clear that the author spoke Greek at a relatively high level and expected the same of his readers (see n. 26); in addition to his distinctive Alexandrian literary style, the author's familiarity with the Ptolemaic court and setting of the

important part of his purpose was to construct for his audience a particular model of interaction between Jews and Greeks. There is, however, less agreement as to what that model was.[20] Many scholars have argued that 3 Maccabees should be understood in direct contrast to another popular Hellenistic Jewish text of roughly the same period, the *Letter of Aristeas*.[21] The *Letter of Aristeas* gives an account of the translation of the Hebrew Torah into Greek at Alexandria in the reign of Ptolemy II Philadelphus. It paints a highly idealized picture of harmony, cooperation and mutual admiration between Greeks and Jews. In contrast, many have argued that 3 Maccabees constructs a model of interaction that is based not on cooperation but on confrontation and mutual hostility. Nothing could be further from the truth. Although the plot that drives the narrative centers on a series of confrontations, the author of 3 Maccabees, precisely like the author of the *Letter of Aristeas*, seeks to construct a model of Jewish identity that will allow Greek-speaking Jews to preserve their traditions and their laws, while at the same time participating fully in the wider Greek world.[22]

The preservation of Jewish tradition and the faithful adherence of the Jewish people to the Jewish law are of central importance to the author of 3 Maccabees. When a conflict occurs between the demands of God's law and the demands of society or the state, God's law must come first. Consequently, the Jews of Jerusalem welcome their victorious king to the city but refuse him admittance to the temple in defiance of all his threats (1:8–29). Likewise, back in Alexandria, the vast majority of the Jews of Alexandria reject Philopator's attempt to seduce them into abandoning their faith. Given a choice between social advancement at the price of apostasy and social degradation or worse, the faithful Jews firmly reject apostasy and seek to evade the decree in other more acceptable ways, such as bribing officials not to register them (2:31–33).

---

bulk of the story in Egypt point clearly to an Egyptian provenance, and the preoccupation with Jewish tradition demonstrates the author's ethnicity. That the author was a Greek-speaking Egyptian Jew, most likely from Alexandria, has been universally assumed by every scholar who has worked with the text; so, e.g., Grimm, *Das zweite, dritte und vierte Buch*, 220; Hadas, *Third and Fourth Books*, 22; Anderson, "3 Maccabees," 510–12; Barclay, *Diaspora*, 192–203; Gruen, *Heritage*, 222–36; Collins, *Between Athens and Jerusalem*, 122–31.

20. For a variety of theories, see, e.g., Hadas, *Third and Fourth Books*, 3; Victor A. Tcherikover, "Jewish Apologetic Literature Reconsidered," *Eos* 48 (1956): 191–93; Anderson, "3 Maccabees," 511–12; Collins, *Between Athens and Jerusalem*, 126; Barclay, *Diaspora*, 192–203.

21. Esp. S. Tracy, "III Maccabees and Pseudo-Aristeas," *YCS* 1 (1928): 241–52; Hadas, *Third and Fourth Books*, 8–10; Collins, *Between Athens and Jerusalem*, 126; and Barclay, *Diaspora*, 192–203.

22. This point is argued at considerably greater length in Johnson, *Historical Fictions*, 141–81. See also Gruen, *Heritage and Hellenism*, 231–34.

Even when confronted with the ultimate sanction, they are willing to submit to death rather than repudiate their law. Apostates are shunned (2:33) and ultimately slaughtered (7:10–15). In each crisis, the hapless Jews place their faith in God to save them, and in each case their faith is rewarded by a series of miracles and divine epiphanies (2:21–22; 5:11–13, 28; 6:18–21). God will protect and reward the pious, and punish the wicked.

That the author of 3 Maccabees is uncompromisingly committed to the preservation of Jewish tradition and law has never been questioned. What has been less often observed is that the author's commitment to the primacy of Jewish law does not imply a permanent state of hostility and confrontation between Jews and non-Jews. On the contrary, the author goes to some pains to establish the fact that under normal circumstances, the preservation of Jewish tradition is entirely compatible with loyalty to the state, harmonious relations between Jewish and non-Jewish neighbors, and active participation in the wider world. The confrontations of the narrative serve only to test and ultimately to vindicate the bonds of mutual respect.

Jews at Court

First and foremost, 3 Maccabees focuses upon the relationship between the Jews and the state. One of the most important themes in the text is the loyalty owed by the Jews to the state. The Jews of Jerusalem initially welcome Philopator and are prepared to celebrate his victory until he threatens to invade the temple. It is highly significant that in this crisis the Jewish elders restrain the calls of the hotheaded young men for armed revolt (1:22–23). Although God's law must come first, the author of 3 Maccabees does not approve of violent resistance. As loyal subjects, the Jews must rely on a combination of what we would call civil disobedience and faith in God. Likewise, the Jews of Alexandria affirm their loyalty even under persecution. The most telling passage is that in which the Jews request permission to execute their apostate comrades (7:11–12). They point out to Philopator that those who abandoned their God for the sake of material advantages are unlikely to prove more loyal to the state than they were to their faith,[23] and the king agrees with them.[24] The author thus demonstrates that piety toward God and loyalty toward the

---

23. 3 Macc 7:11: προφερόμενοι τοὺς γαστρὸς ἕνεκεν τὰ θεῖα παραβεβηκότας προστάγματα μηδέποτε εὐνοήσειν μηδὲ τοῖς τοῦ βασιλέως πράγμασιν.

24. 3 Macc 7:12: ὁ δὲ τἀληθὲς αὐτοὺς λέγειν παραδεξάμενος.

state are simply two sides of the same coin; the one cannot exist without
the other.

Moreover, the author suggests that, under normal circumstances, the
loyalty of the Jews does not go unrewarded. On the contrary, the Jews are
highly regarded and favored by the king. Paradoxically, the conflict
begins when Philopator admires the temple and wants to enter it (1:9–10).
Although much of the subsequent narrative deals with the king's efforts
to persecute the Jews, there is one significant lapse in his indignation.
While under the influence of divine forgetfulness, the king temporarily
forgets his anger against the Jews and immediately begins to praise the
loyalty that they have traditionally shown toward himself and his
family.[25] This temporary state of mind becomes permanent once God
finally opens Philopator's eyes. The reformed Philopator praises the loyalty of the Jews (6:25–26; 7:7), exalts the power of their God (6:28, 33; 7:2,
6, 9) and extends toward the Jews every favor and protection (6:30, 40;
7:1–9, 18, 20). Philopator the persecutor (who, it may be said, resembles
the historical Philopator a good deal more closely than the reformed
Philopator does) is represented as a madman (5:42) acting under the
influence of his notorious companions (2:26; 5:21–22, 34; 6:23–24; 7:3–4);
the reformed Philopator, by contrast, represents the normative ideal from
which the insane Philopator temporarily deviated. Persecution, the
author suggests, is the aberration, while royal favor is the norm.

Jew and Gentile in an Hour of Crisis

To a lesser extent, the author is concerned with the place of the Jews
within Gentile society and their day-to-day relationship with non-Jews.
The author's admiration for Greek culture and his desire to share in it
may be seen first and foremost in his language. His Greek is not the
simple Greek of the uneducated but the artificial and precious language
of the Alexandrian literary elite in this period.[26] The author aspired to be
counted as part of the Hellenized elite and expected the same of his readers. The author also implies that Jews are capable of reaching the highest
levels of power. In the course of the opening narrative of the battle of
Raphia, we learn that Philopator was saved from an assassination
attempt by the quick thinking of a Hellenized Jew at his court named

---

25. 3 Macc 5:31: ἀντὶ τῶν ἀνεγκλήτων ἐμοὶ καὶ προγόνοις ἐμοῖς ἀποδεδειγμένων ὁλοσχερῆ
βεβαίαν πίστιν ἐξόχως Ἰουδαίων.

26. On the style of 3 Macc, see Grimm, *Das zweite, dritte und vierte Buch*, 214–15; Hadas,
Third and Fourth Books, 22; Tcherikover, "Third Book," 1, 18; and Anderson, "3 Maccabees,"
510.

Dositheus (3 Macc 1:2–3).[27] Dositheus subsequently disappears from the narrative, but there are numerous other indications of the author's interest in and familiarity with the royal court. He is intimately familiar with the gossipy details of the reign of the historical Philopator,[28] and his use of putatively authentic official documents (3:12–29; 7:1–9) shows that not only was he familiar with court protocol, but he expected his audience to share that familiarity.

The author also represents the Jews normally enjoying good relations with their neighbors. To be sure, the Jews do have enemies, both at court and among the common people (e.g., 3 Macc 2:26; 3:2; 4:1; 5:3). However, the author stresses that while some people resented the separatism of the Jews in matters of religion and food, the vast majority respected them for their pious way of life (3:2–5). The society of Gentiles need not then become a stumbling block for a traditionally observant Jew. Moreover, whoever the enemies of the Jews may have been, the author makes it clear that they were not the Greeks. The Greeks of Alexandria were horrified by the persecution of the Jews and would have helped them if they could (3:8–10). Thus there is no suggestion that the Jews ought to cut themselves off from their Gentile, and especially their Greek, neighbors. On the contrary, the Greeks, a high status group in the city of Alexandria, are to be cultivated within the necessary limits set by Jewish law.

Overall, then, the author succeeds in constructing a coherent vision of Hellenistic Jewish identity that provides for the continued observance of traditional Jewish law while encouraging the Jews to participate fully in the cultural life of the Hellenized upper classes of Alexandria. The crises narrated by the author permit him to test the limits of this new identity and to demonstrate the lines that an observant Jew might and might not cross. By postulating the worst-case scenario, the author is able to articulate a model for Jewish identity that would encourage the average Hellenized Alexandrian Jew to cope with the far more mundane challenges of life in the Diaspora.

Mining History to Create Identity

It is in relation to the author's ideological purpose, that of communicating his particular vision of Hellenistic Jewish identity, that the peculiar mixture of historical and fictional elements in 3 Maccabees must be understood. If one examines closely the manner in which the author of 3 Maccabees uses history, it becomes apparent that his use of genuine, or

---

27. On Dositheus, see n. 9.
28. For the historical Philopator, see nn. 6 and 7.

putatively genuine, historical material is not random. Rather, he systematically manipulates the historical elements in his narrative in such a way
that they not only give a superficial appearance of historical credibility,
but they also work to support the ideological point he is trying to make.
The author of 3 Maccabees is very much concerned with communicating
a certain kind of truth about the past, but that truth is ideological, not historical. It is more important to the author that his account of the past look
and feel true, and that it support the truth of his main ideological point,
than that it should actually be true in the historical sense.

There are many examples in 3 Maccabees of the way in which the
author uses historical allusions and techniques to buttress the ideological
point he is making, but one will suffice. Third Maccabees contains two
purportedly genuine documents: a royal decree proclaiming the persecution of the Jews and a similar royal decree calling off the persecution and
restoring the Jews to a favored position in the kingdom. These documents
are carefully forged so as to appear authentic. They are written, not in the
author's own rather affected style, but in the bureaucratic idiom of the
Ptolemaic administration. Precisely because they mimic the conventional
formulae of official documents so closely, it can be shown that they were
written not during the reign of Philopator, but over a hundred years later.
For instance, both letters use a conventional opening formula, "Greetings
and good health," not found in official documents before circa 100 B.C.E.[29]
The author imitates the royal correspondence of his own day. This is not
a sign of mere carelessness, but a deliberate stylistic choice. By using the
contemporary bureaucratic style most familiar to his audience, the author
succeeds in lending an air of verisimilitude to his "official" documents.
The fact that such documents could easily be debunked by an expert
reader is irrelevant. It is the impression of accuracy that mattered.

Apart from contributing to the overall illusion of historical accuracy
that the author seeks to convey, the content of these supposedly genuine documents serves to reinforce the author's view of Hellenistic
Jewish identity. In the king's own words, we find reflected the themes
repeatedly stressed by the author throughout the narrative. In the first
letter, the king expresses the idea that the Jews, because of their religious separatism, are likely to betray the state (3 Macc 3:24), but in the
second, the king attributes this opinion to his wicked advisors (7:3–4)
and firmly repudiates the idea, instead praising the steadfast loyalty of
the Jews (7:6–7). The author's insistence upon the loyalty of the Jews to
the state is endorsed in the king's own words. Again, in the first letter,

---

29. For the dating of the formulae, see n. 8.

the king is infuriated by the unwillingness of the Jews to abandon their God (3:18, 23), but in the second letter, the king has nothing but praise for the God who watches over the Jewish people, and he absolves the Jews of all blame (7:6, 9). Thus the importance of fidelity to God's law is officially sanctioned by the very king who had initially persecuted the Jews for their faith. The author's own ideas and views, when articulated in these putatively genuine documents, acquire all the authority of a dusty roll taken directly from the court archives, bearing the official seal of authenticity.

For the author of 3 Maccabees, history is not an end in itself, but simply raw material to be mined and shaped in the service of a particular point of view. The author uses historical details and the citation of documents to create a convincing illusion and to communicate his message more effectively. The version of the past invented by the author of 3 Maccabees was not historically true, but through the suspension of disbelief it expresses a deeper ideological truth. This is history not as it was, but as, in the eyes of the Jews of Alexandria, it ought to have been.

HUMOR AND PARADOX IN THE CHARACTERIZATION OF ABRAHAM IN THE *TESTAMENT OF ABRAHAM*

Jared Ludlow

INTRODUCTION

The *Testament of Abraham* is one of many Second Temple Jewish texts that supplement the biblical story of Abraham. The portrayal of Abraham within the *Testament of Abraham*, however, is one of the most surprising depictions of the patriarch in Jewish literature because it contests the usual representation of Abraham as the paradigm of obedience and humility. Why such a peculiar characterization? Within the secondary literature on this text, more scholars are coming to recognize its comical aspects, although the origin and development of these elements within the transmission history of the manuscripts are still being debated.[1] Some state that the *Testament of Abraham* is a parody or satire of the biblical *Abraham*, a conclusion that would mean the biblical story was at the fore of the author's and intended by that author to be at the fore of the reader's mind.[2] Therefore the extent of intertextual connection between

---

1. See esp. Dale C. Allison Jr., *Testament of Abraham* (Berlin: de Gruyter, 2003), 51–52 and passim; Erich Gruen, *Diaspora: Jews amidst Greeks and Romans* (Cambridge: Harvard University Press, 2002), 183–93; Jared W. Ludlow, *Abraham Meets Death: Narrative Humor in the Testament of Abraham* (JSPSup 41; Sheffield: Sheffield Academic Press, 2002); and a recent conference presentation: Ann Jeffers, "Laughing at Abraham: Parody in the Testament of Abraham" (paper presented at the annual meeting of The Society for Old Testament Studies, University of Birmingham, January 5–7, 2004). Some earlier significant works on this aspect of the text include George W. E. Nickelsburg, "Structure and Message in the Testament of Abraham," in *Studies on the Testament of Abraham* (ed. George W. E. Nickelsburg; SBLSCS 6; Missoula, Mont.: Scholars Press, 1976), 85–93; and Lawrence M. Wills, *The Jewish Novel in the Ancient World* (Ithaca, N.Y.: Cornell University Press, 1995), 247–56.

2. Some have determined that the structures of the text or parallels with traditions about Moses' death are major influences on the characterization of Abraham in the story, aspects which will not be covered in this paper. In *Abraham Meets Death* (50–54), I argue that many of these parallels were coincidences resulting from the use of related characters (righteous man, archangel(s), agent of death, God) and a similar scene: the death of a righteous man after a full life and his natural apprehension toward death, but the differences raise

the *Testament of Abraham* and the biblical Abraham story is a significant issue when one examines Abraham's characterization in this text.

This paper argues that a comic characterization of Abraham is present throughout the text, but it may be going too far (or is not accurate enough) to label it a parody of Abraham. Rather, the characterization of Abraham is of a paradoxical nature. That is to say, while the narrator and other characters provided positive descriptions of Abraham as a righteous, hospitable "friend of God," Abraham's actions and speech contradicted this characterization. This duplicitous characterization was one of many comic elements found especially in the long recension that helped create an entertaining tale of a stubborn, cunning patriarch resisting death.

In addition, observations about Abraham's characterization will be used as data to address questions about the relationship between the two recensions or versions of this text passed down during its transmission history. Why did two different versions develop, and what is the intertextual relationship between them? A comparison of the characterization between the two recensions suggests that the shorter recension (B) is dependent upon A and removes many of these comic elements in its attempt to rehabilitate Recension A's inappropriate characterization of Abraham.

TESTAMENT OF ABRAHAM SUMMARY

The *Testament of Abraham* begins with Abraham's approaching death. The Archangel Michael receives the mission to tell Abraham of his

---

significant questions on how much influence the Moses traditions may have had. See similar caution in Gruen, *Diaspora*, 192: "They [Moses traditions] may well have exerted an influence. But a critical difference exists. Moses, in those traditions, staked a claim on immortality and refused to accept a judgment that would remove him from the world. Abraham had no such pretensions. His posture was procrastination, not recalcitrance." In his recent commentary on the *Testament of Abraham* (24–27), Allison takes to task the minimalist influence conclusion. He includes an impressive chart of narrative aspects that are shared between Abraham in Recension A and Moses in Jewish sources. From a historical standpoint, however, the question remains how the *Testament of Abraham* could adopt so many aspects of Moses traditions that are found in many different Jewish sources? As Allison comments (26–27), "we may in theory imagine *TA* [*Testament of Abraham*] gathering additional parallels to traditions about Moses as time passed, but the Mosaic elements in RecLng. [Recension A] alone do not strike one as secondary additions." Thus the *Testament of Abraham's* parallel traditions would have been present from its earliest inception so how would it know all the aspects of the traditions found in later, disparate texts? In addition some of the possible parallels may just as likely have been influenced by parallels with other Abrahamic stories found in *Jubilees, Philo, Genesis Apocryphon*, etc. See Daniel J. Harrington, "Abraham Traditions in the Testament of Abraham and in the 'Rewritten Bible' of the Intertestamental Period," in Nickelsburg, *Studies on the Testament of Abraham*, 165–71.

impending death so that he can make proper arrangements for his possessions. Michael, however, has a hard time telling Abraham, God's friend, he is about to die; especially after he was so hospitably welcomed by Abraham. After some time, Michael ascends to heaven and declines his mission to tell Abraham of his impending death. God, then, decides to send the notice of Abraham's death to his son Isaac in a dream that Michael is to interpret appropriately. After Isaac recounts his ominous dream and Michael dutifully interprets its true meaning, the angel invites Abraham to make a proper testament and get on his way. But Abraham, instead of obediently following Michael back to God, refuses to follow. Michael again quickly ascends to heaven to check with God on how he should proceed. God tells Michael to deliver a message to Abraham recounting all the blessings God has bestowed on him and to explain the inevitable nature of death. When Michael returns to earth, he finds a penitent Abraham who has only one *meek* request: to see all of God's creations while still in the body. Then he will follow Michael. Michael returns to heaven yet again to secure God's permission for Abraham's heavenly ascension.

As Abraham is taken over the earth to behold all its inhabitants, he sees people committing sins and he repeatedly asks that they be destroyed. Eventually God tells Michael to stop the trip over the earth lest Abraham destroy all its sinful inhabitants, and instead has Abraham taken to the place of judgment so he can learn mercy for sinners. Near the end of the tour of the judgment scene, Abraham expresses repentance then pleads with God to save those he had destroyed earlier. This is accomplished and Michael returns Abraham to his home so he can make the final arrangements for his death. Yet instead of following Michael as he has said he would, Abraham again refuses to make his last testament and follow Michael. Michael ascends to the Lord empty-handed.

God then changes agents: he summons the bitter cup, Death, who will now bring Abraham's soul. Yet, God has him put on beautiful garb and go with soft speech to his friend Abraham rather than appearing as his usual fearsome, bitter self. At first Abraham has a hard time believing that Death is really Death, but finally again refuses to make a proper testament and follow God's agent. Unlike Michael, however, Death does not run to heaven to question how to proceed, but doggedly follows Abraham wherever he goes. Abraham finally asks Death to reveal his true ghastly self. After a fearsome display of Death's many faces, which resulted in the death of all of Abraham's servants, Abraham has enough and asks Death to cover himself. Abraham then asks Death to join him in prayer to restore his servants, which proves successful.

Despite all this display, Abraham still attempts to postpone his fate by first unsuccessfully requesting that Death leave him alone, then asking

Death to teach him the meaning of all his different faces. Finally after a question on unexpected death, Death refuses to answer any more questions but invites Abraham once again to make preparations for his death. Family and servants surround his bed, yet Abraham still does not make a testament and Death has to trick Abraham into grasping his hand whereupon Abraham's soul departs his body and is escorted to paradise by Michael and accompanying angels.

THE RELATIONSHIP OF THE TWO RECENSIONS

This story of the *Testament of Abraham* has been transmitted and translated through the centuries in a variety of manuscripts and languages.[3] An interesting feature of these works is the presence of two basic recensions, or versions A (Long) and B (Short). Both recensions are narrative stories of Abraham and his approaching death; however, there are major differences between them, particularly in plot structure and characterization. Most scholars addressing the relationship of the two recensions have repeated M. R. James's early conclusion that Recension A's *narrative ordering* is more original, but Recension B's *vocabulary* is more original.[4] This stalemate on which recension is closer to the original reflects the common assumption that both recensions as we now have them come from an Ur-source but are not directly dependent on each other. Some even think they come from separate *Vorlage* so are even more distantly related.[5] A close reading of the narratives of both recensions, however, reveals a direct relationship between them with the more comical Recension A coming first and Recension B reacting to and purging the early longer recension of comic elements. Thus the differing narrative strategies of each recension, especially the use of humor by Recension A, offer the clue for unlocking the two recension relationship.

A brief outline of the narrative development of Abraham's character within Recension A shows that Recension A presents a duplicitous Abraham. Later, a few episodes will be highlighted in both recensions to demonstrate the differences between their characterizations of Abraham. The use of humor in Abraham's characterization within Recension A fits with the comic nature of the recension as a whole. Recension B, in

3. For general discussions of the manuscripts see Francis Schmidt, *Le Testament grec d'Abraham: Introduction, édition critique des deux recensions grecques, traduction* (Tübingen: Mohr Siebeck, 1986); and Allison, *Testament of Abraham*.

4. Montague R. James, "The Testament of Abraham," in *Texts and Studies* (ed. J. Armitage Robinson; 10 vols.; Cambridge: Cambridge University Press, 1892), 2.2:49.

5. E.g., E. P. Sanders, "The Testament of Abraham," *OTP* 1:872.

contrast, appears to be an adaptation of the longer recension where most of its comic elements were removed and deliberate ambiguities clarified. As a result of this adaptation, Recension B leaves undeveloped several narrative elements within its own story, evidence of its dependence on Recension A.

COMIC CHARACTERIZATION OF ABRAHAM

Although this text sets the stage for Abraham to make a last testament, the interesting wrinkle that sets this text apart from other testamentary texts is that Abraham repeatedly refuses to make a testament and follow God's agents sent to take his soul. Thus in the end, he dies before any testament is made, and consequently the *Testament of Abraham* is lacking a testament. What happened to the venerable patriarch?

One explanation advanced for why Abraham is characterized as he is in the *Testament of Abraham* is that it is a parody or satire of Abraham. Early in scholarly interpretations of this text, George Nickelsburg argued that the author composed a "startling portrait" of Abraham: "Although he [the author] ascribes to the patriarch some of the virtues traditionally attributed to him (righteousness, hospitality), the author has glaringly omitted the most celebrated of these, viz., Abraham's obedient faith. Indeed, he has created a veritable parody on the biblical and traditional Abraham."[6] Yet, as Erich Gruen points out, "in fact, Abraham nowhere directly defies God. Instead, he questions God's agents as to whether their declarations come from him or represent themselves (15.8, 19.4). And he explicitly affirms willingness to abide by God's will. He merely sought means to postpone its implementation (9.5). Abraham's obedience is not at issue."[7]

Nickelsburg finds none of these parodic features in Recension B, since Abraham makes no refusals and neither the heavenly ascension nor any of the rest of the book indicates any parody.[8] However, in Recension B Abraham requests that the sinners he beheld during his heavenly vision be destroyed just as in Recension A; this feature is one of the aspects of the traditional righteous Abraham that Nickelsburg states

---

6. Nickelsburg, "Structure and Message," 87. Nickelsburg is certainly correct in his insight that, although Abraham haggled in Gen 18:22–23 on behalf of others, in the *Testament of Abraham* he is haggling for his own benefit to avoid death. However, Abraham did return to intercede for others when he prayed that the sinners he had killed would be restored to life, and in his prayer for the balanced soul.

7. Gruen, *Diaspora*, 329 n. 40.

8. Nickelsburg, "Structure and Message," 90.

Recension A is parodying. Thus Recension B does contain parodic elements, however, they are not woven into the narrative as in Recension A, but rather, are most likely remnants from Recension B's adaptation of Recension A.

Lawrence Wills also sees parody of Abraham in the *Testament of Abraham*'s portrayal of Abraham.[9] But Wills sees a change in Abraham's character from the beginning of the story to the end. At first there is a strong satirical tone, which by the end has given way "to somber realizations on the part of Abraham that he will not escape Death's command and that the reality of death is horrible. The work as a whole moves away from the category of satire to a philosophical reflection on the inevitability of death."[10]

As many scholars have looked to Abraham's heavenly ascent to deduce the main message of this text, Wills insightfully points out that Abraham's heightened knowledge of heavenly justice does not satisfy Abraham who continues to resist Death until he is taken by deception.[11] Yet this point also undermines Will's conclusion; for despite his heavenly journey, Abraham continues to refuse the divine messenger and instead requests further delays from Death rather than accepting death's inevitability.

More recently, Ann Jeffers has argued for a Bakhtinian form of parody in which the dialectics of intertextuality require the audience's prior knowledge of a familiar text or story.[12] The parody's "parasitic" relation to its object is evident in characteristics such as exaggeration, incongruity, crude naturalism/behavior, and inappropriate speech/action.

These descriptions of the *Testament of Abraham* as a parody highlight the comic aspects of the text; nevertheless, they do not seem to follow the precise definition of parody, but rather use the term in a more general sense to mean "make fun of" or "mock."[13] A parody "is a composition

---

9. See Gruen's comments regarding this interpretation: "It is going too far to characterize the work as a parody of the pious Abraham. The patriarch's piety is not, in fact, satirized. Rather, it earns him good will, favor, and countless concessions from God and his ministers.... The author does not diminish Abraham's stature but gives him added dimensions—including the very human emotions of spleen, regret, and reluctance to die" (*Diaspora*, 187).

10. Wills, *Jewish Novel*, 255.

11. Ibid.

12. Jeffers, "Laughing at Abraham."

13. Robert Doran correctly states the Nickelsburg does not seem to use the term "parody" in a genre sense, and Doran raises questions about what needs to be done to determine the genre: "If Testament of Abraham is a parody, examples of the literary form parodied need to be provided. Does not much of the humor come from watching Abraham

which always assumes a pre-existing text, [usually serious], which it imitates and distorts, often, but not always, for satiric purposes" mostly by means of exaggeration.[14] For the parody to work, the pre-texts or familiar style must be fairly obvious to the reader since they are the vehicle the author uses for presenting literary humor.[15] Although some of the actions of the characters in the *Testament of Abraham* are comical, it is not a closely imitated work of the "biblical" story of Abraham and the author seems to have a more deliberate purpose than ridicule. The narrator seems to be playing with the testament setting and readers' expectations by repeatedly having God's agents invite Abraham to make a testament and Abraham refusing to do so. Thus if there is any parody in the technical sense, it would be a parody on the testament genre with its standard conventions revolving around the death of a righteous individual.[16]

In searching for improved semantic precision and thus greater accuracy in describing the characterization in the *Testament of Abraham*, it

---

bicker over dying, and does not this simply continue the portrayal of Abraham in Genesis 18 and 23 as a consummate haggler? Are heavenly tours being parodied?" ("Narrative Literature," in *Early Judaism and Its Modern Interpreters* [ed. Robert A. Kraft and George W. E. Nickelsburg; Atlanta: Scholars Press, 1986], 288).

14. Arnold J. Band, "Swallowing Jonah: The Eclipse of Parody," *Prooftexts* 10 (1990): 179–80. Other useful definitions of parody in general terms: "the comic refunctioning of preformed linguistic or artistic material" (Margaret Rose, *Parody: Ancient, Modern, and Post-modern* [Cambridge: Cambridge University Press, 1993], 52); "A conscious (!?) imitation of a literary genre which conveys, through exaggeration, comedy, and humour, criticism of the source genre and the accepted literary and ideological norms that inform it" (Athalya Brenner, "Jonah's Poem Out of and Within Its Context," in *Among the Prophets* [ed. Philip R. Davies and David J. A. Clines; JSOTSup 144; Sheffield: JSOT Press, 1993], 189).

15. John Miles, "Laughing at the Bible: Jonah as Parody," *JQR* 65 (1975): 168. The distinction Miles makes between satire and parody is that "satire is the exposure by comedy of behavior which is standardized and, to that extent, foolish. Parody is that breed of satire in which the standardized behavior to be exposed is *literary*" (168, emphasis added). Another distinction is drawn out by Margaret Rose: "Parody, unlike forms of satire or burlesque which do not make their target a significant part of themselves, is ambivalently dependent upon the object of its criticism for its own reception" (*Parody*, 51). See also Band, "Swallowing," 180: "While satire 'censures wickedness and folly' in human society in general, parody is a literary genre which deals with the refunctioning, or criticism, of other preformed literary and linguistic material." Finally see Ziva Ben-Porat, "Parody's Revenge: or the (Im)possibility of Postmodernist Claims Concerning Parody and Pastiche," in *Parodia, Pastiche, Mimetismo* (ed. Paola Mildonian; Rome: Bulzoni Editore, 1997), 419: "Parody misrepresents a text—i.e. a representation of a 'modelled reality' which is itself already a particular representation of an original alleged reality. It is to be distinguished from satire, which is a critical representation, always comic and often caricatural, of a non-modelled alleged reality. Satire is not a form of rhetorical intertextuality. Its intertextual target (or source) belongs to the user's knowledge-of-the-world frames (i.e. that which is called 'reality')."

16. See Ludlow, *Abraham Meets Death*, 17–28.

seems that *paradox* would better describe the author's intentions than *parody*. A paradox is a statement or action that conflicts with, or is contrary to, expectations. From the descriptions of Abraham throughout the narrative (from the other characters and the narrator), the reader is forming ideas about Abraham and how he should behave, only to have him act differently. His duplicitous actions (stubbornness, craftiness) surprise the reader and cause the reader to pay closer attention to the subsequent didactic section to see how this conflict of character is resolved. Although acquaintance with the traditional Abraham story would deepen the comic effect of such a characterization—Abraham's actions would not only go against the text's description but also his renowned righteousness —a reader ignorant of the biblical story of Abraham would still appreciate the effect. The expectations portrayed within the text, such as a testament scene and Abraham's positive description, and the continuous "reversals" form the basis for Abraham's characterization, not a parody of the traditional (biblical) Abraham. Thus the duplicitous nature of Abraham and the other characters are the primary means of characterization in Recension A.

Narrator's and Characters' Descriptions of Abraham

The narrator of Recension A repeatedly directs the reader's perception of Abraham by describing qualities such as righteousness and hospitality. For example, the narrator illustrates Abraham's hospitality by writing "For he pitched his tent at the crossroads of the oak of Mamre and welcomed everyone—rich and poor, kings and rulers, the crippled and the helpless, friends and strangers, neighbors and passersby—(all) on equal terms did the pious, entirely holy, righteous, and hospitable Abraham welcome" (rec. A 1.1–2).[17]

The other characters' comments about Abraham help form and strengthen the righteous characterization of Abraham. Especially noteworthy are God's descriptions of Abraham since, in religious narratives, God's viewpoint is usually seen as reliable, authoritative, and the standard against which other descriptions should be weighed. God sets the tone in his initial summons to Michael to go down to Abraham by saying "for I have blessed him as the stars of heaven and as the sand by the seashore, and he lives in abundance, (having) a large livelihood and many possessions, and he is very rich. But above all others he is righteous in all goodness, (having been) hospitable and loving until the end of his

---

17. Quotations from E. P. Sanders's translation, "The Testament of Abraham," 1:882.

life" (rec. A 1.5). God repeatedly refers to Abraham as his friend or beloved friend (rec. A 1.6; 4.7; 8.4).[18] During Abraham's heavenly ascension, God exaggerates Abraham's righteousness commanding Michael to stop the chariot lest Abraham destroy everything "for behold, Abraham has not sinned" (rec. A 10.13).

Michael's interactions with Abraham continue the focus on Abraham's righteousness and status as friend of God (rec. A 2.3; 8.2; 9.7; 12.15; 13.2, 4, 14; 14.2; 15.6, 9, 12). When Michael tells God he could not tell Abraham about his imminent death, he explains he had not seen a man like him upon the earth—"merciful, hospitable, righteous, truthful, God-fearing, refraining from every evil deed" (rec. A 4.6). Later, following another of Abraham's refusals, Michael says he refrained from touching Abraham "because from the beginning he has been your friend and he did everything which is pleasing before you. And there is no man like unto him on earth, not even Job, the wondrous man" (rec. A 15.14–15).

The characterization of Abraham as God's righteous friend is further strengthened through Death's dialogues with Abraham (rec. A 16.9). Death tells Abraham that his pleasing form was due to Abraham's righteous deeds, boundless hospitality, and the greatness of his love for God (rec. A 17.7).

All the descriptions and epithets of Abraham by the narrator or put into the mouths of other characters may help form the portrait of a righteous friend of God, but they also provide a foil for the characterization that emerges through Abraham's actions and direct speech. In contrast, Abraham speaks and behaves disobediently and stubbornly.

Abraham's Direct Speech and Actions

In Recension A, Abraham's dialogues and interactions with other characters bring out most strongly the recalcitrant, cunning facets of his character since most of his dialogues are rejections of the messengers, Michael and Death, sent by God to prepare him for his death. Abraham refuses (or delays) to follow God's messengers seven times (rec. A 7.12; 9.3–6; 15.10; 16.16; 17.2; 19.2, 4; 20.4). Even after his recognition of Michael's true mission, Abraham protests, "Now I do know that you are an angel of the Lord, and you were sent to take my soul. Nevertheless, I will not by any means follow you, but you do whatever he [God]

---

18. Abraham was called God's friend in biblical texts as well (e.g., Isa 41:8 and 2 Chr 20:7).

commands" (rec. A 7.12). Abraham's obstinate response puts the burden on Michael to figure out how to fulfill the Lord's command.

Abraham is just as recalcitrant with Death. Even after Abraham comes to accept Death's true identity, he refuses to follow him as well: "I understand what you are saying, but I will by no means follow you" (rec. A 16.16). Instead Abraham rebelliously tries to get away from Death. The first three lines of the narrative describing Abraham's actions follow a narrative pattern of interchange (in an a-b-a-b pattern). Abraham goes into his house, Death follows him; Abraham goes into his room, Death also goes up; Abraham reclines on his couch, Death comes and sits by his feet (rec. A 17.1). This pattern comically represents the frustration brewing inside Abraham until he finally orders Death to leave him (rec. A 17.2).

Thus Abraham's speech and actions do not correspond to the façade of humble obedience. Behind the façade of obedience are feigned contrition, backing out of deals with Michael and Death, and repeated refusals to follow God's messengers. The reader is presented with a paradox: the righteous friend of God depicted by the narrator and other characters including God is also stubborn and cunning. Why this drastic difference in portrayals? Instead of another predictable story about a righteous man who did everything God commanded, Abraham, the epitome of righteousness, constantly rebels against God's will. These repetitive, overexaggerated scenes of stubbornness and cunning go against readers' expectations in order to entertain; this portrayal generates suspense and thereby maintains readers' interest.

Specific Episodes

By examining similar episodes in the two recensions, one can see how their characterizations differed. When Abraham first meets Michael at the beginning of the story in Recension A, he greets Michael as a handsome soldier and frequently refers to him as a "stranger" (rec. A 2.4, 9; 3.7) leaving it ambiguous whether or not he initially recognizes that Michael is a divine messenger. When Abraham washes Michael's feet he tells Isaac that Michael is "tired, having come to us from a long journey" (rec. A 3.7). Abraham's words are full of irony: Michael has come on a long journey, but how dirty would his feet have been? Abraham's ambiguous, ironic comments continue as he asks Isaac to prepare the guest room "for this *man* who is staying as our guest today" (rec. A 4.1), yet he says that Michael "is more honorable than kings and rulers; for even his appearance surpasses all the sons of men" (rec. A 4.3). Abraham's statements create delightful ambiguity for the reader as the reader wonders whether Abraham really knows with whom he is dealing.

Recension B, on the other hand, explicitly discloses through Abraham's internal thought that Abraham does not initially know of Michael's heavenly origin. As Abraham saw Michael approach, "he arose from the ground and welcomed him, *not knowing who he was*" (rec. B 2.2). Thus the narrator presents an Abraham ignorant of Michael's origins. This depiction unambiguously informs the reader that Abraham's subsequent dialogue and hospitable actions are a result of his ignorance.

After their initial meeting, Abraham and Michael walk together toward Abraham's house. This episode illustrates how Recension A provides Abraham's internal thoughts.[19] As they are walking, they pass a talking tree proclaiming a message by God's command: "Holy, holy, holy is the Lord God who is summoning him to those who love him" (rec. A 3.3). The narrator then states "Abraham *hid* the mystery, *thinking* that the Commander-in-chief had not heard the voice of the tree" (rec. A 3.4). Mary Dean-Otting feels that with this simple statement (Abraham thought Michael had not heard the voice), the author establishes Abraham's naiveté,[20] but it seems to me to be more deliberate and cunning than naïve. Why would Abraham attempt to hide something from Michael? It seems to be part of Abraham's "denial" of his inevitable death for he hopes that Michael has not heard that God summons.

This same episode appears in Recension B. When Abraham hears the voice of the singing tree, he *"hid* the mystery in his heart, saying to himself, 'What, then, is the mystery that I have heard?'"* (rec. B 3.4). The internal thought explains that Abraham ignores the voice because of his failure to understand its meaning, through ignorance or naiveté, and his intent to reflect upon it later. This internal statement informs the reader's interpretation of Abraham's subsequent actions in Recension B.

In a third episode, when Abraham washes Michael's feet, the narrator in Recension A explicitly describes some of Abraham's emotions associated with his actions, but does not explain what motivates Abraham's strong emotional response. As Abraham washes Michael's feet, the narrator states that Abraham's heart is moved and he weeps over the stranger (rec. A 3.9). As Michael's tears became precious stones, Abraham

---

19. Internal thought is only given to Abraham in Recension A of the *Testament of Abraham*. Internal thoughts are significant in narratives because they illustrate the degree to which the narrator is either overt or covert. An overt narrator provides internal dialogue or thought as part of the exposition of the character so that the reader can understand the character's actions and perhaps empathize with her or him. Within Abraham's internal thought, the reader can begin to see the hint of paradox between Abraham's early pious descriptions with his later stubborn, crafty actions.

20. Mary Dean-Otting, *Heavenly Journeys: A Study of the Motif in Hellenistic Jewish Literature* (Frankfurt: Lang, 1984), 183.

is astonished (rec. A 3.12). In these descriptions of Abraham's emotions, the reader is not told specifically *why* Abraham reacted in these ways. Recension B, however, brings to the foreground the motives for these ambiguous narrative statements in Recension A. When Abraham asks Isaac to bring water in a vessel so he can wash Michael's feet, he states: "I have an insight (into) what will come to pass, that in this bowl I shall not again wash the feet of a man who is entertained as a guest with us" (rec. B 3.8). Abraham's insight in Recension B indicates a knowledge and/or acceptance of his impending death and thereby reveals to the reader why he is crying.

The ambiguity regarding Abraham's recognition of Michael's true origins within Recension A continues until a puzzling dialogue between Abraham and Sarah. When Sarah first realizes that Michael is an angel of the Lord, she asks Abraham if he knew who this man was (rec. A 6.2). Abraham responds: "I do not know" (rec. A 6.3). Yet after Sarah's explanation of their earlier visitors they had entertained, Abraham responds: "O Sarah, you have spoken truly. Glory and blessing from (our) God and Father! For I too, late this evening, when I was washing his feet in the vessel (which has) the wash basin, said in my heart, 'These feet are (those of one) of the three men that I washed previously'" (rec. A 6.6). Why did Abraham first deny knowing Michael's identity, yet later stated that he had known since earlier washing his feet? Abraham's denial of yet another heavenly manifestation indicates his resistance to his impending death and adds a comical twist since his recognition of Michael comes through Michael's feet! Samuel Loewenstamm remarks, "It is hard to grasp why Abraham remembered Michael's feet better than his general appearance. The motif is seemingly an inapt adaptation of the famous scene in which Eurykleia washes Odysseus' feet and recognizes him by his cicatrix, a clear mark of identity (*Odyssey* 19.386–94.)."[21] If this episode is an adaptation, it strikes me as more comical than inapt.

Abraham's cunning nature is highlighted as he keeps information to himself unless he knows that others already know it. Just as he kept the talking tree incident to himself because he thought Michael had not heard it, so here he does not admit recognition of Michael until he knows Sarah already has recognized him. Then Abraham goes "overboard" in proving to Sarah that he had recognized Michael earlier while washing his feet by pulling out the precious stones that had come from Michael's tears: "If

---

21. Loewenstamm, "Testament of Abraham," 225 n. 4. Loewenstamm pointed out another possible parallel with the *Odyssey* earlier in his article (221): "Abraham's initial failure to identify his visitors is a retarding epic device, well-known from the story of Odysseus' return to his home."

you do not believe me, look at them" (rec. A 6.7). George Nickelsburg describes Abraham as "a disturbed patriarch, afraid to admit that he hears trees talking and sees teardrops turning to pearls."[22] "Disturbed" seems to be too passive; rather Abraham tries to control events instead of meekly submitting to them, thereby showing his "denial" of imminent death. Abraham's deliberateness is revealed by his actions when Michael's tears had earlier turned to precious stones: Abraham "picked up the stones *secretly* and *hid* the mystery, keeping it in his heart alone" (rec. A 3.12), and by his use of them here with Sarah. The author uses the precious stones as a comic element to heighten ambiguity and cunning in Abraham's characterization.

Recension B's account of this confrontation between Abraham and Sarah is very similar to Recension A's, but draws in more aspects from the biblical story of Abraham. When Sarah first calls Michael a man of God, Abraham asks Sarah, "whence do you know that he is a man of God?" (rec. B 6.9). After Sarah tells Abraham that she recognizes Michael as one of the three visitors that had visited them before (cf. Gen 18:1–8), Abraham acknowledges her keen perception and his own recognition of Michael while washing his feet (rec. B 6.12–13). It is a little curious why Abraham delays his acknowledgment of Michael until after asking Sarah how she knew. Is he testing Sarah to see if she really knows? It seems Recension B includes this episode to hearken back to the biblical story, and its structure seems to be dependent on Recension A's parallel episode as just related.

Summary of the Two Recensions

Abraham's duplicitous character advances Recension A's plot by juxtaposing the image of a righteous patriarch with a stubborn, vengeful, yet eager to learn, natural man. Through the narrator and other characters in Recension A, Abraham is referred to as a righteous, hospitable friend of God, yet this description is paradoxically challenged by Abraham's stubborn refusals, secretive actions, feigned contrition, and ultimatums. Ambiguity regarding Abraham's knowledge of the other characters' true identity provides the reader with the pleasures of irony and curiosity.

Recension B's characterization of Abraham, in contrast, brings the story closer to the biblical account of Abraham by including more parallel events with the LXX. In addition, Recension B tries to rehabilitate

---

22. Nickelsburg, "Structure and Message," 86.

Recension A's disrespectful characterization of Abraham. Instead of being secretive and stubborn, as in Recension A, Recension B's Abraham is ignorant or naïve about the characters and some of the events unfolding around him. When Abraham hides the mystery of the talking tree in his heart, his subsequent actions are not efforts to refuse God's messengers or deny his death, but a result of his unawareness. Abraham's naiveté in Recension B creates some ironic statements and even ironic foreshadowing, but without much of the humor of Recension A. Abraham's ignorance of other characters and his premonitions about his death, change Recension A's representation of a cunning Abraham by bringing to the foreground the motivations for his subsequent actions.

Despite Abraham's general righteous portrayal in Recension B, Abraham still lacks mercy and dies without giving a testament. These aspects fit the character driven plot of Recension A, but seem foreign to the plot of Recension B. It seems most likely that they were carried over into Recension B by a redactor of Recension A. In addition, several episodes are introduced into Recension B's story without subsequent development (they are mentioned but not actually connected with the plot of the rest of the story), thus the presence of some narrative elements in Recension B seems to have come from another source, most likely Recension A. For example, in both recensions God has to tell Michael to stop Abraham's heavenly trip because he is destroying all the sinners he saw because he lacks mercy (rec. A10.12–13; rec. B12.12–13). Abraham's lack of mercy provides the occasion for Abraham to learn mercy in Recension A by being taken to the place of judgment, but not so in Recension B. In Recension B, Abraham himself makes the request to be taken to see how the souls are judged *before* he starts destroying the sinners (rec. B10.1). The sequence of plot seems illogical and the statement that Abraham lacks mercy is left dangling in Recension B, whereas the statement is fully developed in Recension A where the plot is, therefore, more coherent. Recension B hints at the tension or paradox between Abraham's positive portrayal and his lack of mercy but does not develop or exploit it in a manner comparable to Recension A.

CONCLUSION

Even though many rightly see the "traditional" Abraham lurking in the background of the story in allusions to biblical events and personality traits, the *Testament of Abraham* does not follow the Genesis account of Abraham's life, thus the comedic result is technically not a parody of Abraham. Rather, the paradoxical characterization within the text stimulates expectations in the reader, only to have them reversed by Abraham's actual speech and actions. Acquaintance with the traditional (biblical) Abraham serves to heighten the effect of surprise and humor but is not necessary for the reader to appreciate the suspense. Rather than falling into the category of "Rewritten Bible," the *Testament of Abraham* expands on the biblical account of Abraham by exploiting a gap in Genesis: Abraham is the only patriarch not to leave a final testament or blessing with his posterity. Rather than filling this gap with a testament, the *Testament of Abraham* exploits the tension and parodies the genre.

The development of the comic aspects in Abraham's characterization in Recension A provides a forum for a sophisticated treatment on death and the figure Death,[23] and a significant discussion on judgment and mercy. Thus Recension A's milieu seems to be one where the community felt comfortable enough with its identity that it could poke fun at some of its heroes without risking alienation. For Recension B, however, the light-hearted touches seem to be too much and it adapts the story without its comedic elements in an effort to tone it down.[24] This conclusion seems to be strengthened by Dale Allison's work on the manuscripts in which he describes several critical notations in the margins condemning the non-sensical aspects of the text.

> One understands their pious mentality. *TA* was, as the works with which it is typically bound show, read as Christian hagiography, and leaders of such services could easily have seen parts of *TA* as potentially unedifying, especially as the text calls readers to emulate Abraham (RecLng. [rec. A] 20:15). How can one imitate a man who refuses to obey God? One recalls how the Chronicler polishes the images of David and Solomon. Some of the manuscripts, not unexpectedly, contain critical marginal comments from later ecclesiastics. A hand in the margin of RecLng. [rec. A]Ms. A attributes the story to heretics. In ms. I we find the remark that *TA* is false, and a marginal note in Q declares the book to be nonsense. The margins of W are full of negative comments—*TA* is mythical, heretical, unbiblical, nonsensical, etc. It is no mystery that *TA* does not exist in Latin and all but disappeared from the West: it was unable to overcome ecclesiastical censure.[25]

---

23. Allison states, "We can run from death, or we can philosophize about it, or we can give it a religious interpretation. But we can also respond with mirth, by combating its sadness with its opposite. In one respect, *TA* addresses death a bit like some Woody Allen films. It is of course far less cynical, but it wraps its teachings about the somber mystery of death in an often amusing tale" (*Testament of Abraham*, 52).

24. Just as the later Greek version of the book of Esther reins in the satirical tendencies of the Hebrew Esther, as pointed out by Wills, *Jewish Novel*, 249.

25. Allison, *Testament of Abraham*, 23. In another place, Allison surmises, "evidently later readers laughed less than earlier readers" (*Testament of Abraham*, p. 52).

Recension B avoids in particular Abraham's stubborn, cunning characterization, a significant part of Recension A, and carries over many plot events that become incoherent in a less comical context. Efforts to retrieve the "original" *Testament of Abraham* suggest that comedy was a significant aspect of the "original" narrative of Abraham's encounter with the bitter cup of death.

PART 3:
EARLY CHRISTIAN NARRATIVE

Resurrection and Social Perspectives in the Apocryphal *Acts of Peter* and *Acts of John*

Judith Perkins

Introduction

In Minucius Felix's *Octavius*, the pagan opponent of Christianity is most outraged by two aspects of the sect. First is the effrontery that such low-status people are offering opinions on "heavenly things" (16.5). The other cause of outrage is the Christians belief in a bodily resurrection: "They say they are reborn after death from the cinders and the ashes" (11.2).[1] Caecilius Natalis, the pagan spokesman, mocks Christians on both counts: "Let your present life, O miserable people, be your gauge of what happens after death. See how some part of you, the greater and better part as you say, experiences want, cold, labor and hunger" (12.2). Caecilius derides Christians' menial status and their belief that the body is a vital part of their personhood—indeed, "the greater and better part" (*ecce pars vestrum et maior, melior, ut dicitis*). Caecilius is a fictional opponent, but Celsus, a historical second-century figure, similarly associates and scorns Christians' low status and their belief in an immortal body (*Contra Celsum* 7.45; 8.49). This association of low status and belief in the resurrected body offers, I suggest, one context for understanding the charged polemic around the nature of the resurrected body in the second century.

The writings of Paul had allowed for a spiritual understanding of the risen body. As Paul said, "It is sown a physical (ψυχικόν) body, it is raised a spiritual (πνευματικόν) body" (1 Cor 15:44). In the second century, however, Justin, Tertullian, Athenagoras, and Irenaeus all refused such a conception and adamantly insisted that the risen body was in no sense

---

* A slightly longer version of this essay was given at the conference "Il contributo delle Scienze Storiche all' interpretazione del Nuovo Testamento," convened by the Pontificio Comitato di Scienze Storiche, in October 2002 and is scheduled to appear in the Proceedings of that conference.

1. Tertullian, *Apology; De Spectaculis* (trans. T. R. Glover et al.; LCL 250; Cambridge: Harvard University Press, 1966).

spiritual, but corporeal, material, indeed, composed of the very flesh worn during life.[2] Why this adamancy? Caroline Bynum asks, "Why did powerful voices among the Christians of the later second century reject more spiritual or gnostic interpretations of the resurrection body?"[3] A possible answer is that proto-Orthodox Christians, through their insistence on an immortal fleshy, material body, worked to disrupt a fundamental premise of the operating Greco-Roman ideological system: disdain for the body and the people associated with it.

The distinction between mind-soul and body historically had provided a foundation for social hierarchy. Plato maintained in the *Republic* (590c) that manual labor was debasing and rendered both slaves and laborers incapable of mastering themselves or controlling their natural animal instincts. Elite Greco-Roman ideology held that the opportunity of living a truly honorable human life was not open to people compelled to work with their bodies or to support bodily necessities.[4] Plato explained in the *Phaedo*, "We are slaves to its [the body's] service and so because of this have no leisure for philosophy" (66d); "the soul can never attain truth as long as it is contaminated by the body, an evil" (66b). Dale Martin aptly observes, "The ancient form of the body/soul dualism thus, not coincidentally, reflects the class structure of society."[5] It was understood that the base occupations of laborers, artisans, trades people, and the like, by their very nature, produced base people.[6] In contrast, those second-century Christians advocating for a resurrection of the fleshly body were refusing Greco-Roman culture's inscription of the body and those associated with it as base and sordid.

Indeed, Christianity ought to be recognized as the institutionalization of this refusal. I have suggested before that the body was key to Christianity's growth as an institution—one that gained strength around

---

2. J. G. Davies, "Factors Leading to the Emergence of Belief in the Resurrection of the Flesh," *JTS* 23 (1972): 448–55.

3. Caroline Walker Bynum, *The Resurrection of the Body in Western Christianity, 200–1336* (Lectures on the History of Religions, New Series 15; New York: Columbia University Press, 1995), 27.

4. William Fitzgerald, "Labor and Laborer in Latin Poetry" *Arethusa* 29 (1996): 391.

5. Dale Martin, *The Corinthian Body* (New Haven: Yale University Press, 1995), 30.

6. Paul Veyne, *From Pagan Rome to Byzantium* (vol. 1 of *A History of Private Life;* ed. Philippe Ariès and George Duby; trans. Arthur Goldhammer; Cambridge: Harvard University Press, 1987), 137. See Cicero, *Off.* 1.150–151; Seneca, *Ep.* 88. These texts reportedly are based on Panaetius and Posidonius. For Roman attitudes toward work, see John H. D'Arms, *Commerce and Social Standing in Ancient Rome* (Cambridge: Harvard University Press, 1981), 20–47, 149–71; Sandra R. Joshel, *Work, Identity, and Legal Status at Rome: A Study of the Occupational Inscriptions* (Norman: University of Oklahoma Press, 1992), 62–91.

the care of bodily needs—of the poor, the sick, the orphaned and wid-owed.[7] For this to occur, however, the cultural devaluation of the body and the people constrained by its needs had to be mitigated. In their doc-trine of the physical resurrection of an immortal body, Christians in the second century were insisting in opposition to contemporary ideology that the material body is an integral and enduring part of the human "self." As the Christians in the *Octavius* were said to believe, the body was "the greater and better part" of themselves, or as Athenagoras testi-fied, "Man, then, who consists of both soul and body, must survive forever" (*Res.* 15.6).

Christians appreciated the novelty of their idea that the material body would experience immortality. They offered it as a unique contri-bution of their faith. As Justin noted, "If the Savior ... had announced as good news the life of the soul only, what new thing would he have brought us in comparison with Pythagoras, Plato, and their like?" (frg. 109). Justin recognized that, in the context of the Greco-Roman world, bodily resurrection was, as he called it, "a new and strange hope" (καινὴν καὶ ξένην ἐλπίδα)[8] with the potential to affect the cultural evalua-tion of the body and the people traditionally associated with its labor and imperatives.

The debate over the nature of the resurrected body therefore had important social implications.[9] Christians advocating a fully material, physical resurrection worked to counteract the traditional social depreci-ation of groups marked by the body, its labor, or its needs. Similarly, groups minimizing physical resurrection were less resistant to the tradi-tional social hierarchies based on the dichotomy of mind-soul and body. Evidence in support of this hypothesis appears in two closely related texts, the apocryphal *Acts of Peter* and the *Acts of John*.[10] These so-called

---

7. Judith Perkins, *The Suffering Self* (London: Routledge, 1995), 8–12, 212–14.

8. Quoted in A. H. C. Van Eijk, "Only That Can Rise Which Has Previously Fallen," *JTS* 22 (1971): 519.

9. I am not suggesting that Christian advocates of the resurrection of the flesh *intended* this social agenda. Rather, James C. Scott's description of the process of cultural change offers a paradigm for understanding the effects of this advocacy: "Cultural forms may not say what they know, nor know what they say, but they mean what they do—at least in the logic of praxis" (*Domination and the Arts of Resistance: Hidden Transcripts* [New Haven: Yale University Press, 1990], 183).

10. For the relationship among the various Acts, see the following work with its list of parallels: F. Stanley Jones, "Principal Orientations on the Relations between the Apoc-ryphal Acts (*Acts of Paul* and *Acts of John; Acts of Peter* and *Acts of John*)," in *Society of Biblical Literature 1993 Seminar Papers* (ed. E. H. Lovering Jr.; SBLSP 32; Atlanta: Scholars Press, 1993), 485–505. For the relationship between the *Acts of John* and the *Acts of Peter*, see Dennis R. MacDonald, "The *Acts of Paul* and the *Acts of John:* Which Came First?" in *Society of*

apocryphal *Acts* are fictive narratives of the second and third centuries that purport to detail the proselytizing adventures of the apostles and share affinities with the Greco-Roman romances with which they are contemporary. Both the *Acts of John* and *Acts of Peter* are considered heterodox, but in the second and early third century, terms such as *heterodox* and *orthodox* must still be considered anachronistic. The *Acts of John*, according to its most recent editors, Eric Junod and Jean-Daniel Kaestli, is an example of popular Christianity on the frontier between gnosticism and "vulgar" Christianity.[11] Junod and Kaestli describe chapters 94–102 and 109 as an "unorthodox" interpolation but date the entire *Acts* to the second century.[12] J. K. Elliott describes the *Acts of Peter* also as a second-century text, a "product of popular piety," and "not a gnostic work" but "influenced to a greater or lesser extent by the unorthodox teachings of the day."[13]

Biblical Literature 1993 Seminar Papers, 623–26; Judith Perkins, "The Acts of Peter as Intertext: Response to Dennis R. MacDonald," in *Society of Biblical Literature 1993 Seminar Papers*, 627–33; Richard I. Pervo "Egging on the Chickens: A Cowardly Response to Dennis R. MacDonald and Then Some," *Semeia* 80 (1997): 43–56; Dennis R. MacDonald, "Which Came First? Intertextual Relationships among the Apocryphal Acts of the Apostles," *Semeia* 80 (1997): 11–42; and Pieter J. Lalleman, "The Relation between the Acts of John and the Acts of Peter," in *The Apocryphal Acts of Peter: Magic, Miracles and Gnosticism* (ed. Jan N. Bremmer; Leuven: Peeters, 1998), 161–78 (with list of parallel passages). The relationship between the *Acts of John* and *Acts of Peter* was a focus of the 1993 Society of Biblical Literature Seminar on Christian Apocrypha. In 1997 a volume of *Semeia* was devoted to an examination of the intertextual relations of the Acts. My study benefited from this work, which pointed out the major points of comparison considered in this paper.

11. Eric Junod and Jean Daniel Kaestli, *Acta Iohannis* (2 vols.; Corpus Christianorum, Series Apocryphorum 1–2; Turnhout: Brepols, 1983), 2:686.

12. Pieter J. Lalleman, *The Acts of John* (Leuven: Peeters, 1998), presents an excellent overview of the structure of the *Acts of John*. He divides the text into three sections (first, chapters 18–86, 106, and 110–115; second, 87–93, 103–105; third, 94–102 and 109) and sees the whole text as forming a unity. Lalleman reviews the debate around the "Gnosticism" of the *Acts of John* (30–39). See Paul G. Schneider, *The Mystery of the Acts of John* (Lewiston, N.Y.: Mellen, 1991), 209–22; "A Perfect Fit: The Major Interpolation in the Acts of John," *Society of Biblical Literature 1991 Seminar Papers* (ed. Eugene H. Lovering Jr.; SBLSP 30; Atlanta: Scholars Press, 1991): 518–32; "The Acts of John: The Gnostic Transformation of a Christian Community," in *Hellenization Revisited: Shaping a Christian Response within the Greco-Roman World* (ed. Wendy E. Helleman; Lanham, Md.: University Press of America, 1994), 241–69, for his discussion of the relationship between the third section and the rest of the Acts. The *Acts of Peter* seems to know the *Acts of John* in its full version; see Pieter J. Lalleman, "Polymorphy of Christ," in *The Apocryphal Acts of John* (ed. Jan N. Bremmer; Kampen: Kok Pharos, 1995), 111 n. 52.

13. J. K. Elliott and M. R. James, *The Apocryphal New Testament: A Collection of Apocryphal Christian Literature in an English Translation* (Oxford: Clarendon, 1993), 392.

Despite their heterodoxy, these *Acts* can provide evidence for the relation between resurrection beliefs and social thinking. For the *Acts of John* and the *Acts of Peter,* while sharing close similarities, differ markedly in their attitudes toward the nature of Jesus' physical body and toward material resurrection (through analogy with their representations of raised human bodies). On these points, the *Acts of Peter,* with its claim for the reality of Jesus' body and its emphasis on the material significance of the raised body, takes an essentially orthodox position. The *Acts of John,* however, with its consistent deemphasis of a material interpretation for either the body of Jesus or the raised body, is far from orthodox. These differences correlate with a contrast in social perspectives. The *Acts of John* displays for the most part the same normative hierarchical assumptions of the surrounding society. But the *Acts of Peter* exhibits a more egalitarian and inclusive focus than the *Acts of John* and offers a stronger affirmation of groups traditionally devalued in the society.

VIEWS ON THE INCARNATION

The *Acts of John* consistently denies Jesus a human body. Junod and Kaestli have argued that the text is not specifically docetic, since the incarnation and the birth and the passion of Jesus are simply ignored without comment.[14] But Pieter Lalleman has countered this argument:

> The familiarity of the author [of the *Acts of John*] ... with the canonical Gospels means that when he is silent about the human quality of Christ, he implicitly denies it. Likewise, the explicit identification of Christ and God is an implicit statement of a docetic position if—as is the case here— it is not counterbalanced by statements regarding Jesus' humanity.[15]

The *Acts of John* stresses the nonhuman nature of Jesus' presence on earth. Polymorphy—Jesus' ability to appear in different forms, sometimes at the same time—is, for example, a feature of a number of the apocryphal *Acts,* but only the *Acts of John* describes a polymorphous Jesus before his resurrection, thereby emphasizing a consistent and continuous unreality for Jesus' human body during his time in this world.[16] When

---

14. Junod and Kaestli, *Acta Iohannis,* 2:493.

15. Lalleman, *Acts of John,* 210. Lalleman notes Peter Weigandt's argument that the Acts of John is the "classic docetic text," (206, citing Peter Weigandt, "Der Doketismus im Urchristentum und in der theologischen Entwicklung des zweiten Jahrhunderts" [Ph. D. diss., Universität Heidelberg, 1961], 39).

16. For discussions of polymorphy, see David R. Cartlidge, "Transfigurations of Metamorphosis Traditions in the Acts of John, Thomas and Peter," *Semeia* 38 (1986): 53–66;

John describes Jesus' call to him and his brother, he tells how his brother
saw a child beckoning, but he saw a young man. Later when he saw an
old bald-headed man, his brother saw a young man (88–89).[17] In John's
account, Jesus is presented almost as a mirage, appearing at the same
time in different physical manifestations to different perceivers.

John also emphasizes the ephemeral nature of Jesus' material body at
the transfiguration. He describes Jesus as absolutely "not like a man
[ἄνθρωπον δὲ οὐδὲ ὅλως]. His feet lit up the ground and his head reached
to heaven" (90.10–11). This whole section of the *Acts* accentuates Jesus'
immateriality. John recounts how Jesus' eyes never closed and how,
when he reclined upon Jesus' breast at table, it sometimes felt "smooth
and tender, and sometimes hard, like stone" (89.12–13; cf. 93.2–4). Jesus
also levitated off the ground, leaving no footprints (93.11–12).

Jesus' post-resurrection body is not a focus in the *Acts of John*, for
Jesus never had a stable material body, never died, and so was never resurrected. The "interpolated" section of the *Acts* makes this point
explicitly: "neither am I he who is upon the cross" (99.4); "therefore I suffered none of the things that they will say of me" (101.1).[18] Jesus is no
human with a body in these *Acts*. John emphasizes, "That is no man I
preach to you to worship, but God unchangeable, God invincible.... If
then you abide in him, you shall possess your soul invincible" (104.1–7).[19]

Lalleman, "Polymorphy of Christ," 97–118; Schneider, *Mystery of the Acts of John;* and Gedaliahu A. G. Stroumsa, "Polymorphie divine et transformations d'un mythologème," in idem,
Savoir et Salut (Paris: Cerf, 1992), 43–63. Origen also refers to a preresurrection polymorphy;
he says that Jesus' propensity to appear differently explains why Judas had to kiss him in
order to identify him (*Contra Celsum* 2.64).

17. References to chapters in the *Acts of John* and *Peter* will appear in the text. References
to the *Acts of John* are to the chapter and line number in the Junod and Kaestli, *Acta Iohannis*.
References to the *Acts of Peter* are to the chapter number and the page and line number in the
Lipsius edition. The translations of *Acts of John*, with some changes, are from Elliott and
James, *Apocryphal New Testament*. Translations from Acts of Peter are based on Elliott and
James, *Apocryphal New Testament;* and Robert Stoops, "Acts of Peter," in *New Testament Apocrypha* (Sonoma, Calif.: Polebridge, forthcoming). Schneider, *Mystery of the Acts of John* (59–62)
suggests the different ages of Jesus seen by perceivers reflect the spiritual maturity of the
viewers. John is more spiritually mature, so he sees an older Jesus. Lalleman, "Polymorphy
of Christ," 105, contests this suggestion on the grounds that Jesus in fact appears in multiple
forms to John, first as a youth and next as an old man: "Judged from that point of view,
John's faith can only be said to be unstable."

18. Lalleman, *Acts of John*, 193, offers an interesting interpretation of what Christ means
when he says he did not suffer and he suffered in the *Acts of John*. Lalleman explains this suffering: "He has come to share man's instability and errantry (96.4–6).... Specific qualities of
the Lord's suffering are his descent from heaven and his incompleteness as a result of his
members' not being unified."

19. All the sections of the *Acts of John* exhibit the same Christomonism; there is no distinction drawn between Christ and God. Christ's humanity is downplayed. The *Acts of Peter*

While the *Acts of Peter* shares with the *Acts of John* a belief in the one-ness of Jesus and God, it offsets this by asserting the reality of Jesus' human being, by insisting that Jesus had a human body, was born of a woman, ate and drank, suffered, died, and was resurrected. The *Acts of Peter* alludes even to Jesus' second coming and final judgment of the dead (28; 75.2). In what sounds like a creedal formula, Peter stresses Jesus' physical reality: "He ate and drank for our sake,[20] although he was nei-ther hungry nor thirsty. He also endured and suffered shameful things for us. He died and rose again because of us" (20; 67.26–28). In his first address to the Roman converts, Peter proclaims Jesus' real birth, death, and resurrection: "God sent his son into the world ... brought forth by the Virgin Mary" (7; 53.21–23)[21] and warns his listeners "not to look for another besides ... this crucified Nazarene who died and rose again on the third day" (7; 54.29–30). The *Acts of Peter* depicts Jesus with a specific human identity, a Nazarene, who was truly born and truly died (23; 71.24–25). Indeed, it is just on these points that Simon Magus will attack Peter: that he believes in "a human being, a Jew and a carpenter's son" (14; 61.28–29).[22] This taunt does not trouble Peter; he accepts it as factual. The *Acts of Peter* explicitly represents Jesus as having a human body, a human identity, even a human occupation.

Attitudes to Human Resurrection

The *Acts'* sharply different conceptions of Jesus' bodily nature corre-spond with a contrast in their attitudes toward the resurrected human body.[23] In the early Christian centuries, the risen body of Christ offered a prototype for the resurrected human body. For example, Irenaeus, an advocate for a resurrected fleshly body, supports his belief with reference to Christ's body: "In the same manner as Christ did rise in the substance

---

is less consistent in its Christology, but see chapter 39 for a similar assimilation of Christ and God.

20. In the *Acts of Peter*, to demonstrate the reality of a dried fish brought back to life (a resurrection), the narrative notes that the fish not only swam, but also ate bread thrown to it (13). Eating seems to be considered a persuasive proof of life.

21 The *Acts of John* does not use the Hebrew Scriptures, but the *Acts of Peter* references their prophecy of the birth of Jesus: "His birth who can declare it" (Isa 53:8); "Behold a Virgin shall conceive in her womb" (Isa 7:13–14). See Robert Stoops, "The Acts of Peter in Intertexual Context," *Semeia* 80 (1997): 57–86, for a discussion of these texts and other biblical citations in the *Acts of Peter*.

22. Lalleman, *Acts of John*, 163.

23. See Bynum, *Resurrection of the Body*; Van Eijk, "Only That Can Rise"; Robert M. Grant, "The Resurrection of the Flesh," *JR* 28 (1948): 120–30 and 188–208; and Gregory J. Riley, *Resurrection Reconsidered: Thomas and John in Controversy* (Minneapolis: Fortress, 1995).

of the flesh ... shall he also raise us up by his own power" (*Haer.* 5.7.1). It is therefore not surprising that such sharply different conceptions of Jesus' bodily nature in the two *Acts* would coincide with divergent attitudes toward the resurrected human body.

Although the *Acts of John* offers repeated examples of resurrections, of people raised from the dead, its focus is not on their resuscitated bodies, but on their new spiritual lives.[24] John demonstrates this perspective when the dead priest of Artemis is raised to show, as he says, "the power of Jesus Christ." John addresses the resurrected priest: "You have been raised but are indeed not really living.... Will you belong to him by whose name and power you have been raised?" (47.11–12). This resurrection is depicted clearly as only preliminary to the conversion that must follow it.[25] The priest's new life begins not with his physical resuscitation, but only when he comes to the faith.

This spiritual emphasis is also explicit in the episode describing the raising of a man killed by his son. When this father is raised, he complains to John that he had already suffered so much from his son, and now "you have called me back to what purpose?" (52.8). John agrees that physical resurrection is not the goal: "If you rise up to the same life, you would be better to remain dead. But rise up to a better life" (52.9–10). In the *Acts of John*, resurrection functions as the symbol for the call to a new life. As Eugene Gallagher notes, the change from death to new life acts as a metaphor. It expresses "an understanding of the powerful changes wrought by conversion."[26] In Paul Schneider's words, "Life after death for the *Acts of John* is the Christian community."[27] Resurrection acts as a trope for conversion.

This image of conversion is not new; Paul and Justin both called baptism a new birth.[28] But in the *Acts of John*, this emphatic metaphoric use of resurrection detaches it from the material realm of physical life and death and imbues it with a primarily spiritual and "realized" meaning. In contrast, the *Acts of Peter's* representations of resurrection emphasizes its physical and social aspects. To see their very different attitudes on resur-

---

24. For resurrections in the *Acts of John*, see Jean Bolyki, "Miracle Stories in the Acts of John," in Bremmer, *Apocryphal Acts of John*, 15–35; Eugene V. Gallagher, "Conversion and Salvation in the Apocryphal Acts of the Apostles," *SecCent* 8 (1991): 13–29; Lalleman, *Acts of John*, 162–65 and passim.

25. Lalleman, *Acts of John*, 165, makes this point with greater clarity.

26. Gallagher, "Conversion and Salvation," 24. Gallagher claims, "the passage from death to life is the *leitmotiv* of the *Acts of John* and the clearest understanding of conversion" (18).

27. Paul G. Schneider, "The Acts of John: The Gnostic Transformation of a Christian Community," in Helleman, *Hellenization Revisited*, 256 n. 13.

28. Rom 6:3–11; 2 Cor 5:17; *1 Apol.* 61.

rection, we can compare the two scenes in the *Acts* that represent multiple resurrections.

Resurrection in the Acts of John

Both *Acts* offer an episode with three resurrections. In the *Acts of John,* the action begins when Callimachus, a wellborn Ephesian (73.10), becomes consumed with desire for Drusiana, the ascetic wife of Andronicus. Learning of his passion, Drusiana is so distraught at being the cause of another's sin that she sickens and dies. Callimachus' desire, however, does not abate, and after her burial he bribes Fortunatus, Andronicus' steward, to open Drusiana's tomb so that he can defile her. On the third day after her death, John and Andronicus come to the tomb and find a strange sight: Callimachus lying with a huge snake sleeping upon him, and next to him, Fortunatus dead (73). Believing he understands what has happened, Andronicus asks John to raise Callimachus so that he can confess. John orders the snake off the man and prays, and Callimachus rises up. He confirms Andronicus' story and describes how he was undressing Drusiana when a beautiful youth covered her with his cloak and said, "Callimachus, die, that you may live" (76.19–20). Then the snake killed Fortunatus and terrified Callimachus into a lifeless state.

Callimachus himself interprets his resurrection from the dead as a conversion. He tells John that the command he heard (that he must die to live) is already fulfilled: "For that unbeliever, godless, lawless man is dead; I am raised (ἐγήγερμαι) by you as a believer, faithful and godly" (76.37–39). Next, Drusiana is raised up, and pitying Fortunatus, she asks that he also be raised. But once raised, Fortunatus runs off, complaining of the Christians' power: "O how far the power of these awful people has spread! I wished I were not raised but remained dead, so as not to see them" (83.7–9). John, declaring that neither Fortunatus' soul nor his nature is changed, begins an extended anathema of Satan and all his issue. John concludes by foretelling a second death for Fortunatus, a death that, the reader soon discovers, has already occurred (86.4–9).

These resurrections all underscore that there are two kinds of resurrections: spiritual and physical. And it is the spiritual that has primary significance.[29] In this narrative, what matters is not Callimachus' physical resuscitation, but his change from a godless man to a believer. Similarly, Fortunatus's physical resurrection, without a spiritual change, is meaningless. It lasts but a few hours. This narrative shares the Greco-

---

29. Bolyki, "Miracle Stories in the Acts of John," 30; Lalleman, *Acts of John,* 163–65.

Roman cultural bias in favor of the mind/spirit over an interest in the body's condition. How little the reality of physical death matters in the perspective of the *Acts of John* is evidenced by the narrative's indeterminacy about the actual physical condition of some of the characters resurrected.[30] Although Callimachus is referred to at one point as a corpse (75.1), it is never clear whether he was actually dead. The serpent never bit him but simply sat on him and terrified him. Since death in this text is never more than a figure, the narrative has little reason to clarify whether Callimachus was dead or simply in a petrified stupor.

This same indifference to a character's physical state occurs in the earlier account of John's raising of Lycomedes and his wife, Cleopatra. Lycomedes' precise condition also is left ambiguous. At his wife's death, he is represented as so overcome with grief that he falls to the ground lamenting. A few sentences later, John describes him as "lifeless" (ἄπνους 21.18). Should the reader take this death from grief seriously?[31] His specific state, however, is not the point in this text, as Cleopatra's response to her resurrection makes clear. Touched by John and bidden to rise, Cleopatra responds, "I will rise master, save your Cleopatra" (23.9–10). As her comment implies, her physical rising is almost irrelevant; her salvation is the new spiritual life she embraces. In the resurrection stories of the *Acts of John*, physical death functions primarily as a symbol of the life before conversion. The materiality of real death barely intrudes into this text.

In the *Acts of John*, "being raised up" is a spiritual marker, a term for spiritual conversion, rather than for a physical transformation.[32] When the pagans of Ephesus, for example, recognize God's power after the destruction of Artemis's temple, they prostrate themselves before John. He instructs them to rise up (Ἀνάστητε 43.4). Similarly, when he gathers the widows into the Ephesian theater to heal them and show Christ's power, John says he will be "raising them up" (ἀνιστῶν 33.11). Converts in this text are not shown being baptized, but rather being raised up, resurrected. Paul Schneider suggests that "resurrection" may have a sacramental connotation in the *Acts of John*. He points out that when John cursed Satan and instructed him to keep away from Christian life, he included in his list of Christian practices, such as fastings, prayers, bap-

---

30. Bolyki, "Miracle Stories in the Acts of John," 32–33; Lalleman, *Acts of John*, 163–64.

31. Greek romance heroes often threaten to die because of the loss of their loved ones. See Perkins, *Suffering Self*, 98–99. Junod and Kaestli, *Acta Iohannis*, 2:547–51, discuss the connections between the *Acts of John* and the romance genre.

32. Knut Schäferdiek, "Herkunft und Interesse der alten Johannesakten," *ZNW* (1983): 247–67.

tism, and eucharist, "their resurrection to God" (ἀπὸ ἀναστάσεως τῆς πρὸς τὸν θεόν; 84.13–14).[33]

This spiritual, metaphorical understanding for resurrection reflected in the *Acts of John* is not exceptional in the spectrum of beliefs that existed in the period.[34] Numerous commentators have pointed out its correspondence with Tertullian's description of his adversaries:

> They say that which is commonly supposed to be death is not really so, namely, the separation of body and soul: it is rather the ignorance of God, by reason of which man is dead to God, and is no less buried in error than he would be in the grave. Wherefore that also must be held to be the resurrection, when a man is reanimated by access to the truth, and having dispersed the death of ignorance, and being endowed with new life by God, has burst forth from the sepulcher. (*Res.* 19)

In this paradigm, resurrection is not a future event, a return to life in a resuscitated body, but an event realized in the present by spiritual change, by recognizing Jesus' call. This conception of resurrection is eminently spiritual; it is very far from a concept of a raised material body.

Resurrection in the Acts of Peter

The case is very different in the *Acts of Peter,* as its scene featuring multiple resurrections evidences.[35] Here Peter and Simon Magus enter into a contest in miracle working. Again three resurrections occur in quick succession. In this narrative, however, the material reality of death and its loss is much more starkly conveyed than was the case in the *Acts of John.* To begin the contest, the prefect orders Simon to cause a slave, a favorite of the emperor, to die and then orders Peter to raise him. Simon speaks a word into the boy's ear, and he dies. But before

---

33. Schneider, "Acts of John," 249.

34. Whether this position is "gnostic" or not is not important to my discussion. See Michael A. Williams, *Rethinking "Gnosticism": An Argument for Dismantling a Dubious Category* (Princeton: Princeton University Press, 1996), 29–51, for the problems with the designation "gnostic." In the second century, many who are considered gnostic defined themselves as Christians. My interest is in the connection of a belief in material resurrection with more egalitarian social attitudes.

35. Christine M. Thomas, "Revivifying Resurrection Accounts: Techniques of Composition and Rewriting in the Acts of Peter Cc. 25–28," in Bremmer, *Apocryphal Acts of Peter,* discusses the narrative construction of this scene. Christine M. Thomas, *The Acts of Peter, Gospel Literature, and the Ancient Novel: Rewriting the Past* (New York: Oxford University Press, 2003), 65–83, offers a valuable study of the narrative processes essential for understanding the prose narratives, including the Gospels of the early Christian period.

Peter can resurrect him, a poor widow comes forward, telling of her dead son. She laments the loss this death has meant for her: "I had only one son, by the labor of his hands he provided for me; he lifted me up; he carried me. Now he is dead, who will give me a hand?" (*Acts of Peter* 25; 73.5–7). The mother emphasizes the real material difference her son made in her life. Peter agrees to help her, and thirty young men volunteer to carry her back to get her son. This text eliminates the vagueness around death seen in the *Acts of John*. It explicitly authenticates the youth's death: "And the young men who had come examined the nose of the boy to see if he were really dead. When they perceived he was dead they comforted the mother" (25). This story precisely and carefully establishes the reality of death, expressly conveying its somber consequences, a mother's sorrow and material loss.

The widow's son is carried back to the forum, where meanwhile Peter has empowered Agrippa to raise up the dead slave. Peter then raises the widow's son, emphasizing the tangible benefits his renewed life will bring to his mother and the community: "Young man arise and walk with your mother as long as you can be of use to her. Afterward you shall be available to me ... and serve as a deacon and bishop" (27). Spiritual change is not the primary focus here, but rather the substantive difference a physical resurrection can make: a mother no longer in need, a community with secured leadership. In this text resurrection may have spiritual implications, but its material effects are equally important.

At this point in the scene (28), another mother of a dead son (in this case, a senator) arrives and begs Peter to raise her son. Peter agrees, but when the body, preceded by its burial riches, arrives, Peter first challenges Simon to raise it. Simon has some success; the body lifts its head, opens its eyes, and bows to Simon. The crowd is swayed by Simon's accomplishment, but Peter chastises them for being foolish, "since you seemingly believe that a dead man rose who has not risen." For, as Peter contends, real life is manifested in the physical and the social: "Let the dead man speak, let him rise, let him untie the grave band from his chin, let him call to his mother" (28; 76.13–15). When Simon is forced to move away from the corpse, it falls back into death. Peter then raises the young senator into full physical being: walking, talking, and donating to the church community (29; 79.10–13). Again the narrative takes care to corroborate the body's dead state. Simon's ability magically to manipulate the corpse underlines its state as simply that of a lifeless object, a thing, open to exploitation.

In both examples of the raised sons in the *Acts of Peter*, the focus is not on spiritual change alone, but on a return to full physical, bodily, and social activity. In this text, resurrection never slights the body, its ability to function as body, to labor and to serve. Resurrection may carry metaphorical implications in the *Acts of Peter,* but in contrast to the *Acts of John,* death's material reality and significance are a parallel concern throughout the narrative.

CORRELATION OF INCARNATION AND
RESURRECTION BELIEFS WITH SOCIAL ATTITUDES

I have proposed that the Christians in the second century who advocated for a material Jesus and a material resurrection worked to resist the operating social hierarchy that depreciated persons identified with the material body. In this paradigm, the *Acts of Peter* should show more concern than the *Acts of John* for people who were traditionally demeaned on the basis of their association with the body—the nonelite. The *Acts of Peter* should also contest the ingrained social attitudes structuring Greco-Roman society and manifest a less hierarchical and more inclusive conception of community. In fact, a reading of the two texts supports the view that incarnation and resurrection beliefs are correlated with social attitudes.

Treatment of the Nonelite

As János Bolyki has observed, the ambience of the *Acts of John* is expressly the world of the upper class: "Wealthy men and their wives— even the leaders of the city—dominate the scene."[36] Bolyki notes that even the one servant featured in the text, Fortunatus, is specifically designated a steward (ἐπίτροπον 70.5); he is not a simple house servant, but an overseer. In the *Acts of John,* the only episode with an explicit social component is the healing of the widows at Ephesus (30–36).[37] In this scene, John reproaches the Ephesians for the sorry state of their poor widows; he has found that only four out of sixty are healthy (30.4–5). John then offers a homily on charity, reminding them that even kings, rulers, and tyrants go naked from this world, liable to everlasting punishment (36.11–13). Beyond this episode, social issues receive scant attention in the *Acts of John.* In this text that denies Jesus a body and regards resurrection as a spiritual event, the physical situation and needs of believers are not a focus.

The *Acts of Peter* provides a striking contrast; social concerns permeate the text.[38] Junod and Kaestli, for example, provide a list of just the

---

36. Bolyki, "Miracle Stories in the Acts of John," 35.

37. Cf. Junod and Kaestli, *Acta Iohannis,* 2:456–65.

38. See Perkins, *Suffering Self,* 124–41; Robert Stoops, "Patronage in the Acts of Peter," *Semeia* 38 (1986): 91–100.

instances in the *Acts of Peter* that correspond with the single scene in the *Acts of John* showing John ministering to the widows.[39] In the *Acts of Peter*, Marcellus, the senator, is described as having ministered to the orphans and widowed of Rome and is shown opening his house to strangers and the poor (8; 55.3–5). Later, after Peter has driven Simon from his house, Marcellus gathers the widows and elderly in his home and gives each a gold piece (19; 66.15). In another scene, Marcellus, Peter, and the other Christians minister to the widows, offering them refreshment and a place to stay (22; 69.1–4). Peter also asks the wealthy mother of the risen senator to give money to the widows (29; 79.10).

The necessity to care for and support the have-nots is a theme repeatedly returned to in the *Acts of Peter*. The narrative also offers an antithetical social comment: those without the faith are depicted as more prone to mistreat those of low status. After Simon subverts Marcellus, for example, Marcellus no longer welcomes strangers, but beats them away from his door (8; 55.16–17). Simon himself apparently mistreats slaves.[40] When Simon leaves Marcellus' house, Marcellus's slaves attack Simon because of the distress he caused them. They beat and stone him and even pour chamber pots over his head (*vasa stericoribus plena* 14; 61.20). The narrative notes that the slaves justified their revenge as both worthy and the will of God (14; 61.24–25). This reference to the slaves' opinions and the indication of God's specific approval of their actions are both signs of this narrative's uncommon attentiveness to the attitudes of slaves.[41]

---

39. Junod and Kaestli, *Acta Iohannis*, 2:457 n. 1.

40. Magda Misset-van de Weg, "'For the Lord Always Takes Care of His Own': The Purpose of the Wondrous Works and Deeds in the Acts of Peter," in Bremmer, *Acts of Peter*, 106.

41. For slavery, see K. R. Bradley, *Slaves and Masters in the Roman Empire: A Study in Social Control* (Collection Latomus 185; Brussels: Latomus, 1984), and *Slavery and Society at Rome: Key Themes in Ancient History* (Cambridge: Cambridge University Press, 1994); Peter Garnsey, *Ideas of Slavery from Aristotle to Augustine* (W. B. Stanford Memorial Lectures; Cambridge: Cambridge University Press, 1996); and Jennifer A Glancy, *Slavery in Early Christianity* (New York: Oxford University Press, 2002). Bradley and Garnsey both note that Christianity's real effects on the institution of slavery were minimal. Slavery was most often used as a metaphor for sin, and its material effects on human persons were ignored. However, *Semeia* 83/84 (1998), entitled *Slavery in Text and Interpretation* (ed. Allan Dwight Callahan et al.), has several papers advocating for a real critique of slavery in early Christianity. This passage discussing the revenge of Marcellus's slaves on Simon is certainly not radical; it notes that the slaves had permission for their attack on Simon (*accepta potestate*), but it does show an unusual concern for a slave perspective. Eubola's slaves also are shown being tortured because of Simon's actions (17).

In another illustration of this sensitivity, Peter is depicted as refusing to raise the young senator unless his mother promises to keep the pledge she made at his death to manumit his slaves:

> Before raising him he said to his mother, "Will these young men whom you have set free in honor of your son be able to serve their master as free men when he is alive? For I know that the spirits of some of them will be wounded when they see your risen son and serve again as slaves. But let them all be free and receive their subsistence as before—for your son shall rise again—and let them be with him." And Peter looked at her for a long time awaiting an answer. (28; 77.7–12)

The narrative both recognizes and comments upon the slaves' aversion to their slavery.[42] Elite literary productions usually mask this reality.[43] Peter's concern for how the slaves would feel, combined with his refusal to raise the boy until their potential hurt is ameliorated, reflects a perspective not often articulated in literary productions of the period.

Diversity and Superiority

The *Acts of Peter* explicitly notes the diversity and inclusiveness of the Christian community. It carefully itemizes its multi-status composition: "The whole crowd of the brethren came together, rich and poor, orphans and widows, the powerful and the weak" (36). The *Acts of John*, however, intimates a community with an implicit hierarchy. The treatment of the Lord's polymorphy in each narrative manifests these different perspectives. As David Cartlidge has suggested, polymorphy in the *Acts of John* projects a hierarchy, while in the *Acts of Peter*, it fosters inclusiveness.[44]

John and his brother James, for example, see Jesus in different forms at the same time. In each case, the Lord is presented as a more mature figure to John. Paul Schneider has read these different manifestations as indications of John's special and greater capacity to receive the Lord and his superior understanding.[45] John himself alludes to his superiority

---

42. Dimitris Kyrtatas, *The Social Structure of Early Christian Communities* (London: Verso, 1987), 66, calls this "the strongest statement in favor of manumission in Christian literature."

43. The Greek novels, for example, reflect the ideology that slaves are devoted to their masters; see Perkins, *Suffering Self*, 56–59.

44. Cartlidge, "Transfigurations of Metamorphosis," 19–36.

45. Lalleman, *Acts of John*, 105, contests Schneider's point, but since so much else in this text supports its innate hierarchy and John's superiority, the fact that John always sees the

when he explains his need to adapt his knowledge to his listeners' capacities: "I indeed am able neither to set forth to you nor to write the things which I saw and heard. Now I must adapt them to your hearing and in accordance with everyone's capabilities" (*Acts of John* 88.3–5). The apostle has special knowledge and must condescend to his listeners so that they may glimpse the Lord's glory (δόξαν 88.7). John continues to emphasize his special status, as he relates how James and Peter became angry with him at the transfiguration because he had spoken with the Lord and how he refused to answer their questions, saying only, "This you shall learn if you ask him" (91.7–8).

Peter also has occasion to describe his experience at the transfiguration when he comes upon a Gospel passage being read on the topic at Marcellus's house. He immediately rolls up the Gospel and begins to discourse upon it (20; 66.30). He explains that Jesus had taken on human form out of his compassion for humankind (*misericordiam* 20; 67.6).[46] The incarnation (absent in the *Acts of John*) is a sign of God's mercy, so that humans might be saved despite their limited vision, as "each saw as his capacity permitted" (*Acts of Peter* 20; 67. 9–10).[47] In the *Acts of Peter*, it is not the apostle with his special knowledge who condescends to his listeners but, rather, the Lord who condescends to all humans and takes on human form out of his desire to be present for all. Peter does not appropriate any superior insight for himself; rather, he emphasizes everyone's limits before the Lord's being. Unlike John, who is depicted at the transfiguration as able to see and hear more than his companions, Peter describes himself as falling down, struck blind by Jesus' brilliance. But the Lord helps him up, appearing in a form he can bear (20; 67. 19–20).

Just as John is portrayed as superior to his companions at the transfiguration, the *Acts of John* appears to share its society's hierarchical conviction that some persons are inherently more worthy than others. This hierarchical stance is particularly evident in what have been called the interpolated chapters (94–102, 109), but this attitude occurs throughout the narrative.[48] In these chapters, the Lord himself instructs John in

more mature vision of Jesus suggests that again he is being depicted as more spiritual than others.

46. Leon Vouaux, *Les Actes de Pierre* (Paris: Letouzey, 1922), 341 n. 3, recognizes that the text's statement here that Jesus took on a "another form," "an image of man" (*effigie hominis videri* 20), might indicate docetism, but he suggests the phrase reflects the imprecision of christological terms of this period.

47. Pervo, "Egging on the Chickens," 50, sums up: in the *Acts of Peter*, "Incarnation was but condescension to human weakness."

48. Schneider, "Acts of John," 241–69. This section has often been termed gnostic, and it does show similarities with attested gnostic themes, especially Valentinian ones. For gnostic

hierarchy when, supposedly hanging on the cross, he appears to him in a cave on the Mount of Olives. The Lord indicates John's privileged knowledge compared with that of the crowd: "John, to the crowd below I am being crucified ... but to you I am speaking" (97.8–10). The Lord explains he is not what they call him: "which is lowly (ταπεινὸν) and not worthy of me" (99.6–7). This lowly and unworthy term appears to be the *human body*. *Jesus* explains that the crowd around the cross below is of a lower nature (ἡ κατωτικὴ φύσις 100.1–2) and tells John to ignore "the many" and disdain those outside the mystery (100.10–11). The Lord's words mark John's superior insight and position and imply a hierarchical community structure; some are by nature lower than others.[49] The Lord explains that those who would know him, know him as a kinsman (συγγενὴς 101.6). His words suggest that believers should recognize a spiritual affinity with the Lord.[50] They are related to the Divine and thus have a special position. John later describes himself laughing at the multitude because of what the Lord has told him about them.[51] It is well known that others (i.e. Gnostics) in the second century called themselves Christians, and like John in the *Acts*, held themselves as superior to the general Christian community.[52] With this attitude, John and these Gnostic Christians would seem simply to impose upon the Christian community the traditional Greco-Roman hierarchal assumptions about social hierarchy.

In contrast, the *Acts of Peter* features not the kinship of some humans with the Divine, but rather the universal and inherent weakness of the human condition. Peter explicitly defines himself to ensure that the Romans do not mistake him for a divine figure. Before his contest in the forum, Peter asserts both his humanity and his failures: "Romans, I am

correspondences, see Junod and Kaestli, *Acta Iohannis*, 2:581–632 and 660–68; Gerard Luttikhuizen, "A Gnostic Reading of the Acts of John," in Bremmer, *Apocryphal Acts of John*, 119–52; Schneider, *Mystery of the Acts of John*, 78–114; and Lalleman, *Acts of John*, 30–38, 199–215. While this section of the *Acts of John* does seem to include more overtly gnostic themes, the text throughout reflects a spiritual understanding for Jesus' body and for human resurrection.

49. Valentinian sources reflect a hierarchical ranking of humans, divided into hylics, psychics, and pneumatics. Note that the lowest and unredeemable category is the material. See Schneider, *Mystery of the Acts of John*, 34–44.

50. This perhaps explains the Lord's comment about some of the chosen who have not understood him: "they are still men" (92.8). It is only when people come to realize their real spiritual nature, that they are divine, that they will understand the Lord. This notion is the foundation of many of the historical gnostic systems; see Kurt Rudolph and R. McL. Wilson, *Gnosis: The Nature and History of Gnosticism* (San Francisco: Harper & Row, 1983), 92–110.

51. My comments on this section are indebted to Gerard Luttikhuizen, "Simon Magus as a Narrative Figure in the Acts of Peter," in Bremmer, *Apocryphal Acts of Peter*, 39–51.

52. See, for example, Irenaeus, *Adv. haer.* 1.8.3.

one of you, I have human flesh and am a sinner" (*carnem portans humanam sed peccator*, 28; 74.29–30). Peter emphasizes his material being (*carnem*) and his sins. Sins and their forgiveness provide a major theme in this narrative.[53] The plot develops from Peter's mission to come to Rome to win back to the faith the Pauline Christians who have apostatized because of Simon's inducements. When he first addresses these Christians, Peter reminds them of God's mercy. He had sent his son into the world, moved by his compassion for humankind (7; 53.28). Peter also reminds them of his own failures. Although he himself had witnessed miracles, he denied the Lord, not once but three times (*et non tantum semel, sed et ter* 7; 54.3). He reassures them: "But the Lord did not blame me, he turned to me and had mercy on the infirmity of my flesh" (*infirmitatem carnis* 7; 54.5–6).

Peter's vision of God's compassion comforts these fallen Christians, and they repent. In his address, Peter also recalls his own miracle experience of walking upon the water. Later Marcellus mentions that Simon had used this very episode and Peter's doubt upon the water to challenge his faith. Such reiterated references to Peter's failings permeate the narrative and present him as a model for God's persistent compassion. Marcellus, the senator, offers another example of human failing. He had supported the Christian community until Simon perverted him. A talking dog Peter sent to castigate Simon persuades Marcellus of the apostle's power, and he begs for forgiveness (9–10). Peter forgives and embraces Marcellus (11; 58.25). But almost immediately, Marcellus again fails in his faith, fearful of reprisals after a demon breaks a statue of the Caesar. Peter rebukes him: "I see you are not the man you were a few minutes ago when you said you were ready to spend everything for the salvation of your soul" (11; 59.12–15). Nevertheless, Peter allows Marcellus to repair the statue.

Worthiness and Forgiveness

The liberality of the Lord's and Peter's forgiveness and compassion for human weakness are touchstones in the *Acts of Peter*. No one is

---

53. Gerald Poupon, "Les Actes de Pierre et Leur Remaniement," *ANRW* 2.25.6:4363–83, has suggested that this emphasis on the multiple opportunities for repentance is the work of a later redactor in the context of the controversy over the treatment of *lapsi*. I am not persuaded by this argument. The theme of failings in faith is too central to Peter's representation to need to be explained as the work of a redactor; moreover the theme structures the entire work in too constitutive a manner to be read as a late addition. Luttikhuizen, "Simon Magus as a Narrative Figure," 40, also disagrees with Poupon's position: "I doubt these are late or about *lapsi*." Stoops also rejects this interpretation ("The Acts of Peter in Intertexual Context," 70).

exempt; there is no hierarchical ordering. The apostle and the senator are as vulnerable to failure as others. The *Acts of John* suggests that some Christians are superior to others on the basis of their heightened spirituality, but in the *Acts of Peter*, all are equalized in their common fallibility. The message of these *Acts* is not the divine kinship of humans, but their collective infirmity.

The *Acts of John* in general reflects a less generous attitude toward human failing. At the transfiguration, for example, when John disturbs the Lord at prayer, he turns on John in the appearance of a small man and pulls his beard. John describes how he was in pain for thirty days. When he questions what a beating would feel like, if such a slight tug could hurt so much, the Lord warns him in the future "not to tempt him who is not to be tempted" (μὴ πειράζειν τὸν ἀπείραστον 90.21–22). The Lord in this narrative is quick to punish and seemingly impatient, although John praises his "patience" (77.18).

The scene in Drusiana's tomb may even intimate that repentance and salvation are not an option for all. At Drusiana's tomb, recall that two men were resurrected, Callimachus and Fortunatus, but only one is saved. Both men were clearly sinners. Callimachus, described as one of the most prominent young men of Ephesus (73.10), had desired necrophilia with Drusiana, and Fortunatus, "the steward," had abetted him. After Callimachus is raised, he tells about the voice he heard declaring his resurrection to a new life, and then he repents, falls at John's feet, and is embraced by the apostle (76–78). But the case is quite different for the second sinner.[54] When Drusiana first proposes that that Fortunatus be raised, Callimachus objects, as the voice he heard did not mention Fortunatus. Callimachus concludes, "If he were good (ἀγαθὸς), God out of mercy would have certainly raised him through the blessed John. He knew that the man should have a bad death" (κακῶς τεθνάναι 81.7–9). Fortunatus is raised, but he wishes he were still dead and runs away.

John announces that Fortunatus has not changed for the good (ἀγαθὸν ψυχὴν 84.2) and condemns him as Satan's offspring. His words suggest that Fortunatus by his very nature was never capable of repentance: "O nature, naturally unsuited for the better ("Ω φύσις ἀφύσικος

---

54. Poupon, "Les Actes de Pierre et Leur Remaniement," 4376, points out the similarities in the depictions of Marcellus and Callimachus in the respective *Acts*. I have written on this passage before (Perkins, "Acts of Peter as Intertext," 627–33). Lallemann, "Acts of John and Peter," 166, suggests that my comparison of Marcellus, Callimachus, and Fortunatus is invalidated by the fact that the latter two were not *lapsi*; his point is well taken. I submit, however, that about the point of the generosity of repentance for sinners in the *Acts of Peter*, the comparison still holds.

πρὸς τὸ κρεῖττον 84.2–3).[55] In John's view, Fortunatus is from another root; he has another nature, as Satan's issue (τοιγαροὖν οἵα ἡ ὁδός σου τοιαύτη καὶ ἡ ῥίζα καὶ ἡ φύσις), and John asks Christ to remove all such issue from the Christian community. The message in this vignette appears to be that some humans by their very nature are prohibited from repentance and salvation. This explains why, as Callimachus said, the voice he heard during his death experience never mentioned Fortunatus. Resurrection from physical death would be wasted upon Fortunatus, as he is incapable of spiritual life. As the narrative comments, "[God] knew that the man should have a bad death" (81.8–9).

In contrast, Peter lays a much less adamant denunciation upon Simon, another who is called a child of the devil (28; 77.2). Peter hopes that he will repent, "for God does not remember evil deeds" (28; 77.3). But when Simon continues to threaten the faith of the Roman converts by flying over the city, Peter appeals to the Lord to stop him. In his prayer, Peter carefully specifies that he does not want Simon killed but simply disabled. Peter's attitude toward Simon keeps open the possibility of his repentance. Neither Peter's words nor his actions suggest he believes that Simon is incapable of salvation. By describing Fortunatus as unsuited by his very nature (φύσις ἀφύσικος) for becoming better (84.2–3), the Acts of John again reinscribes the hierarchical thinking of the contemporary society that restricted some people from a full moral life.

In fact, the scene at Drusiana's tomb can be read as one more refiguration of the most conventional of the elitist social paradigms of Greco-Roman society. Two sinners are represented as raised; one proves worthy of salvation, one does not. The worthy man, Callimachus, also happens to be wellborn, one of the most prominent men of his city. The unworthy man, Fortunatus, is a servant, most likely a slave. This episode not only does nothing to challenge the society's traditional hierarchical assumptions, it actively reinforces them. Characters assume their traditional social roles. The wellborn turn out to be naturally more suited to be better than their social inferiors. So Callimachus is able to use his second chance, but Fortunatus is proved to be naturally unsuited for a better life. This episode, in fact, could be read to imply that favor and kindness are wasted on the lowborn; Fortunatus just throws away his second chance. On the basis of this episode, the Acts of John appears almost reactionary, as if written to counter more egalitarian models of Christianity.

---

55. Bolyki, "Miracle Stories in the Acts of John," 32.

Conclusion

The scenes with multiple resurrections in each of the *Acts* display their different social perspectives. The *Acts of Peter* includes resurrections from diverse status positions; a slave, a poor youth, and a rich one are raised up. In the *Acts of John*, in contrast, two of the three raised are wealthy, and the other, a servant, proves unworthy of his resurrection. The two texts reflect inherently different positions toward inclusiveness and hierarchy. The *Acts of John* displays the bias for hierarchical thinking innate in the society as a whole, and again a servant turns out to be inherently less worthy than an elite person. The *Acts of Peter*, in comparison, moves toward a more inclusive perspective.

These respective social attitudes, moreover, appear to correlate with the texts' different beliefs about the nature of Jesus' body and of human resurrection. The *Acts of John* represents a Jesus without a stable, material human body and uses human resurrection primarily as a trope for spiritual change. This text offers little challenge to traditional social assumptions about status and community. The *Acts of Peter*, in contrast, represents a human, material Jesus. It testifies to his birth, death, and resurrection, his eating and drinking, and his suffering. This narrative also focuses on the physical and social aspects of human resurrections. The *Acts of Peter*, in turn, subverts traditional hierarchies based on status and offers a more inclusive and egalitarian notion of community through its focus on the equality of all humans in their shared dependence on the Lord's mercy.

THE BREASTS OF HECUBA AND THOSE OF THE DAUGHTERS OF JERUSALEM: LUKE'S TRANSVALUATION OF A FAMOUS ILIADIC SCENE

Dennis Ronald MacDonald

INTRODUCTION

For twenty years I have devoted most of my scholarly attention to describing the influence of classical Greek literature—especially poetry and epic—on Hellenistic Jewish and early Christian narratives. My interests in this topic began with the apocryphal *Acts of Andrew*, but gradually spread to include the Gospel of Mark, the book of Tobit, and most recently Luke-Acts.[1] I am convinced that the authors of these works not only consciously imitated Homer, Euripides, and Plato, in many cases they expected their readers to detect that they had done so and to note the religious, moral, or philosophical superiority of their characters and their God. Such contrast imitations, or emulations, were a significant aspect of ancient rhetorical practice and have been observed in the transvaluation of the *Iliad* by the author of the *Odyssey*, of Homeric epic by Aeschylus, Euripides, Herodotus, Hellenistic novelists, and, of course, Vergil, and of Vergil himself by several Latin poets.

Although scholars have recognized such rewritings among classical Greek and Latin authors, few have proposed that Jews and early Christians, too, imitated classical Greek narratives. The chasm between Homer and Luke—for example—was too enormous to bridge: poetry versus prose; Greek religion versus Judaism; eighth century B.C.E. versus late first or early second century C.E. That the author of Luke rewrote literary models is undeniable: he redacted Q and the Gospel of

---

1. See especially *Christianizing Homer: "The Odyssey," Plato, and "The Acts of Andrew"* (New York: Oxford University Press, 1994); *The Homeric Epics and the Gospel of Mark* (New Haven: Yale University Press, 2000); "Tobit and the *Odyssey*," in *Mimesis and Intertextuality in Antiquity and Christianity"* (ed. Dennis R. MacDonald; Harrisburg, Pa.: Trinity Press International, 2001), 11–40; and *Does the New Testament Imitate Homer? Four Cases from the Acts of the Apostles* (New Haven: Yale University Press, 2003).

Mark and emulated several passages of the LXX.[2] That he did so with
Homeric epic, however, is by no means evident to most scholars. For
this one must make a case.

   During the past twenty years I have refined six criteria for establishing genetic, literary connections between two texts. This is how I
described them in my most recent book.

> The first two criteria assess the cultural significance of the proposed
> model. Accessibility, criterion one, pertains to the dating of the proposed
> model relative to the imitation and its physical distribution and popu-
> larity in education, art, and literature. Obviously no author can imitate a
> text that he or she has not read, so the more widespread the circulation
> and popularity of the model, the stronger the case that the author used
> it. Less obvious but no less important is the accessibility of the model to
> the intended readers. Ancient narratives often paraded themselves as
> rewritings of earlier ones to invite comparison; this strategy worked
> only if their readers knew the models well enough to get the point....
> Analogy, the second criterion, asks if other ancient authors imitated the
> same proposed model....
>   The criterion of density [the third] assesses the number or volume
> of similarities between two works. The more parallels one can identify,
> the more convincing is the case for imitation.... The fourth criterion
> examines the relative sequencing of motifs in the two works. If parallels
> appear in the same order, the case strengthens for imitation; conversely,
> if the parallels are random, the case is less compelling.... Density of par-
> allels and similar sequencing may not be sufficient of themselves to
> demonstrate literary dependence insofar as stories of the same genre dis-
> play similarities with no genetic relationship between them at all.
> Proving mimesis often requires satisfaction of the fifth criterion: distinc-
> tive traits. Authors often announced the relationship of their works to
> their models by supplying unusual features as mimetic flags. The flag
> might be a significant name or a telling word, phrase, literary context, or
> motif....
>   These last three criteria—density, order, and distinctive traits—
> provide the glue for holding the model and the imitation together
> hermeneutically. The sixth and final criterion assesses the strategic dif-
> ferences between the two texts: interpretability. As often as not, ancient
> authors borrowed from their models to rival them, whether in style,
> philosophical adequacy, persuasiveness, religious perspective, or

---

2. See especially the work of Thomas Louis Brodie, including "Greco-Roman Imitation
of Texts as a Partial Guide to Luke's Use of Sources," in *Luke-Acts: New Perspectives from the
Society of Biblical Literature Seminar* (ed. Charles H. Talbert; New York: Crossroad, 1984),
17–46; and "Towards Unraveling Luke's Use of the Old Testament: Luke 7.11–17 as an *Imitatio* of 1 Kings 17.17–24," *NTS* 32 (1986): 247–67.

whatever. Such emulations (Greek: ζῆλοι; Latin: *aemulationes*) were most effective when readers recognized the targeted model, so authors often advertised their dependence. For example, Vergil blatantly imitated the Homeric epics in the *Aeneid* but took up the Trojan cause, not the Greek.[3]

LUKE 23:27–31 AND *Iliad* 22

The present study argues that Luke 23:27–31 imitates a famous scene from the *Iliad*.

A large crowd of the people followed him, including women who were beating themselves and wailing for him. Jesus turned to them and said, "Daughters of Jerusalem, do not weep for me; weep rather for yourselves and for your children. For behold days are coming in which people will say: 'Blessed are the sterile, and the wombs that never gave birth, and the breasts that never gave suck.' Then they will begin to say to the mountains, 'Fall on us!' and to the hills, 'Hide us!' For if they do these things to wood that is green, what will happen to the dry?"[4]

Few critical scholars attribute this episode to historical memory insofar as it appears only in Luke and seems to presume the destruction of Jerusalem in 70 C.E. But scholars otherwise dispute its origin. Rudolf Bultmann thought it went back to an Aramaic tradition that ascribed the prophecy to Jesus; others have argued that it is primarily a Lucan redactional creation.[5] Others have examined the text from the perspective of exegetical borrowing in an attempt to locate it more precisely in the process of Lucan composition.[6] Here are some of the texts that scholars have proposed for understanding this passage.

✦ Luke's reference to the "Daughters of Jerusalem" is an echo of prophetic literature, but it is not clear if he is alluding to any particular text: Song 2:7; 5:16; 8:4; Isa 37:22; Zeph 3:14; and Zech 9:9.

---

3. *Does the New Testament Imitate Homer*, 2–6.

4. Luke 23:27–31 (all translations from the Bible and other ancient texts are my own, unless otherwise indicated). See also Luke 21:23, where Jesus expresses pity for women who will be pregnant or nursing at the fall of Jerusalem (cf. Mark 13:17).

5. Rudolf Bultmann, *History of the Synoptic Tradition* (trans. John Marsh; New York: Harper & Row, 1963), 37; Joseph A. Fitzmyer, *The Gospel according to Luke* (2 vols.; AB 28–28A; New York: Doubleday, 1985), 1495.

6. E.g., Raymond E. Brown, *The Death of the Messiah: From Gethsemane to the Grave* (2 vols.; New York: Doubleday, 1994), 917–32.

✦ Jesus' statement that these women should weep for themselves and their children often is read as an allusion to Zech 12:10–14 LXX:

> And I will pour on the house of David and on the inhabitants of Jerusalem a spirit of grace and compassion, and they will look on me whom they have mocked, they will mourn over him as over a beloved son, and they will be tormented as over a firstborn son. In that day wailing will increase in Jerusalem as one mourns the cutting of a pomegranate orchard in the valley. The land will mourn tribe by tribe; each tribe by itself and their women by themselves.... [What follows is a series of lamentations by the tribes and their women.] All the tribes that are left—a tribe [will mourn] by itself, and their women by themselves.

Zechariah 12:10–14 appears elsewhere in the New Testament for understanding the death of Jesus and so may also have informed Luke (e.g., John 19:37, Matt 24:30, and Rev 1:7).

✦ The expression "days are coming in which" (Luke 23:29) is common in the LXX, such as Jer 7:32; 16:14; and 29:31.

✦ Scholars frequently cite the oracle in Isa 54:1 LXX as a parallel to Luke 23:29: "Rejoice, O sterile woman who does not bear; break out in song and cry out, you who never was in labor, because the children of the desolate woman will be more than those of the one who has a husband, says the Lord."[7] In Isaiah, God tells Zion to rejoice because God will make it prosper. In Jesus' comments in Luke, however, the women are to rejoice in the very fact that they have no children when Jerusalem falls. It is quite possible that Luke reversed the meaning of the text intentionally, but the reversal of the text is subtle and by no means transparent.

✦ The commands to the mountains in Luke echo an oracle in Hosea concerning the fall of Samaria:

Hosea 10:8b LXX	Luke 23:30
καὶ ἐροῦσιν τοῖς ὄρεσιν	τότε ἄρξονται λέγειν τοῖς ὄρεσιν
Καλύψατε ἡμᾶς,	Πέσατε ἐφ᾽ ἡμᾶς,
καὶ τοῖς βουνοῖς	καὶ τοῖς βουνοῖς
Πέσατε ἐφ᾽ ἡμᾶς	Καλύψατε ἡμᾶς.

---

7. Brown, *Death of the Messiah*, 923.

The imprecision of the statement in Luke may indicate quotation from memory; in any case, there seems to be no redactional advantage for Luke to have reversed the commands to the mountains and the hills.

✦ Ezek 17:24 LXX, like Jesus' statement in Luke, also contrasts the "green tree" and the "dry," but the text sheds little light on the passage in Luke.

In sum, nearly every aspect of this text has a potential parallel in Jewish scriptures, especially in the LXX.

One also might examine this text intertextually with Luke 11: 27–28. "While he [Jesus] was saying these things, a woman from the crowd raised her voice and said to him, 'Blessed is the womb that bore you and the breasts that you sucked.' But he said, 'Blessed rather are those who hear the word of God and observe it.'" The beatitude means something like "Your mother is so fortunate to have a son like you!"[8] Beatitudes are common in ancient texts, but there seems to exist no precise equivalent to this one. Luke 11:27 may be an original creation based on Prov 23:25 LXX: "May your father and mother be glad in you; may the woman who bore you rejoice." One can make a strong case that Luke's beatitude originally appeared in Q. Even though Matthew does not have an exact equivalent to it, Matthew does contain a version of Mark 3:31–35, which likewise speaks of those who do the will of God as Jesus' true family; it appears in the same context as Luke's beatitude. That is, both statements follow the Q saying about the return of the unclean spirit (Matt 12:46–50 and Luke 11:27–28).

Gospel of Thomas logion 79 combines Luke's beatitude (11:27) and Jesus' statement to the daughters of Jerusalem (Luke 23:29). This text is extremely important for our purposes, for if *Thomas* were independent of the Synoptics, as many scholars assume, it would seem to witness to traditions known also to Luke. I will argue, however, that for this text, the author of *Thomas* almost certainly combined two passages that he discovered in the text of Luke. Thomas combined them; Luke kept them distinct. I translate logion 79 from the retrotranslation in *Synopsis quattuor evangeliorum* (15th ed.):

A woman from the crowd said to him, "Blessed is the womb that bore you and the breasts that suckled you." He said to her, "Blessed are those who hear the word of the Father and truly observe it. For days will come

---

8. Scholars usually relate the beatitude to Gen 49:25; among the blessings of Jacob to his sons is the "blessing of the breasts and of the womb," namely, children.

and you will say, 'Blessed is the womb that did not conceive and the breasts of those who did not give milk.'"

I will return to this matter at the end of this study.

My discussion to this point is quite traditional, and one can find some version of it in most critical commentaries on Luke. But I want to propose a radically different intertextual reading of the text, one that to my knowledge has never been considered. Without denying the influence of the biblical texts I mentioned earlier, I propose that Luke modeled this passage after Hecuba's supplication near the beginning of *Iliad* 22. Hector was on his way to face Achilles, who would slay him. His parents, Priam and Hecuba, watching the event from the walls, begged him not to fight.

> The old man cried out in grief, beat [κόψατο] his head with his hands, raised them up, and cried out in great anguish imploring his dear son who had stopped before the gates furiously eager to fight Achilles. The old man spoke pathetically to him with arms outstretched: "Hector, dear son, please do not take a stand against this man alone without others lest you quickly meet your fate, conquered by the son of Peleus.... While I am still alive, have pity on me—unhappy and unlucky—whom the Father, the son of Cronos will destroy at the threshold of old age with a harsh lot after seeing many woes: my sons perishing, my daughters dragged off, my treasures pillaged, little children [τέκνα] dashed to the ground in dread combat, my daughters-in-law hauled off by the destructive hands of the Achaeans.... "

> His mother, for her part, mourned and shed tears; unclasping the fold of her garment with one hand, she held out a breast with the other. As she shed tears, she said, "Hector, my child, have regard for these and take pity on me, if ever I gave you the breast that banishes worry. Remember these, dear child, and ward off the enemy from inside the wall; do not stand there as a champion against him. For if he kills you, I will never weep for you upon a bier, dear scion, whom I bore."[9]

Hecuba fears that Achilles would not return the corpse of her son for a fitting burial. Hector was not deterred and went to his death.

---

9. *Il.* 22.33–40, 69–65, and 79–87. The exposure of the breasts has later parallels. According to Herodotus, Egyptian women exposed their breasts to mourn the dead (*History* 2.85). Tacitus claimed that German women paraded on the walls of the city with their breasts exposed to encourage their husbands to fight more courageously and to keep them from becoming slaves (*Germania* 8.1).

This famous passage derives its power in part from the dilemma that it presents to Hector. On the one hand, he was eager to face Achilles from a sense of duty and honor. Earlier he had told Andromache that he never backed down from a fight and had learned always to seek glory at the front ranks of battle.[10] Only cowards shrink from danger; no one can escape his or her fate. On the other hand, Hector was an exemplary family man—loyal son and brother, loving husband, tender father—so the pleas of his parents would have been especially compelling for him. He needed to choose between public honor and private compassion. Powerful, too, is the juxtaposition of the two extremes of life: birth represented by Hecuba's breasts and Hector's impending death. Hecuba's plea is made all the more compelling for her radical gesture: her public nudity and risk of shame.

The parallels between this passage and Luke 23:27–31 are haunting. In both a young hero is about to die and people—especially women—mourn him and beat themselves (κόψατο/ἐκόπτοντο). In their speeches, Priam and Jesus each predict the fall of a city and the tragic fate of its women and children, or τέκνα. Both texts mention women's breasts to dramatize the scene.

The parallels between Hecuba's appeal and Luke 23:27–31 meet the criteria for a direct literary connection that I presented at the beginning of this paper. The first criterion is *accessibility*. The *Iliad* was the most famous book in Greek antiquity and the death of Hector was one of its most famous episodes. Indeed, it is the tragic climax of the entire epic. Furthermore, the death and burial of Hector was a favorite topic for visual artists, and no book rivaled the *Iliad* as a model for education in literacy.[11]

The second criterion is *analogy*, evidence that other authors imitated the same putative model. As one might expect, this powerful scene had many literary imitators. Seneca opened his *Trojan Women* with Hecuba still mourning the death of Hector and asking her Trojan sisters to let down their hair, disrobe to the waist, and beat their breasts, and they did

---

10. *Il.* 6.440–446.

11. On the death and burial of Hector in art see Susan Woodford, *The Trojan War in Ancient Art* (Ithaca, N.Y.: Cornell University Press, 1993), 81–87. "Priam's visit to Akhilleus was the most popular scene to be represented in Greek art of all the episodes in the Iliad" (Nicholas Richardson, *The Iliad: A Commentary: Volume 6, Books 21–24* [Cambridge: Cambridge University Press, 1993], 291). Homer's primacy in Greek literary education is universally acknowledged. For a helpful, recent discussion see Raffaella Cribiore, *Gymnastics of the Mind: Greek Education in Hellenistic and Roman Egypt* (Princeton: Princeton University Press, 2001), 194–97. See also the relevant discussions of curriculum in Teresa Morgan, *Literate Education in the Hellenistic and Roman Worlds* (New York: Cambridge University Press, 1998).

so.[12] Euripides wrote that as Neoptolemus was about to slay Hecuba's daughter Polyxena, she recalled her mother's sweet breasts.[13] According to Quintus Smyrnaeus, Hecuba had a dream in which her breasts dribbled blood onto the tomb of Achilles where Polyxena was slain.[14]

A fragment of the poet Stesichorus depicts the mother of a monster appealing to her son not to face Heracles in a fight. "I, unhappy woman, miserable in the child I bore, miserable in my sufferings; but I beseech you, Geryon, if ever I offered you my breast ... at your dear (mother's side) gladdened ... by (your feasting).' (With these words she opened) her fragrant robe .... "[15] Heracles later slew him.

Aeschylus, too, imitated the Homeric scene. Before Orestes killed his mother Clytemnestra, she begged him: "Stop, my son! Have respect for this breast, my child, at which, as you slumbered, with tender gums you sucked nourishing milk."[16] Her final utterance was: "So this is the serpent I birthed and suckled!"[17]

In Euripides' *Daughters of Troy*, Andromache tells her baby boy, Astyanax, just before his murder during the sack of Troy, "In vain did this breast give you suck when you were in swaddling bands, vainly did I suffer and struggle with labors."[18] Euripides wrote also of the tragic fight for the throne of Thebes between Polyneices and Etiocles, the sons of Oedipus and Jocasta. Just before they fought, Jocasta tried to make peace. "With tears and mourning visible to all; she offered her breast to her children, she offered it as a suppliant would a plea."[19]

The Latin poet Statius retold the story of the Theban civil war and made much of Euripides' reference to Jocasta's breast, adding other

12. Seneca, *Troades* 83–116.

13. Euripides, *Hecuba* 424.

14. Quintus Smyrnaeus, *Posthomerica* 14.272–278.

15. Stesichorus frg. 13, *Greek Lyric III* (trans. David A. Campbell; LCL 476; Cambridge: Harvard University Press, 1991), 73.

16. Aeschylus, *Libation-Bearers* 896–98; cf. 903: "I nursed you."

17. *Libation-Bearers* 928. Euripides' Orestes says that as he and his sister Electra slew her, Clytemnestra appealed to their pity by opening her robe and exposing her breast to them (Electra 1206–1209). See also Euripides, *Orestes* 527, 568, and 841, and *Greek Anthology* 9.126, apparently a rhetorical exercise on this topic. Naked breasts became a cliché for grief in ancient fiction. According to Sophocles, a woman wronged by her son bared her breasts before committing suicide (*Trachiniae* 923–926). Euripides wrote that as Polyxena was about to be slain on Achilles' tomb, she opened her robe, exposed her breasts, and invited the soldier to stab her there. Out of pity, he cut her neck instead, allowing her to cover herself from the gaze of men as she died (*Hecuba* 557–570). Ovid rewrote the scene, keeping Polyxena's daring final gesture of defiance (*Metamorphoses* 13.453–480; cf. 490–493, where Hecuba beats and scratches her breasts).

18. Euripides, *Daughters of Troy* 758–763; cf. Euripides, *Andromache* 510–512.

19. Euripides, *Phoenician Maidens*, 1567–1569.

details from *Iliad* 22. Outraged that her two sons could not make peace with each other, she bared her breasts, beat on the gate, and insisted on entry "by virtue of this womb." She then entreated one of her sons to take pity on his mother.[20] Despite her pleas, her children continued to rage against each other, and before they slew each other, she tried again by going to one boy "nude, with bloody chest."[21] She dared him to slay her, since he obviously had no regard for her gray hair, breasts, or womb.[22]

In the final book of Vergil's *Aeneid*, the Latin King Latinus and Queen Amata beg Turnus, their champion, not to fight in a passage patently modeled after the pleas of Priam and Hecuba to Hector. Latinus appeals to Turnus because the victory of the Trojans is inevitable and ends by begging him to pity his old father.[23] Conspicuously absent from Amata's appeal is Hecuba's dramatic exposure of her breasts, but it would be inappropriate for her to do so: Turnus was not her son but her would-be son-in-law.

Iliad 22.81–87	*Aeneid* 12.54–63
As she **shed tears** she said, "*Hector*, my child, *have regard for these* and *take pity on me*, if ever I gave you the breast that banishes worries. Remember these breasts, dear child, and ward off the enemy from inside the wall; *do not stand as a champion against him. For if he kills you, I will never weep for you upon a bier, dear scion*, whom I bore."	And the queen, disturbed about the new terms of the fight and prepared to die, *wept* and held her ardent son-in-law: "*Turnus, by these tears*, by whatever *respect for Amata may touch your soul*—you who now are my only hope, you are my comfort in old age, under your power is the glory and sovereignty of the Latins, in you resides all our declining house—I ask only this: *give up attacking Trojans.* *The same calamities of battle await both you and me*, Turnus. Together with you I will leave this hateful light; *never as a slave will I see Aeneas as my son-in-law.*"

---

20. *Thebaid* 7.479–510.
21. *Thebaid* 11.315–318; cf. 10.694–696.
22. *Thebaid* 11.341–342.
23. Vergil, *Aen.* 12.18–45.

In both columns a matron begs a beloved young warrior to have respect for her sorrow by refusing to fight a mightier foe, and in both the youth ignores her request.

The imitations cited thus far are poetic, but the scene had prose imitators as well. In Chariton's novel the parents of Chaereas, the protagonist, try to deter him from leaving to search for his beloved Callirhoe. His mother embraced his knees, tore open her dress, and held out her breasts, quoting Homer's Hecuba: "Child, have regard for these and take pity on me, if ever I gave you the breast that banishes worry."[24] In each of these examples it is likely that *Iliad* 22 informs the text.

Second Maccabees narrates a story with striking parallels to this tradition of supplicating breasts, but they are not so distinctive as to require imitation of *Iliad* 22 directly. The Seleucid ruler Antiochus IV tortured to death seven brothers and their mother. Before the death of the seventh and youngest brother, the mother whispers to him, "Son, have pity on me who carried you about in the womb for nine months, gave you suck for three years, nurtured you, brought you to this age in life, and provided you food. . . . Do not fear this executioner but be worthy of your brothers; accept death, so that I may receive you back with your brothers in God's mercy."[25] Because of her hope in the resurrection, she asked her son to die bravely; Hecuba had asked Hector to stay safely within the walls.

The author of 4 Maccabees rewrote the story of the mother of the seven martyrs but clearly felt uncomfortable with its anatomical details. Instead of telling her sons to have regard for her womb and breasts, she says, "Remember that it is through God that you participate in the world and have the benefit of life; for this reason you must endure every labor for God's sake."[26] In another version of her speech to her sons, this one at the end of the book, she again avoids explaining how to make babies.

> I was a pure virgin and never crossed the threshold of my father's house; thus I preserved the built-up rib. No corrupter in some desolate spot ruined me, no ravisher in some field. Never did the corrupter, the deceitful snake, befoul the purity of my virginity. I remained with my husband throughout my prime. The father of these grown lads has died. He is blessed, because he lived his life with good children and did not suffer this moment of being deprived of them. When he was still with you boys, he taught you the law and the prophets.[27]

---

24. Chariton, *Chaereas and Callirhoe* 3.5.
25. 2 Macc 7:27 and 29.
26. 4 Macc 16:18–19.
27. 4 Macc 18:7–9.

Gregory of Nazianzus, on the other hand, was no Byzantine Victorian and directly contrasted the mother of the seven martyrs in 2 Maccabees with Homer's Hecuba. Whereas Hecuba feared that Hector would die at the hands of Achilles, Gregory wrote that the mother in 2 Maccabees feared that the youngest son would not have the courage to die. "She considered delay, not death, as danger." The mother's whisper to her son becomes in Gregory a dramatic gesture apparently inspired by *Iliad* 22: "She exposed her breasts, recalled her nursing, let down her gray hair, and presented her old age as the gift of a suppliant."[28]

A spectacular reversal of genders for this scene appears in the *Martyrdom of Perpetua and Felicitas,* where she goes to her death courageously like Hector and her father, like Hecuba, appeals to her to renounce her faith and thus save her life.

Iliad 22.81–87	*Martyrdom of Perpetua and Felicitas* 5.2–4
As she *shed tears* she said, "*Hector,* my child, *have regard for these* and *take pity on me, if ever I gave you* the breast that banishes worries.	... saying: "*Daughter, take pity on my gray hairs. Take pity on your father, if I am worthy* to be called your father, if I have raised you to this flowering of age with these hands, if I favored you above all your brothers. Do not abandon me to public shame.
Remember these breasts, dear child, and ward off the enemy from inside the wall; *do not stand as a champion against him.* For if he kills you, I will never weep for you upon a bier, dear scion,* whom I bore."	Consider your brothers; *consider your mother* and your aunt, *consider your child who cannot live without you. Abandon your resolve!* You will destroy us all, for *none of us will be able to speak openly if something happens to you.*"

Again later, her father begs her to recant: "He began to rip out his beard and throw it on the ground, and he prostrated himself on the

---

28. *Oratio 15. In Machabaeorum laudem* (PG 35.916–917).

ground, disparaged his old age and spoke such words that would move all creation."[29] But he failed to move her to recant.

Perpetua's friend, Felicitas, had given birth to a girl in jail. One of her sisters took the girl and nursed her, but Felicitas was still lactating when she was led to her death. She "rejoiced that she had given birth safely so that she should fight the beasts, from blood to blood, from midwife to gladiator, a postpartum bath in the form of a second baptism."[30] The following passage tells how they were escorted from prison into the arena.

> After they were stripped naked and placed in netting, they were brought out. The crowd was horrified when they observed that one of them was but a delicate child and the other had recently given birth with milk trickling from her breasts. So the women were recalled and dressed in loose-fitting tunics. Perpetua first was thrown [by the heifer] and landed on her bottom [in lumbos]. There she sat up and pulled up her tunic that had ripped on the side to cover her thighs, concerned more about modesty than pain. And then, after asking for a hairpin, she arranged her disheveled hair, for it was indecent for a martyr to die with unkempt hair, lest she be seen in her hour of glory to be in mourning [plangere, literally, "to be beating her breasts in lamentation"].[31]

As Herbert Musurillo rightly notes, Perpetua's concern for modesty at the moment of her death directly imitates the death of Polyxena in the *Hecuba* of Euripides. These examples should suffice to show that Hecuba's appeal to Hector in *Iliad* 22 generated a vibrant literary tradition about women exposing their breasts in appeals for pity before the deaths of their children.[32] Criterion 2, *analogy,* is clearly satisfied.

Criterion three is *density* or *volume;* criterion four is *order.* The higher the density of parallels between two texts (and more often these parallels appear in the same order), the more likely the case for mimesis.

---

29. *Martyrdom of Perpetua and Felicitas* 9.2.

30. Ibid., 8.3.

31. Ibid., 20.2–5.

32. Herbert Mursillo, trans., *The Acts of the Christian Martyrs* (OECT; Oxford: Oxford University Press, 1972), 129. Clement of Alexandria cited Homer's reference to Hecuba's "breast that banishes worries" as though his Christian readers would have recognized its source (*Paidagogos* 1.6.43).

Iliad 22.25–89	Luke 23:27–31
✦ Hector is on his way to fight Achilles.	Jesus is on the way to the cross.
✦ Priam and other Trojans, including the women, saw Hector outside the gates; the old man "*beat* [κόψατο] *his head* with his hands ... *and cried out in anguish.*"	"A large crowd of the people followed him, including women who *were beating* [ἐκόπτοντο] *themselves and wailing for him.*"
✦ "His mother, for her part, mourned and *shed tears;* unclasping the fold of her garment with one hand, she held out a breast [μαζόν] with the other. As she *shed tears,* she said, 'Hector, *my child* [τέκνον], have regard for these and take pity on me, if ever I gave you *the breast* [μαζόν] that banishes worry. Remember these, dear *child* [τέκνον], and ward off the enemy from inside the wall; do not stand there as a champion against him.'"	"Jesus turned to them and said, 'Daughters of Jerusalem, *do not weep* for me; *weep rather for yourselves and for your children* [τέκνα]. For behold days are coming in which people will say: 'Blessed are the sterile, and the wombs that never gave birth, and *the breasts* [μαστοί] that never gave suck.'"
✦ [Hos 10:8: "And *they will say to the mountains, 'Hide us!' and to the hills, 'Fall on us!'* "]	"Then *they will* begin to *say to the mountains, 'Fall on us!' and to the hills,* 'Hide us!'"
✦ [In his speech to Hector, Priam had predicted the fall of Troy and emphasized the plight of the women and children.]	"For if they do these things to wood that is green, what will happen to the dry?" Jesus here predicts the fall of Jerusalem and emphasizes the plight of the women and children.
✦ [Priam foresaw "*little children* [τέκνα] *dashed to the ground* in dread combat."]	[In 19:44 Jesus laments over Jerusalem and says, "You and your *children* [τέκνα] in you they will *dash to the ground.*"]

The notion that in times of adversity it is better for women not to have had children is common in ancient literature.[33] This precise sentiment does

---

33. E.g., Euripides, *Alcestis* 880–888; *Andromache* 394–410; Seneca the Elder, *Controversiae* 2.5.2; Tacitus, *Annales* 2.75; and Apuleius, *Apology* 85.571.

not appear in the *Iliad*, but when Hector dies, Hecuba wishes to die with him. "O my child, I am so miserable! Why will I now live suffering cruelly while you are dead? Night and day throughout the city you were my boast, a help to all the Trojan men and Trojan women in the city, who used to welcome you like a god."[34] Hecuba's desire to die because of the deaths of her many children became proverbial.[35]

Notice also the parallels between the mourning of the Trojans for Hector and that of the crowd for Jesus.

Iliad 22.405–409	Luke 23:48
"His mother tore her hair, threw far away her shining veil, and wailed at the top of her lungs *when she saw her child.* And his dear father cried out in grief, and around them the people gave themselves to *wailing and groaning* throughout the city."	"And the entire crowd present at this spectacle, *when they saw what had happened,* they *beat their breasts* and returned home."

In light of Jesus' earlier instructions to the women (Luke 23:48), these lamentations at Jesus' death may have been both for Jesus and for women and their offspring.

Criterion five is *distinctive traits.* With respect to these parallels, the only significant lexical similarities between these two accounts are uses of κόπτω, τέκνα, and μαζός/μαστός. But at the level of motifs one finds a rather distinctive constellation of traits: a dying hero, weeping women, exposed breasts, and predictions of the fall of a city.

The final criterion is *interpretability,* the ability of the parallels to enrich one's understanding of a text, especially through contrasts, that is, through emulation. Jesus resembles Hector insofar as he, too, goes courageously to his fate, but he also provides a contrast. Hector refused to show compassion for Hecuba by recklessly going off to fight. Jesus, however, does show compassion, for he tells the women to weep for themselves and their children. Put another way, Hector had to make a choice between heroism in the face of death or compassion for his parents.

---

34. *Il.* 22.430–435. One may recall that Vergil's Amata commits suicide after the death of Turnus. See also *Aen.* 9:481–497, where the mother of Euryalus wants to die now that her son is dead. This passage is an imitation of Hecuba's lamentation in Il. 22.

35. E.g., Euripides, *Hecuba* 167–168, 213–214, 231, and 383–388; Quintus Smyrnaeus, *Posthomerica* 14.300–301; and Tryphiodorus, *The Taking of Ilios* 403–404 and 686–687.

Jesus, on the other hand, demonstrates both courage and compassion. Notice also that the women and children of Troy would suffer because, with Hector dead, the destruction of the city was certain. Luke's Jesus predicts that the women and children of Jerusalem would suffer because by killing Jesus the Jewish authorities doomed the city to destruction (see also 20:9–19).

It would seem reasonable to conclude that Luke modeled this passage after *Iliad* 22 primarily and used biblical images for elaboration. If this is the case, the parallel in the *Gospel of Thomas* does not witness to a tradition independent of Luke but to the text of Luke itself.

Luke 11:27–28	*Gospel of Thomas* 79
While he [Jesus] was saying these things, *a woman from the crowd* raised her voice and *said to him, "Blessed is the womb that bore you and the breasts that you sucked."* But *he said, "Blessed* rather *are those who hear the word of God and observe it."*	*A woman from the crowd said to him, "Blessed is the womb that bore you and the breasts that suckled you."* *He said* to her, *"Blessed are those who hear the word of the Father and* truly *observe it."*

Luke 23:29	
For behold *days are coming* in which people will say: *"Blessed are the sterile, and the wombs that never gave birth, and the breasts* that never gave suck."	*For days will come* and you *will say, "Blessed* is *the womb that did not conceive and the breasts* of those who did not give milk."

Already in the first line in *Thomas* one sees possible evidence of Lucan redaction insofar as it seems to presuppose a narrative context: "A woman from the crowd...." The parallels between *Thomas* and Luke 11 are nearly identical, including the reference to the plural construction "blessed are those...." But the parallels with Luke 23 are a different matter. First, *Thomas* alters the plural "Blessed are...." to the singular, "Blessed is...." In Luke the women are blessed because they would not have to see their children killed in the war. In *Thomas* the woman is blessed because she, in observing "the word of the Father," chooses not to have sex. This would explain the absence of Luke's reference to women who are sterile and the change from "never gave birth" in Luke to "did not conceive" in *Thomas*. Notice also that *Thomas* omits entirely any reference to the fall of Jerusalem; it focuses entirely on sexuality. In each of these changes, *Thomas* seems to be secondary to Luke; indeed, each can be explained as a redaction of Luke as a direct source. There is no reason to think that *Thomas* knew a pre-Lucan tradition about the blessing of the breasts. The only thing pre-Lucan about 23:27–31 are allusions to the LXX (Hos 10:8 most obviously) and to *Iliad* 22.

The example of Homeric imitation in Luke 23:27–31 is but one of many that appear throughout Luke-Acts. In *Does the New Testament Imitate Homer?* I propose four examples from Acts that also seem to imitate the *Iliad*, the casting of lots to replace Judas among the twelve echoes the casting of lots in book 7 to select Ajax to fight Hector; the vision to Cornelius echoes the lying dream to Agamemnon at the beginning of book 2; the angel's rescue of Peter from prison in chapter 12 echoes Hermes' rescue of Priam from Achilles in book 24; and Paul's farewell address to the Ephesian elders in chapter 20 echoes Hector's famous farewell to Andromache in book 6. Imitations of the *Odyssey* similarly appear throughout Luke-Acts. It may well be that the detection of literary imitation is one of the most neglected topics in discussions of early Christian narrative composition; Homeric epic may be the most neglected target of such imitations.

255-273

THE CHORAL CROWDS IN THE
TRAGEDY ACCORDING TO ST. MATTHEW

J. R. C. Cousland

INTRODUCTION

The Christian church father Tertullian famously sniffed, "What has Athens to do with Jerusalem?" If recent scholarship furnishes any indication, one would have to reply, "Quite a bit." Dennis MacDonald has lately produced a volume that remarks on the similarities between *The Homeric Epics and the Gospel of Mark,* concluding that "Mark imitated Homeric epic and expected his readers to recognize it,"[1] while Lawrence Wills in *The Quest of the Historical Gospel* establishes that "the *Life of Aesop* ... is the closest [literary] parallel to Mark and John."[2] My purpose here, however, is to explore a more time-honored connection with classical literature, specifically that between Greek tragedy and the Gospels.[3] The recognition of the dramatic character of the Gospels, particularly the passion narratives, goes back to at least the tenth century C.E.,[4] and the relation between Greek tragedy and the Gospels continues to be explored

---

1. Dennis R. MacDonald, *The Homeric Epics and the Gospel of Mark* (New Haven: Yale University Press, 2000), 189. See, in addition, idem, *Does the New Testament Imitate Homer? Four Cases from the Acts of the Apostles* (New Haven: Yale University Press, 2003), 1–15.

2. Lawrence M. Wills, *The Quest of the Historical Gospel* (London: Routledge, 1997), 177–78.

3. On tragedy and the Bible, see J. Cheryl Exum, *Tragedy and Biblical Narrative* (Cambridge: Cambridge University Press, 1992), esp. 1–15. The conceptual similarities between tragedy and the Gospels are discussed by Roger L. Cox, "Tragedy and the Gospel Narratives," *Yale Review* 57 (1968): 545–70, though Cox does not discuss the question of the literary *Gattung* of tragedy. Finally, see the illuminating assessment by Alfred Breitenbach: "Drama," in *Neues Testament und Antike Kultur* (ed. Kurt Erlemann and Karl Leo Noethlichs; vol. 1 of *Prolegomena-Quellen-Geschichte*; Neukirchen-Vluyn: Neukirchener, 2004), 102–5.

4. St. Ethelwold (ca. 908–984) is said to have applauded the "praiseworthy custom" of representing the death and resurrection of Jesus. This "drama" was performed using dialogue and mime in conjunction with the church's liturgy; cf. *ODCC*, s.v. "Drama, Christian."

by scholars such as Stephen H. Smith and Winfried Verberg, again with particular reference to the passion narrative.[5]

One feature that has yet to receive the attention it merits is the place of the Gospel crowds in relation to the chorus in Greek tragedy. Note that in making this connection, I do not mean to imply that Jesus and the Gospel writers were necessarily acquainted with Greek tragedy. Nevertheless, the possibility cannot be ruled out of hand: it is sometimes argued that Jesus' use of the term "hypocrite" demonstrates an acquaintance with Greek drama, picked up from visits from Nazareth to the theater in the nearby Hellenized city of Sepphoris.[6] Nor is it unlikely that so sophisticated an author as Luke should be unfamiliar with drama, especially as he may paraphrase Euripides in Acts: "It hurts to kick against the goads" (26:14; cf. Bacch. 795).[7] Yet, since it is difficult to establish direct influence, I will simply bracket the question, and examine whether, within the two literary genres, tragedy and Gospel, the crowds and the chorus display similarities in the way they are characterized and in the type of functions they perform. Given constraints of space, I have elected to compare the crowds of a single Gospel, namely, Matthew, with the tragic chorus as a whole, being cognizant that there will be an inevitable amount of distortion in comparing one Gospel to a corpus of tragedies.

Are the Gospel crowds analogous to the choruses of Greek tragedy? Certain obvious similarities do emerge, one of the most evocative being the

---

5. A. J. Lunn, "Christ's Passion as Tragedy," *SJT* 43 (1990): 209–31; Stephen H. Smith, "A Divine Tragedy: Some Observations on the Dramatic Structure of Mark's Gospel," *NovT* 37 (1995): 209–31; Winfried Verburg, *Passion als Tragödie: Die literarische Gattung der antiken Tragödie als Gestaltungsprinzip der Johannespassion* (SBS 182; Stuttgart: Katholisches Bibelwerk, 1999). See further Robert L. Brawley, *Luke-Acts and the Jews: Conflict and Conciliation* (SBLMS 33; Atlanta: Scholars Press, 1987), 135–38; Jo-Ann A. Brant, *Dialogue and Drama: Elements of Greek Tragedy in the Fourth Gospel* (Peabody, Mass.: Hendrickson, 2004), 178–86; Morna Hooker, "The Beginning of the Gospel" in *The Future of Christology* (ed. Abraham J. Malherbe and Wayne Meeks; Minneapolis: Fortress, 1993), 19–21; Petri Merenlahti, *Poetics for the Gospels? Rethinking Narrative Criticism* (London: T&T Clark, 2002), 38–39; Joseph B. Tyson, *The Death of Jesus in Luke-Acts* (Columbia: University of South Carolina Press, 1986), 29–47; Dan O. Via, *Kerygma and Comedy in the New Testament: A Structuralist Approach to Hermeneutic* (Philadelphia: Fortress, 1975), 98–103.

6. Cf. BDAG, s.v. "ὑποκριτής." On Jesus' possible acquaintance with tragedy from theater at Sepphoris, see R. Batey, "Jesus and the Theatre," *NTS* 30 (1984): 563–74; and Martin Hengel, *The "Hellenization" of Judaea in the First Century after Christ* (London: SCM, 1989), 74; John Meier, *A Marginal Jew* (New York: Doubleday, 1991–), 3:621 for dissenting views.

7. In Acts 17:28, Luke has Paul cite Aratus (*Phaenomena* 5) and possibly Epimenides (*Cretica*) and Cleanthes (*Hymn to Zeus*). Paul himself cites Menander's *Thais* (218) at 1 Cor 15:33, though this passage may well have become proverbial; cf. Anthony C. Thiselton, *The First Epistle to the Corinthians* (NIGTC 7; Grand Rapids: Eerdmans, 2000), 1254.

corporate character and persona of the two groups. Although both consist of numerous individuals, they generally speak and react as if they were a single person. There is, in addition, a certain obvious similarity in function: the responses of the two groups amplify the significance of an actor's actions, without necessarily authoritatively pronouncing upon them.

At the same time there are some very profound differences. The Greek chorus assumes a major role in all the great tragedians. They are present in the orchestra for almost the entirety of the play, and their role is of corresponding importance. Their utterances figure prominently: according to Paulsen, the average choral component in Aeschylus is about 48 percent, in Sophocles 21 percent and 20 percent in Euripides.[8] In Matthew, by contrast, the crowds are only mentioned explicitly some fifty times. Moreover, the very character of their speech is fundamentally dissimilar. The chorus, accompanied by an *aulos*, sings choral songs that feature lyric poetry of a frequently "high" and often intense quality, while the crowds, when they speak at all, utter laconic, even banal, prose.[9] Utterances apart, the role of the crowds in the Gospels is very limited. If it is appropriate to describe the tragic chorus as a character, it can justly be asked whether this is also true for the crowds of the Gospels. Is there really enough of a torso on which to place a mask? Finally, there is a prominent religious and ritual component to the choruses of Greek tragedy. Their dancing and singing explicitly and implicitly celebrated Dionysus, the god of drama, and the dramatic productions in which music and dance figured were a main constituent of many of his religious festivals. These activities indicate that the chorus were not simply literary figures;[10] their role also had a strong performative function associated with religious ritual.[11] Albert Henrichs, in

---

8. The older study by E. A. Phoutrides ("The Chorus of Euripides," *Harvard Studies in Classical Philology* 27 [1916]: 79–81) emerges with slightly different percentages: Aeschylus 43 percent; Sophocles 20 percent; Euripides 21 percent. The higher proportion of the chorus in Aeschylus is largely due to three of his surviving plays having only two actors. Thomas Paulsen, "Die Funktionen des Chores in der Attischen Tragödie" in *Das antike Theater: Aspekte seiner Geschichte, Rezeption und Aktualität* (ed. G. Binder and Bernd Effe; Bocumer Altertumswissenschaftliches Colloquium 33; Trier: Wissenschaftlicher Verlag, 1998), 92, furnishes the following percentages for the role of the chorus: *Persians*, 46 percent; *Seven against Thebes*, 49 percent; *Suppliant Women*, 60 percent.

9. Cf. Michael Silk, "Style, Voice and Authority in the Choruses of Greek Drama" in *Der Chor im antiken und modernen Drama* (ed. Peter Reimer and Bernhard Zimmermann; Drama 7; Stuttgart: Metzler, 1999), 1–26.

10. David Wiles (*Tragedy in Athens: Performance Space and Theatrical Meaning* [Cambridge: Cambridge University Press, 1997], 88–113) draws attention to the importance of mimetic dance as a feature of the chorus.

11. Claude Calame, "Performative Aspects of the Choral Voice in Greek Tragedy: Civic Identity in Performance" in *Performance Culture and Athenian Democracy* (ed. Simon Goldhill and Robin Osborne; Cambridge: Cambridge University Press, 1998), 125–53.

particular, has stressed the self-referentiality of the chorus, which emphasizes their role as conscious participants in religious ritual and not simply
as actors in a literary production.[12] By contrast, the Gospel crowds are
simply literary figures, and it may even be said, if half-humorously, that
the Gospel of Matthew seems to suggest that the crowds are not a chorus;
Jesus addresses the crowds, saying of "this generation," "We piped to
you and you did not dance" (Matt 11:17a).

Having made these caveats, however, there does appear to be
enough in the way of similarities to warrant a comparison. If nothing
else, an elucidation of the differences between the two groups should
help to clarify the varieties of *Gattung*. The following examination will
begin by addressing the corporate character of the two groups.

THE GREEK CHORUS

"Generalization about the role of the chorus in Greek tragedy is noto-
riously perilous."[13] So cautions David Bain. Yet recent years have shown
that not a few are prepared to countenance the risk: there has been a veritable explosion of scholarship devoted to the Greek chorus.[14] And while
there is arguably some measure of agreement about details of staging,
there is comparatively less about the function and role of the chorus,
especially in tragic performance. Rather than preferring one or two of
these positions, the following account will provide an overview of some

12. Albert Henrichs, "'Why Should I Dance?' Choral Self-Referentiality in Greek
Tragedy," *Arion* 3 [1995]: 56–111, offers a richly modulated discussion of the ritual role of the
chorus.

13. David Bain, *Actors and Audience* (Oxford: Oxford University Press, 1977), 58–59.

14. See, in addition to the works cited above: William Arrowsmith, "Chorus," in *The
New Princeton Encyclopedia of Poetry and Poetics* (Princeton: Princeton University Press, 1993),
201–2; Helen H. Bacon, "The Chorus in Greek Life and Drama," *Arion* 3 (1995): 6–24; Simon
Goldhill, "Collectivity and Otherness: The Authority of the Tragic Chorus" in *Tragedy and the
Tragic: Greek Theatre and Beyond* (ed. M. S. Silk; Oxford: Clarendon, 1996), 244–56; John
Gould, "Tragedy and Collective Experience" in Silk, *Tragedy and the Tragic*, 217–43; Paulsen,
"Die Funktionen des Chores in der Attischen Tragödie," 69–92; Rush Rehm, *Greek Tragic
Theatre* (London: Routledge, 1992), 51–61. For recent works devoted to the role of the chorus
in individual dramatists or plays, see the bibliography in Paulsen, "Funktionen," 91, and
Marsh McCall, "The Chorus of Aeschylus' *Choephori*" in *Cabinet of the Muses* (ed. Mark Grif-
fith and Donald Mastronarde; Atlanta: Scholars Press, 1990), 17–30. On the role of the chorus
in Greek Comedy, see Anton Bierl, *Der Chor in der alten Komödie: Ritual und Performativität*
(Leipzig: Saur, 2001); L. P. E. Parker, *The Songs of Aristophanes* (Oxford: Clarendon, 1997); and
Bernhard Zimmermann, "Chor und Handlung in der griechischen Komödie," in Reimer and
Zimmermann, *Chor*, 49–59.

of the dominant points of view and examine whether they have any overlap with Matthew's portrayal of the crowds.

First, however, it would be useful to provide an encapsulation of
what is often agreed upon.[15] The chorus' origin, like that of drama itself,
remains obscure. In all likelihood, however, the chorus emerged out of
the ritual dithyrambic choruses who sang and danced in honor of Dionysus at his annual festivals. By the time of Aeschylus, they had become an
established component of tragedy, so much so, in fact, that the term
"chorus" became metonymous for drama.[16]

Starting with their "corporate character," it would be as well to discuss what the two terms "corporate" and "character" mean. By corporate,
I mean that, in general, the chorus acts as a whole, speaks with one voice,
and contains no distinctive individuals. There are a few instances where
an individual might converse with another non-choral character, as when
speeches are attributed to the *koryphaios*, the chorus leader, or sti-
chomythia, an exchange of lines between an actor and a member of the
chorus. Even here, however, these individuals can be taken as representative of the whole.[17] And although the chorus can shift from first-person
singular to first-person plural, Kaimio has demonstrated that this phenomenon is typically a function of emphasis.[18] Where there is a
fragmentation of point of view in the chorus, it is often expressive of hor-
rific occurrences, such as happens to the chorus of old men upon their
hearing Agamemnon's death cries.[19]

The notion of character is more difficult. In discussions of Greek
tragedy the question has been the subject of much heated debate over the
last century. In his seminal work on Sophocles, Tycho von Wilamowitz,
the son of the famed classicist, argued that there was no such thing as
unified character or psychological verisimilitude—what characters said

---

15. For a valuable compendium of ancient sources that treat the chorus and other features of ancient drama, see Eric Csapo and William Slater, *The Context of Ancient Drama* (Ann
Arbor: University of Michigan, 1995), 349–68. Their analysis of the chorus, however, tends to
overestimate its "decline."

16. Bacon ("Chorus in Greek Life," 6) remarks that "for the Athenians of the archaic and
classical periods a play, whether a tragedy or a comedy, was first and foremost a chorus. A
poet who wished to produce a play went before an Athenian magistrate and, in the official
phrase, 'asked for a chorus.'" See the evidence on the choregic system listed in Csapo and
Slater, *Context*, 139–57 and more fully in Peter Wilson, *The Athenian Institution of the Khoregia:
The Chorus, the City and the Stage* (Cambridge: Cambridge University Press, 2000).

17. This point would be disputed by Silk, "Style, Voice and Authority," 16.

18. Maarit Kaimio, *The Chorus of Greek Drama within the Light of the Person and Number
Used* (Commentationes Humanarum Litterarum 46; Helsinki: Societas Scientiarum Fennica,
1970), 242.

19. Cf. Gould, "Collective Experience," 223; and Aeschylus, *Agamemnon* 1348–71.

was purely a feature of their situation and was designed to maximize the dramatic effect of an individual scene.[20] If recent critical opinion has tended to restore to tragedy the notion of a coherent protagonist,[21] debate about the dramatic consistency of the chorus continues. Rush Rehm, for instance, contends that we should "put to rest the notion that the chorus has a single, consistent character within a play."[22] On the other hand, the work by Rösler, Burton, and Gardiner on the Sophoclean chorus and Thiel on Aeschylus' *Agamemnon* has tended to stress the degree to which the chorus figures as a consistent character, integral to the drama itself.[23] Helpful in this regard is Mastronarde's recognition that the chorus possesses an "intradramatic" position as a "group with a particular fictional identity" and an "extradramatic" position as a "collective voice less tied to a particular identity."[24] A great deal depends on the playwright and the play, and even the phase of the playwright's work. Stephen Esposito convincingly argues that by contrast with his earlier plays, in Sophocles' later plays, "the chorus moved into the arena of the actors, on occasion even seeming to be an actor."[25]

In terms of their composition, most of the tragic choruses are the creation of the playwright, in part because of the limited numbers of larger groups in Greek mythology, but also because established groups such as the Argonauts or the heroes in *Seven Against Thebes* contained such well-known mythological figures—Jason, Polyneices—that they could hardly be expected to remain anonymous.[26] The anonymity of the chorus is also a function of dramatic expediency. Because the chorus is left "on stage"

---

20. Tycho von Wilamowitz-Moellendorff, *Die dramatische Technik des Sophokles* (Philosophische Untersuchungen 22; Berlin: Weidmann, 1917), 39.

21. See, for instance, the papers on character in Aeschylus and Sophocles by E. P. Easterling, reprinted in *Greek Tragedy* (ed. Ian McAusland and P. Walcot; Oxford: Oxford University Press, 1993), esp. 12–16, 58–65.

22. Rehm, *Greek Tragic Theatre*, 59.

23. Reginald W. B. Burton, *The Chorus in Sophocles' Tragedies* (Oxford: Clarendon, 1980); Cynthia P. Gardiner, *The Sophoclean Chorus: A Study of Character and Function* (Iowa City: University of Iowa Press, 1987); Wolfgang Rösler, "Der Chor als Mitspieler: Beobachtungen zur 'Antigone,'"*Antike und Abendland* 29 (1983): 107–24; Rainer Thiel, *Chor und tragische Handlung im 'Agamemnon' des Aischylos* (Beiträge zur Altertumskunde 35; Stuttgart: Teubner, 1993).

24. Donald Mastronarde, "Knowledge and Authority in the Choral Voice of Euripidean Tragedy," *Syllecta Classica* 10 (1999): 88.

25. Stephen Esposito, "The Changing Roles of the Sophoclean Chorus," *Arion* 4 (1996): 108.

26. Gould ("Collective Experience," 223 n. 28) notes one instance where there may have been a named character in the tragic chorus—Hypermestra in Aeschylus's *Danaids*. Whether Hypermestra was actually a member of the chorus is still disputed.

for most of the tragedy, it would be considerably more difficult to construct a play, if they represented known mythological characters.[27] This anonymity of the chorus has also been seen as expressive of their marginality as a group,[28] though this is not always the case. Kaimio has shown that in several plays by Aeschylus—especially the *Persians*—there is a representative element to the chorus, especially in contrast to Euripides where the chorus is conceived more vaguely with neither its collective nor its individual character much emphasized.[29]

THE FUNCTION OF THE CHORUS

It has long been recognized that the chorus performs a variety of functions.[30] Rather than list them all, I propose to mention four that have proven to be influential. It goes without saying that there is little agreement among scholars about the chorus' function and that many would dispute one or even all of those put forward here.

The Chorus as Actor

A first function of the chorus is as an actor in the drama.[31] This assessment is as early as Aristotle. He affirms that "one should regard the chorus as one of the actors; as part of the whole, participating in the action, not as in Euripides but as in Sophocles" (*Poetics* 18.19).[32] The distinction that Aristotle draws here between Euripides and Sophocles is not entirely clear, but Mastronarde has plausibly suggested that Euripides' choral songs tend to have an indirect connection with the episode just concluded and are slow to address the events unrolling in the tragic plot. The result is a withdrawal from the action, and a retarding of the linear dramatic momentum. By contrast, Sophocles' choral songs do relate to

---

27. Cf. Martin Hose, *Studien zum Chor bei Euripides* (Beiträge zur Altertumskunde 10; Stuttgart: Teubner, 1990), 1:16–17.

28. Gould ("Collective Experience," 219–24) emphasizes their marginality; Goldhill ("Collectivity," 252–54) effectively demonstrates that this marginality is not so pronounced as Gould would suggest. Cf. Mastronarde, "Knowledge," 90.

29. Kaimio, *Chorus*, 240, 244.

30. E.g., Walther Kranz, *Stasimon* (Berlin: Weinmannsche Buchhandlung, 1933), 171.

31. Plays that feature the chorus as a major character would include Aeschylus's *Eumenides* and *Suppliant Women*. The chorus contributes to the action in Aeschylus's *Libation-Bearers* and Euripides' *Ion*. They figure as victims in Aeschylus's *Agamemnon*, Sophocles' *Oedipus tyrannus*, and Euripides' *Daughters of Troy*.

32. Horace (*Ars* 193–194), perhaps in dependence on Aristotle, envisages a similar role for the chorus: "actoris partis chorus officiumque virile defendat."

the actor's present concerns and are emotionally linked to the situation of the actor. The result is that Sophocles' chorus tends to maintain the tension between episodes and advance the dramatic momentum.[33]

The Intensification of Drama

A second related function is one proposed by Walther Kranz, who argues that the choruses intensify the drama.[34] Typically, the chorus does not heighten the drama by initiating important action, as their role is essentially passive.[35] This is not to deny that there are plays where they do contribute substantially to the events on the stage, but, on the whole, they respond to the actions as they are initiated and performed by the actors. The rationale for such a stance is suggested by (Pseudo-)Aristotle in his *Problems* where he explains why active or steady musical modes are not appropriate to the chorus: "For the characters on the stage are imitating heroes; and in the old days only the leaders were heroes, but the rest of the folk, to whom the chorus belong, were only men" ([*Probl.*] 19.48).[36] The actor sets the agenda, the chorus respond to it. Their particular province, therefore, is not action but reaction; they do not engage in reasoned discourse, but in emotional responses. As A. M. Dale has remarked, "It is an unbroken law, all through the history of Greek tragedy, that though a Chorus may join in the dialogue to a limited extent, it must never make a set speech, a 'rhesis', never marshal arguments, try to prove or refute a contention, or speak a descriptive set piece."[37] Instead, their part is to express fears, hopes and judgments.[38] In so doing, they amplify the significance of a given action and help to interpret it for the audience.

Idealized Spectators

One of the most famous and enduring theories about choral functions was proposed 150 years ago by August Wilhelm Schlegel, who argued that the chorus represented the "idealized spectator" (*der idealisierte*

---

33. Mastronarde, "Knowledge," 98–100.

34. Kranz, *Stasimon*, 171.

35. Mastronarde, "Knowledge," 92.

36. Aristotle, *Problems* (trans. Walter S. Hett; 2 vols.; LCL 316–317; Cambridge: Harvard University Press, 1961), 1:413.

37. Amy M. Dale, "The Chorus in the Action of Greek Tragedy" in idem, *Collected Works* (Cambridge: Cambridge University Press, 1969), 211.

38. Jean-Pierre Vernant and Pierre Vidal-Naquet, *Myth and Tragedy in Ancient Greece* (New York: Zone Books, 1988), 34.

Zuschauer). The chorus is dissociated from the tragedy in a manner in keeping with their physical position between the *skênê* with the actors and the audience. The chorus, in Schlegel's words, "represented in general, first, the common mind of the nation, and then the general sympathy of all mankind."[39] They speak for the assembled audience, and say what an audience member might be presumed to say. Thus, the chorus often expresses conventional societal perceptions and truisms as well, and represents the viewpoint of established morality. As the repository of collective memory, the chorus is also able to impart the traditional wisdom of the community. Just how enduring this idea has proved can be ascertained from the fact that Martin Hose's recent monograph on the Euripidean chorus has sought to rehabilitate it.[40]

A related version of this view has also been advanced by Jean-Pierre Vernant and Pierre Vidal-Naquet, who maintain that the chorus functions as representatives of the collective city body: "the mouthpiece of the city."[41] The chorus, when they confronted the "hero marked by his immoderation, represented a collective truth, an average truth, the truth of the city."[42] As the collective, they carry on unchanged whatever fate the actor might experience.

The Embodiment of the "Other"

A converse approach has recently been advanced by John Gould.[43] He contends that instead of embodying the city of the citizen, the chorus embodies the "other:"

> [I]ts essential role within the tragic fiction resides ... in its giving collective expression to an experience alternative, even opposed to that of the "heroic" figures who most often dominate the world of the play; however, they express, not the values of the *polis*, but far more often the experience of the excluded, the oppressed and the vulnerable. That "otherness" of experience is indeed tied to its being the experience of a

---

39. August Wilhelm Schlegel, "Vorlesungen über dramatische Kunst und Literatur" in *Sämmtliche Werke* (ed. Eduard Böcking; 16 vols.; Hildesheim: Olms, 1971–72), 5:76.

40. Hose, *Chor bei Euripides*, 1.32–9. Compare Arrowsmith's ("Chorus," 201) designation of the chorus as "society in miniature."

41. Vernant and Vidal-Naquet, *Myth and Tragedy*, 311. See further, Oddone Longo, "The Theater of the *Polis*," in *Nothing to Do with Dionysos?* (ed. John J. Winkler and Froma I. Zeitlin; Princeton: Princeton University Press, 1990), 16–17.

42. Vernant and Vidal-Naquet, *Myth and Tragedy*, 311.

43. Gould, "Collective Experience," 217–43.

"community", but that community is not that of the sovereign (adult, male) citizen-body.[44]

The chorus, then, can be marked by its alterity in relation to the actors, but arguably to the audience as well.

MATTHEW'S CROWDS

In order to consider how the above précis of the chorus fits with Matthew's portrayal of the crowds, it would be useful to examine briefly the place of the crowds in the First Gospel. Matthew's crowds appear in the Gospel at the outset of Jesus' public ministry, just before the Sermon on the Mount: "great crowds followed him from Galilee, the Decapolis, Jerusalem, Judea, and from beyond the Jordan" (Matt 4:25).[45] These crowds continue to follow Jesus over the course of his public ministry to Israel, and last appear in Jesus' trial before Pontius Pilate, where they are incited by their leaders to ask for Jesus' crucifixion. Their involvement in his trial is exceptional, however. For the most part, they form an admiring retinue who marvel at Jesus' words and deeds and give expression to their astonishment intermittently in direct speech. They contrast noticeably with the two other main groups of the Gospel, the Jewish leaders and Jesus' disciples. The Jewish leaders, while nominally consisting of figures such as the scribes, Pharisees, Sadducees, chief priests and Herodians, manifest a singular persona. They are implacably opposed to Jesus, and ultimately serve as the architects of his betrayal and death. The disciples, by contrast, are the antithesis of the Jewish leaders. They are committed to Jesus; they follow him and help him to perform his ministry. They recognize his identity as the Son of God. The three groups, therefore, describe a spectrum of response to Jesus, with the crowds situated in the middle.

If the scholarship devoted to the Gospel crowds is not so considerable as that to the Greek chorus, it is still contested.[46] Worthy of remark is the fact that Matthew's version of the crowds is largely his own construct.

---

44. Ibid., 224.

45. The Gospel crowds have also been fruitfully compared with groups in other genres of literature; cf. Richard Ascough, "Narrative Technique and Generic Designation: Crowd Scenes in Luke-Acts and in Chariton," *CBQ* 58 (1996): 69–81.

46. On the crowds in Matthew, see Warren Carter, "The Crowds in Matthew's Gospel," *CBQ* 55 (1993): 54–67; J. R. C. Cousland, *The Crowds in Matthew's Gospel* (NovTSup 102; Leiden: Brill, 2002); Meier, *Marginal Jew*, 3:19–39; Martin Meiser, *Die Reaktion des Volkes auf Jesus* (BZNW 96; Berlin: de Gruyter, 1998), 223–61; Paul S. Minear, "The Disciples and the Crowds in the Gospel of Matthew," *AThR* supp. ser. 3 (1974): 28–44; Wolfgang Schenk, *Die Sprache des Matthäus* (Göttingen: Vandenhoeck & Ruprecht, 1987), 349–52.

If we can safely assume that Mark is his source, it is certainly noteworthy that he drops over half of Mark's thirty-eight references to the crowds, keeping only eighteen while adding thirty-two of his own. So while his overall portrayal of the crowds has been shaped by the structure and parameters established by Mark, the individual representations are effectively his own.

The Character of the Crowds

The crowds in Matthew display some of the same features as the chorus. They contain no named characters, and they too, act as a whole and largely speak with one voice.[47] Further, in the explicit authorial descriptions of the crowds, (absent, of course, in Greek tragedy) they are, almost without exception, treated as a single entity.[48] Whatever the crowds do, or however they react, they do it in concert. If undeniably pallid and etiolated, they nevertheless display certain features that are largely consistent and characteristic. Over the course of Jesus' public ministry they are repeatedly astonished at Jesus' teaching (7:28; 22:33) and fearful or dumbfounded at his thaumaturgy (9:8, 33; 12:33; 15:31). Moreover, they are repeatedly described as following him (4:25; 8:1; 12:15; 14:13; 19:2; 20:19). Such traits are hardly the exclusive preserve of the crowds, but they are imputed to them with such regularity, that they could be said to become defining characteristics.

Despite these features, E. P. Sanders has said that "the crowds in the Gospels and Acts serve the convenience of the narrator,"[49] and it could certainly be argued that his observation holds true for the Matthean crowds. Matthew apparently uses the same crowds to acclaim Jesus in the triumphal entry and to revile him and condemn him to death in the passion narrative.[50] That the crowds are capable of such a striking *volte-face* could suggest that Matthew is not particularly concerned with consistency of characterization—the same deficiency that von Wilamowitz finds in the chorus—but the sort of all-purpose dial-a-crowd so familiar in Josephus's *Jewish War*. This apparent lack of consistency has led both Wolfgang Schenk and Paul S. Minear to posit differing groups of

---

47. At 12:47 there is one textually doubtful occasion where a member of the crowds—τις—addresses Jesus, but apart from that all utterances are attributed to the crowd.

48. There is one exception at 9:18–26, where ὄχλος appears to signify a delimited group of mourners.

49. E. P. Sanders, *Jesus and Judaism* (London: SCM, 1985), 289.

50. Minear ("Crowds," 35), on the basis of this contradictory behavior, postulates two sets of crowds.

crowds within the Gospel. Schenk has proposed that the crowds consist of discrete entities, arguing that the recurring use of "great crowds" (ὄχλοι πολλοὶ) without the article signals the appearance of a new and distinct group six times within the Gospel, with the other occurrences of crowds (ὄχλοι) being anaphoric and referring back to the most recent mention of "great crowds."[51] Minear, by contrast, would argue for only two discrete groups, one favorably disposed to Jesus' ministry and another involved in his Passion.

Neither claim is wholly convincing. Schenk's distinction simply does not hold. He observes, for instance, that 8:1 states that "great crowds" (ὄχλοι πολλοὶ) followed Jesus, a datum that leads him to infer that "a new group" is signified here.[52] Yet 7:28–9, the verses immediately prior to 8:1, also mention crowds—but not "great crowds"—who are amazed at Jesus' teaching. Can it be that Matthew is really distinguishing between one set of crowds at 7:28–9 and a new set introduced in the very next verse, especially when he provides no other basis for distinguishing between them? What possible reason would Matthew have for differentiating between the two?

Minear argues for two distinct groups on the basis of their differing attitudes toward Jesus.[53] Yet in the arrest narrative Matthew has Jesus address the crowds explicitly (26:55) and asks why they did not arrest him when he was teaching in the temple, a query that recalls their earlier astonishment at his teaching in the temple (22:33). The effect is to link the groups—they did not arrest Jesus because they were marvelling at his message. The crowds are portrayed, therefore, as a unity even though they reverse their stance. The import of this reversal will be considered more fully below.

The Function of the Crowds

Moving from the question of character to function, further points of contact between the Greek chorus and the crowds become evident.

The Crowds as Actor

The crowds are actors in the Gospel in the sense that they advance the action in the manner of Sophocles over Euripides. The very brevity of their spoken remarks means that there is no delay or withdrawal from the action. At points, their responses to Jesus even engender action. Their

---

51. Schenk, *Sprache*, 349–50.
52. Ibid., 350.
53. Minear, "Crowds," 35.

surmise, "Can this be the Son of David?" (Matt 12:23), prompts the Pharisees to retort, "It is only by Beelzebul, the ruler of demons, that this fellow casts out the demons" (12:24) which, in turn, sets up a long rejoinder by Jesus. A similar situation arises when the crowds acclaim Jesus as the Son of David in the triumphal entry into Jerusalem (21:9). Their spontaneous outburst causes the entire city to fall into turmoil, wanting to know who Jesus was. While these actions are still largely responses to Jesus, there is a clear sense that the crowds despite their passivity participate in the action. The same is true in their role in the trial of Jesus, where in response to their leaders' persuasion, they call for Jesus' crucifixion and help impel Pilate to put him to death (27:22–23).

On other occasions, where the crowds' acclaim closes an episode, their reaction often serves as a bridge to the next narrative segment so that there is no real hiatus in the action as it unrolls through the Gospel.

The Intensification of Drama

In regard to the second function, there is an obvious sense in which the crowds heighten the drama. In the first place, the crowds' actions are almost entirely conceived as responses to Jesus. Their following him, it is true, is not initiated by him, but can still be regarded as their response to his person. Otherwise, their fear, astonishment, amazement, glorification of God, and outbursts are reactions to Jesus' words and deeds. On the limited number of occasions where the crowds express themselves in direct discourse, their reactions are best described as outbursts since they are frequently preceded by expressions of wonder. For instance, we are told of the crowds' astonishment first; "the crowds marvelled, saying 'Never was anything like this seen in Israel'" (Matt 9:33), or they "were amazed, and said 'Can this be the son of David?'" (12:23). Their clearest assessments of the identity of Jesus as "Son of David" and "prophet" occur in the emotionally charged context of the triumphal entry. All of these reactions are designed to amplify the extraordinary quality of Jesus' words and deeds. It is no surprise that the first mention of the crowds' astonishment (7:28) follows immediately upon the teaching of the Sermon on the Mount, nor that the ensuing sequence of ten miracles should also conclude with an amazed outburst (9:33). All this is relatively straightforward. The crowds' utterances bring the implied reader to consider afresh the singular quality of Jesus' words and deeds.

One may add, however, that in their consideration of Jesus and his deeds, the crowds' utterances betray little of the social emphasis of the Greek chorus. For if the chorus' concern is largely horizontal, the crowds' concern is almost exclusively vertical, that is to say, fixated on God and his dealings with them. Instead of the heroic mythical past being brought into the present to clarify the present, the present is clarified by being grafted onto the past, attached to the continuum of God's dealings with his people.

In the same way, the crowds' rejection of Jesus at the Gospel's end heightens the tragic aspect of Jesus' passion. The people he had taught and healed now completely forsake him. They contribute to Jesus' heroic abandonment.

Idealized Spectators

Can the crowds also be construed as "idealized spectators" who, in this instance, would embody the "general sympathy" of all potential hearers/readers? Superficially at least, there is a sense in which the crowds do evoke the "general sympathy" of the Gospel's implied audience. It was just mentioned above how the crowds react with wonder when confronted with the Sermon on the Mount and the catena of ten miracle stories. Yet the implied readers will have been confronted with three extensive and remarkable chapters of Jesus' dicta (chs. 5–7), as well as a detailed exposition of Jesus' miracle-working (chs. 8–9), and it would hardly be unnatural or unexpected that they should react with a corresponding sense of wonder. This is borne out in part by the fact that they would have so few other models in the Gospel with which to identify immediately. The disciples in Matthew are endued with such a sufficient understanding of Jesus that they are rarely astonished, while the Jewish leaders are so implacably opposed to him that they regularly impute his activities to Satan. The crowds figure as the conventional *via media*: Vernant's "average truth." The crowds act as repositories of traditional wisdom, just as the chorus commonly furnishes mythological *exempla*. They know of God's dealings with Israel in the past and are able to advert to them. Moreover, it is the crowds who introduce the title Son of David into the narrative and who interpret Jesus in light of Israel's past.

At the same time, Matthew would impugn some of their "average truth." For him, the crowds are in no way *idealized* figures, and his implied readers are to dissociate themselves from at least part of the perspective of the crowds. This insight emerges most clearly in Matthew chapter thirteen, where the perceptions of the crowds are shown to be inadequate: "Their ears are hard of hearing and they have shut their eyes; so that they might not look with their eyes, and listen with their ears, and understand" (13:15). They are unable to penetrate Jesus' parables or, even worse, to realize that they need to be penetrated. The disciples, by contrast, do recognize that they require further interpretation from Jesus and ask him for more (13:36): to them, we are told, it has been given to know "the secrets of the kingdom of heaven" but to the crowds it has not

(13:11). The disciples, therefore, are represented as the idealized figures in the Gospel. They fully comprehend the mystery of Jesus' person, and for this reason do not generally marvel at Jesus' deeds; instead they worship him (viz. 2:11; 14:33; 28:9, 17). Thus, if Matthew does intend a collective group in his Gospel to figure as idealized spectators to his implied readers, it is not the crowds but the disciples who would best suit this role. The crowds represent a common sensibility.

The Embodiment of the "Other"

One would expect, therefore, that the crowds were meant to embody the enfranchised collective. Paradoxically, the crowds function more as exemplars of "otherness." The chief reason is that Matthew contrasts two "public" groups: the crowds and their leaders. It is the latter group that corresponds to the privileged males of Athenian society. They possess wealth, power and knowledge. They establish legislation and the crowds are constrained to submit to it. The crowds, by contrast, display strong suggestions of marginality in their depiction. The sick and needy figure in their number, as do women and children. They are vulnerable and oppressed and in need of teaching and guidance: "like sheep without a shepherd" (9:36). They embody a nonofficial perspective.

Crowds versus Chorus

In summarizing the above findings, it is safe to say that the crowds do share some of the functions that are associated with the tragic chorus. Even if some fit better than others, there is still a fair measure of overlap, at least for the categories of function that I have chosen.

So far, then, the discussion has concentrated on the similarities between the chorus and the crowds. Yet, as noted above, there is a very major respect in which the two differ and that is when the crowds perform a *volte-face*, where they completely reverse their previous stance towards Jesus. We have noted that, generally speaking, the attitude of the Greek chorus is static and does not change appreciably. The chorus of the daughters of Oceanus in *Prometheus Bound* proclaim their friendship to Prometheus in the *parodos* and reaffirm it in the *exodos*. In only a few plays can it be said that the chorus fundamentally changes its disposition. In the *Medea* the chorus' initial sympathy for Medea (357–63) turns to horror at her pitiless murder of her own children (1260–1270). In the *Orestes* too the chorus apparently changes, condemning Orestes' matricide (819–21) but later acquiescing to the plan to kill Helen (1104). Or again, in Aescyhlus' *Eumenides*, the outraged Furies' promise to blight the land (780–91) is transformed into the promise of a blessing through Athena's use of *peithō*, persuasion, to mollify them (885; 971). Nevertheless, these transformations are generally explicable within the context the plays provide. The murder of one's own children is naturally repugnant, just as Helen is said to deserve the hatred of all other women (1153–54), while the Furies relent upon being presented with the prospect of receiving honor and veneration from the Athenians. Athena gives them a better offer.

Yet in Matthew the transformation is far more abrupt, so abrupt that, as mentioned above, some scholars have sought to isolate two separate crowds. What is more, the crowds, despite their passivity, are considerably less static than the other figures in the Gospel. The disciples and Jewish leaders do not appreciably change over the course of the work, and neither does Jesus. The crowds are the only ones who change.

Indeed, it is arguable that the constituents that Aristotle gives to the optimal tragic plot, reversal (*peripeteia*) and recognition (*anagnōrisis*), can best be distinguished in the actions of the crowds—if they are to be found in the Gospel at all. In Matthew, it is the arrival of Jesus in Jerusalem—the triumphal entry (21:1–11) that precipitates both. Having earlier entertained and dismissed the idea that he might be the Son of David, the crowds finally come to recognize and acclaim him at the triumphal entry. More importantly, they acclaim him as "the prophet Jesus from Nazareth in Galilee" (21:11) to the residents of Jerusalem when they are asked about Jesus' identity. Matthew, alone of the Gospels, has the crowds make this attribution here, and it is one that is repeated at 21:46, where we are told that the crowds "held him to be a prophet," a passage also unique to Matthew. At this decisive point, they become aware of his identity and share it with inhabitants of Jerusalem.

This realization sets in motion Jesus' tragic destiny. Identifying Jesus as a prophet invokes the notion of the "violent fate of the prophets" (23:37), the idea that all of the Hebrew prophets had been persecuted and put to death by their own people. As expressed by Stephen in the book of Acts, this charge runs: "You stiff-necked people ... Which of the prophets did your fathers not persecute? And they killed those who announced beforehand the coming of the Righteous One" (Acts 7:51–52).[54] The crowds' recognition that Jesus is a prophet, therefore, is ominous. While the causal link is, perhaps, not as explicit as in a Greek tragedy, it can be argued that it is the crowds' calling attention to Jesus, and particularly to Jesus' status as prophet, that leads to his passion. In calling attention to Jesus' status as a prophet, they also tacitly acknowledge that they belong to a people who have put their prophets to death. The significance of the

---

54. Cf. Odil H. Steck, *Israel und das gewaltsame Geschick der Propheten: Untersuchungen zur Überlieferung des deuteronomistischen Geschichtsbildes im Alten Testament, Spätjudentum und Urchristentum* (WMANT 23; Neukirchen-Vluyn: Neukirchener, 1967), 63–64, 289–316.

identification made at the triumphal entry becomes even more determinative in the final words of Jesus' public ministry: Jesus' apostrophe to Jerusalem castigates the city for "killing the prophets and stoning those who are sent to you" (23:37). As these are the last words Jesus utters publicly before his arrest and death, there is little doubt of their bearing on him, nor, for that matter, of his prophetic awareness of his impending fate. Jesus, the prophet from Nazareth in Galilee, is going to be killed at the crowd's instigation. The crowds' discovery of Jesus, therefore, is a momentous one. Their recognition of Jesus as a prophet—slowly to be sure—institutes his reversal in fortune. What is more, it also provides an explanation for the treachery of the crowds. Since they represent Israel, it is necessary that the crowd should fulfil their particular destiny and revile Jesus. This template—the violent fate of the prophets—is the only rationale provided by the Gospel for the crowds' profound change in disposition.

What this suggests, therefore, is that the metatextual character of the crowds is determinative for Matthew's representation. Matthew's crowds resemble the choruses of Greek tragedy in being a largely anonymous assemblage of local figures: one could envision a chorus of the "townspeople of Capernaum." Yet such an impression is misleading. Several utterances of the crowds suggest that their character is more broadly conceived than their limited role would suggest. Especially noteworthy is the occurrence of the word "Israel" in connection with them. When confronted with Jesus' thaumaturgy, they "glorified the God of Israel" (15:31) or marvelled saying "Never was anything like this seen in Israel" (9:33).[55] This latter remark is worthy of closer attention. Surely it means more than "this is unprecedented" or "within the geographical framework of Israel this is unique."[56] Rather, as the temporal indicator "never" suggests, it is a reference to *Heilsgeschichte*, to the history of God's dealings with Israel. This being so, however, one wonders why this utterance should be put in the crowds' mouth. Why should they be particularly qualified to talk about Israel's salvation history unless they themselves were participants in it? The natural inference is that they are to be taken as exemplars of the people of Israel. A similar impression is afforded by 27:25. There the crowds, presumably in concert with the chief priests and elders, are described as "all the people" (πᾶς ὁ λαὸς).

---

55. This remark is characteristically Jewish and may even have a liturgical stamp; cf. J. R. C. Cousland, "The Feeding of the Four Thousand *Gentiles?* Matthew 15:29–38 as a Test Case," *NovT* 41 (1999): 1–23.

56. Graham Harvey, *The True Israel: Uses of the Names Jew, Hebrew and Israel in Ancient Jewish and Early Christian Literature* (AGJU 35; Leiden: Brill, 1996), 235 n. 34.

This identification has considerable implications for the character of the crowd. It suggests that there is intratextuality and extratextuality at work here, though in a manner that inverts Mastronarde's conception. At the intratextual level, the crowds are characterized as the occasional recipients of Jesus' ministry, and finally as the dupes of their leaders in Jesus' death. At the extratextual level, however, they embody the people of Israel. The character of the crowds is attenuated in respects because Matthew can draw on metatextual representations that supplement his portrayal. Just as Euripides can rely on Homer's depiction of Helen to establish the context for his own *Helen,* so too can Matthew rely on the Hebrew scriptures to provide the context for his depiction of the crowds as Israel. Jesus' description of the crowds as "sheep without a shepherd" (9:36) or as "lost sheep of the House of Israel" (10:6) draws on a profusion of related images of Israel found in Ezekiel and elsewhere to develop the crowds' marginalized quality. Matthew further draws on ideas present in Nehemiah (viz. 9:26) and elsewhere to inform the crowds' role in enacting the violent fate of the prophets. Both these rather incongruous portrayals have their root in depictions of Israel presented in the Hebrew Bible.

The implication of this identity is that the Gospel deals with the crowds at times as though they were a named character with all the setting and context that comes with it. Gould has said that the "hero has a name which is central to his identity," while the chorus articulates experience without a name.[57] But in carrying the name Israel, the crowds evoke and articulate all that the name represents, namely, the entire history of Yahweh's past involvement with Israel. In the Gospel they act out of this history and assume thereby a role closer to that of an actor than a chorus, as is evidenced by the *volte-face* described above. They embrace their tragic destiny in rejecting Jesus. Indeed, it can be argued that their fate is even more tragic than that of Jesus. In Matthew, the outcome for Jesus is ultimately comic. He is rejected by his people, suffers horribly and dies a gruesome death it is true, but in the end he is resurrected and endowed with all authority (28:16–20). The crowds, by contrast, experience the messianic words and deeds of Jesus, penetrate his identity, only to reject him, their true messiah, and fall under the mendacious sway of an oppressive and deluded leadership. The crowds' role and destiny is ultimately tragic. They do not continue on as the chorus does. Once they have rejected Jesus, the crowds are no longer referred to—after that they are symbolically united with their leadership. Clearly, the two dramatic

---

57. Gould, "Collective Experience," 222–23.

curves are used to provide contrast. With Christ's assumption of divine status in the resurrection, the crowds relinquish their previous status as God's chosen people. Both Jesus' and the crowds' trajectories follow a parallel tragic downward slant. But with the resurrection, the two, symbolically, separate profoundly.

CONCLUSIONS

What the foregoing suggests about the crowds, therefore, is that they have a dual character and a dual function. Matthew is able to endue them with a double role; on the one level they represent the assembled multitudes who react to Jesus in many of the ways that a chorus reacts to the actors. On a metatextual level, however, they assume the identity of a known actor—Israel—and their function is to enact the mythological template laid down for Israel. In the same way that Oedipus is fated to kill his father and marry his mother, there is a suggestion that Israel is foredoomed to reject the prophet Jesus. They enact their own tragedy. Thus, the crowds do resemble the tragic chorus in a number of respects; where they differ is in performing an additional function within the tragic tenor of Matthew's Gospel. Their refusal to dance when the pipes are played is, in the end, portentous and shows the crowds assuming their own tragic destiny as Israel.

THE SUMMARIES OF ACTS 2, 4, AND 5
AND PLATO'S *REPUBLIC*

Rubén R. Dupertuis

INTRODUCTION

In earlier critical interpretation, the descriptions of the early Christian community of goods in the longer summaries of Acts 2:42–47 and 4:32–35, along with the related summary in Acts 5:12–16, often played a starring role in the quest for the sources underlying the narrative of Acts.[1] In more recent interpretation, especially since the work of Martin Dibelius and Henry Cadbury,[2] the summaries, or at least parts of them, are generally attributed to the author of Acts. Three other points also elicit general agreement. First, the summaries are commonly understood to be generalizations based on more specific traditions, such as the gifts of Barnabas and Ananias and Sapphira (4:36–5:11). Second, the summaries are inseparable from the surrounding events on both narrative and linguistic grounds.[3] And third, some of the characterizations in the summaries are understood to indicate some degree of idealization in light of Hellenistic utopian ideals.[4] Most interesting in this regard is the

---

1. See Jacques Dupont, *The Sources of Acts* (trans. Kathleen Pond; New York: Herder & Herder, 1964), 17–61, for a survey and analysis of earlier source theories.

2. Martin Dibelius, "Style Criticism of the Book of Acts," in *Studies in the Acts of the Apostles* (ed. H. Greeven; New York: Scribner's, 1956), 1–25; Henry J. Cadbury, *The Making of Luke-Acts* (New York: MacMillan, 1927), 58–59, 324–25; idem, "The Summaries in Acts," in *The Acts of the Apostles: Additional Notes* (vol. 5 of *The Beginnings of Christianity*; ed. Henry J. Cadbury and Kirsopp Lake; London: Macmillan, 1933), 392–402.

3. See especially Maria Anicia Co, "The Major Summaries in Acts (Acts 2,42–47; 4,32–35; 5,12–16): Linguistic and Literary Relationship," *ETL* 68 (1992): 49–85.

4. The following are representative but not exhaustive: Lucien Cerfaux, "La composition de la premiere partie du Livre des Actes," *ETL* (1936): 667–91; idem, "La première communauté chrétienne à Jérusalem (Act., II, 41–V, 42)," *ETL* 16 (1939): 5–31; Heinrich Zimmerman, "Die Sammelberichte der Apostelgeschichte," *BZ* 5 (1961): 71–82; Hans Conzelmann, *A Commentary on the Acts of the Apostles* (trans. J. Limburg et al.; Philadelphia: Fortress, 1987), 24–25; Ernst Haenchen, *The Acts of the Apostles: A Commentary* (trans. R. McL. Wilson; Philadelphia: Westminster, 1971), 191–96, 230–35; Eckhard Plümacher, *Lukas als*

description of the early Christian community in Jerusalem as having "all things in common [ἅπαντα κοινά]" (Acts 2:44, 4:32), and being of "one heart and soul [καρδία καὶ ψυχὴ μία]" (4:32).

THE SUMMARIES AND HELLENISTIC IDEALS

While many interpreters believe that idealization of some sort on Luke's part may be involved, there has been much discussion regarding exactly what the literary relationship between Acts and the Hellenistic traditions might be and which particular group of ideas provides the most helpful comparison. Hans Conzelmann read the description of the early Christian community as an idealization based on the widespread literary *topos* of property sharing often associated with utopian dreams or stories of primeval times.[5] Ekhard Plümacher and, especially, David Mealand both saw a more direct literary connection between Acts and parallels in Plato's *Republic*.[6] Others however suggest that the complex of images in these summaries is best seen in light of the Greek friendship ideals.[7] Still other interpreters do not see much of a connection between these passages and Greek utopian literature at all.[8]

A number of interpreters have objected to the notion that the author of Acts intentionally alluded to Plato's *Republic* or Greek utopian ideals in order to portray the twelve apostles and the early Christian community

---

hellenistischer Schriftsteller (Göttingen: Vandenhoeck & Ruprecht, 1972), 16–18; David L. Mealand, "Community of Goods and Utopian Allusions in Acts II–V," *JTS* 28 (1977): 96–99; Jacques Dupont, "Community of Goods in the Early Church, " in *The Salvation of the Gentiles: Studies in the Acts of the Apostles* (New York: Paulist, 1979), 85–102; S. Scott Bartchy, "Community of Goods in Acts: Idealization or Social Reality?" in *The Future of Early Christianity: Essays in Honor of Helmut Koester* (ed. Birger Pearson; Minneapolis: Fortress, 1991), 309–18; Alan C. Mitchell, "The Social Function of Friendship in Acts 2:44–47 and 4:32–37," *JBL* 111 (1992): 255–72; Gregory E. Sterling, "'Athletes of Virtue': An Analysis of the Summaries in Acts (2:41–47; 4:32–35; 5:12–16)," *JBL* 113 (1994): 679–96.

5. Conzelmann, *Acts*, 24.

6. Plümacher, *Lukas*, 16–18; Mealand, "Community of Goods," 96–99.

7. Dupont, "Community of Goods"; and especially, Mitchell, "Social Function." The *topos* of friends having all things in common can be found in the following: Aristotle, *Eth. nic.* 9.8.2; 9.9.1–2; Plutarch, *Adul. am.* 65a and *Amic. mult.* 94c, 96d; Diogenes Laertius, 8.10; Cicero, *Off.* 1.51. Other instances are noted by Pieter W. van der Horst, "Hellenistic Parallels to the Acts of the Apostles (2,1–47)," *JSNT* 25 (1985): 49–60; and idem, "Hellenistic Parallels to Acts (Chapters 3 and 4)," *JSNT* 35 (1989): 37–46.

8. Brian Capper, "The Palestinian Cultural Context of Earliest Christian Community of Goods," in *The Book of Acts in Its First Century Setting* (ed. R. Bauckham; vol. 4 of *The Book of Acts in Its Palestinian Setting*; Grand Rapids: Eerdmans, 1995), 323–57. See also Jean Danielou, "La communauté de Qumrân et l'organization de l'Eglise ancienne," *RHPR* 35 (1955): 104–15.

as belonging to an ideal or golden age of the church. David Seccombe doubts that "a Christian writer, as immersed in the Old Testament as Luke, would consciously have imitated pagan mythological conceptions in his presentation of the Christian movement."[9] Seccombe goes on to make a distinction between being unconsciously influenced by Hellenistic culture and education into an appreciation of Hellenistic ideals—which he believes to be the case with the author of Acts—and "consciously striving toward a utopian goal."[10] A similar distinction is made by Hans-Josef Klauck, who understands the author of Acts to have been conscious of using the language of Hellenistic social utopias in his description of the early Christian community, but is quick to point out that there is no direct dependence, just influence of patterns of speech.[11]

The discussion generally revolves around the question of Luke's intentional portrayal of the early Christian community in light of Greek utopian ideals. The mechanism by which to explain the lexical and thematic similarities between the description of the Christians in Acts and utopian traditions has generally been some form of a literary *topos*.[12] I will suggest below that recent awareness of the widespread practice of literary imitation in the Greco-Roman world with its emphasis on the imitation of models has made difficult the task of making a distinction between the use of a widespread *topos* or motif and a direct allusion to a specific author or text. Furthermore, I will suggest that the portrayal of the early Christian community in Jerusalem is modeled in part on Plato's guardians as described in the *Republic* and related dialogues.

EDUCATION AND MIMESIS

Literate education in the Greco-Roman world involved working through a series of steps that were designed, in the long run, to lay the groundwork of rhetorical training. The dominant feature of literate edu-

---

9. David P. Seccombe, *Possessions and the Poor in Luke-Acts* (SNTSU 6; Linz: Fuchs, 1982), 200.

10. Seccombe, *Possessions and the Poor*, 201.

11. Hans-Josef Klauck, "Gütergemeinschaft in der klassischen Antike, im Qumran und im Neuen Testament," *RevQ* 11 (1982–83): 72.

12. The exceptions are Mealand, "Community of Goods," 97–99, who suggested the possibility of a direct literary connection, and Cerfaux, "La première communauté," who understood the summaries to have come from one of a series of sources the author of Acts used for his narrative of the early church. The similarities between the summaries and utopian traditions derived from Plato were to him so striking, that he posited a Hellenistic provenance for the source.

cation was the imitation of that which had been done with success.[13] Immediately after memorizing the alphabet and copying lists of words students began copying and memorizing maxims and lines of poetry, followed by copying, memorizing, expanding and paraphrasing longer passages (often taken from Homer). Finally, for a limited and usually elite few came grammatical and rhetorical exercises, which were, once again, based in the imitation of models.

At the primary and secondary educational levels the imitation of models was fairly straight-forward. At a more advanced compositional level, the ways in which one text served as a model for another was more complex. Authors were taught to imitate more than one model, culling the best from different writers like a bee collects pollen from various flowers, and arranging and assorting the raw materials into a new compound. Seneca states:

> We should follow, men say, the example of the bees, who flit about and cull the flowers that are suitable for producing honey, and then arrange and assort in their cells all that they have brought it.... It is not certain whether the juice which they obtain from the flowers forms at once into honey, or whether they change that which they have gathered into this delicious object by blending something therewith and by a certain property of their breath.... We should so blend those several flavours into one delicious compound that, even though it betrays its origin, yet it nevertheless is a clearly different thing from that whence it came. (*Ep.* 84.3–5)[14]

---

13. On literary *mimesis* in antiquity see George C. Fiske, *Lucilius and Horace: A Study in the Classical Theory of Imitation* (Madison: University of Wisconsin, 1920; repr., New York: Herder & Herder, 1964); Stephen Hinds, *Allusion and Intertext: Dynamics of Appropriation in Roman Poetry, Roman Literature and its Contexts* (Cambridge: Cambridge University Press, 1998), 1–51; Richard McKeon, "Literary Criticism and the Concept of Imitation in Antiquity," in *Critics and Criticism* (ed. Ronald S. Crane; Chicago: University of Chicago Press, 1952), 147–75; D. A. Russell, "De Imitatione," in *Creative Imitation in Latin Literature* (ed. David A. West and Anthony J. Woodman; Cambridge: Cambridge University Press, 1979), 1–16; Ellen Finkelpearl, "Pagan Traditions of Intertextuality in the Roman World," in *Mimesis and Intertextuality in Antiquity and Christianity* (ed. Dennis R. MacDonald; SAC; Harrisburg, Pa.: Trinity Press International, 2001), 78–90. For recent discussions of education in the Greco-Roman world see Raffaella Cribiore, *Writing, Teachers, and Students in Graeco-Roman Egypt* (Atlanta: Scholars Press, 1996); idem, *Gymnastics of the Mind: Greek Education in Hellenistic and Roman Egypt* (Princeton: Princeton University Press, 2001); Teresa Morgan, *Literate Education in the Hellenistic and Roman Worlds* (Cambridge: Cambridge University Press, 1998); and Ronald F. Hock, "Homer in Greco-Roman Education," in MacDonald, *Mimesis and Intertextuality*, 56–77.

14. Seneca, *Epistles* (trans. Richard M. Gummere; 3 vols; LCL; Cambridge: Harvard University Press, 1917–25), 2:277, 279.

Sometimes reliance on a model was announced or advertised and some-times it was disguised. Imitation of a model was not limited to word choice, but encompassed literary style, themes and was done across genres. With imitation as the dominant compositional ethos, creativity was measured by how writers handled traditional subjects and themes, not by an author's ability to spin new tales. Horace tells would-be writ-ers that "it is hard to treat in your own way what is common: and you are doing better in spinning into acts a song of Troy than if, for the first time, you were giving the world a theme unknown and unsung" (*Ars* 128–130).[15]

An important aspect of learning to write was a competitive relation-ship with the model. Great models did not deter would-be writers, but acted as a challenge, inviting them to weigh in on a given theme. It may be partly as a result of this principle of composition that *topoi* develop. The long list of imitators of Homer's storms in the *Odyssey* is a good example.[16] Regarding this principle of improvement or rivalry, Seneca states, "he who writes last has the best of the bargain; he finds already at hand words which when marshaled in a different way, show a new face" (*Ep.* 79.6).[17] At the primary and secondary stages of education, Homer, and to a lesser degree Euripides and Menander, dominated the curricu-lum; at the level of rhetorical training and in the writings of the literary elite, however, there are a larger number of authors alluded to and used as models.[18] Plato's writings come to fore at this point.[19]

Of the many implications of the practice of literary mimesis for the study of early Christian literature, the following are of importance for this study.[20] First, if someone learned to write Greek, we can assume

---

15. Horace, *Satires, Epistles, and Ars poetica* (trans. H. Rushton Fairclough; LCL; Cam-bridge: Harvard University Press, 1978), 461.

16. See the discussion in Dennis R. MacDonald, "The Shipwrecks of Odysseus and Paul," *NTS* 45 (1999): 93–94.

17. Seneca, *Epistles* (Gummere, 2:205).

18. Morgan, *Literate Education*, 67–89.

19. In Theon's late first-century C.E. manual of preliminary rhetorical exercises, for example, passages from Plato's *Republic, Symposium, Phaedo, Timaeus,* and the *Phaedrus* are proposed as models. For a translation of the extant *progymnasmata,* see George A. Kennedy, ed. and trans., *Progymnasmata: Greek Textbooks of Prose Composition and Rhetoric* (SBLWGRW 10; Atlanta: Society of Biblical Literature, 2003).

20. The two scholars who have explored the implications in the greatest depth are Thomas L. Brodie and Dennis R. MacDonald. For the former, see "Greco-Roman Imitation of Texts as a Partial Guide to Luke's Use of Sources," in *Luke-Acts: New Perspectives from the Society of Biblical Literature* (ed. Charles H. Talbert; New York: Crossroad, 1984), 17–46; "The Accusing and Stoning of Naboth (1 Kgs 21:8–13) as One Component of the Stephen Text," *CBQ* 45 (1984): 417–32; "Luke-Acts as an Imitation and Emulation of the Elijah-Elisha

familiarity with those authors and texts typically used as models in the educational system, including Homer, Euripides, and, by the early stages of rhetorical training, Plato. Second, it is possible to create a hierarchy, of sorts, when comparing numerous instances of a *topos* or theme given the preponderance of certain authors as targets for imitation. Third, the importance of mimesis in educational training and literary practice calls into question the use of religious boundaries to decide whether a Christian or Jewish author would have been familiar with certain classical texts.[21] It is more likely that a mimetic literary ethos, not piety, determines an author's literary models. That the author of Acts should use models as diverse as the Septuagint, Homer, and Plato should not be surprising;[22] diverse allusions to traditional literary themes are to be expected as part of standard compositional practices.

The importance of the role of mimesis in composition, both at the educational and literary levels, opens the door for another look at the relationship between the major summaries in Acts and the parallels in Plato's writings.

THE PERFECT POLIS

Primarily through the description of the ideal state in the *Republic* and the *Laws*, Plato was quite possibly the single most influential writer in the development of utopian traditions, including the extraordinary journey, the idyllic primeval age and the political utopia.[23] In the *Republic*, Socrates' pursuit of justice leads to the founding of a hypothetical state based on the separation of functions and the specialization of labors—

Narrative," in *New Views on Luke and Acts* (ed. Earl Richards; Collegeville, Minn.: Liturgical Press, 1990), 78–85; and "Towards Unraveling the Rhetorical Imitation of Sources in Acts: 2 Kings 5 as One Component of Acts 8,9–40," *Bib* 67 (1986): 41–67. For the latter, see especially *Christianizing Homer: "The Odyssey," Plato, and "The Acts of Andrew"* (Oxford: Oxford University Press, 1994); and *The Homeric Epics and the Gospel of Mark* (New Haven: Yale University Press, 2000).

21. See, for example, J. R. C. Cousland, "Dionysus Theomachos? Echoes of the *Bacchae* in 3 Maccabees," *Bib* 82 (2001): 539–48; and Dennis R. MacDonald, "Tobit and the *Odyssey*," in MacDonald, *Mimesis and Intertextuality*, 11–40.

22. For Luke's imitation of the Septuagint, see Brodie's work referenced in n. 20 above. For Luke's imitation of Homer see Dennis R. MacDonald, "Luke's Eutychus and Homer's Elpenor: Acts 20:7–12 and *Odyssey* 10–12," *Journal of Higher Criticism* 1 (1994): 5–24; and idem, "Shipwrecks," 88–107. For Luke's possible imitation of Plato, see John Kloppenborg, "*Exitus Clari Viri*: The Death of Jesus in Luke," *TJT* 8 (1992): 106–20; Gregory Sterling, "*Mors philosophi*: The Death of Jesus in Luke," *HTR* 94 (2001): 383–402.

23. On Greek utopianism, see John Ferguson, *Utopias of the Classical World* (Ithaca, N.Y.: Cornell University Press, 1975); and Doyne Dawson, *Cities of the Gods: Communist Utopias in Greek Thought* (New York: Oxford University Press, 1992).

more importantly, each person is to work in an area to which his or her nature is suited. This state is to be ruled by a special class of guardians—part warriors, part philosophers—who, like farmers and builders specifically trained and skilled in their respective arts, are specifically bred, trained and sustained for the all important art of ruling and defending a state. Society is essentially divided into three groups: (1) a group of ruler guardians; (2) a larger group of warrior guardians whose job it is to defend the state; and (3) a producing class made up of everybody else.

In order to guarantee a just leadership and avoid corruption one of the more well known aspects of Plato's ideal state emerges: the guardians would not be permitted to own property or accumulate wealth in any way. The more extreme aspect of this communal arrangement is the common possession of wives and children.[24] The material sharing of possessions leads to a form spiritual unity and complete ideological harmony that, in turn, leads to achieving a just state.

In two later and related dialogues, the *Timaeus* and the *Critias*, Plato historicizes (and mythologizes) his hypothetical state suggesting it actually existed in a time that antedated the contemporary, and therefore incomplete, historical record. This long forgotten Athens, then, stood as the ideal primeval state from which the contemporary Athens had devolved and to which it could aspire. The fact that Plato takes his "hypothetical state" and places it in "history," however idealized and remote, will be extremely important in the subsequent development of utopian and golden age motifs. Also important is the fact that Plato's guardians stand at the point where images of ideal leaders, an ideal polity, golden ages and the corrupting potential of money converge.[25]

Plato's influence on subsequent utopian traditions is hard to overestimate. Moses Hadas has suggested that "there is a strong probability that [Plato] was the most important single intellectual factor in the process of Hellenization and that his is the major responsibility for shaping the east's eventual contribution to the west."[26] Images of far-off lands and philosophical utopias after Plato are largely dependent

---

24. This was not an invitation to libertinism, but an extension of Plato's attempt to protect the guardians from anything that might lead them to place their own interests over the interests of the state.

25. Plato appears to be largely responsible for introducing a concern for the corrupting power of money and possessions into traditional pictures of the golden age; see H. C. Baldry, *Ancient Utopias* (University of Southampton Inaugural Lecture; Southampton, U.K.: University of Southampton, 1956); and David M. Schaps, "Socrates and the Socratics: When Wealth Became a Problem," *CW* 96 (2003): 131–59.

26. Moses Hadas, "Plato the Hellenizer," in idem, *Hellenistic Culture: Fusion and Diffusion* (New York: Columbia University Press, 1959), 73.

on him.[27] Plato also appears to have influenced the portrayal of the Essenes by both Philo (*Prob.* 81–84) and Josephus (*Ant.* 18.18–22; *B.J.* 2.119–161). In particular, the structure of the latter's discussion in *B.J.* 2.119–161 appears to be shaped by Plato's treatment of the ideal state in the *Republic*.[28]

COMPARING THE EARLY CHRISTIAN COMMUNITY IN ACTS AND PLATO'S GUARDIANS

In his brief but important note on the community of goods in Acts and utopian ideals, Mealand showed that the wording in Acts 2:44 and 4:32 is closer to Plato's descriptions of the guardians than any instances of the friendship maxim in Aristotle's writings or elsewhere.[29] In addition to the lexical similarities, there are a number of general similarities and correspondences between the descriptions of early Christian community life in the summaries of Acts 2 and 4 and the descriptions of the guardians in *Resp.* 2–5.

First, both occur in the context of the founding of a new city or nation and the establishment of a new constitution. Numerous echoes of the Sinai traditions in Exod 19 and later Jewish writers suggest that the Pentecost events in Acts 2 provide the charter for the newly inaugurated kingdom of God (Acts 1:3, 6).[30] Recently there has been increased attention

---

27. For a discussion of Plato's influence on Hellenistic utopias, especially those of Euhemerus and Iambulus, see Lawrence Giangrande, "Les Utopies Hellenistiques," *CEA* 5 (1976): 17–33. For Hellenistic philosophical utopias, see Dawson, *Cities of the Gods.*

28. Tessa Rajak, "Ciò che Flavio Giuseppe Vide: Josephus and the Essenes," in *Josephus and the History of the Greco-Roman World: Essays in Memory of Morton Smith* (ed. Fausto Parente and Joseph Sievers; Leiden: Brill, 1994), 149–51.

29. Mealand, "Community of Goods," 98. Another reason for preferring the Platonic parallels is that both Acts and Plato discuss the complete absence of personal possessions, which is not the case in the friendship tradition. Furthermore, the line between friendship and utopian ideals cannot be too neatly drawn, since by his use of the maxim, κοινὰ τὰ φίλων, to justify the guardians' κοινωνία, Plato needs to be seen as part of the trajectory. Subsequent uses of the property-sharing ideal often mention Plato: Iamblichus, *Vita Pythagora* 30.167; Strabo, *Geographica* 7.3.7; and Clement of Alexandria, *Strom.* 3.2.10.

30. There are numerous parallels between Acts 2 and Philo's account of the giving of the law in *Decal.* 33.46–7. These include the gathering of all the people in one place, the appearance of sound and fire, and xenolalia. Charles Talbert concludes his analysis of the similarities by stating, "The echoes are unmistakable. Sound, fire, and speech understood by all people were characteristic of the Sinai theophany. The same ingredients are found in the Pentecostal events. The Sinai theophany and the establishment of the Mosaic covenant would be brought to mind as surely as would Elijah by the description of John the Baptist's dress in Mark 1:6. The typology of Acts 2:1–11, then, is that of making a covenant" (*Reading Acts: A Literary and Theological Commentary on the Acts of The Apostles* [New York: Crossroad, 1997], 43).

to the similarities between the beginning of Acts and the ways in which the founding of a city was typically described in Greek and Roman literature. Hubert Cancik has demonstrated that the beginning of Acts uses the tropes and language commonly used by historiographers to describe the beginning of an institution.[31] Similarly, David Balch has argued that Luke-Acts presents Jesus as the founder of a new πολιτεία preserved and perpetuated after his death by his followers.[32] And Todd Penner has suggested that Acts, with special mention of the events narrated in ch. 2, is part of a "discourse [that] is fundamentally civic in nature."[33] However hypothetical and utopian, in the *Republic* Plato recounts the various stages of the establishment of a truly just πολιτεία—it is, in the most literal way possible, the founding of a new city.[34]

Second, both describe a way of life in which the κοινωνία among the citizens or members is marked by the absence of private possessions. In the *Republic* the term κοινωνία appears primarily in relation to the distinctive communal arrangements of the guardians.[35] Similarly, κοινός occurs in this section primarily in the context of sharing property, possessions and other goods.[36] In Luke-Acts, the term κοινωνία appears only in Acts

---

31. Hubert Cancik, "The History of Culture, Religion, and Institutions in Ancient Historiography: Philological Observations Concerning Luke's History," *JBL* 116 (1997): 673–95. Also, Walter T. Wilson's analysis of the Greco-Roman tropes of the founding of a city can profitably be applied to the beginning of Acts ("Urban Legends: Acts 10:1–11:18 and the Strategies of Greco-Roman Foundation Narratives," *JBL* 120 [2001]: 77–99).

32. "ΜΕΤΑΒΟΛΗ ΠΟΛΙΤΕΙΩΝ—Jesus as Founder of the Church in Luke-Acts: Form and Function," in *Contextualizing Acts: Lukan Narrative and Greco Roman Discourse* (ed. Todd Penner and Caroline Vander Stichele, SBLSymS 20; Atlanta: Society of Biblical Literature, 2003), 139–88.

33. Todd Penner, "Civilizing Discourse: Acts, Declamation and the Rhetoric of the Polis," in Penner and Vander Stichele, *Contextualizing Acts*, 65–104.

34. The interlocutors function as the city's founders, having the power to construct as they see fit and to legislate accordingly. The language of establishing a city occurs throughout *Resp.* 3–5: οἰκίζομεν (4.420b); πρόσταγμα (4.423c); πόλιν κατῳκίζομεν (4.433a); νομοθετήσωμεν (3.417b). It is the interlocutors who determine that a permanent overseer should be selected from among the older and wiser guardians (3.412a–414b) and provide the city's first rulers with a myth of origins justifying laws and requirements (3.414b–417b).

35. *Resp.* 5.449c, 449d, 450b, 461e, 464a, 464b, 466d, 476a.

36. The guardians are to live together (κοινῇ ζῆν) (3.416e); Plato twice uses the proverb, κοινὰ τὰ φίλων, regarding sharing of all things, including wives and children (4.424a, 5.449c); both male and female guardians are to have all in common (κοινῇ ... πάντα) and are to be given the same nurture and education (5.451e); females and males should share all tasks (ἅπαντα τὰ ἔργα) (453a); all women shall be common (κοινάς) to the men (5.457d); they are to have houses and meals in common (οἰκίας τε καὶ ξυσσίτια κοινὰ ἔχοντες) (5.458c–d); all are to spend their stipend in common (κοινῇ πάντας) (5.464b–c). Plato's summaries of the ideal state's constitution in the related dialogues also use the same phrase: πάντα κοινὰ (*Tim.* 18c, cf. 18b); ἅπαντα δὲ πάντων κοινὰ (*Crit.* 110d).

2:42, while the cognate κοινός appears in two clusters in Acts. It appears a number of times in Acts 10–11 in relation to Jewish purity laws likely meaning "unclean,"[37] and in the summaries in 2:44 and 4:32, where it is used in relation to the sharing of possessions and the absence of private property. The meaning of κοινωνία in its present context is best seen in relation to community of goods (v. 44).[38] As Mealand has shown, the construction Luke uses in Acts 4:32, οὐδὲ ... ἴδιον, closely resembles the way in which Socrates repeatedly describes the absence of possessions among the guardians, which is first described as οὐσίαν κεκτημένον μηδεμίαν μηδένα ἰδίαν (Resp. 3.416d).[39]

Third, in both Acts and the Republic the communal holding of possessions is linked to the authority of the leaders. This is more readily apparent in the Republic, where attributes that determine good leadership, such as unity, are said to be dependent on the κοινωνία of the guardians (5.462c, 5.464a). The authority of the apostles in Acts 1–6 also appears to be tied to their relationship to possessions. This can be seen in the structure of the summaries: in both, statements about the power and authority of the apostles appear to interrupt descriptions of the community of goods (2:43; 4:33). The final summary in 5:12–16 drops the community of goods entirely, focusing on the apostles' miracle-working powers. The emphasis on the apostles' collective authority is justified by the nearly miraculous unity and unanimity among members crystallized in the community of goods. The power of the apostles and the community's social organization go together.[40]

A fourth point of similarity is that both feature two separate principal discussions of the communal organization of group. In the context of the founding of the city, in Resp. 3.415d–417a Socrates describes for the first time how the guardians' daily activities and household arrangements should be organized. In Resp. 5.461e–466d Socrates again addresses the communal holding of property and possessions, but focuses on the unity among the guardians made possible by their social

---

37. This meaning of the term is consonant with the predominant use of the term in the Gospels of Mark and Matthew.

38. Dupont, "Community of Goods," 86–87.

39. Mealand, "Community of Goods," 97. Similar constructions occur elsewhere as well: in extending the communalism to wives and children: ἰδίᾳ δὲ οὐδενὸς οὐδὲν τοιοῦτον κεκτημένου (5.458c); and in repeating the requirements in order to show that the guardians' achieve the greatest good as a result of their polity: μηδὲν ἴδιον ἐκτῆσθαι (5.464d). The same expression is used in Resp. 5.457d in reference to having only one wife and in the summaries of the guardians' polity in Tim. 18b and Crit. 110c.

40. Daniel Marguerat, "La mort d'Ananias et Saphira (Ac 5:1–11) dans la stratégie narrative de Luc," NTS 39 (1993): 216.

arrangements. In Acts also there are two descriptions of the communal life of the early Christians in Jerusalem featuring possessions in common. And, like the two corresponding sections in the *Republic*, the summary in Acts 2 focuses on the daily life of the community while that in Acts 4 focuses on the unity of the group.

Acts 2:42–3:11 *and* Resp. 3.414–417

The goal of Socrates' new city is to show that justice is not the rule of the stronger and that its practice is in everyone's best interest. For this reason it is important for Plato to provide mechanisms that will guarantee the success of the state by keeping its leaders from becoming corrupt. The two most significant features of the guardians' life are their education and, as mentioned above, communal living arrangements that require a special relationship to possessions. Together, they protect against the corruption of the rulers, ensuring complete unity and harmony within society and among the guardians.

In the *Republic* the subject of the proper education of the guardians comes up immediately after they are mentioned for the first time (2.374e–376e). Socrates spends considerable time outlining what education in the ideal state should look like, memorably banishing the poets in favor of literature that will not pollute the guardians with tales of promiscuous gods and other unwholesome themes.[41] Having created suitable guardians by virtue of a good education and established appropriate tests to make sure only the most capable become rulers (3.412b–414b), Socrates sets out to "arm these sons of earth and conduct them under the leadership of the rulers" (3.415d).[42] After selecting the proper place for their camp, Socrates introduces the requirements with the following two related statements:

> [We may affirm] that they must have the right education [παιδείας], whatever it is, if they are to have what will do most to make them gentle to one another and their charges.... In addition, moreover, to such an education a thoughtful man would affirm that their houses [οἰκήσεις] and possessions [οὐσίαν] provided for them ought to be such as not to

---

41. While the centrality of education for both establishing and maintaining the state is discussed elsewhere as well, *Resp.* 2.374e–403d systematically deals with different aspects of the education of the guardians: proper speech or stories regarding the gods, proper stories about men, acceptable forms of diction, music and the importance of gymnastics.

42. All text and translations of the *Republic* are from Paul Shorey's translation (2 vols.; LCL 237, 276; Cambridge: Harvard University Press, 1935–37).

interfere with the best performance of their own work as guardians and not to incite them to wrong the other citizens." (416c–d)

The quality of the guardians' leadership is dependent on both their education and relationship to possessions.[43] Luke's picture of the daily life of the early Christian community similarly begins with a general statement in which education (διδαχή) and fellowship (κοινωνία) are linked (Acts 2:42).[44] Although details of the apostles' teaching are not given, it should probably be seen in light of the forty-day period of instruction (1:3) and the preaching of the apostles prominent not only in the early chapters of Acts but throughout the narrative. As in the *Republic*, in Acts 2:43 a related statement about the quality of the leaders follows. Unlike the description of the guardians, however, the focus in Acts is not on the potential for corruption, but on the apostles' power and legitimacy signaled by their ability to perform miraculous deeds and the fear these abilities engendered in others. The nature of the authority is different, but in both true leaders and property sharing go together.

In both the *Republic* and in Acts specifics about the community follow. The guardians' requirements are:

[1] In the first place, none must possess any private property save the indispensable.
[2] Secondly, none must have any habitation or treasure house which is not open for all to enter at will.
[3] Their food, in such quantities as are needful for athletes of war sober and brave, they must receive as an agreed stipend from the other citizens as the wages of their guardianship, so measured that there shall be neither superfluity at the end of the year or any lack.
[4] And resorting to a common mess like soldiers on a campaign they will live together.

---

43. The link between the two suggested here is made more explicit later in the dialogue: "For if a right education makes of them reasonable men they will easily discover everything of this kind—and other principles that we now pass over, as that the possession of wives and marriage, and the procreation of children and all that sort of thing should be made as far as possible the proverbial goods of friends that are common" (*Resp.* 4.423e–424a).

44. Interpreters have long disagreed on where the summary begins. Some take v. 41 as the beginning (C. K. Barrett, *Acts of the Apostles* [2 vols; ICC; Edinburgh: T&T Clark, 1994–98], 1:161–2; F. F. Bruce, *The Acts of The Apostles: The Greek Text with Introduction and Commentary* [London: Tyndale, 1951; repr., Grand Rapids: Eerdmans, 1990], 131). I follow those interpreters who take v. 41 as the end of the preceding section and v. 42 as the beginning of the paragraph (Conzelmann, *Acts*, 23; Haenchen, *Acts*, 190–91; and Ben Witherington III, *The Acts of the Apostles: A Socio-rhetorical Commentary* [Grand Rapids: Eerdmans, 1998], 156).

[5] Gold and silver, we will tell them, they have of the divine quality from the gods always in their souls, and they have no need of the metal of men nor does holiness suffer them to mingle and contaminate that heavenly possession with the acquisition of mortal gold. (416d–417a [Shorey; LCL])[45]

Implicit in the first prescription is the notion, made clearer in the third, that what goods the guardians have are to be supplied by the producing class. The first detail Luke gives about the community also concerns the absence of private property: all were "together and had all things in common; and they sold their possessions and goods and distributed them to all as any had need" (Acts 2:44–45). The way in which Plato describes the absence of private possession among the guardians here—κεκτημένον μηδεμίαν μηδένα ἰδίαν—is strikingly similar to Acts' reprisal of the community of goods in 4:32: οὐδὲ εἷς τι τῶν ὑπαρχόντων αὐτῷ ἔλεγεν ἴδιον εἶναι. Like Plato, Luke's first specific description of the Christians' κοινωνία qualifies the absence of personal possessions with a statement about basic needs; Plato does so with the phrase ἀν μὴ πᾶσα ἀνάγκη, while Luke adds ἄν τις χρείαν εἶχεν. Furthermore, the Christian community's practice of selling possessions is analogous to the supply of goods the guardians are to receive from the producing class.

In both what follows addresses the activities of daily life. Plato's second requirement stipulates that there are to be no boundaries regarding houses. The emphasis is not on houses as personal possessions, although this is implied, but on the absence of personal or private boundaries creating an openness between the guardians. The third requirement addresses another basic need, food, the simplicity of which is suggested by the reference to the rations of soldiers at war. Socrates also requires that that the guardians live together [κοινῇ ζῆν] and take their meals in a common mess [ξυσσίτια]. Like the guardians, the Christians in Jerusalem share meals in each other's homes. The awkward phrase κλῶντές τε κατ᾽ οἶκον ἄρτον may be a way of suggesting the absence of personal boundaries between homes as stipulated in Socrates' second requirement. It also suggests that, like the guardians' third requirement, the Christians share meals and live together. The simple quality of the guardians food may also be echoed in Acts 2:46. One of the two attributes describing the way in which they share their nourishment, ἀφελότητι, occurs only here in the New Testament and is probably best understood as simplicity. [46]

---

45. The numbering in brackets is mine.

46. Barrett sees the term as an alternative to ἁπλότης, which is used in the same sense in Eph 6:5; Col 3:22; 1 Chr 29:17; Wis 1:1. Further support for taking the term to mean "simple"

The parallels with the founding of the guardians city in the *Republic* do not end here. The fifth stipulation prohibits the guardians from handling or acquiring gold or silver in order to keep them from the corrupting power of money. To justify this, the guardians are to be told that they already have silver and gold (χρυσίον δὲ καὶ ἀργύριον) in their natures, making them the possessors of a more valuable treasure (3.416e). While Acts 3:1–10 begins a new episode, the central point of the prohibition of money is preserved. Peter responds to a begging paralytic's request for alms saying, "I have no silver and gold [ἀργύριον καὶ χρυσίον οὐχ ὑπάρχει μοι] but I give you what I have; in the name of Jesus Christ of Nazareth, walk" (3:6). The man is helped to his feet and finds that he is healthy. The first part of Peter's response is very nearly the same phrase that the founders tell the guardians to justify their being kept from handling money. In both the *Republic* and Acts the denial of silver and gold is justified by the possession of something of much greater value that is of divine origin.[47]

The real irony of the guardians' polity is that what appears at first to be a sacrifice on their part in not being able to own possessions or accumulate wealth has a final reward that outweighs any inconvenience they might at first experience. By putting the interests of the state before their own the guardians gain, finally, more for themselves than they could have otherwise: "So living they would save [σώζοιντό] themselves and save [σώζοιεν] their city" (3.417a). The first major summary in Acts ends with a notice of the community's growth: "And the Lord added to their number day by day those who were being saved [σωζομένους]" (2:47). Luke, like Plato, concludes the first description of the community's daily life with an eye on the final reward at stake: the salvation available through the new manifestation of the kingdom of God inaugurated by the outpouring of the Holy Spirit.

Acts 4:32–5:16 and Resp. *5.462–466*

The function of the absence of private property in the ideal state is to prevent leaders from acting in their own self-interest, thus guaranteeing

---

comes from the Vulgate, where it is translated as *simplicitas*. Barrett also notes that ἀφηλῶς is used in for simple meals in Athenaeus, *Deip.* 10.419d (*Acts*, 1:171).

47. There is also a possible parallel between the location of the guardian's residences and the mysterious Beautiful (ὡραίαν) Gate at which the beggar sits (Acts 3:2, 10). The very first element in the description of the guardians' community life is the location of the camp: "And when they have arrived they must look out for the fairest (καλλίστον) site in the city for their encampment" (415e).

the all-important unity of the state. The goal for the guardians is to achieve "a kind of concord and harmony ... a kind of beautiful order" (4.430e) in which all members of the city, both "the rulers and the ruled are of one mind" (4.431e). Plato's second extended discussion of the guardians' social organization is instigated by the interlocutors' desire to hear more about the community of wives and children, which he briefly mentioned earlier in the dialogue (4.423e). In *Resp.* 5.462–466 Plato puts the newly constructed polity to the test to make sure it leads to the desired unity. Socrates asks, "Do we know of any greater evil for a state than the thing that distracts it and makes it many instead of one, or a greater good than that which binds it together and makes it one?" (5.462b). The ideal unity is depicted as the unity of body and soul in a single organism (5.462c). The primary cause of individualization and disunity, he continues, "is when the citizens do not utter [φθέγγωνται] in unison such words as 'mine' and 'not mine' [τό τε ἐμὸν καὶ τὸ οὐκ ἐμόν] .... The city, then, is best ordered in which the greatest number use the expression 'mine' and 'not mine' [λέγουσι τὸ ἐμὸν καὶ τὸ οὐκ ἐμόν] of the same things in the same way" (5.462c). A few passages later, we find this idea repeated: "these citizens, above all others, will have one and the same thing in common which they will name [ὀνομάσουσι] mine, and by virtue of this communion they will have their pleasures and pains in common" (5.464a). To assuage any doubt, Socrates further roots this unity precisely in the sharing of property, and in this case, its extreme manifestation in the community of wives and children: "And is not the cause of this [*referring to unity*], besides the general constitution of the state, the community [κοινωνία] of wives and children among the guardians?" (5.464a). The guardians' community of goods guarantees that the language of unity is accompanied by actions (5.463e).

The unity of the early Christian community finds its clearest expression in the summary of Acts 4:32–35. The three points emphasized in *Resp.* 5.462–64—(1) the greatest good is acting as a single organism, (2) which can be realized in unanimous expression, (3) and can be achieved because of a polity in which there is no private property—are present in Acts 4:32 where the Christians are described as being of "one heart and soul," and none among them says "any of the things which he possessed was his own, but they had everything in common."

The first characteristic of the community's life listed—being of one heart and soul—corresponds to Plato's ideal of the group functioning as a single organism.[48] The guardians' unity of expression regarding

---

48. The phrase may be, as some have suggested, an intentional combination of Semitic and Greek idiom. See, for example, Deut 6:5 (Dupont, "Community of Goods," 92).

possessions is emphasized in the requirement that all say "mine" and "not mine" of the same things, which is stated repeatedly throughout the section.[49] Luke similarly portrays the Christians as not saying (ἔλεγεν) any had personal possessions. This verse is often understood as contradicting the absolute community of goods implied in 2:45 and 4:34–35. Given the other similarities to the *Republic*, rather than understanding the use of λέγω as evidence of a different source, of Luke's depiction of multiple property-sharing systems simultaneously,[50] or of a subjective community of goods,[51] the formulation allows the early Christians to fulfill the greatest good of a state in their unity of verbal expression regarding possessions. Furthermore, as in the *Republic*, Luke preserves the link between unanimous verbal expression and communal holding of possessions in v. 32 by following the statement that no one claimed personal possessions with the adversative particle ἀλλ' introducing the community's practice, ἦν αὐτοῖς ἅπαντα κοινά. Luke describes the early Christian community in v. 32 in essentially the same terms and in the same order that Plato assesses the guardians' polity in *Resp.* 5.462a–464b.

In *Resp.* 5.464c Plato provides a brief summary of the requirements first established in *Resp.* 3.416c–417a emphasizing the absence of private possessions and the support of the guardians by the producing class. After highlighting the power of the apostles' witness in v. 33, Luke describes the early Christian community in similar terms. Luke, who is not creating a state *de novo*, lists the goods of which the Christians divested themselves. Just as *Resp.* 5.464c repeats the earlier stipulations in 3.416c–d, Acts 4:34 repeats the absence of possessions first mentioned in 2:42–47. The differences from the first to the second discussions are analogous. In *Resp.* 3.416c–d, Plato specifically lists only possessions as something the guardians must not have, while houses are used to emphasize the communal living of the guardians and lands are not mentioned at all. Similarly, in Acts 2:44–45 only possessions and goods (κτήματα and ὑπάρξεις) are specifically identified as the things the Christians sell. The second discussion in *Resp.* 5.464c has houses (οἰκίας), lands (γῆν) and other property (κτῆμα). Similarly, in Acts 4:34–35 Luke lists houses

---

49. φθέγγωνται and λέγουσι in 5.462c; ξυμφωνήσουσιν in 5.463e; ἐλέγομεν in 5.463e; ἐμὸν ὀνομάζοντας in 5.464c.

50 Justin Taylor, "The Community of Goods among the First Christians and among the Essenes," in *Historical Perspectives: From the Hasmoneans to Bar Kokhba in Light of the Dead Sea Scrolls: Proceedings of the Fourth International Symposium of the Orion Centre for the Dead Sea Scrolls and Associated Literature, 27–31 January 1999* (ed. David Goodblatt et al.; Leiden: Brill, 2001), 153.

51. John Dominic Crossan, *The Birth of Christianity: Discovering What Happened in the Years Immediately after the Execution of Jesus* (San Francisco: HarperSanFrancisco, 1998), 469–76.

(οἰκιῶν) and, using a different term, adds lands (χωρίων). Luke does not list a third item, but his use of κτήτωρ is interesting as it appears only here in the New Testament.[52] The use of the term is not surprising, however, given that the related noun κτῆμα and verbs κτάομαι and κτᾶσθαι appear in nearly every description of the community of goods among the guardians in *Resp.* 2–5 and occur in *Resp.* 5.464c–d three times.[53] Finally, it is worth noting the similarity between the producing classes' support of the guardians—repeated in *Resp.* 5.464c—and the practice of laying the proceeds of the goods sold at the apostles' feet, which accomplishes the same thing. This act also emphasizes the authority of the apostles within the group and shows that, like the guardians, the words of unity are realized in deeds (cf. *Resp.* 5.463e).

Two other similarities are worth noting. First, another important aspect of Plato's ideal state is the separation between the guardian class (comprised of both the warrior and ruler guardians) and the rest of society. There is also an important distinction between the ruler guardians (who are generally the eldest) and the rest of the guardian class. Regarding their relationship, Plato states:

> "As for an older man, he will always have the charge of ruling and chastising the younger." "Obviously." "Again, it is plain that the young man, except by the command of the rulers, will probably not do violence to an elder or strike him, or, I take it, dishonour him in any other way. There being two competent guardians to prevent that, fear [δέος] and awe [αἰδώς], awe restraining him from laying hands on one who may be his parent, and fear in that others will rush to the aid of the sufferer, some as sons, some as brothers, some as fathers." (5.465b [Shorey, LCL])

In Acts also there is some distance between the leaders (the apostles) and the rest of the Christian community. This is first singled out in the qualifications necessary to become an apostle when Judas is replaced (1:21–22). In the summaries and surrounding episodes the relationship between the apostles and the rest of the community is characterized as one of fear and awe. Immediately following the reference to the κοινωνία of the apostles in Acts 2:42 and immediately preceding the description of the community of goods in the first summary is a description of the reaction to the apostles' miraculous powers: "And fear [φόβος] came upon every soul; and many wonders and signs were done through the

---

52. The term κτῆμα occurs four times in the New Testament: Mark 10:22 and its parallel in Matt 10:22 and in this section of Acts at 2:45 and 5:1. Of seven instances of κτᾶσθαι in the New Testament, five are in Luke-Acts.

53. See, for example, *Resp.* 3.416d, 416e, 417a; 4.423e; 5.458d, 464c, 464d, 464e.

apostles" (2:43). A similar reaction is reported of the Christian community in response to the miraculous deaths of Ananias and Sapphira:
"And great fear came upon the whole church, upon all who heard of
these things" (5:11). The theme appears again in the third and related
major summary: "Now many signs and wonders were done among the
people by the hands of the apostles. And they were all together in
Solomon's portico. None of the rest dared join them, but the people
held them in high honor" (5:12–13). There has been some debate regarding the referent of "the rest" (λοιπῶν). Some interpreters take the term to
refer to non-Christians or outsiders.[54] Another possible interpretation,
which I prefer, takes λοιπῶν as referring to a distinction between the
apostles and the rest of the Christian community based on other Christians' fear of what happened to Ananias and Sapphira, fear or anger of
Jewish authorities, and the narrator's presentation of the apostles in the
previous two summaries as qualitatively different beings.[55] This distance between the apostles and other Christians whom they lead
parallels the distance and somewhat fearful relationship between the
different groups of guardians in Plato's ideal state. Admittedly, there is
a major difference between the two: while the guardians are feared for
possible familial ties, the apostles are feared and respected for their miracle-working power.

Second, the distance between the guardian classes and the rest of the
population is related to the division of labor: everybody in the ideal state
is to do only what is suited to his or her nature. The guardians are not to
do any activity that is beneath them in order to allow them to focus on
their specialized duties (Resp. 395c, 416c). An interesting parallel in Acts
is the appointment of the Seven to cover serving tables in order to free the
disciples to do the more important task of preaching the gospel (6:1–11).
Somewhat surprisingly, despite the text's emphasis on their different
role, the narrative goes on to describe the activity of Stephen, one of the

---

54. Haenchen states, "Round this group of Christians holy awe draws its protective
circle: none of the 'rest,' the non-Christians, dare mix with the listening believers" (Acts, 245).
Conzelmann attributes the "apparent contradiction between verses 12 and 14 [to] mere
clumsiness on the part of the narrator" and suggests that λοιπῶν clearly refers to non-Christians (Acts, 39).

55. Witherington reads λοιπῶν as referring to "the rest of the Christians who were
afraid to join the apostles in the temple in view of what happened the first time—namely,
the arousal of the anger of the Jewish authorities and the trial of the Christian leaders"
(Acts, 225). Similarly, Luke Timothy Johnson reads the verse as referring to the other Christians' fear of approaching the apostles in the wake of the fate that had just befallen Ananias
and Sapphira (The Acts of the Apostles [Sacra Pagina 5; Collegeville, Minn.: Liturgical Press,
1992], 95).

Seven, as having much the same function and role in the preaching of the gospel that the members of the Twelve did.[56]

Conclusion

As the table below illustrates, the parallels between Plato's description of the guardians in his ideal state and the description of the earliest Christian community in the summaries of Acts are dense and extend beyond the important lexical agreements of a few key phrases into significant thematic parallels.

Support of the Guardians/Apostles

Guardians concentrate on philosophy, training and affairs of the state	Apostles lead the community in teaching, fellowship breaking of bread, and prayers
	they perform signs and wonders
Guardians are supported by the producing class	Apostles are supported by other Christians (who lay the proceeds of goods sold at their feet)
in order to concentrate on being guardians (because all classes should do what is suited to their natures)	The Seven are elected so the apostles do not spend their time serving tables instead of preaching

Lifestyle

They live in simple houses in an area set apart	Eat in each other's homes
They eat and train and are educated together	Worship, break bread and learn the apostle's teaching together
Possessions are held in common, no one has private property	Possessions are held in common, no one has private property
They have neither excess nor need, food as needed	Proceeds of goods sold are distributed to all as needed, no one is needy

---

56. Luke Timothy Johnson, *The Literary Function of Possessions in Luke-Acts* (SBLDS 39; Missoula, Mont.: Scholars Press, 1977), 212–13.

Importance of Unity

Success of the community depends on unity and being in agreement	Christian community is of "one heart and soul"

Importance of Education

The right education will ensure guardians will be able to handle rigors of communal living	They devoted themselves to the apostles' teaching and fellowship

Silver and Gold

Guardians do not need silver or gold because what they have is greater: silver and gold is built into their natures	Apostles do not need silver or gold because what they have is greater: the power to heal in the name of Jesus

Division of Society

Ruler guardians	Apostles (the Twelve)
The more numerous warrior guardians	Growing Christian community
The rest of the working classes	Everybody else (non-Christians)

I suggest that the Luke's portrait of the early Christian community in the summaries is specifically modeled on Plato's description of the guardians in the *Republic*. Reading the summaries in light of his literary model may help explain at least a few the inconsistencies often noted in the section. At face value, there is an apparent inconsistency regarding whether the community of goods depicted by Luke is mandatory or voluntary. Acts 2:44–45, 4:34–45 suggest that all Christians sold all their possessions, while elsewhere in Acts Christians are depicted as owning property (12:12, 21:9, 21:16), keeping their wealth after conversion (8:27–40) and being in need of outside financial help (11:27–30).[57] Furthermore, that the Christians say they do not have personal possessions in

---

57. In addition, Paul's decidedly noncommunal lifestyle in the second half of Acts is in stark contrast with the description of the early Christian community: Paul presents his self-supporting lifestyle as a model for others in his speech to the Ephesian elders (20:34–35); Paul is depicted by the author of Acts as having the means to pay for an expensive Nazirite vow (21:26); and Paul's living arrangements in Rome may suggest some wealth (28:30–31).

Acts (4:32) and Peter's response to Ananias (5:4) can suggest that participation was voluntary. The use of λέγω in 4:32, as I have suggested above, can more properly be explained as Luke's attempt to have the Jerusalem community achieve the ideal of unity of expression required of the guardians by Plato. The apparent interruption of both the summaries in Acts 2 and 4 by a notice about the authority of the apostles (2:43, 4:33) need not be seen as evidence that Luke switched to a different source. In the *Republic* the guardians' authority and superior leadership is dependant precisely on adhering to the stipulations regarding communal life and the absence of personal possessions. Although he may not do it as smoothly, Luke likewise pairs the two. That Peter and John have no money in Acts 3:1–11 can be understood to be at odds with the idea that they were in charge of the community's purse.[58] This too can be understood in light of Luke's imitation of *Resp.* 3.416–417 in the preceding summary. There is one more intriguing inconsistency in the narrative that might be explained in light of Luke's use of the *Republic* as a model. In Acts 2:46–47 the Jerusalem Christians break bread in each other's homes, but in 4:32 they are depicted as selling their homes along with other possessions. This can be explained by Luke's modeling of the two summaries on the two different descriptions of the guardians' polity in *Resp.* 3.415–417 and 5.462–464. In both first discussions houses are mentioned to underscore the communal living arrangements, while in both second discussions houses are listed among the possessions.

Luke Timothy Johnson has noted that many of these minor inconsistencies "probably demand of the author a concern he did not have."[59] In light of Luke's apparent use of the *Republic* as literary model, these difficulties might be understood as narrative inconsistencies the author sacrificed in order to score more important allusive, theological, and apologetic points. Immediately following the symbolic founding of God's kingdom on earth, Luke presents the credentials of the leaders of this new polity using the narrative language of Plato's philosopher-kings.

---

58. See the discussion in Thomas E. Phillips, *Reading Issues of Wealth and Poverty in Luke-Acts* (SBEC 48; Lewiston, N.Y.: Mellen, 2001), 200–202. Phillips argues that the summary in Acts 2:42–47 does not indicate that the apostles had personal access to the community's resources, and that the statement in 3:6 need not be seen as a contradiction of the preceding summary.

59. *Literary Function of Possessions*, 10 n. 1.

A Biography of a Motif: The Empty Tomb in the Gospels, the Greek Novels, and Shakespeare's *Romeo and Juliet*

Andy M. Reimer

Introduction

Given that this paper will track the literary motif of the empty tomb through the canonical Gospels, the Greek romance novels, and on through a Shakespearean play using a biographical format, it is appropriate that its formulation is only explicable in autobiographical terms. This hypothesis on the historical and literary links between these texts owes its conception to my coincidental reading of several works. First, I purchased a one-volume complete works of Shakespeare in a little bookshop in Sheffield when I arrived there in 1994. For the first time in my life, I actually read Shakespeare's comedies, having had to endure a steady diet of Shakespearean tragedy in my high school education and never having revisited the bard since. Also for the first time in my life, I read the Greek romance novels at my doctoral supervisor's suggestion (much to the amusement of my wife). I was immediately struck by correlations in the plot lines—children mixed up at birth, servants as masters and masters as servants, and the near misses and ever elusive meeting that would solve the plot's complication, to name just the most obvious. I thought surely considerable research must have been done on the link between Greek novels and Shakespearean plays—subsequent research indicated others have noted the similarities, but typically simply in passing.[1] Then I read G. W. Bowersock's *Fiction as History: Nero to Julian*[2] in which he suggests that the Gospel stories could have been a contributing factor in the rising fortunes of fictional works in the Neronian and post-Neronian world.[3]

---

1. See below nn. 39 and 40.

2. Glen W. Bowersock, *Fiction as History: Nero to Julian* (Berkeley and Los Angeles: University of California Press, 1994).

3. The novelty of Bowersock's hypothesis is certainly evident if one glances at E. L. Bowie and S. J. Harrison's summary of scholarship on the ancient romance novels, especially

For the most part, Bowersock's hypothesis has been met with disbelief and, curiously, written reviews have been somewhat sparse. Certainly there appears to be no extensive written rebuttal.[4] In the end I feel somewhat like Robert M. Grant—this is simply too interesting a thesis not to pursue further.[5] The following is, therefore, an attempt to pursue the implications of Bowersock's hypothesis by following a motif that can be found in the four canonical Gospels, at least two of the Greek novels and in a deconstructed fashion in a grand Shakespearean tragedy—that is the motif of the empty tomb.

I shall approach the task of tracing this motif through these three types of literature on two tracks. First, I am interested, at least in a cursory fashion, to explore the genetic dependence of one on the other. This will be the difficult sell given the incredulity with which Bowersock's hypothesis has been received. It has also proven difficult given the present state of Shakespearean source criticism and the fact that I am a neophyte to the whole discipline of Shakespearean studies. Second, I want to explore on the level of narrative, how the motif is being used in each of these three genres and what insights an intertextual reading produces. I am using the term intertextual here from a reader response, rather than source critical, perspective. Within biblical studies, in recent years, source critics have begun to exploit the term to speak about literary borrowings between ancient writers. Likewise, a recent work on Shakespearean intertextuality uses the term to speak about the intentional adaptation of one text by another.[6] I am salvaging the term intertextuality to speak of what occurs in the interpreter's head, a head filled with particular texts that impinge on any interpretive activity. In keeping with this latter literary, rather than historical, task, I shall engage the motif of the empty tomb by treating it as an entity with a life story and my investigation as biography. Like any good biography, we begin with birth.

---

their summary of scholarship on the origins of the Greek novel and its relationship to other ancient literatures; "The Romance of the Novel," *JRS* 83 (1993): 159–78 (165).

4. Keith Hopkins, while entertained by Bowersock's work, remains unconvinced largely due to his conviction that Christianity and its literature are an unknown commodity in the first-century Roman Empire; "Past alternative: Review of G. W. Bowersock's *Fiction as History*," *The Times Literary Supplement* 4846 (Feb. 16, 1996): 29. Simon Swain's short review suggests he is ultimately more convinced by the differences between the Gospel stories and ancient fiction. While not ruling out contacts, he refuses to accept they are as significant as Bowersock suggests, "Review of G. W. Bowersock, *Fiction as History. Nero to Julian*," *JRS* 86 (1996): 216–17.

5. See the sympathetic review offered by Robert M. Grant, *Church History* 66 (1997): 307–8.

6. Stephen J. Lynch, *Shakespearean Intertextuality: Studies in Selected Sources and Plays* (CDTS 86; Westport, Conn.: Greenwood, 1998), 1–3.

THE BIRTH OF THE EMPTY-TOMB MOTIF

A. The Conception of the Empty Tomb

The birth of the empty-tomb tradition is shrouded in a sort of mystery and wrapped up in a deep religious piety, precisely where one gets a whiff of moral scandal. As such, its birth is not entirely unlike the birth of the character who first leaves an empty tomb behind to be discovered. There are those who would have us believe that the empty-tomb accounts we find in the canonical Gospels owe their existence to a group of women in Jerusalem who went out to what they believed was Jesus' tomb and found it void of Jesus' body.[7] In this case the empty-tomb motif of later narrative fame is first conceived when that discovery is reported by the first participants. In the words of Geza Vermes,

> [I]n the end, when every argument has been considered and weighed, the only conclusion acceptable to the historian must be that the opinions of the orthodox, the liberal sympathizer and the critical agnostic alike—and even perhaps of the disciples themselves—are simply interpretations of the one disconcerting fact: namely that the women who set out to pay their last respects to Jesus found to their consternation, not a body, but an empty tomb.[8]

At a popular level, most Christian readers prefer this account of the matter but other strongly held opinions circulate widely in the biblical scholarly guild. In particular, Dominic Crossan has argued long and hard for the past two decades that the empty-tomb story had no existence before its birth at the hands of the writer of the Gospel of Mark.[9]

---

7. Notable scholars who hold to some form of an empty-tomb discovery as historically plausible include Christopher Rowland, *Christian Origins* (London: SPCK, 1985), 189–93; Raymond E. Brown, *The Virginal Conception and Bodily Resurrection of Jesus* (New York: Paulist, 1973), 117–25; Geza Vermes, *Jesus the Jew: A Historian's Reading of the Gospels* (Philadelphia: Fortress, 1973), 37–41. Popular writers on Jesus, even those who make no claim to faith or express outright skepticism, frequently assume some form of an empty-tomb discovery actually happened, e.g., A. N. Wilson, *Jesus: A Life* (New York: Norton, 1992), 241–2. A convenient list of scholars who hold to some form of historical nucleus in the Markan empty-tomb tradition can be found in Gerald O' Collins, "The Resurrection: The State of the Questions," in *The Resurrection: An Interdisciplinary Symposium on the Resurrection of Jesus* (ed. Stephen T. Davis et al.; Oxford: Oxford University Press, 1997), 14.

8. Vermes, *Jesus the Jew*, 41.

9. Dominic Crossan's major work on the passion and resurrection narratives, which forms the foundation for his subsequent tomes, is *The Cross that Spoke: The Origins of the Passion Narrative* (San Francisco: Harper & Row, 1988). See also *The Historical Jesus: The Life of a Mediterranean Jewish Peasant* (Edinburgh: T&T Clark, 1991), 395–416; *Jesus: A Revolutionary*

Others are content to decry certainty and allow the story of the empty tomb to remain shrouded behind a cloud of "critical distance," the contemporary historical investigator forever banished not just from entering the tomb, but even from approaching the graveyard.[10] Is it a case of an actual resurrection complete with the discovery of an empty tomb? A pious fiction invented by an early Christian preacher? A story created to cover the scandal of a Savior left on a cross for weeks, abandoned by his followers, never to receive a proper burial? An elaborate ruse complete with a "tomb robbery" of some sort? A simple misunderstanding in a dark graveyard?

For our purposes these questions can remain unanswered. For our biography to succeed, one need only be convinced of the following: the empty-tomb accounts found in the Gospels are based on oral traditions that go back several decades before the writing of the Gospels as we know them today. As we shall notice in a moment, the earlier the empty-tomb stories about Jesus circulated, the greater the likelihood of this being the source of empty-tomb narratives in the novels. In particular, for Bowersock's hypothesis to fly, Christian empty-tomb stories must be floating about Nero's Rome. Here in particular Crossan's reconstruction of the Gospel sources is most problematic with its claim that Mark is the virginal mother of the empty-tomb motif. Space does not permit a full-blown refutation of this position, but a few salient points need to be brought forward.

Those who argue for a very late invention of the empty-tomb accounts will frequently point to the absence of this narrative in the Pauline letters, and particularly its absence in 1 Cor 15:3–8 where the topic is such that one might reasonably expect this story to appear. However the gap between the terse creedal statements of 1 Cor 15:3–5 and the Gospels' empty-tomb stories should not be exaggerated.[11] Verse 4 draws

---

Biography (San Francisco: HarperSanFrancisco, 1994), 159–92; and *The Birth of Christianity* (San Francisco: HarperSanFrancisco, 1998), 550–73.

10. E. P. Sanders's concluding chapter on the resurrection is a good example of how typically biblical scholars skirt the issue of the empty tomb and the manner of resurrection, in his case with his nigh reverential, "we cannot reconstruct what really happened.... I do not see how to improve on the evidence, or how to get behind it" (*The Historical Figure of Jesus* [London: Penguin, 1993], 278). Frequently the empty-tomb stories are brushed over in a haste to point out their irrelevance to some belief in some form of resurrection that does not necessitate the involvement of the corpse of the historical Jesus. See Marcus Borg's perspective laid out in Marcus J. Borg and N. T. Wright, *The Meaning of Jesus: Two Visions* (San Francisco: HarperSanFrancisco, 1999), 130–31; or Luke Timothy Johnson, *The Real Jesus: The Misguided Quest for the Historical Jesus and the Truth of the Traditional Gospels* (San Francisco: HarperSanFrancisco, 1996), 135–36.

11. Arguments for or against the correlation of 1 Cor 15 and the Gospel empty-tomb accounts have been rehearsed often enough—for two more recent examples see, in favor of

attention to entombment with its use of ἐτάφη, while the phrase ἐγήγερται τῇ ἡμέρᾳ τῇ τρίτῃ would suggest a belief in a definitive moment of resurrection rather than simply an amorphous collection of visionary appearances at unspecified moments following the death of Jesus. Indeed if the phrase ἐξ ἀναστάσεως νεκρῶν in Rom 1:4 is read as a "resurrection from among the corpses"[12] Paul's familiarity with a resurrection account that involves a missing body in a tomb ought not to be ruled out. Ultimately, an argument against an early empty-tomb tradition from 1 Cor 15 remains an argument from silence and furthermore betrays a typically underdeveloped imagination in terms of what early Christian teaching and preaching consisted.[13] While the Western Protestant preaching tradition and to some extent the whole of the Western theological tradition is fixated on Pauline epistolary discourse, the Gospels point to early church rhetoric having a narrative component that we would claim was nonexistent if all we had was the Pauline materials. The Pauline epistolary materials, concerned as they are to solve specific problems in specific locales, can hardly be seen as offering conclusive evidence as to the vitality, depth and breadth of the narrative component of early Christian teaching. The Gospels and especially Mark, however, do suggest something about that vitality.

The most basic evidence for the preexistence of the Markan empty-tomb account, however, is the very puzzling form it takes in our earliest manuscript evidence. The abrupt opening, dangling conclusion, and staccato-like simplicity of Mark have in recent years been viewed with a certain admiration by contemporary readers as a case of narrative artistry and design.[14] However, one is rather suspicious that these readers are caught

---

correspondence, N. T. Wright, *The Challenge of Jesus: Rediscovering Who Jesus Was and Is* (Downers Grove, Ill.: InterVarsity Press, 1999), 140–49, and in favor of discrepancy Robert Funk and the Jesus Seminar, *The Acts of Jesus: The Search for the Authentic Deeds of Jesus* (San Francisco: HarperSanFrancisco, 1998), 453–55, 465–67. Critical commentaries likewise visit the issue without fail, e.g., Hans Conzelmann, *1 Corinthians* (trans. James W. Leitch; Philadelphia: Fortress, 1975), 255–56; Anthony C. Thiselton, *The First Epistle to the Corinthians: A Commentary on the Greek Text* (NIGTC; Grand Rapids: Eerdmans, 2000), 1197–203. N. T. Wright offers a rather lengthy treatment of 1 Cor 15 in his more recent tome, *The Resurrection of the Son of God* (Minneapolis: Fortress, 2003), 312–60, esp. 321.

12. Rowland, *Christian Origins*, 190. See also νεκρός in LSJ.

13. Even conceding Paul thinks of Jesus as having been "raised from among the corpse," admittedly one does not have any real positive evidence of Paul's awareness of an empty-tomb story proper. But that said, we have little direct evidence of Paul's awareness of most early Jesus stories. Given Paul seems of so little use in establishing what the early church claimed Jesus actually did or said, I would arguing using him to establish what the early church story tellers didn't say is problematic.

14. To cite but two recent examples of recent works lauding the literary artistry of Mark: Edwin R. Broadhead, *Mark* (Sheffield: Sheffield Academic Press, 2001), and Mitzi L.

up in what Kermode's describes as "our desire for the well-formed—or our wish to induce well-formedness where it is not apparent."[15] Rather more plausible to my mind is that these features of Mark are indicative of the intended readership—that is, this is a quick and ready collection of well-known stories both to the writer and intended readers. While the early church tradition that Mark was a less than orderly written account of Peter's preaching may be fictional, it is a plausible fiction to the extent that these written materials surely represent the repertoire of the first and second generation of church preachers and teachers.[16]

In the end we are thrown into a very subjective question of plausibility. Which is more believable? Would the friends of "Mark" have gathered around for a first reading of the manuscript and remarked how delightfully deconstructive the piece was? Would they have noted and appreciated the literary features that so engage contemporary literary critics such as: Mark's jagged opening; the dangling unresolved ending allowing readers to conclude the story as they wish; the cryptic naked man at the arrest who might be the author, or perhaps the ideal reader who identifies with the failed disciples but later shows up at the empty tomb; and the portrayal of the original disciples as incompetent fools?[17]

Minor, *The Power of Mark's Story* (St. Louis: Chalice, 2001). A thorough and masterful analysis of Mark's startling ending from a narrative critical perspective can be found in Paul L. Danove, *The End of Mark's Story: A Methodological Study* (Leiden: Brill, 1993).

15. Frank Kermode, *The Genesis of Secrecy* (Cambridge: Harvard University Press, 1979), 65. My own suspicions about the role of contemporary readerly creativity in the construction of "narrative critical" analyses of the Gospels (i.e., narrative critics "make" as much as they "discover" the narrative structure they encounter) was generated by my reading of Stephen D. Moore, *Literary Criticism and the Gospels: The Theoretical Challenge* (New Haven: Yale University Press, 1989). Moore especially calls attention to the fact that narrative unity is an a priori of narrative critical approaches, not its well reasoned conclusions (*Literary Criticism*, 52; see also Stephen D. Moore, *Poststructuralism and the New Testament: Derrida and Foucault at the Foot of the Cross* (Minneapolis: Fortress, 1994), 68, 74–81.

16. Eusebius quotes Papias (ca. 135 C.E.) as follows: "And the Presbyter used to say this, 'Mark became Peter's interpreter and wrote accurately all that he remembered, not, indeed, in order, of the things said and done by the Lord. For he had not heard the Lord, nor had he followed him, but later on, as I said, followed Peter, who used to give teaching as necessity demanded but not making, as it were, an arrangement of the Lord's oracles, so that Mark did nothing wrong in thus writing down single points as he remembered them. For to one thing he gave attention, to leave out nothing of what he had heard and to make no false statement in them'" (3.39, from *Eusebius: The Ecclesiastical History* [trans. Kirsopp Lake; 2 vols.; LCL; Cambridge: Harvard University Press, 1926], 1:297).

17. A key problem with Crossan's characterization of Mark's intent as seriously revisionistic is that it does not square very well with the evidence of the immediate and widespread use of Mark that the two-source hypothesis requires. See, for example, "Historical Jesus as Risen Lord," in Crossan et al., *The Jesus Controversy: Perspectives in Conflict* (Harrisburg, Pa.: Trinity Press International, 1999), 8–26; or a previous work, *Jesus: A Revolutionary Biography,*

Or is it more likely that the first listeners of Mark would have noted their familiarity with most of the stories and seen the written collection as a quick and useful tool for a variety of local and itinerant teaching duties.[18] It seems to me that if the two-source hypothesis is correct, and even more interesting, if John is familiar with Mark, then the very presence of these additional Gospels suggests something along these lines.[19] Mark was a good little collection of Jesus' material one could use, but in the end fell short as a complete literary document and so needed to be replaced.[20] At the very least, three attempts later and we had the makings of a fourfold Gospel canon. While Crossan demands a reading of Mark as a radically revisionistic writer, if one reads Mark as essentially preservationist, as I would argue we ought to, the natural conclusion is that empty-tomb accounts were in circulation before they were incorporated into the collections of Jesus' traditions we now know as Matthew, Mark, Luke, and

---

123–92; the latter is a popularization of the material covered in more technical detail in *The Historical Jesus: The Life of a Mediterranean Jewish Peasant* (San Francisco: HarperSanFrancisco, 1991), 354–416. I am more convinced by the sort of portrayals of Mark's development along the lines of those offered by Larry W. Hurtado, "The Gospel of Mark: Evolutionary or Revolutionary Document?" *JSNT* 40 (1990): 15–32.

18. My general picture of the early church as in some ways akin to ancient "schools" owes its existence to Loveday Alexander, "Paul and the Hellenistic Schools: The Evidence of Galen," in *Paul in His Hellenistic Context* (ed. Troels Engberg-Pedersen; Edinburgh: T&T Clark, 1994), 60–83. Also influential in this hypothesis has been Arthur Darby Nock, whose work suggests that wrapping our contemporary minds around this church-school correlation may require us to realize that the ancient "school" was more like a "church" (*Conversion: The Old and the New in Religion from Alexander the Great to Augustine of Hippo* [Oxford: Clarendon, 1933], esp. 202–3). In terms of understanding the construction of Mark, I must confess to finding a past generation of cranky dissidents on Markan structure at times more convincing than the contemporary literary critics. For example, Ernest Best, "Mark's Preservation of the Tradition," in *The Interpretation of Mark* (ed. W. Telford; Philadelphia: Fortress, 1985), 119–33; or John C. Meagher, *Clumsy Construction in Mark's Gospel: A Critique of Form and Redaktionsgeschichte* (Toronto Studies in Theology 3; New York: Mellen, 1979).

19. On John's knowledge of Mark, Richard Bauckham puts forward an ingenious argument favoring not just John's knowledge of Mark, but a writing of John intended to augment and correct Mark ("John for Readers of Mark" in *The Gospels for All Christians: Rethinking the Gospel Audiences* [ed. Richard Bauckham; Grand Rapids: Eerdmans, 1998], 147–71). Dwight Moody Smith speculates in this direction but is much more cautious in "When Did the Gospels Become Scripture?" *JBL* 119 (2000): 3–20, esp. 19–20. Martin Hengel's revisitation of the construction of the fourfold Gospel canon also argues that "John … presupposes both [Mark and Luke] but deliberately gives a quite different account" (*The Four Gospels and the One Gospel of Jesus Christ* [trans. John Bowden; Harrisburg, Pa.: Trinity Press International, 2000], 39).

20. Smith argues that authors of Matthew and Luke intend to rewrite and thus replace Mark ("When Gospels Become Scripture," 10). On John he is more circumspect, merely speculating that John is "improving" Mark by setting him aside and starting again (19).

John.[21] Again it should be stressed that this view is *not* in the end premised on the historicity of the empty-tomb story itself—Gerd Lüdemann's work on the resurrection narratives is one example of a scholar who argues for the pre-existence of Mark's empty-tomb narrative quite apart from accepting its historicity.[22]

The Birth of the Empty Tomb in the Canonical Gospels

The story in its most basic form is found in Mark 16:1–8. It starts with a group of women, namely, Mary Magdalene, Mary the mother of James, and Salome purchasing spices when the Sabbath comes to an end. They arise very early and head out to Jesus' tomb (μνημεῖον) intent on anointing his body with the purchased spices (ἄρωμα). The narrator then jumps to their arrival at the tomb, reporting in a flashback their conversation to that point concerning who they could enlist to roll the stone (λίθος) away from the entrance of the tomb. As stated, they have arrived and the downcast women look up and realize the large stone has already been rolled away (ἀποκεκύλιστια). They enter the tomb and to their alarm (ἐξεθαμβήθησαν) discover a white clad young man on the right hand side. He instructs them not to be alarmed, informs them that he is aware that they are seeking Jesus of Nazareth who was crucified, tells them that he has been raised (ἠγέρθη) and is no longer on the premises, and then draws attention to the site where his body had been placed. He then instructs the women to report to his disciples and Peter that Jesus is going ahead of them into Galilee and there they will see him as Jesus had promised them. The women flee the tomb, saying nothing to anyone, on account of their fear (ἐφοβοῦντα γάρ). And with that ends Mark's Gospel, at least Mark's Gospel in our earliest manuscript evidence. While contemporary scholars have waxed eloquent about the power of this dangling conclusion, ancient readers seem to have had other sensibilities and the variety of other possible endings in the Markan manuscript tradition as well as the other Gospels writers that take up his story suggests precisely what those sensibilities were.[23]

---

21. Evidence to the contrary, namely, the conviction that Mark invented the empty-tomb story in the 70s, is laid out with some clarity in Funk and the Jesus Seminar, *Acts of Jesus*, 450–67.

22. Gerd Lüdemann, *What Really Happened to Jesus: A Historical Approach to the Resurrection* (trans. John Bowden; Louisville: Westminster John Knox, 1995), 26–32.

23. The most convincing argument I have heard favoring the conclusion of Mark at 16:8 and offering a sensible reading on that basis is by Larry Hurtado, "The Women, The Tomb, and the Conclusion of Mark" (paper presented at the British New Testament Conference, Birmingham, September 5, 2003).

Of the three remaining canonical accounts, Luke's lies the closest to this Markan version (24:1–12). Luke too makes special note of the early dawn (ὄρθρος) departure for the tomb (μνημεῖον) by women, later named as Mary Magdalene, Joanna, Mary the mother of James and other unnamed women. Luke implies they are going to anoint Jesus body, although all he reports is the preparation and transportation of the spices (ἄρωμα). This larger crew is not reported to be concerned about moving the stone, but upon arrival discovers the stone (λίθος) rolled away (ἀποκεκυλισμένον) from the tomb. They enter the tomb and search unsuccessfully for the body and this leaves them at a loss (ἀπορέω). At this point two figures in shining clothing (ἐν ἐσθῆτι ἀστραπτούσῃ) appear, reducing the women to prostrated fearfulness (ἔμφοβος). They are asked why they seek the living among the dead, are told Jesus is not in the tomb but has risen (ἠγέρθη),[24] and are reminded of Jesus' predictions given while in Galilee. Luke's larger group of women do a fine job of carrying out the instructions of the two figures, although they are later met with disbelief by the men. Peter then runs off to the tomb, not quite entering but stooping and peering in, sees the cast aside grave linens and departs with amazement (θαυμάζω). The UBS[3] has serious reservations about the originality of the Peter incident in Luke, offering it only a "D" rating, no doubt suspicious that John has crept into the account. However, the UBS[4] offers a "B" rating on the grounds of rather overwhelming and early evidence for this reading.

Matthew reduces Mark's party of women to two, Mary Magdalene and the "other" Mary, rather than inflating it as Luke has, and also fails to offer any rationale for the dawn (ἐπιφώσκω) visit to the tomb (τάφος) (28:1). But Matthew has given us something unique among the four Gospels: a Roman guard and a sealed tomb that will ensure no grave robbing takes place in the name of feigned prophecy fulfillment (27:62–66). Matthew also resolves the mystery of exactly how that stone rolled. While the narrative is not entirely clear, it appears that the women are in attendance with the guard when an earthquake hits and a descending angel, with a shining face (ἀστραπή) and snowy white clothing, rolls back the stone (λίθος) and sits on it (28:2–3). The male guards are seized with fear (φόβος) and in a fine touch of irony collapse as if dead (ὡς νεκροί). The women are told not to be fearful by the descending angel, they are informed that Jesus is not there but has risen (ἠγέρθη) as

---

24. The line οὐκ ἔστιν ὧδε, ἀλλὰ ἠγέρθη was given a "D" rating in the UBS[3] but has that moved up to a "B" rating in the UBS[4]. The "D" reflects a suspicion that this is a superfluous copying over of material by a later editor on the basis of the Markan account; the "B" rating better reflects the very early and broad support for including this line.

promised (as per Mark), and are then invited to come and see the site where his body was placed. Also in line with Mark are the instructions that they are to report their findings and travel on to Galilee where Jesus preceded them. The narrator does not directly narrate the women's entry into the tomb, only their departure from the tomb and their experience of fear (φόβος) and great joy en route to report to the disciples. They then encounter Jesus, who provokes further prostration, but adds very little to the angel's words or instructions. The guards, in contrast, report what they have seen to the chief priests who bribe them into stating that what took place was precisely what the guards were there to prevent: the theft of Jesus' body by his disciples (28:11–15).

John's account, while tracking in that uniquely Johannine manner, begins remarkably similar to the synoptics (20:1–18). He reduces the party of women to one, Mary Magdalene, but she too departs in the wee hours of the morning (πρωῒ σκοτίας ἔτι οὔσης) for the tomb (μνημεῖον) and discovers the stone (λίθος) removed (ἠρμένον) from the tomb. We are not told what exactly Mary does or sees at this point, but rather are informed that she runs off to Peter and the "other disciple" and reports the removal of the Lord from the tomb and her ignorance of where those removing him might have placed him. Curiously, the ignorance is reported in the first person plural (οἴδαμεν) implying, in a puzzling way given the structure of this narrative, that there are others who are already aware of the empty tomb before this first narrated report.[25] Peter and the anonymous disciple then engage in a foot race to the tomb, with the "other disciple" arriving first but stopping shy of entering, simply peering in the entrance to see the abandoned grave linens. Peter enters and is rewarded with a closer look at the grave clothes and the separated head wrappings. The other disciple now seems to work up the courage to enter, and seeing what Peter saw, believes, although the narrator informs us of their ignorance of Scripture and the necessity of Jesus' resurrection from the dead (ἐκ νεκρῶν ἀναστῆναι). The male disciples return home, leaving Mary weeping at the tomb. It is at this point we have angelic visitations—two figures as in Luke, also dressed in white as per Mark and Matthew, sitting where Jesus had once lain, and noticed only as Mary in her weeping bends over to look into the tomb once more. They ask her the cause of her weeping. She states what she said earlier to the disciples, assuming someone has made off with Jesus' body, and turns around to see Jesus—although of course it takes an exchange between the two for

---

25. Obviously, if one argues for Johannine familiarity with one or more synoptic accounts this is easily accounted for as a slip generated by a knowledge of more than one woman visiting the tomb and departing perplexed.

this to become apparent to her. She is given instructions to report to Jesus' disciples his impending ascension and she does so. These then are the canonical empty-tomb stories in brief.

THE EMPTY TOMB HITS PUBERTY

We will leave our empty-tomb motif in its infancy and early childhood and move on to its adolescence, now with hormones coursing through its veins and all the melodrama of young love. We are talking, of course, about the empty-tomb stories of the Greek romance novels.

By way of aside I ought to mention a bawdy tale with an empty tomb in a Latin novel that, we can be certain, was written after Christian empty-tomb stories were circulating in Nero's Rome—Petronius' *Satyricon*. Here a faithful wife remains in the tomb of her dead husband, while nearby a soldier is guarding crosses to prevent robbers' remains from being removed and properly buried. The wife and soldier eventually end up in a three night sexual tryst in the dead husband's tomb. The parents of one of the crucified, seeing the guard is lax, steal the body and bury it. The guard, suicidal over the empty cross, certain of his punishment, is prevented from ending his life only by the quick thinking virtuous wife. She offers her husband's body to be placed on the empty cross and the following day onlookers wondered "by what means the dead man ascended the cross" (*Satyricon* 111–112). Ironically, while there are all sorts of inversions (perhaps perversions?) of the Gospel stories of crucifixion, entombment and resurrection, this story has the most in common with Crossan's *Cross Gospel*—both offer an empty cross, the *Satyricon* furthermore an empty cross *on the third day*.[26] And in a bit of delightful intertextuality that only Derrida could fully appreciate, the centurion assigned to guard the tomb in the *Cross Gospel* is named Petronius. Whether Petronius is intentionally playing off Christian stories is, perhaps, unknowable—although intertextual readings have incredible potential, as they do in the Greek novels to which we now return

The romance novel, which offers us the clearest connection with the Gospel empty-tomb stories, is one of the earliest of the extant Greek romance novels, Chariton's *Callirhoe*. In recent years it has become fashionable to date this novel as early as the first century B.C.E. Erwin Rhode in 1876 thought of this particular novel as a late degenerate version of the

---

26. Crossan, *The Cross That Spoke*,16. Crossan's "original stratum" for the *Cross Gospel* (as per) can be reconstructed by the modern reader by taking a modern translation of the *Gospel of Peter* such as that offered by James K. Elliott (*The Apocryphal New Testament* [Oxford: Clarendon, 1993], 154–58), and reading from 2.5b–10.49.

genre, dating to perhaps the fifth or sixth century C.E. B. E. Perry writing in 1930 moved the novel to among the earliest and placed it in the second century C.E., while E. H. Haight suggested a pre-150 C.E. date in 1943.[27] Writing in 1973, Antonios Papanikolaou suggested the first century B.C.E. date.[28] In the end the real difficulty with Papanikolaou's argument is that he is placing great emphasis Chariton's *failure* to "atticize" in a manner akin to the sophists of the second century, despite showing enough familiarity with classic Greek works to suggest the necessary skills for such a move. However, even should one accept this argument, it only eliminates the second century C.E., and perhaps the very late first century C.E., it hardly necessitates driving all the way back into the first century B.C.E. G. P. Goold questions Papanikolaou's certainty in the end, and opts for a range between 25 B.C.E. and 50 C.E.[29] Consuelo Ruiz-Montero has done the most detailed linguistic analysis and ultimately finds Papanikolaou's conclusions skewed by a failure to compare Chariton with *Atticist* documents alongside his comparison with *koiné.* Ruiz-Montero is convinced the language is better dated to "the last years of the first century A.D. or the beginning of the second."[30] B. P. Reardon's "guess" is approximately the middle of the first century C.E.[31] For Bowersock's hypothesis to work all one really needs is to stick with Reardon's "guess." As Bowersock correctly points out, Suetonius does offer evidence that Claudius' Rome was all too familiar with stories about Christ.[32] And the fact that Christians could function as a scapegoat for the burning of Rome strongly implies that Christians were a well known commodity in Nero's Rome.[33]

If I am correct in suggesting we cannot be definite on the date of Callirhoe, and that a mid-first century range is a good guess, indeed that even a date as late as the 60s C.E. is as plausible as any, *then I would wish to*

---

27. B. E. Perry, "Chariton and His Romance from a Literary-Historical Point of View," *AJP* 51 (1930): 93 n. 1; Elizabeth H. Haight, *Essays on the Greek Romances* (New York: Longmans, Green & Co., 1943), 12.

28. Antonios Papanikolaou, *Chariton-Studien: Untersuchen zur Sprache und Chronologie der griechischen romane* (Hypomnemata 37; Göttingen: Vandenhoeck & Ruprecht, 1973).

29. G. P. Goold, ed. and trans., *Chariton and Callirhoe* (LCL 481; Cambridge: Harvard University Press, 1995), 2.

30. Consuelo Ruiz-Montero, "Aspects of the Vocabulary of Chariton of Aphrodisias," *CQ* 41 (1991): 484–89.

31. Bryan P. Reardon, "Introduction to *Chaereas and Callirhoe*," in *Collected Ancient Greek Novels* (ed. Bryan P. Reardon; Berkeley and Los Angeles: University of California Press, 1989), 17. See also Bryan P. Reardon, "A. Chariton" in *The Novel in the Ancient World* (ed. Gareth Schmeling; Leiden: Brill, 1996): 309–35, esp. 312–25.

32. Bowersock, *Fiction as History*, 119; Suetonius, *Claudius* 25.4.

33. Tacitus, *Annals* 15.44.2–5.

argue strongly for its tradition-dependence on Christian empty-tomb stories such as we find later preserved in our four canonical Gospels.[34] I am not suggesting the *Scheintod* motif is necessarily borrowed from the Gospel tradition.[35] Rather, I wish to argue more narrowly *that using an early dawn discovery of an empty tomb in which the stone has been rolled away from the entrance is simply too similar not to suggest narrative dependence.* In Chariton's novel, Callirhoe has suffered a vicious kick from her new husband, who has been tricked by rival suitors into believing his bride is having an affair. She is hastily buried complete with enormous finery, and revives naturally in the tomb, awakening amidst funeral wreaths and ribbons and the prevalent smell of spices (ἄρωμα). Panic ensues, then weeping resignation, only to have her eternal rest disturbed by tomb robbers who are intent on bagging the funeral loot. They attack the tomb with crowbars and succeed in emptying the tomb of all its contents, including Callirhoe who now begins her traveling adventures around the Mediterranean. We follow the story of Callirhoe for a considerable period of time before the narrator returns to Syracuse in book 3 to tell what happened the morning after the burial.

The grave robbers, working in the dark of night, had failed to close up the tomb upon departing. Chaereas, we are told, waited until dawn (περίορθρος) to visit the tomb (τάφος), bringing with him wreaths and libations, but in actuality, intent on killing himself at his wife's tomb

---

34. Ronald Hock, "The Greek Novel," in *Greco-Roman Literature and the New Testament: Selected Forms and Genres* (ed. David E. Aune; SBLSBS 21; Atlanta: Scholars Press, 1988), 127–46 (134); and "Why New Testament Scholars Should Read Ancient Novels," in *Ancient Fiction and Early Christian Narrative* (ed. Ronald F. Hock et al.; SBLSymS 6; Atlanta: Scholars Press, 1998), 121–38, deserves a great deal of credit for his efforts in bringing work on ancient fiction into the study of early Christian narratives such as the Gospels. Curiously, on two occasions where he lays out a case for New Testament scholars consulting ancient novels and numerous parallels cited, the empty-tomb stories are mentioned in passing only once. It ought to be noted that Hock is considerably more cautious than the sort of scholarship represented by this paper—namely, he is not arguing for direct dependence between any of these ancient documents, only a shared sociocultural and linguistic milieu which allows one to illuminate the other. In the final editing stages of this article, I managed to begin N. T. Wrights's *The Resurrection of the Son of God* and there discovered his fascinating engagement with Chariton's *Callirhoe*, including a willingness to speculate that Bowersock's hypothesis as it pertains to the empty tombs is "by no means impossible" (68–73, esp. 72).

35. Indeed, I am not suggesting that the Gospel tradition is the primary source for most of the themes in the Greek novels—the *Scheintod* motif along with other features of the Greek novels can be found in Mediterranean literature that has been circulating for millennia as Graham Anderson points out in *Ancient Fiction: The Novel in the Graeco-Roman World* (London: Helm, 1984), 1–24. For an article that highlights the complexity of accounting for the Greek novel's existence, see Consuelo Ruiz-Montero's "The Rise of the Greek Novel," in Schmeling, *Novel in the Ancient World*, 29–85.

because he could not bear being separated from her. Arriving at the tomb, he discovers the stone (λίθος) has been moved (κεκινημένους)[36] and the entrance is wide open. The sight leaves him astonished (ἐκπλήσσω) and gripped by fearful perplexity (δεινῆς ἀπορίας). In his astonishment he remains outside the tomb until the swift messenger Rumor brings out the people of Syracuse to the opened tomb. Hermocrates, ruler of Syracuse and father of Callirhoe, gives the order and an unnamed man is sent in and he returns with an accurate report. As unbelievable as it may seem (ἄπιστον ἐδόκει), the corpse is not lying there (τὸ μηδὲ τὴν νεκρὰν κεῖσθαι). Chaereas decides to see for himself, but upon searching the tomb, is able to find nothing. Other disbelieving members of the crowd also enter, until finally someone notices the stolen funeral offerings and offers the explanation of tomb robbers. While the crowd offers a variety of undisclosed speculations, Chaereas himself is convinced this is the work of the gods, Callirhoe herself possibly being a goddess. Whatever the distraught groom may believe about Callirhoe and a possible heavenly translation, he sets himself to engage in a search by land and sea and even sky, if he must, to catch up to Callirhoe. Hermocrates, presumably in a hunt for the tomb robbers, sends out warships on a Mediterranean wide search. The classic chase around the Mediterranean, which is so much the hallmark of the Greek romance novel, has now begun in earnest for Chaereas.

It is fascinating to note parallels between Chariton's empty-tomb story and those of the Gospels. Remember on a source-critical level I am suggesting that Chariton is familiar with Christian empty-tomb stories along the lines of those preserved in retellings in the canonical Gospels. In terms of a purely literary intertextual reading, Chariton shares features with all four Gospels. As with all of the accounts, it begins in the early dawn, and like Mark and Luke, those heading to the tomb bear materials to finish the task of mourning the dead. As in Mark, Luke, and John, the person or persons arriving discover the stone covering the entrance of the tomb to have already been moved. Emotions of bewilderment and fear common to all the Gospel accounts are experienced here as well. Then in a curious parallel to John, Chariton has his hero hesitate on entering, another enters first, and only then does the hero enter and believe in the departure of the body having seen it for himself. Of course, if the text offered by UBS[4] is original, one has a similar phenomenon in Luke where the disciples do not believe the report of those who first entered the tomb, although Peter is willing to check out the matter for himself. As with both

---

36. Chariton, like Mark, Luke, and John, uses a perfect passive to describe the discovery of the moved stone.

the first tomb entries in John and the implied tomb inspection of Matthew, Chariton's tomb is well and truly empty—Luke and Mark and Mary's second visit in John all have figures awaiting those who enter the tomb, even if the tomb is empty of the body in question. The divergent opinions on what has become of the body in Chariton finds an echo in John especially with the varying reactions of Peter, the "other" disciple, and Mary (whose words in 20:2 and 15 imply some sort of tomb "robbery"). Finally, in an inversion of Matthew's empty-tomb story, in Chariton grave robbery is precisely the right conclusion that those discovering the empty tomb ought to draw. In Matthew, of course, in a move fraught with irony, the guards are first requested to prevent grave robbery and the spread of a false rumor, but upon failing in that duty, they are subsequently paid to spread the false rumor of grave robbery.

It appears that for the most part, the received view on Xenophon's *An Ephesian Tale* is that it is scavenging Chariton's work at a number of points. Graham Anderson specifically points to the tomb episode in *An Ephesian Tale* as an example of Xenophon's borrowing from Chariton.[37] Xenophon's work moves at a breathless pace compared to Chariton, and one is sometimes left with the distinct impression that our author is on a mission to see that every possible Greek romance novel plot device finds expression in his work, and, if possible, finds multiple expression. We pick up the tale in book 3, chapter 4, already having been warned by an oracle earlier in the novel that tombs will be a part of the couple's

---

37. "Introduction to An Ephesian Tale," in Reardon, *Collected Ancient Greek Novels*, 126. While the theory of Xenophon having borrowed story lines from Chariton has generally had widespread support, it should be noted that Bernhard Kytzler expresses some misgivings on establishing direct literary links, although he would concede some sort of connection and continues to suggest a second century C.E. date, "B. Xenophon of Ephesus" in Schmeling, *Novel in the Ancient World*, 336–359 (esp. 346–348). James N. O'Sullivan's hypothesis that Xenophon is actually our earliest example of the Greek novel and as such demonstrates that an oral tradition lies behind the genre as a whole could potentially wreck our tidy biography—Xenophon predating even a late first century Chariton makes our case for borrowing of motif from early Christian stories more problematic (*Xenophon of Ephesus: His Compositional Technique and the Birth of the Novel* [Berlin: de Gruyter, 1995]). John R. Morgan, review of J. N. O'Sullivan, *Xenophon of Ephesus: His Compositional Technique and the Birth of the Novel, JHS* 116 (1996): 199–200, finds the argument fascinating but ultimately raises some serious questions about what O'Sullivan's evidence may or may not establish (G. Schmeling is likewise fascinated, although noncommittal; review of J. N. O'Sullivan, *Xenophon of Ephesus, AJP* 117 [1996]: 660–63). Arguably, one could concede O'Sullivan's argument that Xenophon's composition betrays qualities of oral story-telling without that necessarily implying an early date—while the datable features of Xenophon (terms for officials in Egypt and Cilicia) are not much to go on and open to debate, they really are as close to hard evidence as exists and these suggest a second century date (Kytzler, "Xenophon," 347–48).

unhappy adventures (1.7). Anthia is in Tarsus, having been rescued from
a robbers' lair by Perilaus who is now intent on marrying her while she
remains intent on being true to her lost husband Habrocomes. She has the
fortune of meeting with a down and out physician from Ephesus,
Eudoxus, who reminds her of her hometown. As the day of the wedding
approaches, she ends up in a private conversation with Eudoxus, pouring
out her love and loyalty for Habrocomes who she is now convinced is
dead. She asks for a poison in order to commit suicide, promising to fund
Eudoxus' long desired return to Ephesus. Unbeknownst to Anthia,
Eudoxus returns not with a lethal poison but simply a sleeping-potion,
which allows him to gain what he needs to return home without having
Anthia's death on his conscience. When Anthia is alone in the bridal
chamber, she orders a cup of water, throws in the poison while in the pri-
vacy of the chamber, and collapses into a deep sleep. Thereafter follows
the typically hasty entombment and Anthia awakens in tomb and is
eventually comforted by the fact that she will be allowed to starve to
death inside. As expected, the sumptuous funeral leads pirates into temp-
tation and they remove the goods and the girl. Unlike Chariton, one
really does not have an empty-tomb discovery story directly narrated,
but only alluded to—not unexpected in this novel which packs in so
many twists and turns and endless adventures that at least some must be
mentioned merely in passing. The narrator informs us that Perilaus
learns that the tomb has been broken into, the body is gone, and he is left
grief-stricken. In a retelling of the account by an old woman in the presence of Habrocomes, we are told that the "pirates found out what was
buried with her, opened the grave, took the treasure, and spirited away
the body. And on that account Perilaus is searching far and wide" (3.9).[38]
Habrocomes too is convinced that he must set out on a quest to find
Anthia's body and when he does, embrace it, and be buried with her. The
empty-tomb discovery story has been so condensed as almost to disappear. It remains implied but not narrated. What does remain of the motif
are the explanations offered by those who discover the empty tombs—in
this case they are immediately convinced tomb robbers have departed
with a dead corpse. We are now a considerable distance from the Gospel
narratives and their version of the empty-tomb story, although the suspicion that individuals have robbed the grave and an incorrect belief that
the former tomb occupant is dead is comparable to Matthew's guards
and John's perplexed Mary Magdalene.

---

38. Translation taken from Graham Anderson, "An Ephesian Tale," in Reardon, *Collected Ancient Greek Novels*, 153.

The Empty Tomb in Glorious Death

Xenophon's *Ephesian Tale* evokes for contemporary readers a recollection of Shakespeare's *Romeo and Juliet* and the plot device that draws the play to its tragic conclusion.[39] In Geoffry Bullough's *Narrative and Dramatic Sources of Shakespeare,* Xenophon's *Ephesiaca* and the story we have just recalled is briefly stated under the heading of "Previous Versions of the Story."[40] Kermode likewise begins with *Ephesiaca* in discussing Shakespeare's sources.[41] Bullough traces the evolution of this motif through Masuccio's *Il Novellino* of 1476, a further development of the story in Luigi da Porto's *Istoria novellamente ritrovata di due Nobili Amanti* published in 1530, a French adaptation of Masuccio by Adrian Sevin in *Halquadrich and Burglipha* in 1542, a poem by Clízia in Venice in 1553, and ultimately to an adaptation of da Porto in Bandello's *novella* which was translated into French by Boiastuau in 1554. William Painter ultimately brought the work into English in *Palace of Pleasure* in 1567 but most scholars conclude that Shakespeare's main source for Romeo and Juliet was Arthur Brooke's long poem *The Tragicall Historye of Romeus and Juliet,* published in 1562 and also based on Boiastuau. Bullough describes Brooke's poem as "a leaden work which Shakespeare transmuted to gold,"[42] and other Shakespearean critics follow suit referring to Brooke's poem as "pedestrian, long-winded...in a lumbering pseudo-high style" and speak of the "miracle ... [of] what Shakespeare was able to make from it."[43] And it is to Shakespeare's *Romeo and Juliet* we now turn to in

---

39. Obviously I am not the first to see this connection; Anderson mentions it ("Introduction to *An Ephesian Tale,*" 125). Haight's clever synopsis of the Greek novels also makes this connection (*Greek Romances,* 58).

40. Geoffrey Bullough, ed., *Narrative and Dramatic Sources of Shakespeare* (vol. 1 of *Early Comedies, Poems, Romeo and Juliet;* 10 vols.; London: Routledge & Kegan Paul; New York: Columbia University Press, 1957), 269. Stuart Gillespie, *Shakespeare's Books: A Dictionary of Shakespeare Sources* (London: Athlone, 2001), 204–8, suggests possible direct but more likely distant links between Greek romance and Shakespeare, mentioning Xenophon's *Ephesiaca* in passing but not linking it directly to *Romeo and Juliet.* John W. Velz, *Shakespeare and the Classical Tradition: A Critical Guide to Commentary, 1660–1960* (Minneapolis: University of Minnesota Press, 1968), items 0178, 0207, 1900, 1909, 1963, 2096, 2294, notes at least seven scholarly works on Shakespeare that suggest a link between *Ephesiaca* and *Romeo and Juliet.* The follow-up volume compiled by Lewis Walker, *Shakespeare and the Classical Tradition: An annotated Bibliography 1961–1991* (New York: Routledge, 2002), items 2461–76, does not suggest any additional works linking *Ephesiaca* and *Romeo and Juliet* in the thirty years following Velz's volume.

41. Frank Kermode, "Romeo and Juliet" in *The Riverside Shakespeare* (ed. G. Blakemore Evans and J. J. M. Tobin; 2nd ed.; Boston: Houghton Mifflin, 1997), 1101.

42. Bullough, *Narrative,* 277–78.

43. G. Blakemore Evans, ed., *Romeo and Juliet* (Cambridge: Cambridge University Press, 1984), 8. Kermode describes Brooke's poem as "a very dull work" ("Romeo," 1101).

order to see our empty-tomb motif meet its most glorious demise, a death befitting such a fascinating birth and adolescence.

The demise of the empty-tomb motif begins with plans to create an empty tomb. We will enter the play here, in the exchange between Juliet and Friar Lawrence as he attempts to dissuade her from committing suicide now that Romeo has been exiled and her Father insists on her marrying County Paris. Friar Lawrence states,

> If rather than to marry County Paris,
> Thou hast the strength of will to slay thyself,
> Then it is likely thou wilt undertake
> A thing like death to chide away this shame,
> That cop'st with Death himself to scape from it;
> And if thou darest, I'll give thee remedy. (IV.i.71–75)[44]

Juliet responds in the affirmative, willing to endure all manner of horrible fates to prevent marriage to Paris, including entombment. Her words resonate in a curious and perhaps ironic fashion given the descriptions of Jesus' tombs in the Gospels (Matt 27:60, Luke 23:53, John 19:41),

> Or bid me go into a new-made grave,
> And hide me with a dead man in his shroud.

Friar Lawrence then offers Juliet a forty-two hour sleeping potion to be taken the night before her wedding. He lays out a plan in which she will be placed in the Capulet family vault, Romeo will be informed of the plan by letter, and both the Friar Lawrence and Romeo shall be present in the tomb when she awakens and the latter shall sweep her off to Mantua (IV.i.90–117). Unlike the fearful women of the Gospel accounts, or for that matter the terror stricken Callirhoe of Chariton who awakens in a tomb, Juliet is to put off "womanish fear" and indeed she responds with, "Give me, give me! O, tell not me of fear!" (IV.i.119–121). Xenophon's brave Anthia would be proud. Later, however, she is haunted by fears: fear of the potion being deadly, fear of waking too soon and being stifled in the vault or going mad at the sight of the bodies (IV.iii.14–54). Ironically, her fears are misplaced—the potion is not deadly, although Romeo's dagger will be, she will not wake too soon, but entirely too late, and she shall indeed slay herself, not at the sight of her kinsmen's bodies, but at the sight of Romeo's body. The problem with this empty-tomb plan is here

---

44. All quotions drawn from *The Riverside Shakespeare*.

foreshadowed—the empty tomb is already occupied and will only grow increasingly so as the plan is enacted.

Romeo, upon discovering Juliet's entombment, sets out as did Chaereas to end his life at the tomb, and as did the women in the Gospels, he purchases necessary materials to finish a task at the tomb. Only here it is death dealing poison rather than body preserving spices (V.i.85–86). Perhaps what goes most awry in this attempted empty-tomb scenario is the failure to observe correct timing—so much grief could have been prevented if only the tomb visits had been made at early dawn rather than at night. Both Paris and his page and Romeo and his servant Balthasar are intent on a midnight visit to Juliet's tomb. The page's warning and Romeo's torch provokes Paris to hide. Romeo arrives much as the tomb robbers of Chariton with tools in hand, forcing open the entrance. Once again, the empty-tomb scenario is violated—it will be left for the Friar Lawrence and Balthasar to discover a tomb with an *open* entrance. And indeed it is Romeo's attempted opening of the tomb that provokes Paris into a deadly duel. Romeo ultimately enters the tomb with an extra body—not a promising sign at all. In a strange twist, Romeo finds a full tomb and sees death where there is in reality life, while Chaereas finds an empty tomb and also sees death where there is in reality life. But like the Gospel stories, even this less than empty tomb is not without a dazzling presence, a shimmering personality. Upon entering and seeing Juliet's body, Romeo says,

> A grave? O no, a lanthorn, slaught'red youth;
> For here lies Juliet, and her beauty makes
> This vault a feasting presence full of light (V.iii.84–86)

And having added Paris to the tomb already containing Tybalt and Juliet, Romeo ingests his poison and adds to the crowded tomb. Friar Lawrence and Balthasar, as we just suggested, are the ones left to experience the tomb with the stone rolled away. As in John and *Callirhoe*, we have here two men, with only one willing to enter immediately. It is not in the end a woman who experiences fear at the tomb in Shakespeare, but a man—Friar Lawrence,

> Stay then, I'll go alone.
> Fear comes upon me.
>
> O, much I fear some ill unthrifty thing. (V.iii.134–135)

Friar Lawrence, despite the bloodied entrance, goes in to "seek the living among the dead" as the angels in Luke put it (24:5). However, despite finding Juliet alive, he cannot even at this stage procure a partially emptied tomb—his fear drives him back out of the tomb and Juliet is left behind with Romeo's dagger. Finally here we are back to a woman making a discovery in a tomb—unfortunately in an inversion of the Gospel stories the tomb that was expected to be empty is surprisingly full. Eventually a whole host of persons shall find their way into this less than empty tomb—and the tomb is simply bursting with individuals dead and alive by the closing dialogue. Only after the last lines are spoken, does the tomb rid itself of the living, leaving the numerous dead behind in silence. The empty-tomb motif meets death.

Epilogue

Fans of Fox Television's X-Files frequently witness the resurrection of the empty-tomb motif. It seems the empty tomb cannot itself be held in a grave any more than Jesus in the stories of the early Christians or heroines in the Greek romance novel. The creative afterlife of the empty-tomb motif suggests that the power of good storytelling may have had a good deal more to do with the success early Christianity had in converting pagans than doctrinal sophistication. Beyond the New Testament epistles so loved by German liberal Protestants and American fundamentalists lie the New Testament Gospels and the book of Acts, which speak to this storytelling tradition; beyond the second-century church fathers lie the apocryphal Gospels and Acts, which testify to the enduring vein of Christian storytelling.[45] It should not surprise us, therefore, that the Christian stories too could find their way into the most entertaining of pagan storytelling and that these stories would have a staying power that continues to this very day.

---

45. The link between the popularity of ancient novels and that of second-century apocryphal narratives circulating within Christianity has been most pressed by Richard Pervo on numerous occasions including his essay, "The Ancient Novel Becomes Christian," in Schmeling, *Novel in the Ancient World*, 685–709.

BIBLIOGRAPHY

EDITIONS AND TRANSLATIONS OF ANCIENT LITERATURE

Achilles Tatius. *Leucippe and Clitophon*. Translated by John J. Winkler. Pages 170–284 in *Collected Ancient Greek Novels*. Edited by Bryan P. Reardon. Berkeley and Los Angeles: University of California Press, 1989.

Aelian. *Aelian: Historical Miscellany*. Translated by Nigel G. Wilson. LCL 486. Cambridge: Harvard University Press, 1997.

Aeschylus. *Seven against Thebes*. Pages 20–52 in *Aeschylus: Prometheus Bound, The Suppliants, Seven against Thebes, and The Persians*. Translated by Philip Vellacott. Harmondsworth, U.K.: Penguin, 1961.

———. *The Persians*. Pages 122–52 in *Aeschylus: Prometheus Bound, The Suppliants, Seven against Thebes, and The Persians*. Translated by Philip Vellacott. Harmondsworth, U.K.: Penguin, 1961.

Allen, Thomas W., ed. *Homeri Opera*. 5 vols. Oxford: Oxford University Press, 1946.

Anderson, Hugh. "3 Maccabees." *OTP* 2:509–29.

Aphthonius, *Aphthonii Progymnasmata*. Pages 1–51 in Rhetores Graeci 10. Edited by Hugo Rabe. Leipzig: Teubner, 1926.

Apuleius. *Apuleius: The Golden Ass*. Translated by Patrick G. Walsh. New York: Oxford University Press, 1995.

Aristotle. *The Poetics*. Edited and translated by Stephen Halliwell, W. Hamilton Fyfe, and Doreen C. Innes. LCL 199. Cambridge: Harvard University Press, 1995.

Athenaeus *Deipnosophistae*. Translated by G. B. Gulick. 7 vols. LCL. Cambridge: Harvard University Press, 1937.

Athenagoras. *Legatio and de Resurrectione*. Edited by William R. Schoedel. OECT. Oxford: Clarendon, 1972.

Burchard, C., trans. "Joseph and Aseneth." *OTP* 2:177–247.

Chariton. *Callirhoe*. Edited and translated by G. P. Goold. LCL 481. Cambridge: Harvard University Press, 1995.

———. *Callirhoe*. Pages 21–224 in *Collected Ancient Greek Novels*. Edited by Bryan P. Reardon. Berkeley and Los Angeles: University of California Press, 1989.

———. *Charitonis Aphrodisiensis de Chaerea et Callirhoe Amatoriarum Narrationum Libri Octo*. Edited by Warren E. Blake. Oxford: Oxford University Press, 1938.

Elliot, James K., and M. R. James, eds. *The Apocryphal New Testament: A Collection of Apocryphal Christian Literature in an English Translation*. New York: Clarendon, 1993.

Euripides. *Iphigenia among the Taurians*. Pages 152–311 in *Euripides IV*. Edited and translated by David Kovacs. LCL 10. Cambridge: Harvard University Press, 1999.

———. *Trojan Women*. Pages 15–143 in *Euripides IV*. Edited and translated by David Kovacs. LCL 10. Cambridge: Harvard University Press, 1999.

Eusebius. *Ecclesiastical History*. Translated by Kirsopp Lake. 2 vols. LCL. Cambridge: Harvard University Press, 1959.

Ezekiel the Tragedian. *The Exagoge*. Pages 50–67 in *The Exagoge of Ezekiel*. Edited and translated by Howard Jacobson. Cambridge: Cambridge University Press, 1983.

Freedman, H., and Maurice Simon, trans. *Exodus Rabbah*. London: Soncino, 1939.

Gregory of Nazianzus. *Oratio in laudem Basilii*. Edited by J.-P. Migne. PG 35. Paris: Migne, 1844–64.

Hadas, Moses, trans. *The Third and Fourth Books of Maccabees*. New York: Harper, 1953.

Hanhart, Robert, ed. *Maccabaeorum liber III*. 2nd ed. Septuaginta, Vetus Testamentum graecum 9/3. Göttingen: Vandenhoeck & Ruprecht, 1980.

Hermogenes. *Hermogenis Opera*. Pages 1–27 in Rhetores Graeci 6. Edited by Hugo Rabe. Stuttgart: Teubner, 1913.

Homer. *The Iliad*. Translated with an introduction by Richmond Lattimore. Chicago: University of Chicago Press, 1951.

———. *The Iliad*. Edited by William Wyatt. Translated by A. T. Murray. 2 vols. LCL 170–171. Cambridge: Harvard University Press, 1925.

———. *The Odyssey*. Translated by Richmond Lattimore. New York: Harper & Row, 1965, 1967.

Horace. *Ars poetica*. Pages 450–89 in *Satires, Epistles, and Ars poetica*. Translated by H. Rushton Fairclough. LCL 194. Cambridge: Harvard University Press, 1978.

Junod, Eric, and Jean Daniel Kaestli, eds. *Acta Iohannis*. 2 vols. Corpus Christianorum, Series Apocryphorum 1–2. Turnhout: Brepols, 1983.

Lipsius, Richard A., and Max Bonnet, eds. *Acta Apostolorum Apocrypha*. Vol. 2. Darmstadt: Olms, 1891–98. Repr., Darmstadt: Olms, 1959.

Musurillo, Herbert, ed. and trans. *The Acts of the Christian Martyrs*. OECT. Oxford: Clarendon, 1972.

Nicolaus. *Nicolai Progymnasmata*. Pages 1–79 in Rhetores Graeci 11. Edited by Joseph Felten. Leipzig: Teubner, 1913.

Origin. *Origen: Contra Celsum*. Edited by Henry Chadwick. Cambridge: Cambridge University Press, 1953.

Plato. *Republic*. Translated by Paul Shorey. 2 vols. LCL 237, 276. Cambridge: Harvard University Press, 1935–37.

———. *The Republic*. Translated by Benjamin Jowett in *The Republic of Plato: An Ideal Commonwealth*. New York: Willey, 1901.

Plutarch. *Isis and Osiris*. Pages 7–191 in *Moralia V*. Translated by F. C. Babbitt. LCL 306. Cambridge: Harvard University Press, 1936.

———. *The Rise and Fall of Athens: Nine Greek Lives by Plutarch*. Translated by Ian Scott-Kilvert. Harmondsworth, U.K.: Penguin, 1960.

Quintilian. *The Orators Education*. Edited and translated by Donald A. Russell. 5 vols. LCL 124–127, 494. Cambridge: Harvard University Press, 2002.

Rahlf, Alfred, ed. *Septuagint*. Stuttgart: Deutsche Bibelgesellschaft, 1935.

Rufus of Perinthus. *Techne Rhetorike*. Pages 399–407 in *Rhetores Graeci*. Edited by Leonard Spengel and Caspar Hammer. Leipzig: Teubner, 1894.

Sanders, E. P., trans. "The Testament of Abraham." *OTP* 1:871–902.

Schmidt, Francis. *Le Testament grec d'Abraham: Introduction, edition critique des deux recensions grecques, traduction*. Tübingen: Mohr Siebeck, 1986.

Seneca. *Epistles*. Translated by Richard M. Gummere. 3 vols. LCL 75–77. Cambridge: Harvard University Press, 1917–25.

Shinan, A., ed. *Midrash Shemot Rabbah* [Hebrew]. Tel-Aviv: Dvir, 1984.

Shutt, R. J. H., trans. "Letter of Aristeas." *OTP* 2:7–34.

Stesichorus. In *Greek Lyric III*. Translated by David A. Campbell. LCL 476. Cambridge: Harvard University Press, 1991.

Stoops, Robert, trans. *New Testament Apocrypha*. Sonoma, Calif.: Polebridge, forthcoming.

Tertullian. *Treatise on the Resurrection: De Resurrectione Carnis Liber*. Edited by Ernest Evans. London: SPCK, 1960.

Theodor, Julius, and Chanoch Albeck, eds. *Bereshit Rabbah* [Hebrew]. Jerusalem: Wahrman, 1965.

Theon. *Progymnasmata*. In *Rhetores Graeci*. Edited by Christian Walz. 9 vols. Tübingen: Cottae, 1832–36. Repr., Osnabrück: Zeller, 1968.

Vergil. *Virgil Aeneid Book VIII*. Edited by K. W. Gransden. Cambridge: Cambridge University Press, 1976.

———. *The Aeneid of Virgil: Books 7–12*. Edited by R. D. Williams. London: Macmillan, 1973.

Vermes, Geza, trans. *The Dead Sea Scrolls in English*. 4th ed. London: Penguin, 1995.

Xenophon. *Anabasis*. Translated by Carleton L. Brownson. Revised by John Dillery. LCL 90. Harvard: Harvard University Press, 1998.

———. *Cyropaedia*. Translated by Walter Miller. 2 vols. LCL 51–52. Cambridge: Harvard University Press, 1914.

———. *Xenophon: The Persian Expedition*. Translated by Rex Warner. Harmondsworth, U.K.: Penguin, 1949.

Xenophon of Ephesus. *An Ephesian Tale*. Pages 125–69 in *Collected Ancient Greek Novels*. Edited by Bryan P. Reardon. Translated by Graham Anderson. Berkeley and Los Angeles: University of California Press, 1989.

Ziegler, Joseph, ed. *Susanna, Daniel, Bel et Draco*. Septuaginta, Vetus Testamentum graecum16. Göttingen: Vandenhoeck and Ruprecht, 1999.

Secondary Scholarship

Achtemeier, Paul J. *1 Peter*. Edited by E. J. Epp. Hermeneia. Minneapolis: Fortress, 1996.

Adams, Percy G. *Travel Literature and the Evolution of the Novel*. Lexington: University Press of Kentucky, 1983.

Adrados, F. Rodríguez. *History of the Graeco-Latin Fable*. Translated by Leslie A. Ray. 3 vols. Mnemosyne, Bibliotheca Classica Batava, Supplementum 201. Leiden: Brill, 1999.

Albertz, Rainer G. "Bekehrung von oben als 'messianische Programm': Die Son-derüberlieferung der Septuaginta in Dan 4–6." Pages 46–62 in *Theologische Probleme der Septuaginta und der hellenistischen Hermeneutik*. Edited by Henning Graf Reventlow. Veröffentlichungen der Wissenschaftlichen Gesellschaft für Theologie 11. Munich: Kaiser & Gütersloher, 1997.

Albrektson, Bertil. "Reflections on the Emergence of a Standard Text of the Hebrew Bible." Pages 49–65 in *Congress Volume: Göttingen, 1977*. Edited by John A. Emerton. VTSup 29. Leiden: Brill, 1978.

Alexander, Loveday. "Paul and the Hellenistic Schools: The Evidence of Galen." Pages 60–83 in *Paul in His Hellenistic Context*. Edited by Troels Engberg-Pedersen. Edinburgh: T&T Clark, 1994.

———, ed. *Images of Empire*. JSOTSup 122. Sheffield: Sheffield Academic Press, 1991.

Allison, Dale C., Jr. *Testament of Abraham*. Berlin: de Gruyter, 2003.

Anderson, Graham. *Ancient Fiction: The Novel in the Graeco-Roman World*. London: Helm, 1984.

———. *The Novel in the Graeco-Roman World*. Totowa, N.J.: Barnes & Noble, 1984.

———. "Introduction to An Ephesian Tale," Pages 125–28 in *Collected Ancient Greek Novels*. Edited by Bryan P. Reardon. Berkeley and Los Angeles: University of California Press, 1989.

Anderson, Hugh. *The Jews of Egypt*. Translated by Robert Cornman. Philadelphia: Jewish Publication Society, 1995.

Arrowsmith, William. "Chorus." Pages 201–2 in *The New Princeton Encyclopedia of Poetry and Poetics*. Princeton: Princeton University Press, 1993.

Ascough, Richard, "Christianity in Caesarea Maritima." Pages 153–79 in *Religious Rivalries and the Struggle for Success in Caesarea Maritima*. Edited by Terence L. Donaldson. Waterloo, Ont.: Wilfrid Laurier University Press, 2000.

———. "Narrative Technique and Generic Designation: Crowd Scenes in Luke-Acts and in Chariton." *CBQ* 58 (1996): 69–81.

Austin, Rita G., *P Vergili Maronis Aeneidos Liber Primus*. Oxford: Clarendon, 1971.

———. *P Vergili Maronis Aeneidos Liber Quartus*. Oxford: Clarendon, 1982.

———. *P Vergili Maronis Aeneidos Liber Sextus*. Oxford: Clarendon, 1977.

Bacon, Helen H. "The Chorus in Greek Life and Drama." *Arion* 3 (1995): 6–24.

Bain, David. *Actors and Audience*. Oxford: Oxford University Press, 1977.

Balch, David L. "ΜΕΤΑΒΟΛΗ ΠΟΛΙΤΕΙΩΝ—Jesus as Founder of the Church in Luke-Acts: Form and Function." Pages 139–88 in *Contextualizing Acts: Lukan Narrative and Greco Roman Discourse*. Edited by Todd Penner and Caroline Vander Stichele. SBLSymS 20. Atlanta: Society of Biblical Literature, 2003.

———. "The Suffering of Isis/Io and Paul's Portrait of Christ Crucified (Gal. 3:1): Frescoes in Pompeian and Roman Houses and in the Temple of Isis in Pompeii." *JR* 83 (2003): 24–55.

Baldry, H. C. *Ancient Utopias*. University of Southhampton Inaugural Lecture. Southhampton, U.K.: University of Southhampton, 1956.

Balsdon, John P. V. D. *Roman Women: Their History and Habits*. New York: Barnes & Noble, 1962.

Band, Arnold J. "Swallowing Jonah: The Eclipse of Parody." *Prooftexts* 10 (1990): 179–95.

Barclay, John M. G. *Jews in the Mediterranean Diaspora: From Alexander to Trajan (323 BCE- 117 CE)*. Edinburgh: T&T Clark, 1996.

Barrett, Anthony A. *Agrippina: Sex, Power, and Politics in the Early Empire*. New Haven: Yale University Press, 1996.

Barrett, Charles K. *Acts of the Apostles*. 2 vols. ICC. Edinburgh: T&T Clark, 1994–98.

Bartchy, S. Scott. "Community of Goods in Acts: Idealization or Social Reality?" Pages 309–18 in *The Future of Early Christianity: Essays in Honor of Helmut Koester*. Edited by Birger Pearson. Minneapolis: Fortress, 1991.

Batey, Richard A. "Jesus and the Theatre." *NTS* 30 (1984): 563–74.

Bauckham, Richard. "John for Readers of Mark." Pages 147–71 in *The Gospels for All Christians: Rethinking the Gospel Audiences*. Edited by Richard Bauckham. Grand Rapids: Eerdmans, 1998.

Bauer, Walter. "Jesus' Earthly Appearance and Character." Pages 433–36 in vol. 1 of *New Testament Apocrypha*. Edited by Edgar Hennecke. Translated by R. McL. Wilson. Philadelphia: Westminster, 1963.

Baumgartner, Walter. *Das Buch Daniel*. Giessen: Töpelmann, 1926.

Beck, Roger. "Ritual, Myth, Doctrine, and Initiation in the Mysteries of Mithras: New Evidence from a Cult Vessel." *JRS* 90 (2000): 145–80.

Ben-Porat, Ziva. "Parody's Revenge: Or the (Im)possibility of Postmodernist Claims Concerning Parody and Pastiche." Pages 417–23 in *Parodia, Pastiche, Mimetismo*. Edited by Paola Mildonian. Rome: Bulzoni, 1997.

Benson, Larry D. *The Riverside Chaucer*. 3rd ed. Boston: Houghton Mifflin, 1987.

Bernard, John D., ed. *Vergil at 2000: Commemorative Essays on the Poet and His Influence*. New York: AMS Press, 1986.

Best, Ernest. "Mark's Preservation of the Tradition." Pages 119–33 in *The Interpretation of Mark*. Edited by William Telford. Issues in Religion and Theology 7. Philadelphia: Fortress, 1985.

Beye, Charles Rowan. *Ancient Epic Poetry: Homer, Apollonius, Virgil*. Ithaca, N.Y.: Cornell University Press, 1993.

Bickermann, Elias J. "Makkabaerbucher (III)." PW 27:799.

Bierl, Anton. *Der Chor in der alten Komödie: Ritual und Performativität*. Leipzig: Saur, 2001.

Black, Fiona. "Lost Prophecies! Scholars Amazed! *Weekly World News* and the Bible." Pages 20–43 in *Culture, Entertainment and the Bible*. Edited by George Aichele. JSNTSup 309. Sheffield: Sheffield Academic Press, 2000.

Bludau, August. *Die alexandrinische Übersetzung des Buches Daniels und ihr Verhältnis zum massoretischen Texten*. Freiburg: Herder, 1897.

Boitani, Piero. *English Medieval Narrative in the Thirteenth and Fourteenth Centuries*. Cambridge: Cambridge University Press, 1982.

Bolyki, Janos. "Miracle Stories in the Acts of John." Pages 15–35 in *Apocryphal Acts of John*. Edited by Jan N. Bremmer. Kampen: Kok Pharos, 1995.

Bonner, Stanley F. *Education in Antiquity: From the Elder Cato to the Younger Pliny*. Berkeley and Los Angeles: University of California Press, 1977.

Bonz, Marianne Palmer. *The Past as Legacy: Luke-Acts and Ancient Epic*. Minneapolis: Fortress, 2000.

Booth, Alan. "Elementary and Secondary Education in the Roman Empire." *Florilegium* 1 (1979): 1–14.

Borg, Marcus J., and N. T. Wright. *The Meaning of Jesus: Two Visions*. San Francisco: HarperSanFrancisco, 1999.

Bosworth, Brian. "Augustus, the Res Gestae and Hellenistic Theories of Apotheosis." *JRS* 89 (1999): 1–18.

Bowersock, Glen W. *Fiction as History: Nero to Julian*. Berkeley and Los Angeles: University of California Press, 1994.

Bowie, Ewen L., and Stephen J. Harrison. "The Romance of the Novel." *JRS* 83 (1993): 159–78.

Bovon, Francois. "The Synoptic Gospels and the Noncanonical Acts of the Apostles." *HTR* 81 (1998): 19–36.

Bradley, Keith R. *Slaves and Masters in the Roman Empire: A Study in Social Control*. Collection Latomus 185. Brussels: Latomus, 1984.

———. *Slavery and Society at Rome*. Key Themes in Ancient History. Cambridge: Cambridge University Press, 1994.

Branca, Vittore. *Boccaccio: The Man and His Works*. Translated by Richard Monges. New York: New York University Press, 1976.

Brant, Jo-Ann A. *Dialogue and Drama: Elements of Greek Tragedy in the Fourth Gospel*. Peabody, Mass.: Hendrickson, 2004.

Breitenbach, Alfred. "Drama." Pages 102–5 in *Neues Testament und Antike Kultur*. Vol. 1 of *Prolegomena-Quellen-Geschichte*. Edited by Kurt Erlemann and Karl Leo Noethlichs. Neukirchen-Vluyn: Neukirchener, 2004.

Bremmer, Jan N. *The Apocryphal Acts of John*. Vol. 1 of *Studies on the Apocryphal Acts of the Apostles*. Kampen: Kok Pharos, 1995.

———. *The Apocryphal Acts of Paul and Thecla*. Vol. 2 of *Studies on the Apocryphal Acts of the Apostles*. Kampen: Kok Pharos, 1996.

———. *The Apocryphal Acts of Peter: Magic, Miracles and Gnosticism*. Vol. 3 of *Studies on the Apocryphal Acts of the Apostles*. Leuven: Peeters, 1998.

Bremmer, Jan N., and Lourens van den Bosch. *Between Poverty and the Pyre: Moments in the History of Widowhood*. New York: Routledge. 1995.

Brenner, Athalya. "Jonah's Poem Out of and Within Its Context" Pages 183–92 in *Among the Prophets: Language, Image, and Structure in the Prophetic Writings*. Edited by Philip R. Davies and David J. A. Clines. JSOTSup 144. Sheffield: JSOT Press, 1993.

Brilliant, Richard. "'Let the Trumpets Roar!' The Roman Triumph." Pages 221–29 in *The Art of Ancient Spectacle*. Edited by Bettina Bergmann and Christine Kondoleon. Studies in the History of Art 56. New Haven: Yale University Press, 1999.

Broadhead, Edwin R. *Mark*. Sheffield: Sheffield Academic Press, 2001.

Brodie, Thomas Louis. "The Accusing and Stoning of Naboth (1 Kgs 21:8–13) as One Component of the Stephen Text." *CBQ* 45 (1984): 417–32.

———. "Greco-Roman Imitation of Texts as a Partial Guide to Luke's Use of Sources." Pages 17–46 in *Luke-Acts: New Perspectives from the Society of Biblical Literature Seminar*. Edited by Charles H. Talbert. New York: Crossroad, 1984.

———. "Luke-Acts as an Imitation and Emulation of the Elijah-Elisha Narratives." Pages 78–85 in *New Views on Luke and Acts*. Edited by Earl Richards. Collegeville, Minn.: Liturgical Press, 1990.

————. "Towards Unraveling Luke's Use of the Old Testament: Luke 7.11–17 as an *Imitatio* of 1 Kings 17.17–24." *NTS* 32 (1986): 247–67.

Broek, Roelof van den. *The Myth of the Phoenix according to Classical and Early Christian Traditions.* Leiden: Brill, 1971.

Brosend, William F., II. "The Means of Absent Ends." Pages 348–62 in *History, Literature and Society in the Book of Acts.* Edited by Ben Witherington III. Cambridge: Cambridge University Press, 1996.

Brown, Raymond E. *The Death of the Messiah: From Gethsemane to the Grave.* 2 vols. New York: Doubleday, 1994.

————. *The Virginal Conception and Bodily Resurrection of Jesus.* New York: Paulist, 1973.

Bruce, F. F. *The Acts of the Apostles: The Greek Text with Introduction and Commentary.* London: Tyndale, 1951. Repr., Grand Rapids: Eerdmans, 1990.

Bullough, Geoffrey, ed. *Narrative and Dramatic Sources of Shakespeare.* Vol. 1 of *Early Comedies, Poems, Romeo and Juliet.* 10 vols. London: Routledge & Kegan Paul; New York: Columbia University Press, 1957.

Bultmann, Rudolf. *History of the Synoptic Tradition.* Translated by John Marsh. New York: Harper & Row, 1963.

Burton, Reginald W. B. *The Chorus in Sophocles' Tragedies.* Oxford: Clarendon, 1980.

Bynum, Caroline Walker. *The Resurrection of the Body in Western Christianity, 200–1336.* Lectures on the History of Religions, New Series 15. New York: Columbia University Press, 1995.

Cadbury, Henry J. *The Making of Luke-Acts.* New York: MacMillan, 1927.

————. "The Summaries in Acts." Pages 392–402 in *The Acts of the Apostles: Additional Notes.* Vol. 5 of *The Beginnings of Christianity.* Edited by Henry J. Cadbury and Kirsopp Lake. London: MacMillan, 1933.

Calame, Claude. "Performative Aspects of the Choral Voice in Greek Tragedy: Civic Identity in Performance." Pages 125–53 in *Performance Culture and Athenian Democracy.* Edited by Simon Goldhill and Ryan Osborne. Cambridge: Cambridge University Press, 1998.

Cameron, Averil. *Christianity and the Rhetoric of Empire: The Development of Christian Discourse.* Berkeley and Los Angeles: University of California Press, 1994.

Cancik, Hubert. "The History of Culture, Religion and Institutions in Ancient Historiography: Philological Observations Concerning Luke's History." *JBL* 116 (1997): 673–95.

Capper, Brian. "The Palestinian Cultural Context of Earliest Christian Community of Goods." Pages 327–57 in *The Book of Acts in Its First Century Setting.* Edited by R. Bauckham. Vol. 4 of *The Book of Acts in Its Palestinian Setting.* Grand Rapids: Eerdmans, 1995.

Carter, Warren. "The Crowds in Matthew's Gospel." *CBQ* 55 (1993): 54–67.

Cartlidge, David R. "Transfigurations of Metamorphosis Traditions in the Acts of John, Thomas and Peter." *Semeia* 38 (1986): 53–66.

Cartlidge, David R., and J. Keith Elliott. *Art and Christian Apocrypha.* New York: Routledge, 2001.

Cenival, Françoise de. *Le Mythe de l'Oeil du Soleil.* Demotische Studien 9. Sommerhausen: Zauzich, 1988.

Cerfaux, Lucien. "La composition de la premiere partie du Livre des Actes." *ETL* (1936): 667–91.

Certeau, Michel de. "History: Science and Fiction." Pages 37–52 in *The Certeau Reader*. Edited by Graham Ward. Oxford: Blackwell, 2000.

Chaucer, Geoffery. *The Canterbury Tales*. Oxford: Clarendon, 1989.

Clark, Raymond J. *Catabasis: Vergil and the Wisdom-Tradition*. Amsterdam: Gruner, 1978.

Co, Maria Anicia. "The Major Summaries in Acts (Acts 2,42–47; 4,32–35; 5,12–16): Linguistic and Literary Relationship." *ETL* 68 (1992): 49–85.

Cohen, Jakob. *Judaica et Aegyptiaca, de Maccabaeorum libro III Quaestiones historicae*. Groningen: Waal, 1941.

Collart, Paul. *Les Papyrus Bouriant*. Paris: Champion, 1926.

Collins, John J. *Between Athens and Jerusalem: Jewish Identity in the Hellenistic Diaspora*. Grand Rapids: Eerdmans, 2000.

———. *Daniel: A Commentary on the Book of Daniel*. Hermenia. Minneapolis: Fortress, 1993.

———. "New Light on the Book of Daniel from the Dead Sea Scrolls." Pages 180–96 in *Perspectives in the Study of the Old Testament and Early Judaism: A Symposium in Honour of Adam S. van der Woude on the Occasion of His 70th Birthday*. Edited by Florentino García Martínez and Ed Noort. NovTSup 73. Leiden: Brill, 1998.

———. *The Scepter and the Star: The Messiahs of the Dead Sea Scrolls and Other Ancient Literature*. Garden City, N.Y.: Doubleday, 1995.

Condren, Edward I. *Chaucer and the Energy of Creation: The Design and the Organization of the Canterbury Tales*. Gainesville: University Press of Florida, 1999.

Conte, Gian Biagio. *The Rhetoric of Imitation*. Translated and edited by Charles Segal. Ithaca, N.Y.: Cornell University Press, 1986.

Conzelmann, Hans. *Acts of the Apostles: A Commentary*. Translated by James Limburg, A. Thomas Kraabel, and Donald H. Juel. Hermeneia. Philadelphia: Fortress, 1987.

———. *1 Corinthians*. Translated by James W. Leitch. Philadelphia: Fortress, 1975.

Cooper, Helen. *The Structure of the Canterbury Tales*. Athens: University of Georgia Press, 1983.

Cotter, Wendy. "Cornelius, the Roman Army and Religion." Pages 279–301 in *Religious Rivalries and the Struggle for Success in Caesarea Maritima*. Edited by Terence L. Donaldson. Waterloo, Ont.: Wilfrid Laurier University Press, 2000.

Cousland, J. R. C. *The Crowds in Matthew's Gospel*. NovTSup 102. Leiden: Brill, 2002.

———. "Dionysus *Theomachos*? Echoes of the *Bacchae* in 3 Maccabees." *Bib* 82 (2001): 539–48.

———. "The Feeding of the Four Thousand *Gentiles*? Matthew 15:29–38 as a Test Case." *NovT* 41 (1999): 1–23.

Cox, Roger L. "Tragedy and the Gospel Narratives." *Yale Review* 57 (1968): 545–70.

Craven, Toni. *Artistry and Faith in the Book of Judith*. SBLDS 70. Chico, Calif.: Scholars Press, 1983.

Cribiore, Raffaella. *Education in Greek and Roman Antiquity*. Edited by Yun Lee Too. Leiden: Brill, 2001.

———. *Gymnastics of the Mind: Greek Education in Hellenistic and Roman Egypt.* Princeton: Princeton University Press, 2001.

———. *Writing, Teachers, and Students in Graeco-Roman Egypt.* American Studies in Papyrology 36. Atlanta: Scholars Press, 1996.

Crossan, John Dominic. *The Birth of Christianity: Discovering What Happened in the Years Immediately after the Execution of Jesus.* San Francisco: HarperSanFrancisco, 1998.

———. *The Cross That Spoke: The Origins of the Passion Narrative.* San Francisco: Harper & Row, 1988.

———. "Historical Jesus as Risen Lord." Pages 8–26 in *The Jesus Controversy: Perspectives in Conflict.* Edited by John Dominic Crossan, Luke Timothy Johnson, and Werner H. Kelber. Harrisburg, Pa.: Trinity Press International, 1999.

———. *The Historical Jesus: The Life of a Mediterranean Jewish Peasant.* San Francisco: HarperSanFrancisco, 1991.

———. *Jesus: A Revolutionary Biography.* San Francisco: HarperSanFrancisco, 1994.

———. *The Jesus Controversy: Perspectives in Conflict.* Harrisburg, Pa.: Trinity Press International, 1999.

Csapo, Eric, and William Slater. *The Context of Ancient Drama.* Ann Arbor: University of Michigan Press, 1995.

Dale, A. M. "The Chorus in the Action of Greek Tragedy." Pages 210–20 in idem, *Collected Works.* Cambridge: Cambridge University Press, 1969.

Danove, Paul L. *The End of Mark's Story: A Methodological Study.* Leiden: Brill, 1993.

D'Arms, John H. *Commerce and Social Standing in Ancient Rome.* Cambridge: Harvard University Press, 1981.

Davies, J. G. "Factors Leading to the Emergence of Belief in the Resurrection of the Flesh." *JTS* 23 (1972): 448–55.

Dawson, Doyne. *Cities of the Gods: Communist Utopias in Greek Thought.* New York: Oxford University Press, 1992.

Dean-Otting, Mary. *Heavenly Journeys: A Study of the Motif in Hellenistic Jewish Literature.* Frankfurt: Lang, 1984.

Debut, Janine. "De l'usage des listes de mots comme fondement de la pédagogie dans l'antiquité." *REA* 85 (1983): 261–74.

———. "Les documents scholaires." *ZPE* 63 (1986): 251–78.

Deissmann, Gustav Adolf. *Bible Studies.* Edinburgh: T&T Clark, 1901.

Dibelius, Martin. *Studies in the Acts of the Apostles.* Edited by Heinrich Greeven. London: SCM, 1956.

———. "Style Criticism of the Book of Acts." Pages 1–25 in *Studies in the Acts of the Apostles.* Edited by Heinrich Greeven. New York: Scribner's, 1956.

Di Lella, Alexander A., and Louis F. Hartman. *The Book of Daniel.* AB 23. New York: Doubleday, 1978.

Dihle, Albrecht. *Greek and Latin Literature of the Roman Empire. From Augustus to Justinian.* London: Routledge, 1994.

DiTommaso, L. *A Bibliography of Pseudepigrapha Research.* JSPSup 39. Sheffield: Sheffield Academic Press, 2001.

Donaldson, Terence L., ed. *Religious Rivalries and the Struggle for Success in Caesarea Maritima.* Waterloo, Ont.: Wilfrid Laurier University Press, 2000.

Donelson, Lewis R., "Cult Histories and the Sources of Acts." *Bib* 68 (1987): 1–21.

Doody, Margaret. *The True Story of the Novel.* New Brunswick, N.J.: Rutgers University Press, 1996.

Doran, Robert. "Narrative Literature." Pages 287–310 in *Early Judaism and Its Modern Interpreters.* Edited by Robert A. Kraft and George W. E. Nickelsburg. Atlanta: Scholars Press, 1986.

Dupont, Jacques. "Community of Goods in the Early Church." Pages 85–102 in *The Salvation of the Gentiles: Studies in the Acts of the Apostles.* New York: Paulist, 1979.

———. *The Sources of Acts.* Translated by Kathleen Pond. New York: Herder & Herder, 1964.

Eagleton, Terry. *Literary Theory: An Introduction.* Oxford: Blackwell, 1983.

Easterling, P. E. "Constructing Character in Greek Tragedy." Pages 82–99 in *Characterization and Individuality in Greek Literature.* Edited by Christopher Pelling. Oxford: Clarendon, 1990.

Edmondson, Jonathan C. "The Cultural Politics of Public Spectacle in Rome and the Greek East, 167–166 B.C.E." Pages 77–95 in *The Art of Ancient Spectacle.* Edited by Bettina Bergmann and Christine Kondoleon. Studies in the History of Art 56. New Haven: Yale University Press, 1999.

Elam, Kier. *The Semiotics of Theatre and Drama.* London: Routledge, 1980.

Epstein, Morris. *Tales of Sendebar.* Philadelphia: Jewish Publication Society of America, 1967.

Esposito, Stephen. "The Changing Roles of the Sophoclean Chorus." *Arion* 4 (1996): 85–114.

Evans, G. Blakemore and J. J. M. Tobin, eds. *Riverside Edition of Shakespeare.* 2nd ed. Boston: Houghton Mifflin, 1997.

Exum, J. Cheryl. *Tragedy and Biblical Narrative.* Cambridge: Cambridge University Press, 1992.

Farrell, Joseph. "The Virgilian Intertext." Pages 222–238 in *The Cambridge Companion to Virgil.* Edited by Charles Martindale. Cambridge: Cambridge University Press, 1997.

Fehling, Detlev. *Herodotus and His "Sources": Citation, Invention and Narrative Art.* Translated by J. G. Howie. Leeds: Cairns, 1989.

Ferguson, John. *Utopias of the Classical World.* Ithaca, N.Y.: Cornell University Press, 1975.

Finkelpearl, Ellen. "Pagan Traditions of Intertextuality in the Roman World." Pages 78–90 in *Mimesis and Intertextuality in Antiquity and Christianity.* Edited by Dennis R. MacDonald. Harrisburg, Pa.: Trinity Press International, 2001.

Fiske, George C. *Lucilius and Horace: A Study of the Classical Theory of Imitation.* Madison: University of Wisconsin Press, 1920. Repr., New York: Herder & Herder, 1964.

Fitzgerald, William. "Labor and Laborer in Latin Poetry." *Arethusa* 29 (1996): 389–418.

Fitzmyer, Joseph A. *The Acts of the Apostles.* AB 31. New York: Doubleday, 1997.

———. *The Gospel according to Luke.* 2 vols. AB 28–28A. New York: Doubleday, 1985.

Flint, Peter. "The Daniel Tradition at Qumran." Pages 329–67 in *The Book of Daniel: Composition and Reception.* Edited by John J. Collins and Peter W. Flint. VTSup

83. Leiden: Brill, 2001.

Flinterman, Jaap-Jan. "De Tweede Sofistiek: Een Portie Gebakken Lucht?" *Lampas* 29 (1996): 135–54.

Fraser, Peter M. *Ptolemaic Alexandria*. 3 vols. Oxford: Oxford University Press, 1972.

Fuks, Alexander. "Dositheos Son of Drimylos: A Prosopographical Note." *JJP* 7–8 (1954): 205–9.

Funk, Robert, et al. *The Acts of Jesus: The Search for the Authentic Deeds of Jesus.* San Francisco: HarperSanFrancisco, 1998.

Gabba, Emilio. "True History and False History in Classical Antiquity." *JRS* 71 (1981): 50–62.

Gallagher, Eugene V. "Conversion and Salvation in the Apocryphal Acts of the Apostles." *SecCent* 8 (1991): 13–29.

Gardiner, Cynthia P. *The Sophoclean Chorus: A Study of Character and Function.* Iowa City: University of Iowa Press, 1987.

Garnsey, Peter. *Ideas of Slavery from Aristotle to Augustine.* W. B. Stanford Memorial Lectures. Cambridge: Cambridge University Press, 1996.

Garnsey, Peter, and Richard Saller. *The Roman Empire. Economy, Society and Culture.* Berkeley and Los Angeles: University of California Press, 1987.

Giamatti, A. Bartlett. *The Earthly Paradise and the Renaissance Epic.* New York: Norton, 1966.

Giangrande, Lawrence. "Les Utopies Hellenistiques." *Cahiers d'Etudes Anciennes* 5 (1976): 17–33.

Gill, Christopher, and Timothy P. Wiseman, eds. *Lies and Fiction in the Ancient World.* Austin: University of Texas Press, 1993.

Gillespie, Stewart. *Shakespeare's Books: A Dictionary of Shakespeare Sources.* London: Athlone, 2001.

Gittes, Katharine S. *Framing the Canterbury Tales: Chaucer and the Medieval Frame Narrative Tradition.* Contributions to the Study of World Literature 41. New York: Greenwood, 1991.

Glancy, Jennifer A. *Slavery in Early Christianity.* New York: Oxford University Press, 2002.

Gleason, Kathryn L. "Ruler and Spectacle: The Promontory Palace." Pages 208–27 in *Caesarea Maritima: A Retrospective after Two Millennia.* Edited by Avner Raban and Kenneth G. Holum. DMOA 21. Leiden: Brill, 1996.

Goldhill, Simon. "Collectivity and Otherness: the Authority of the Tragic Chorus." Pages 244–56 in *Tragedy and the Tragic: Greek Theatre and Beyond.* Edited by Michael S. Silk. Oxford: Clarendon, 1996.

Gould, John. "Tragedy and Collective Experience." Pages 217–43 in *Tragedy and the Tragic: Greek Theatre and Beyond.* Edited by Michael S. Silk. Oxford: Clarendon, 1996.

Grant, Robert M. "The Resurrection of the Flesh." *JR* 28 (1948): 120–30, 188–208.

———. Review of G. W. Bowersock, *Fiction as History: Nero to Julian. CH* 66 (1997): 307–8.

Green, John R. *Theatre in Ancient Greek Society.* London: Routledge: 1994.

Greenblatt, Stephen. *Marvelous Possessions: The Wonder of the New World.* Chicago: University of Chicago Press, 1991.

Grimm, Carl L. W. *Das zweite, dritte und vierte Buch der Maccabaer*. Vol. 4 of *Kurzgefaßtes exegetisches Handbuch zu den Apokryphen des alten Testaments*. Leipzig: Hirzl, 1857.

Gruen, Erich S. *Diaspora: Jews amidst Greeks and Romans*. Cambridge: Harvard University Press, 2002.

———. *Heritage and Hellenism: The Reinvention of Jewish Tradition*. Berkeley and Los Angeles: University of California Press, 1998.

Gruenwald, Ithamar. *Apocalyptic and Merkavah Mysticism*. Leiden: Brill, 1980.

Gunkel, Hermann. "Esther." *RGG*² 2:378–79.

Gutman, Yehoshua. *The Beginnings of Jewish-Hellenistic Literature* [Hebrew]. Jerusalem: Bialik Institute, 1958.

———. "The Historical Value of 3 Maccabees" [Hebrew]. *SXOLIA* 3 (1959): 49–72.

Hacham, Noah. "The Third Book of Maccabees: Literature, History and Ideology" [Hebrew]. Ph.D. diss. Hebrew University of Jerusalem, 2002.

Hadas, Moses. *Hellenistic Culture: Fusion and Diffusion*. New York: Columbia University Press, 1959.

———. "Plato the Hellenizer." Pages 72–81 in idem, *Hellenistic Culture: Fusion and Diffusion*. New York: Columbia University Press, 1959.

Haenchen, Ernst. *The Acts of the Apostles: A Commentary*. Translated by B. Noble and G. Shinn. Philadelphia: Westminster, 1971.

Haight, Elizabeth H. *Essays on the Greek Romances*. New York: Longmans, Green and Co., 1943.

Halliwell, Stephen. "Traditional Greek Conceptions of Character." Pages 34–58 in *Characterization and Individuality in Greek Literature*. Edited by Christopher Pelling. Oxford: Clarendon, 1990.

Hamilton, Richard. *Choes and Anthesteria: Athenian Iconography and Ritual*. Ann Arbor: University of Michigan Press, 1992.

Harland, Philip A. *Associations, Synagogues, and Congregations: Claiming a Place in Ancient Mediterranean Society*. Minneapolis: Fortress, 2003.

Harrington, Daniel J. "Abraham Traditions in the Testament of Abraham and in the 'Rewritten Bible' of the Intertestamental Period." Pages 165–71 in *Studies on the Testament of Abraham*. Edited by George W. E. Nickelsburg. SBLSCS 6. Missoula, Mont.: Scholars Press, 1976.

Harvey, Graham. *The True Israel: Uses of the Names Jew, Hebrew and Israel in Ancient Jewish and Early Christian Literature*. AGJU 35. Leiden: Brill, 1996.

Hemer, Colin. *The Book of Acts in the Setting of Hellenistic History*. Winona Lake, Ind.: Eisenbrauns, 1990.

Hengel, Martin. *The Four Gospels and the One Gospel of Jesus Christ*. Translated by John Bowden. Harrisburg, Pa.: Trinity Press International, 2000.

———. *The "Hellenization" of Judea in the First Century after Christ*. London: SCM, 1989.

———. *Judaism and Hellenism: Studies in Their Encounter in Palestine during the Early Hellenistic Period*. 2 vols. Philadelphia: Fortress, 1974.

Henrichs, Albert. "'Why Should I Dance?' Choral Self-Referentiality in Greek Tragedy." *Arion* 3 (1995): 56–111.

Henry, Mary Madeleine. *Prisoner of History: Aspasia of Miletus and Her Biographical Tradition*. New York: Oxford University Press, 1995.

Hertel, Johannes. *Das Pañcatantra. Seine Geschichte und seine Verbreitung.* Leipzig: Teubner, 1914.

Hinds, Stephen. *Allusion and Intertext: Dynamics of Appropriation in Roman Poetry, Roman Literature and Its Contexts.* Cambridge: Cambridge University Press, 1998.

Hock, Ronald F. "The Greek Novel." Pages 127–46 in *Greco-Roman Literature and the New Testament: Selected Forms and Genres.* Edited by David E. Aune. SBLSBS 21. Atlanta: Scholars Press, 1988.

———. "Homer in Greco-Roman Education." Pages 55–71 in *Mimesis and Intertextuality in Antiquity and Christianity.* Edited by Dennis R. MacDonald. Harrisburg, Pa.: Trinity Press International, 2001.

———. "The Rhetoric of Romance." Pages 445–65 in *Handbook of Classical Rhetoric in the Hellenistic Period 330 B.C.–A.D. 400.* Edited by Stanley E. Porter. Leiden: Brill, 1997.

———. "Why New Testament Scholars Should Read Ancient Novels." Pages 121–38 in *Ancient Fiction and Early Christian Narrative.* Edited by Ronald F. Hock, J. Bradley Chance, and Judith Perkins. SBLSymS 6. Atlanta: Scholars Press, 1998.

Hock, Ronald F., J. Bradley Chance, and Judith Perkins, eds. *Ancient Fiction and Early Christian Narrative.* SBLSymS 6. Atlanta: Scholars Press, 1998.

Hock, Ronald F., and Edward N. O'Neil. *The Chreia in Ancient Rhetoric.* Vol. 1 of *The Progymnasmata.* SBLTT 27. Atlanta: Scholars Press, 1986.

Holladay, Carl R. "The Portrait of Moses in Ezekiel the Tragedian." Pages 447–52 *Society of Biblical Literature 1976 Seminar Papers.* SBLSP 15. Chico, Calif.: Scholars Press, 1976.

Hooker, Morna. "The Beginning of the Gospel." Pages 18–28 in *The Future of Christology.* Edited by Abraham J. Malherbe and Wayne Meeks. Minneapolis: Fortress, 1993.

Holzberg, Niklas. *The Ancient Novel: An Introduction.* London: Routledge, 1995.

———. "De Griekse Briefroman." *Hermeneus* 67 (1995): 71–77.

Hopkins, Keith. "Novel Evidence for Roman Slavery." *Past & Present* 138 (February 1993): 3–27.

———. "Past Alternative: Review of G. W. Bowersock's *Fiction as History.*" *The Times Literary Supplement* 4846 (Feb. 16, 1996): 29.

Horst, Pieter W. van der. "Hellenistic Parallels to the Acts (Chapters 3 and 4)." *JSNT* 35 (1989): 37–46.

———. "Hellenistic Parallels to the Acts of the Apostles (2,1–47)." *JSNT* 25 (1985): 49–60.

———. "Moses' Throne Vision in Ezekiel the Dramatist." *JJS* 34 (1983): 21–29.

Hose, Martin. *Studien zum Chor bei Euripides.* Beiträge zur Altertumskunde 10. Stuttgart: Teubner, 1990.

Humphreys, W. Lee. "A Life-Style for Diaspora: A Study of the Tales of Esther and Daniel." *JBL* 92 (1973): 211–23.

Hunger, Herbert. *Die hochsprachliche profane Literatur der Byzantiner.* 2 vols. Munich: Beck, 1978.

Hurtado, Larry W. "The Gospel of Mark: Evolutionary or Revolutionary Document?" *JSNT* 40 (1990): 15–32.

————. "The Women, The Tomb, and the Conclusion of Mark." Paper presented at the British New Testament Conference. Birmingham, Sept. 5, 2003.

Jacobson, Howard. "Mysticism and Apocalyptic in Ezekiel's Exagoge." *Illinois Classical Studies* 6 (1981): 272–93.

James, Montague R. "The Testament of Abraham." Pages 1–130 in vol. 2 of *Texts and Studies*. Edited by J. Armitage Robinson. Cambridge: Cambridge University Press, 1892.

Jeansonne, S. P. *The Old Greek Translation of Daniel 7–12*. CBQMS 19. Washington, D.C.: Catholic Biblical Association of America, 1988.

Jeffers, Ann. "Laughing at Abraham: Parody in the Testament of Abraham." Paper presented at the annual meeting of The Society for Old Testament Studies. University of Birmingham, Jan. 5–7, 2004.

Jenkyns, Richard. *Classical Epic: Homer and Virgil*. Classical World Series. Bristol, U.K.: Bristol Classical Press, 1992.

————. *Virgil's Experience Nature and History: Times, Names, and Places*. Oxford: Clarendon, 1998.

Johnson, Lee A. "A Literary Guide to Caesarea Maritima." Pages 35–56 in *Religious Rivalries and the Struggle for Success in Caesarea Maritima*. Edited by Terence L. Donaldson. Waterloo, Ont.: Wilfred Laurier University Press, 2000.

Johnson, Luke Timothy. *The Acts of the Apostles*. Sacra Pagina 5. Collegeville, Minn.: Liturgical Press, 1992.

————. *The Literary Function of Possessions in Luke-Acts*. SBLDS 39. Missoula, Mont.: Scholars Press, 1977.

————. *The Real Jesus: The Misguided Quest for the Historical Jesus and the Truth of the Traditional Gospels*. San Francisco: HarperSanFrancisco, 1996.

Johnson, Sara R. *Historical Fictions and Hellenistic Jewish Identity*. Berkeley and Los Angeles: University of California Press, 2004.

————. "Mirror, Mirror: Third Maccabees, Historical Fictions and Jewish Self-Fashioning in the Hellenistic Period." Ph.D. diss. University of California at Berkeley, 1996.

Jones, F. Stanley. "Principal Orientations on the Relations between the Apocryphal Acts (*Acts of Paul* and *Acts of John*; *Acts of Peter* and *Acts of John*)." Pages 485–505 of *Society of Biblical Literature 1993 Seminar Papers*. Edited by E. H. Lovering Jr. SBLSP 32. Atlanta: Scholars Press, 1993.

Joshel, Sandra R. *Work, Identity, and Legal Status at Rome: A Study of the Occupational Inscriptions*. Norman: University of Oklahoma Press, 1992.

Junod, Eric, and Jean Daniel Kaestli, eds. *Acta Iohannis*. 2 vols. Corpus Christianorum Series Apocryphorum. Turnhout: Brepols, 1983.

Kaimio, Maarit. *The Chorus of Greek Drama within the Light of the Person and Number Used*. Commentations Humanarum Litterarum 46. Helsinki: Societas Scientarum Fennica, 1970.

Kasher, Aryeh. *The Jews in Hellenistic and Roman Egypt: The Struggle for Equal Rights*. Tübingen: Mohr Siebeck, 1985.

Kasher, Rimon. "The Mythological Figure of Moses in Light of Some Unpublished Midrashic Fragments." *JQR* 88 (1997): 19–42.

Kaster, Robert A. "Notes on 'Primary' and 'Secondary' Schools in Late Antiquity." *TAPA* 113 (1983): 323–46.

Kennedy, George. *Progymnasmata: Greek Textbooks of Prose Composition and Rhetoric*. SBLWGRW 10. Atlanta: Society of Biblical Literature, 2003.

Kerenyi, Karoly. *Der antike Roman: Einführung und Textauswahl*. Darmstadt: Wissenschaftliche Buchgesellschaft, 1971.

———. *Die griechisch-orientalische Romanliteraatur in religionsgeschichtlicher Beleuchtung*. Tübingen: Mohr Siebeck, 1927.

Kermode, Frank. *The Genesis of Secrecy*. Cambridge: Harvard University Press, 1979.

Kloppenborg, John S. "Ethnic and Political Factors in the Conflict at Caesarea Maritima." Pages 227–48 in *Religious Rivalries and the Struggle for Success in Caesarea Maritima*. Edited by Terence L. Donaldson. Waterloo, Ont.: Wilfred Laurier University Press, 2000.

———. "*Exitus Clari Viri*: The Death of Jesus in Luke." *TJT* 8 (1992): 106–20.

Koester, Helmut. *History, Culture, and Religion of the Hellenistic Age*. Vol. 1 of *Introduction to the New Testament*. New York: de Gruyter, 1982.

———. *History and Literature of Early Christianity*. Vol. 2 of *Introduction to the New Testament*. New York: de Gruyter, 1982.

Koff, Leonard M. *Chaucer and the Art of Storytelling*. Berkeley and Los Angeles: University of California Press, 1988.

Koff, Leonard M., and B. Deen Schildgen, eds. *The Decameron and the Canterbury Tales: New Essays on an Old Question*. Madison, N.J.: Fairleigh Dickinson University Press, 2000.

Konstan, David. "The Invention of Fiction." Pages 3–17 in *Ancient Fiction and Early Christian Narrative*. Edited by Ronald F. Hock, J. Bradley Chance, and Judith Perkins. SBLSymS 6. Atlanta: Scholars, 1998.

Kranz, Walther. *Stasimon*. Berlin: Weinmannsche Buchhandlung, 1933.

Kratz, Reinhard G. *Translatio imperii: Untersuchungen zu den aramäischen Danielerzählungen und ihrem theologiegeschichtlichen Umfeld*. WUNT 63. Neukirchen-Vluyn: Neukirchener, 1991.

Kraus, Christina S., and Anthony J. Woodman. *Latin Historians*. Greece and Rome: New Surveys in the Classics 27. Oxford: Oxford University Press, 1997.

Kuch, Heinrich. "Funktionswandlungen des Antiken Romans." Pages 52–81 in *Der antike Roman: Untersuchungen zur literarischen Kommunikation und Gattungsgeschichte*. Edited by Heinrich Kuch. Berlin: Akademie Verlag, 1989.

Küchler, Max. *Frühjüdische Weisheitstraditionen*. Fribourg: Universitätsverlag, 1979.

Kugel, James. *In Potiphar's House: The Interpretive Life of Biblical Texts*. San Francisco: HarperSanFrancisco, 1990.

Kuhl, Curt. *Die drei Männer im Feuer*. BZAW 55. Giessen: Töpelmann, 1930.

Kussl, Rolf. *Papyrusfragmente griechischer Romane: Ausgewählte Untersuchungen*. Tübingen: Narr, 1991.

Kuttner, Ann. "Hellenistic Images of Spectacle, from Alexander to Augustus." Pages 97–123 in *The Art of Ancient Spectacle*. Edited by Bettina Bergmann and Christine Kondoleon. Studies in the History of Art 56. New Haven: Yale University Press, 1999.

Kyrtatas, Dimitris. *The Social Structure of Early Christian Communities*. London: Verso, 1987.

Kytzler, Bernhard. "Xenophon of Ephesus." Pages 336–59 in *The Novel in the Ancient World*. Edited by Gareth Schmeling. Leiden: Brill, 1996.

Lanckan, J. "Ḥarṭummîn—die Traumspezialisten?" *BN* 119/120 (2003): 101–17.

Lalleman, Pieter J. *The Acts of John*. Leuven: Peeters, 1998.

———. Polymorphy of Christ." Pages 97–118 in *The Apocryphal Acts of John*. Edited by Jan N. Bremmer. Kampen: Kok Pharos, 1995.

———. "The Relation between the Acts of John and the Acts of Peter." Pages 161–78 in *The Apocryphal Acts of Peter: Magic, Miracles and Gnosticism*. Edited by Jan N. Bremmer. Leuven: Peeters, 1998.

———. "The Resurrection in the Acts of Paul." Pages 126–41 in *The Apocryphal Acts of Paul and Thecla*. Edited by Jan N. Bremmer. Kampen: Kok Pharos, 1996.

Lattimore, Richard. *The Poetry of Greek Tragedy*. Baltimore: Johns Hopkins University Press, 1958.

Lavagnini, Bruno. *Le Origini del romanzo Greco*. Pisa: Mariotti, 1921.

Lebram, Jürgen-Christian. *Das Daniel Buch*. Zürich: Theologischer Verlag, 1984.

Lehnardt, A. *Bibliographie zu den Jüdischen Schriften aus hellenistisch-römischer Zeit*. JSHRZ 6/2. Gütersloh: Gütersloher Verlagshaus, 1999.

Levenson, Jon D. *Esther: A Commentary*. Louisville: Westminster John Knox, 1997.

Lichtheim, Miriam. *The Late Period*. Vol. 3 of *Ancient Egyptian Literature*. Los Angeles: University of California Press, 1980.

Llewellyn, Nigel. "Virgil and the Visual Arts." Pages 117–40 in *Virgil and His Influence: Bimillennial Studies*. Edited by Charles Martindale. Bristol, U.K.: Bristol Classical Press, 1984.

Lloyd, Geoffrey E. R. *Demystifying Mentalities*. Cambridge: Cambridge University Press, 1990.

Loewenstamm, Samuel. "The Testament of Abraham and the Texts concerning Moses' Death." Pages 219–25 in *Studies on the Testament of Abraham*. Edited by George W. E. Nickelsburg. SBLSCS 6. Missoula, Mont.: Scholars Press, 1976.

Longo, Oddone. "The Theater of the *Polis*." Pages 12–19 in *Nothing to Do with Dionysos*. Edited by John J. Winkler and Froma I. Zeitlin. Princeton: Princeton University Press, 1990.

Lüdemann, Gerd. *Das frühe Christentum nach den Traditionen der Apostelgeschichte*. Göttingen: Vandenhoeck & Ruprecht, 1987.

———. *What Really Happened to Jesus: A Historical Approach to the Resurrection*. Translated by John Bowden. Louisville: Westminster John Knox, 1995.

Ludlow, Jared W. *Abraham Meets Death. Narrative Humor in the Testament of Abraham*. JSPSup 41. Sheffield: Sheffield Academic Press, 2002.

Lunn, A. J. "Christ's Passion as Tragedy." *SJT* 43 (1990): 209–31.

Luttikhuizen, Gerard. "A Gnostic Reading of the Acts of John." Pages 119–52 in *The Apocryphal Acts of John*. Edited by Jan N. Bremmer. Kampen: Kok Pharos, 1995.

———. "Simon Magus as a Narrative Figure in the Acts of Peter." Pages 39–51 in *The Apocryphal Acts of Peter: Magic, Miracles and Gnosticism*. Edited by Jan N. Bremmer. Leuven: Peeters, 1998.

Lynch, Stephen J. *Shakespearean Intertextuality: Studies in Selected Sources and Plays*. Contributions in Drama and Theatre Studies 86. Westport, Conn.: Greenwood, 1998.

MacDonald, Dennis R. *The Acts of Andrew and the Acts of Andrew and Matthias in the City of the Cannibals*. Atlanta: Scholars Press, 1990.

———. "*The Acts of Paul* and the *Acts of John*: Which Came First?" Pages 623–26 in *Society of Biblical Literature 1993 Seminar Papers*. Edited by E. H. Lovering Jr. SBLSP 32. Atlanta: Scholars Press, 1993.

———. *Christianizing Homer: The Odyssey, Plato, and The Acts of Andrew*. New York: Oxford University Press, 1994.

———. *Does the New Testament Imitate Homer? Four Cases from the Acts of the Apostles*. New Haven: Yale University Press, 2003.

———. *The Homeric Epics and the Gospel of Mark*. New Haven: Yale University Press, 2000.

———. *The Legend and the Apostle: The Battle for Paul in Story and Canon*. Philadelphia: Westminster, 1983.

———. "Luke's Eutychus and Homer's Elpenor: Acts 20:7–12 and *Odyssey* 10–12." *Journal of Higher Criticism* 1 (1994): 5–24.

———. "The Shipwrecks of Odysseus and Paul." *NTS* 45 (1999): 88–107.

———. "Tobit and the *Odyssey*." Pages 11–40 in *Mimesis and Intertextuality in Antiquity and Christianity*. Edited by Dennis R. MacDonald. Harrisburg, Pa.: Trinity Press International, 2001.

———. "Which Came First? Intertextual Relationships among the Apocryphal Acts of the Apostles." *Semeia* 80 (1997): 11–41.

———, ed. *Mimesis and Intertextuality in Antiquity and Christianity*. Harrisburg, Pa.: Trinity Press International, 2001.

Mack, Burton L. "A Radically Social Theory of Religion." Pages 123–36 in *Secular Theories on Religion: Current Perspectives*. Edited by Tim Jensen and Mikael Rothstein. Copenhagen: Museum Tusculanum Press, 2000.

Macurdy, Grace H. *Hellenistic Queens: A Study of Woman Power in Macedonia, Seleucid Syria, and Ptolemaic Egypt*. Chicago: Ares, 1985.

Malina, Bruce J., and Jerome H. Neyrey. *Portraits of Paul: An Archaeology of Ancient Personality*. Louisville: Westminster John Knox, 1996.

Marguerat, Daniel. "La mort d'Ananias et Saphira (Ac 5:1–11) dans la stratégie narrative de Luc." *NTS* 39 (1993): 209–26.

———. *La première histoire du christianisme: les Actes des apôtres*. Paris: Cerf, 1999.

Marrou, Henri Irénée. *Histoire de l'éducation dans l'antiquité*. Paris: Seuil, 1965.

———. *A History of Education in Antiquity*. Translated by George Lamb. New York: Sheed & Ward, 1956. Repr., Madison: University of Wisconsin Press, 1982.

Martin, Dale. *The Corinthian Body*. New Haven: Yale University Press, 1995.

Martin, Luther H. "The Anti-individualistic Ideology of Hellenistic Culture." *Numen* 41 (1994): 117–40.

———. "Secrecy in Hellenistic Religious Communities." Pages 101–22 in *Secrecy and Concealment: Studies in the History of Mediterranean and Near Eastern Religions*. Edited by Hans G. Kippenberg and Guy G. Stroumsa. SHR 65. Leiden: Brill, 1995.

Martindale, Charles, ed. *The Cambridge Companion to Virgil*. Cambridge: Cambridge University Press, 1997.

———. *Virgil and his Influence: Bimillennial Studies*. Bristol, U.K.: Bristol Classical Press, 1984.

Mastronarde, Donald. "Knowledge and Authority in the Choral Voice of Euripidean Tragedy." *Syllecta Classica* 10 (1999): 87–104.

McAusland, Ian, and P. Walcot, eds. *Greek Tragedy.* Oxford: Oxford University Press, 1993.

McCall, Marsh. "The Chorus of Aeschylus' Choephori." Pages 17–30 in *Cabinet of the Muses.* Edited by Mark Griffith and Donald Mastronarde. Atlanta: Scholars Press, 1990.

McClure, John A. "Late Imperial Romance." *Raritan* 10 (1991): 111–30.

McCutcheon, Russell T. "Redescribing 'Religion' as Social Formation: Toward a Social Theory of Religion." Pages 51–72 in *What Is Religion? Origins, Definitions, and Explanations.* Edited by Thomas A. Idinopulos and Bryan C. Wilson. Leiden: Brill, 1998.

McKeon, Richard. "Literary Criticism and the Concept of Imitation in Antiquity." Pages 147–75 in *Critics and Criticism.* Edited by Ronald S. Crane. Chicago: University of Chicago Press, 1952.

McLean, Bradley H. "Epigraphical Evidence in Caesarea Maritima." Pages 57–64 in *Religious Rivalries and the Struggle for Success in Caesarea Maritima.* Edited by Terence L. Donaldson. Waterloo, Ont.: Wilfrid Laurier University Press, 2000.

Meagher, John C. *Clumsy Construction in Mark's Gospel: A Critique of Form- and Redaktionsgeschichte.* Toronto Studies in Theology 3. New York: Mellen, 1979.

Meeks, Wayne. *The Prophet-King: Moses Traditions and the Johannine Christology.* NovTSup 14. Leiden: Brill, 1967.

Meier, John. *A Marginal Jew: Rethinking the Historical Jesus.* 3 vols. New York: Doubleday, 1991–.

Meiser, Martin. *Die Reaktion des Volkes auf Jesus.* BZNW 96. Berlin: de Gruyter, 1998.

Merkelbach, Reinhold. *Roman und Mysterium in der Antike.* Munich: Beck, 1962.

Merkle, Stefan. "Telling the True Story of the Trojan War: The Eyewitness Account of Dictys of Crete." Pages 183–96 in *The Search for the Ancient Novel.* Edited by James Tatum. Baltimore: Johns Hopkins University Press, 1994.

Miles, Gary B. and Archibald W. Allen. "Vergil and the Augustan Experience." Pages 13–41 in *Vergil at 2000: Commemorative Essays on the Poet and His Influence.* Edited by John D. Bernard. New York: AMS Press, 1986.

Miles, John. "Laughing at the Bible: Jonah as Parody." *JQR* 65 (1975): 168–81.

Milik, Józef T. "Daniel et Susanne á Qumrân." Pages 337–59 in *De la Tôrah au Messie: Etudes d'exegèse et d'herméneutique bibliques offertes á Henri Cazelles.* Edited by Maurice Carrez, Joseph Doré, and Pierre Grelot. Paris: Desclée, 1981.

Minear, Paul S. "The Disciples and the Crowds in the Gospel of Matthew." *Anglican Theological Review Supplement Series* 3 (1974): 28–44.

Minor, Mitzi L. *The Power of Mark's Story.* St. Louis: Chalice, 2001.

Misset-van de Weg, Magda. "'For the Lord Always Takes Care of His Own': The Purpose of the Wondrous Works and Deeds in the Acts of Peter." Pages 97–110 in *The Acts of Peter: Magic, Miracle and Gnosticism.* Edited by Jan N. Bremmer. Leuven: Peeters, 1998.

Mitchell, Alan C. "The Social Function of Friendship in Acts 2:44–47 and 4:32–37." *JBL* 111 (1992): 255–72.

Modrzejewski, Joseph M. "How to Be a Jew in Hellenistic Egypt?" Pages 65–92 in *Diasporas in Antiquity.* Edited by Shaye J. D. Cohen and Ernest S. Frerichs. Atlanta: Scholars Press, 1993.

Moore, C. A. *Esther.* AB 7B. Garden City, N.Y.: Doubleday, 1971.

———. *Judith.* AB 40. Garden City, N.Y.: Doubleday, 1985.

Moore, Stephen D. *Literary Criticism and the Gospels: The Theoretical Challenge.* New Haven: Yale University Press, 1989.

———. *Poststructuralism and the New Testament: Derrida and Foucault at the Foot of the Cross.* Minneapolis: Fortress, 1994.

Morgan, John R. "Introduction." Pages 1–12 in *Greek Fiction: The Greek Novel in Context.* Edited by John R. Morgan and Richard Steinman. London: Routledge, 1994.

———. "Make-Believe and Make Believe: The Fictionality of the Greek Novels." Pp. 175–229 in *Lies and Fiction in the Ancient World.* Edited by Christopher Gill and Timothy P. Wiseman. Exeter: University of Exeter Press, 1993.

———. Review of J. N. O'Sullivan, *Xenophon of Ephesus: His Compositional Technique and the Birth of the Novel. JHS* 116 (1996): 199–200.

Morgan, Teresa. *Literate Education in the Hellenistic and Roman Worlds.* New York: Cambridge University Press, 1998.

Morse, Ruth. *Truth and Convention in the Middle Ages.* Cambridge: Cambridge University Press, 1991.

Muchiki, Yoshiyuki. *Egyptian Proper Names and Loanwords in North-West Semitic.* SBLDS 173. Atlanta: Society of Biblical Literature, 1999.

Müller, Hans-Peter. "Mantische Weisheit und Apokalyptik." Pages 268–93 in *Congress Volume: Uppsala, 1971.* VTSup 22. Leiden: Brill, 1972.

Munck, Johannes. *The Acts of the Apostles.* AB 31. Garden City, N.Y.: Doubleday, 1967.

Murray, Michele. "Jews and Judaism in Caesarea Maritima." Pages 127–52 in *Religious Rivalries and the Struggle for Success in Caesarea Maritima.* Edited by Terence L. Donaldson. Waterloo, Ont.: Wilfrid Laurier University Press, 2000.

Mussies, Gerard. "Joseph's Dream (Matt 1,18–23) and Comparable Stories." Pages 177–86 in *Text and Testimony: Essays on New Testament and Apocryphal Literature in Honour of A. F. J. Klijn.* Edited by T. Baarda et al. Kampen: Kok, 1988.

Newman, J. K. *The Concept of Vates in Augustan Poetry.* Collections Latomus 89. Brussels: Latomus, 1967.

Nickelsburg, George W. E. "4Q551: A Vorlage to the Story of Susanna or a Text Related to Judges 19." *JJS* 48 (1997): 349–51.

———. *Jewish Literature Between the Bible and the Mishnah.* Philadelphia: Fortress, 1981.

———. "Structure and Message in the Testament of Abraham." Pages 85–93 in *Studies on the Testament of Abraham.* Edited by George W. E. Nickelsburg. SBLSCS 6. Missoula, Mont.: Scholars Press, 1976.

Niditch, Susan, and Robert Doran. "The Success Story of the Wise Courtier: A Formal Approach." *JBL* 96 (1977): 179–93.

Nilsson, Martin P. *The Dionysiac Mysteries of the Hellenistic and Roman Age.* Lund: Gleerup, 1957.

———. *Geschichte der Griechischen Religion.* 2 vols. Munich: Beck, 1967–74.

Nock, Arthur Darby. *Conversion: The Old and the New in Religion from Alexander the Great to Augustine of Hippo.* Oxford: Clarendon, 1933.

O'Collins, Gerald. "The Resurrection: The State of the Questions." Pages 5–28 in *The Resurrection: An Interdisciplinary Symposium on the Resurrection of Jesus.* Edited by Stephen T. Davis, Daniel Kendall, and Gerald O'Collins. Oxford: Oxford University Press, 1997.

O'Sullivan, James N. *Xenophon of Ephesus: His Compositional Technique and the Birth of the Novel.* Berlin: de Gruyter, 1995.

Otto, Walter F. *Dionysus: Myth and Cult.* Bloomington: Indiana University Press, 1965.

Pack, Roger A. *The Greek and Latin Literary Texts from Greco-Roman Egypt.* 2nd ed. Ann Arbor: University of Michigan Press, 1965.

Painter, R. Jackson. "Greco-Roman Religion in Caesarea Maritima." Pages 105–25 in *Religious Rivalries and the Struggle for Success in Caesarea Maritima.* Edited by Terence L. Donaldson. Waterloo, Ont.: Wilfrid Laurier University Press, 2000.

Papanikolaou, Antonios D. *Chariton-Studien: Untersuchungen zur Sprache und Chronologie der griechischen Romane.* Hypomnemata 37. Göttingen: Vandenhoeck & Ruprecht, 1973.

Parente, F. "The Third Book of Maccabees as Ideological and Historical Source." *Henoch* 10 (1988): 143–82.

Parker, L. P. E. *The Songs of Aristophanes.* Oxford: Clarendon, 1997.

Paul, A. "Le Troisème livre des Macchabées." *ANRW* 2.20.1:298–336.

Paulsen, Thomas. "Die Funktionen des Chores in der Attischen Tragödie." Pages 69–92 in *Das antike Theater: Aspekte seiner Geschichte, Rezeption und Aktualität.* Edited by G. Binder and Bernd Effe. Bocumer Altertumswissenschaftliches Colloquium 33. Trier: Wissenschaftlicher Verlag, 1998.

Penner, Todd. "Civilizing Discourse: Acts, Declamation and the Rhetoric of the Polis." Pages 65–104 in *Contextualizing Acts: Lukan Narrative and Greco-Roman Discourse.* Edited by Todd Penner and Caroline Vander Stichele. SBLSymS 20. Atlanta: Society of Biblical Literature, 2003.

Perdrizet, P. "Le Fragment de Satyros sur les dèmes d'alexandrie." *REA* 12 (1910): 217–47.

Perkins, Judith. "The Acts of Peter as Intertext: Response to Dennis MacDonald." Pages 627–33 in *Society of Biblical Literature 1993 Seminar Papers.* Edited by E. H. Lovering Jr. SBLSP 32. Atlanta: Scholars Press, 1993.

———. "Space, Place, Voice in the Acts of the Martyrs and the Greek Romance." Pages 117–37 in *Mimesis and Intertextuality in Antiquity and Christianity.* Edited by Dennis R. MacDonald. Harrisburg, Pa.: Trinity Press International, 2001.

———. *The Suffering Self: Pain and Narrative Representation in the Early Christian Era.* London: Routledge, 1995.

Perry, B. E. "Chariton and His Romance from a Literary-Historical Point of View." *AJP* 51 (1930): 93–134.

Pervo, Richard I. "The Ancient Novel Becomes Christian." Pages 685–709 in *The Novel in the Ancient World*. Edited by Gareth Schmeling. London: Brill, 1996.

———. "Egging on the Chickens: A Cowardly Response to Dennis MacDonald and Then Some." *Semeia* 80 (1997): 43–56.

———. "Johannine Trajectories in the Acts of John." *Apocrypha* 3 (1992): 47–68.

———. "A Nihilist Fabula: Introducing the Life of Aesop." Pages 77–120 in *Ancient Fiction and Early Christian Narrative*. Edited by Ronald F. Hock, J. Bradley Chance, and Judith Perkins. SBLSymS 6. Atlanta: Scholars Press, 1998.

———. *Profit with Delight*. Philadelphia: Fortress, 1987.

Phillips, Thomas E. *Reading Issues of Wealth and Poverty in Luke-Acts*. Studies in the Bible and Early Christianity 48. Lewiston, N.Y.: Mellen, 2001.

Phoutrides, E. A. "The Chorus of Euripides." *Harvard Studies in Classical Philology* 27 (1916): 77–170.

Pleket, H. W. "An Aspect of the Imperial Cult: Imperial Mysteries." *HTR* 58 (1965): 331–47.

Porten, Bezalel. "Settlement of Jews at Elephantine and Arameans at Syene." Pages 451–70 in *Judah and the Judeans in the Neo-Babylonian Period*. Edited by Oded Lipschits and Joseph Blenkinsopp. Winona Lake, Ind.: Eisenbrauns, 2003.

Porten, Bezalel, and Ada Yardeni. *Textbook of Aramaic Documents from Ancient Egypt*. Jerusalem: Hebrew University of Jerusalem, 1993.

Posener, Georges. *Le Papyrus Vandier*. Cairo: Institut Français d'Archéologie Orientale, 1986.

Pound, Ezra. *ABC of Reading*. New York: New Directions, 1960.

Poupon, Gerald. "Les Actes de Pierre et Leur Remaniement." *ANRW* 2.25.6:4363–83.

Preisigke, Friedrich, and Emil Keissling. *Wörterbuch der griechischen Papyrusurkunden*. Berlin: Erben, 1925–31.

Raban, Avner, and Kenneth G. Holum, eds. *Caesarea Maritima: A Retrospective after Two Millennia*. DMOA 21. Leiden: Brill, 1996.

Rajak, Tessa. "Cio che Flavio Giuseppe Vide: Josephus and the Essenes." Pages 140–60 in *Josephus and the History of the Greco-Roman World: Essays in Memory of Morton Smith*. Edited by Fausto Parente and Joseph Sievers. Leiden: Brill, 1994.

Reardon, Bryan P. "A. Chariton." Pages 309–35 in *The Novel in the Ancient World*. Edited by Gareth Schmeling. Leiden: Brill, 1996.

———, ed. *Collected Ancient Greek Novels*. Berkeley and Los Angeles: University of California Press, 1989.

Rehm, Rush. *Greek Tragic Theatre*. London: Routledge, 1992.

Richardson, Nicholas. *The Iliad: A Commentary*. Cambridge: Cambridge University Press, 1993.

Richardson, Peter. "Archaeological Evidence for Religion and Urbanism in Caesarea Maritima." Pages 11–34 in *Religious Rivalries and the Struggle for Success in Caesarea Maritima*. Edited by Terence L. Donaldson. Waterloo, Ont.: Wilfrid Laurier University Press, 2000.

Riley, Gregory J. "Mimesis of Classical Ideals in the Second Christian Century." Pages 91–103 in *Mimesis and Intertextuality in Antiquity and Christianity*. Edited by Dennis R. MacDonald. Harrisburg, Pa.: Trinity Press International, 2001.

————. *Resurrection Reconsidered: Thomas and John in Controversy.* Minneapolis: Fortress, 1995.

Ritner, Robert K. *The Mechanics of Ancient Egyptian Magical Practice.* SAOC 54. Chicago: Oriental Institute of the University of Chicago, 1993.

Robbins, Vernon. "Luke-Acts: A Mixed Population Seeks a Home in the Roman Empire." Pages 202–21 in *Images of Empire.* Edited by Loveday Alexander. JSOTSup 122. Sheffield: Sheffield Academic Press, 1991.

————. "Narrative in Ancient Rhetoric and Rhetoric in Ancient Narrative." Pages 369–84 in *Society of Biblical Literature 1996 Seminar Papers.* SBLSP 35. Atlanta: Scholars Press, 1996.

Roberts, Michael. *Biblical Epic and Rhetorical Paraphrase in Late Antiquity.* Liverpool: Cairns, 1985.

Rohde, Erwin. *Der griechische Roman und seine Vorläufer.* Leipzig: Breitkopf & Hartel, 1876. 3rd ed. Leipzig: Breitkopf & Hartel, 1914.

Rose, Margaret. *Parody: Ancient, Modern, and Post-modern.* Cambridge: Cambridge University Press, 1993.

Rösler, Wolfgang. "Der Chor als Mitspieler. Beobachtungen zur 'Antigone.'" *Antike und Abendland* 29 (1983): 107–24.

Rowland, Christopher. *Christian Origins.* London: SPCK, 1985.

Rudolph, Kurt, and R. McL Wilson. *Gnosis: The Nature and History of Gnosticism.* San Francisco: Harper & Row, 1983.

Ruiz-Montero, Consuelo. "Aspects of the Vocabulary of Chariton of Aphrodisias." *CQ* 41 (1991): 484–89.

————. "Caritón de Afrodisias y los Ejericios prepartorios de Elio Teón." Pages 709–13 in *Treballs en honor de Vergilio Bejarano.* Edited by L. Ferreres. Barcelona: Publicacions de Universitat de Barcelona, 1991.

————. "Chariton von Aphrodisias: Ein Überblick." *ANRW* 2.34.2:1006–54.

————. "The Rise of the Greek Novel." Pages 29–85 in *The Novel in the Ancient World.* Edited by Gareth Schmeling. Leiden: Brill, 1996.

Russell, Donald A. "De Imitatione." Pages 1–16 in *Creative Imitation in Latin Literature.* Edited by David A. West and Anthony J. Woodman. Cambridge: Cambridge University Press, 1979.

————. *Greek Declamation.* New York: Cambridge University Press, 1983.

Ryholt, Kim. *Carlsberg Papyri 4: The Story of Petese Son of Petetum and Seventy Other Good and Bad Stories (P. Petese).* Carsten Niebuhr Institute Publications 23. Copenhagen: Museum Tusculanum Press, 1999.

————. "An Elusive Narrative Belonging to the Cycle of Stories about the Priesthood at Heliopolis." Pages 361–66 in *Acts of the Seventh International Conference of Demotic Studies, Copenhagen, 23–27 August 1999.* Edited by Kim Ryholt. CNI Publications 27. Copenhagen: Museum Tusculanum Press, 2002.

Saïd, Edward. *Culture and Imperialism.* New York: Vintage, 1993.

Sanders, E. P. *The Historical Figure of Jesus.* London: Penguin, 1993.

————. *Jesus and Judaism.* London: SCM, 1985.

Scarcella, Antonio M. "The Social and Economic Structures of the Ancient Novels." Pages 221–76 in *The Novel in the Ancient World.* Edited by Gareth Schmeling. London: Brill, 1996.

Schäferdiek, Knut. "Herkunft und Interesse der alten Johannesakten." *ZNW* 74 (1983): 247–67.

Schaps, David M. "Socrates and the Socratics: When Wealth Became a Problem." *Classical World* 96 (2003): 131–59.

Schenk, Wolfgang. *Die Sprache des Matthäus*. Göttingen: Vandenhoeck & Ruprecht, 1987.

Schlegel, August Wilhelm. *Vorlesungen über dramatische Kunst und Literatur in sämmtliche Werke*. Edited by Eduard Böcking. 16 vols. Hildesheim: Olms, 1971–72.

Schmeling, Gareth. Review of James N. O'Sullivan, *Xenophon of Ephesus: His Compositional Technique and the Birth of the Novel*. *AJA* 117 (1996): 660–63.

———. *Xenophon of Ephesus*. Twayne's World Authors Series. Boston: Twayne, 1980.

Schmidt, Francis. *Le Testament grec d'Abraham. Introduction, édition critique des deux recensions grecques, traduction*. Tübingen: Mohr Siebeck, 1986.

Schneider, Paul. "The Acts of John: The Gnostic Transformation of a Christian Community." Pages 241–69 in *Hellenization Revisited: Shaping a Christian Response within the Greco-Roman World*. Edited by Wendy E. Helleman. Lanham, Md.: University Press of America, 1994.

———. *The Mystery of the Acts of John*. Lewiston, N.Y.: Mellen, 1991.

———. "A Perfect Fit: The Major Interpolation in the Acts of John." Pages 518–32 in *Society of Biblical Literature 1991 Seminar Papers*. SBLSP 30. Atlanta: Scholars Press, 1991.

Schoedel, William R. *A Commentary on the Letters of Ignatius of Antioch*. Philadelphia: Fortress, 1985.

Schürer, Emil. *The History of the Jewish People in the Age of Jesus Christ*. Revised and translated by Geza Vermes, Fergus Millar, and Martin Goodman. 3 vols. Edinburgh: T&T Clark, 1986.

Scott, James C. *Domination and the Arts of Resistance: Hidden Transcripts*. New Haven: Yale University Press, 1990.

Scullard, Howard H. *The Elephant in the Greek and Roman World*. London: Thames & Hudson, 1974.

Seccombe, David P. *Possessions and the Poor in Luke-Acts*. SNTSU 6. Linz: Studien zum Neuen Testament und seiner Umwelt, 1982.

Silk, Michael. "Style, Voice, and Authority in the Choruses of Greek Drama." Pages 1–26 in *Der Chor im antiken un modernen Drama*. Edited by Peter Reimer and Bernhard Zimmerman. Drama 7. Stuttgart: Metzler, 1999.

Slater, Niall W. "From Harena to Cena: Trimalchio's Capis (Sat. 52.1–3)." *CQ* 44 (1994): 549–51.

Sly, Dorothy I. "The Conflict over Isopoliteia: An Alexandrian Perspective." Pages 249–65 in *Religious Rivalries and the Struggle for Success in Caesarea Maritima*. Edited by Terence L. Donaldson. Waterloo, Ont.: Wilfrid Laurier University Press, 2000.

Smith, Dwight Moody. "When Did the Gospels become Scripture?" *JBL* 119 (2000): 3–20.

Smith, Stephen H. "A Divine Tragedy: Some Observations on the Dramatic Structure of Mark's Gospel." *NovT* 37 (1995): 209–31.

Snell, B. "Die Jamben in Ezechiels Moses-Drama." *Glotta* 44 (1966): 25–32.

Spargo, John Webster. *Virgil the Necromancer: Studies in Virgilian Legends.* Harvard Studies in Comparative Literature 10. Cambridge: Harvard University Press, 1934.

Spiegelberg, Wilhelm. *Der ägyptische Mythus vom Sonnenauge (Der Papyrus der Tierfabeln, "Kufi") nach dem leidener demotischen Papyrus I 384.* Strassburg: Strassburger Druckerei und Verlagsanstalt, 1917.

———. *Demotische Texte auf Krügen.* Demotische Studien 5. Leipzig: Hinrichs, 1912.

Stark, Isolde. "Religiöse Elemente im antiken Roman." Pages 135–49 in *Der antike Roman: Untersuchungen zur literarischen Kommunikation und Gattungsgeschichte.* Edited by Heinrich Kuch. Berlin: Akademie Verlag, 1989.

Steck, Odil H. *Israel und das gewaltsame Geschick der Propheten: Untersuchungen zur Überlieferung des deuteronomistischen Geschichtsbildes im Alten Testament, Spätjudentum und Urchristentum.* WMANT 23. Neukirchen-Vluyn: Neukirchener, 1967.

Steiner, Richard C. "An Aramaic Text in Demotic Script." *COS* 1:309–27.

Stephens, Susan A., and John J. Winkler. *Ancient Greek Novels: The Fragments.* Princeton: Princeton University Press, 1995.

Sterling, Gregory E. "'Athletes of Virtue': An Analysis of the Summaries of Acts (2:41–47; 4:32–35; 5:12–16)." *JBL* 113 (1994): 679–96.

Sternberg, Meir. *The Poetics of Biblical Narrative.* Bloomington: Indiana University Press, 1987.

Stoops, Robert. 1986. "The Acts of Peter in Intertexual Context." *Semeia* 80 (1997): 57–86.

———. "Christ as Patron in the Acts of Peter." *Semeia* 56 (1992): 143–57.

———. "Patronage in the Acts of Peter." *Semeia* 38 (1986): 91–100.

Stroumsa, Gedaliahu A. G. "Polymorphie Divine et Transformation d'un Mythologème." Pages 43–63 in *Savoir et Salut.* Paris: Cerf, 1992.

Strugnell, John. "Notes on the Text and Metre of Ezekiel The Tragedian's Exagôgê." *HTR* 60 (1967): 449–57.

Swain, Simon. *Hellenism and Empire: Language, Classicism and Power in the Greek World A.D. 50–250.* Oxford: Clarendon, 1996.

———. Review of G. W. Bowersock, *Fiction as History: Nero to Julian. JRS* 86 (1996): 216–17.

Sweet, Matthew. *Inventing the Victorians.* London: Faber & Faber, 2001.

Takacs, Sarolta A. *Isis and Sarapis in the Roman World.* Leiden: Brill, 1995.

Talbert, Charles H. *Reading Acts: A Literary and Theology Commentary on the Acts of the Apostles.* New York: Crossroad, 1997.

———, ed. *Luke-Acts: New Perspectives from the Society of Biblical Literature Seminar.* New York: Crossroad, 1984.

Tarrant, R. J. "Aspects of Virgil's Reception in Antiquity." Pages 56–72 in *The Cambridge Companion to Virgil.* Edited by Charles Martindale. Cambridge: Cambridge University Press, 1997.

Taylor, Justin. "The Community of Goods among the First Christians and among the Essenes." Pages 147–61 in *Historical Perspectives: From the Hasmoneans to Bar Kokhba in Light of the Dead Sea Scrolls: Proceedings of the Fourth International*

Symposium of the Orion Centre for the Dead Sea Scrolls and Associated Literature, 27–31 January 1999. Edited by David Goodblatt, Avital Pinnick, and Daniel R. Schwartz. Leiden: Brill, 2001.

Tcherikover, Victor A. "Jewish Apologetic Literature Reconsidered." *Eos* 48 (1956): 169–93.

———. "The Third Book of Maccabees as a Historical Source of Augustus' Time." *ScrHier* 7 (1961): 1–26.

Thiel, Rainer. *Chor und tragische Handlung im 'Agamemnon' des Aischylos.* Beiträge zur Altertumskunde 35. Stuttgart: Teubner, 1993.

Thiselton, Anthony C. *The First Epistle to the Corinthians: A Commentary on the Greek Text.* NIGTC. Grand Rapids: Eerdmans, 2000.

Thomas, Christine M. *The Acts of Peter, Gospel Literature, and the Ancient Novel: Rewriting the Past.* New York: Oxford University Press, 2003.

———. "At Home in the City of Artemis. Religion in Ephesos in the Literary Imagination of the Roman Period." Pages 81–117 in *Ephesos Metropolis of Asia: An Interdisciplinary Approach to Its Archaeology, Religion, and Culture.* Edited by Helmut Koester. Valley Forge, Pa.: Trinity Press International, 1995.

———. "Revivifying Resurrection Accounts: Techniques of Composition and Rewriting in the Acts of Peter cc. 25–28." Pages 65–83 in *The Apocryphal Acts of Peter: Magic, Miracle and Gnosticism.* Edited by Jan N. Bremmer. Leuven: Peeters, 1998.

Thomson, James A. K. *The Art of the Logos.* London: Allen & Unwin, 1935.

Tondriau, Julien. "Les Thiases Dionysiaques royaux de la cour Ptolémaïque." *ChrEg* 21 (1946): 149–71.

———. "Un Thiase Dionysiaque à Péluse sous Ptolémée IV Philopator." *BSAA* 37 (1948): 3–11.

Too, Yun Lee, ed. *Education in Greek and Roman Antiquity.* Leiden: Brill, 2001.

Tov, Emanuel. "Criteria for Evaluating Textual Readings: The Limitations of Textual Rules." *HTR* (1982): 429–48.

———. "A Modern Textual Outlook Based on the Qumran Scrolls." *HUCA* 53 (1982): 11–27.

———. *The Text-Critical Use of the Septuagint in Biblical Research.* Jerusalem Biblical Studies 3. Jerusalem: Simor, 1981.

Toynbee, Jocelyn M. C. *Animals in Roman Life and Art.* Baltimore: Johns Hopkins University Press, 1973.

Tracy, S. "III Maccabees and Pseudo-Aristeas." *YCS* 1 (1928): 241–52.

Trenkner, Sophie. *The Greek Novella in the Classical Period.* Cambridge: Cambridge University Press, 1958.

Tyson, Joseph B. *The Death of Jesus in Luke-Acts.* Columbia: University of South Carolina Press, 1986.

———. "The Jewish Public in Luke-Acts." *NTS* 30 (1984): 574–83.

Ulrich, Eugene. "Double Literary Editions of Biblical Narratives and Reflections on Determining the Form to be Translated." Pages 1–16 in *Perspectives on the Hebrew Bible: Essays in Honor of Walter J. Harrelson.* Edited by James L. Crenshaw. Macon, Ga.: Mercer University Press, 1980.

———. "From Literature to Scripture: Reflections on the Growth of a Text's Authoritativeness." *DSD* 10 (2003): 3–25.

———. "Horizons of Old Testament Textual Research at the Thirtieth Anniversary of Qumran Cave 4." *CBQ* 46 (1984): 613–36.

———. "Pluriformity in the Biblical Text, Text Groups, and Questions of Canon." Pages 23–41 in *The Madrid Qumran Congress: Proceedings of the International Congress on the Dead Sea Scrolls, Madrid 18–21 March, 1991.* Edited by Julio Trebolle Barrera and Luis Vegas Montaner. STDJ 11. Leiden: Brill, 1992.

Unnik, Willem C. van. *Tarsus or Jerusalem: The City of Paul's Youth.* Translated by George Ogg. London: Epworth, 1962.

Van Eijk, A. H. C. "Only That Can Rise Which Has Previously Fallen." *JTS* 22 (1971): 517–29.

Van Tilborg, Sjef. *Reading John in Ephesus.* NovTSup 83. Leiden: Brill, 1996.

Velz, John W. *Shakepeare and the Classical Tradition: A Critical Guide to Commentary, 1660–1960.* Minneapolis: University of Minnesota Press, 1968.

Verberg, Winifred. *Passion als Tragödie: Die literarische Gattung der antiken, Tragödie als Gestaltungsprinzip der Johannespassion.* Stuttgarter Bibelstudien 182. Stuttgart: Katholisches Bibelwerk, 1999.

Verheyden, Jozef, ed. *The Unity of Luke-Acts.* BETL 142. Leuven: University Press, 1999.

Vermes, Geza. *Jesus the Jew: A Historian's Reading of the Gospels.* Philadelphia: Fortress, 1973.

Vernant, Jean-Pierre, and Pierre Vidal-Naquet. *Myth and Tragedy in Ancient Greece.* New York: Zone Books, 1988.

Versnel, Henk S. *Inconsistencies in Greek and Roman Religion I: Transition and Reversal in Myth and Ritual.* Studies in Greek and Roman Religion 2. Leiden: Brill, 1993.

———. "Religieuze Stromingen in het Hellenisme." *Lampas* 21 (1988): 111–36.

———. "Two Carnivalesque Princes: Augustus and Claudius and the Ambiguity of Saturnalian Imagery." Pages 99–122 in *Karnivaleske Phänomene in antiken und nachantiken Kulturen und Literaturen.* Edited by Siegmar Döpp. Stätten und Formen der Kommunikation im Altertum 1. Trier: Wissenschaftlicher Verlag, 1993.

Veyne, Paul. *Did the Greeks Believe in Their Myths? An Essay on the Constitutive Imagination.* Translated by Paula Wissing. Chicago: University of Chicago Press, 1988.

———. *From Pagan Rome to Byzantium.* Vol. 1 of *A History of Private Life.* Edited by Philippe Ariès and George Duby. Translated by Arthur Goldhammer. 5 vols. Cambridge: Harvard University Press, 1987.

Via, Dan O. *Kerygma and Comedy in the New Testament: A Structuralist Approach to Hermeneutic.* Philadelphia: Fortress, 1975.

Vleeming, Sven P. and Jan W. Wesselius. *Studies in Papyrus Amherst 63: Essays on the Aramaic texts in Aramaic/Demotic Papyrus Amherst 63.* 2 vols. Amsterdam: Juda Palache Instituut, 1985–90.

Vouaux, Leon. *Les Actes De Pierre.* Paris: Letouzey, 1922.

Walker, Lewis. *Shakespeare and the Classical Tradition: An Annotated Bibliography 1961–1991.* New York: Routledge, 2002.

Webb, Ruth. "The *Progymnasmata* as Practice." Pages 289–316 in *Education in Greek and Roman Antiquity.* Edited by Yun Lee Too. Leiden: Brill, 2001.

Weigandt, Peter. "Der Doketismus im Urchristentum und in der theologischen Entwicklung des zweiten Jahrhunderts." Ph.D. diss. University of Heidelberg, 1961.

Wenthe, Dean. "The Old Greek Translation of Daniel 1–6." Ph.D. diss. University of Notre Dame, 1991.

Wesseling, Berber. "The Audience of the Ancient Novels." Pages 67–79 in *Groningen Colloquia on the Novel*. Edited by Heinz Hofmann. Groningen: Forsten, 1988.

Wesselius, Jan Wim. "The Writing of Daniel." Pages 291–310 in *The Book of Daniel: Composition and Reception*. Edited by John J. Collins and Peter W. Flint. VTSup 83. Leiden: Brill, 2001.

White, Hayden. *The Content of the Form: Narrative Discourse and Historical Representation*. Baltimore: Johns Hopkins University Press, 1990.

Wieneke, Joseph. "Ezechielis Iudaei poetae Alexandrini: Fabulae Quae Inscribitur." Ph.D. diss. University of Münster, 1931.

Wilamowitz, Tycho von. *Die dramatische Technik des Sophokles*. Philosophische Untersuchungen 22. Berlin: Weidmann, 1917.

Wiles, David. *Tragedy in Athens: Performance Space and Theatrical Meaning*. Cambridge: Cambridge University Press, 1997.

Williams, D. S. "3 Maccabees: A Defense of Diaspora Judaism?" *JSP* 13 (1995): 17–29.

Williams, Michael A. *Rethinking "Gnosticism": An Argument for Dismantling a Dubious Category*. Princeton: Princeton University Press, 1996.

Williams, R. D., ed. *P Vergili Maronis Aeneidos Liber Quintus*. Oxford: Clarendon, 1971.

———. ed. *Vergili Maronis Aeneidos Liber Tertius*. Oxford: Clarendon, 1962.

Willrich, Hugo. "Dositheos Drimylos' Sohn." *Klio* 7 (1907): 293–94.

Wills, Lawrence M. *The Jew in the Court of the Foreign King: Ancient Jewish Court Legends*. Minneapolis: Fortress, 1990.

———. *The Jewish Novel in the Ancient World*. Ithaca, N.Y.: Cornell University Press, 1995.

———. *The Quest of the Historical Gospel*. London: Routledge, 1997.

Wilson, A. N. *Jesus: A Life*. New York: Norton, 1992.

Wilson, Peter. *The Athenian Institution of the Khoregia: The Chorus, the City and the Stage*. Cambridge: Cambridge University Press, 2000.

Wilson, Robert R. "From Prophecy to Apocalyptic: Shape of Israelite Religion." *Semeia* 21 (1982): 79–95.

Wilson, Walter T. "Urban Legends: Acts 10:1–11:18 and the Strategies of Greco-Roman Foundation Narratives." *JBL* 120 (2001): 77–99.

Winston, David. "New Light on an Old Drama." *Jud* 35 (1986): 109–13.

Winter, Bruce. "The Importance of the Captatio Benevolentiae in the Speeches of Tertullus and Paul in Acts." *JTS* 42 (1991): 505–31.

Wiseman, Timothy P. "Lying Historians: Seven Types of Mendacity." Pages 122–46 in *Lies and Fiction in the Ancient World*. Edited by Christopher Gill and Timothy P. Wiseman. Exeter: University of Exeter Press, 1993.

Witherington, Ben, III. *The Acts of the Apostles: A Socio-rhetorical Commentary*. Grand Rapids: Eerdmans, 1998.

Woodford, Susan. *The Trojan War in Ancient Art*. Ithaca, N.Y.: Cornell University Press, 1993.

Woodman, Anthony J. *Rhetoric in Classical Historiography: Four Studies*. London: Routledge 1988.

Wright, N. T. *The Challenge of Jesus: Rediscovering Who Jesus Was and Is*. Downers Grove, Ill.: InterVarsity Press, 1999.

———. *The Resurrection of the Son of God*. Minneapolis: Fortress, 2003.

Zauzich, Karl-Theodor. "Demotische Fragmente zum Ahikar-Roman." Pages 180–85 in *Folia Rara*. Edited by Herbert Francke, Walther Heissig, and Wolfgang Treue. Wiesbaden: Steiner, 1976.

Zeitlin, Froma I. "Playing the Other: Theater, Theatricality, and the Feminine in Greek Drama." Pages 63–96 in *Nothing to Do with Dionysos? Athenian Drama in its Social Context*. Edited by John J. Winkler and Froma I. Zeitlin. Princeton: Princeton University Press, 1990.

Ziebarth, Erich. *Aus der antiken Schule: Sammlung griechischer Texte auf Papyrus, Holztafeln, Ostraka*. 2nd ed. Bonn: Marcus & Marcus, 1913.

Zimmermann, Bernhard. "Chor und Handlung in der griechischen Komödie." Pages 49–59 in *Chor im antiken und modernen Drama*. Edited by Peter Reimer and Bernhard Zimmermann. Drama 7. Stuttgart: Metzler, 1999.

CONTRIBUTORS

Jo-Ann A. Brant, Professor of Bible and Religion, Goshen College, Goshen Indiana

J. R. C. Cousland, Associate Professor of Religious Studies, University of British Columbia, Vancouver, British Columbia, Canada

Rubén Rene Dupertuis, Visiting Assistant Professor of Religion, Centre College, Danville, Kentucky

Noah Hacham, Post-Doctoral Fellow, The Orion Center for the Study of the Dead Sea Scrolls and Associated Literature, Department of Jewish History, The Hebrew University, Jerusalem, Israel

Charles W. Hedrick, Distinguished Professor of Religious Studies Emeritus, Southwest Missouri State University, Springfield, Missouri

Gerhard van den Heever, Senior Lecturer of New Testament Studies, University of South Africa, Pretoria, South Africa

Ronald F. Hock, Professor of Religion, University of Southern California, Los Angeles, California

Tawny L. Holm, Associate Professor of Religious Studies, Indiana University of Pennsylvania, Indiana, Pennsylvania

Sara R. Johnson, Associate Professor of Classics, University of Connecticut, Storrs, Connecticut

Jared W. Ludlow, Associate Professor of History and Religion, Brigham Young University-Hawaii, Laie, Hawaii

Dennis R. MacDonald, John Wesley Professor of New Testament and Christian Origins, Claremont School of Theology, and Director of the Institute for Antiquity and Christianity at Claremont Graduate University, Claremont, California

Chaim Milikowsky, Professor of Talmud, Bar-Ilan University, Ramat-Gan, Israel

Judith B. Perkins, Professor of Classics and Humanities, Saint Joseph College, West Hartford, Connecticut

Richard I. Pervo, Saint Paul, Minnesota

Andy Reimer, Associate Professor of Biblical Studies, Alliance University College, Calgary, Alberta, Canada

Chris Shea, Professor of Classics and Chair, Department of Modern Languages & Classics, Ball State University, Muncie, Indiana

Gareth L. Schmeling, Distinguished Professor of Classics, University of Florida, Gainesville, Florida

Index of Ancient Sources

Apocrypha

OLD TESTAMENT PSEUDEPIGRAPHA

DEAD SEA SCROLLS

RABBINIC LITERATURE

NEW TESTAMENT APOCRYPHA AND PSEUDEPIGRAPHPA

INDEX OF MODERN AUTHORS

INDEX OF SUBJECTS

Printed in the United States
37222LVS00005B/79-141

9 781589 831667

12.2.05